Informix Power Reference

ISBN 0-13-080906-3

9 780130 809063

90000

PRENTICE HALL PTR INFORMIX SERIES

To See a Complete List of Informix Press Titles, Point to
    http://www.prenhall.com/~informix

Informix
Power
Reference

Art Taylor

Prentice Hall PTR
Upper Saddle River, New Jersey 07458
http://www.phptr.com

Library of Congress Catologing-in-Publication Data

Taylor, Art
    Informix power reference/Art Taylor.
       p. cm. --(Prentice Hall PTR Informix series)
    Includes index.
    ISBN 0-13-080906-3
    1. Database management--Software. 2. Informix software.
    I. Title. II. Series.
    QA76.9.D3T396 1999   98-41668
005.75'65--dc21   CIP

Editorial/Production Supervision: *Kerry Reardon*
Acquisitions Editor: *John Anderson*
Buyer: *Alexis R. Heydt*
Cover Design: *Anthony Gemmellaro*
Cover Design Direction: *Jerry Votta*
Art Director: *Gail Cocker-Bogusz*
Series Design: *Claudia Durrell Design*
Marketing Manager: *Miles Williams*
Manager, Informix Press: *Sandy Emerson*

 © 1999 Prentice Hall PTR
Prentice-Hall, Inc.
A Simon & Schuster Company
Upper Saddle River, NJ 07458

 Informix Press
Informix Software, Inc.
4100 Bohannon Drive
Menlo Park, CA 94025

The following are worldwide trademarks of Informix Software, Inc., or its subsidiaries, registered
in the United States of America as indicated by ®, and in numerous other counties worldwide:
INFORMIX®, Informix DataBlade® Module, Informix Dynamic Scalable Architecture™, Informix Illustra™
Server, InformixLink®, INFORMIX®-4GL, INFORMIX®-4GL Compiled,
INFORMIX®-CLI, INFORMIX®-Connect, INFORMIX®-ESQL/C, INFORMIX®-MetaCube™,
INFORMIX®-Mobile, INFORMIX®-NET, INFORMIX®-NewEra™ INFORMIX®-NewEra™ Viewpoint™,
INFORMIX®-NewEra™ Viewpoint™ Pro, INFORMIX®-OnLine, INFORMIX®-OnLine Dynamic Server™,
INFORMIX®-OnLine Workgroup Server, INFORMIX®-OnLine Workstation, INFORMIX®-SE,
INFORMIX®-SQL, INFORMIX-Superview™, INFORMIX®-Universal Server

All other product names mentioned herein are the trademarks or registered trademarks of their
respective owners.

The publisher offers discounts on this book when ordered in bulk quantities. For more
information, call the Corporate Sales Department at 800-382-3419; FAX: 201-236-714,
email corpsales@prenhall.com or write Corporate Sales Department, Prentice Hall PTR,
One Lake Street, Upper Saddle River, NJ 07458

Prentice Hall books are widely used by corporations and government agencies for training,
marketing, and resale.

Printed in the United States of America

10 9 8 7 6 5 4 3 2 1

ISBN 0-13-080906-3

Prentice-Hall International (UK) Limited, *London*
Prentice-Hall of Australia Pty. Limited, *Sydney*
Prentice-Hall Canada Inc., *Toronto*
Prentice-Hall Hispanoamericana, S.A., *Mexico*
Prentice-Hall of India Private Limited, *New Delhi*
Prentice-Hall of Japan, Inc., *Tokyo*
Simon & Schuster Asia Pte. Ltd., *Singapore*
Editora Prentice-Hall do Brasil, Ltda., *Rio de Janeiro*

To Hannah and Eric,
the best there is

Contents

A database is the core, the center of an application, a very critical component of the application architecture. Vital application information flows in and out of this component. Failures or flaws in the database could have a severe impact on the entire application.

For this reason, because of this criticality, the correct administration of the database is of paramount importance. For an application to run without incident, the database used must operate correctly and efficiently. Smooth database operation requires not only proper administration, but a proper physical and logical design of the database, a design that should match the needs of the application using the database.

As an Informix database administrator, you must understand the full range of engine operations: from how the engine uses machine resources (CPU and disk), how data integrity is maintained through logging mechanisms, archive and recovery facilities, and most importantly, database monitoring and tuning. Starting with a discussion of basic terms and concepts and proceeding through a discussion of the engine architecture, this book covers each of these topics in turn.

As an Informix application developer, you must understand the operation of the database to correctly architect an application. Flexible data organization through static database fragmentation is a an important feature of the Informix database and if understood and used correctly, can improve performance for many applications. This book covers Informix fragmentation in detail, explaining how this important feature can be used to improve performance for data retrieval and ease data administration by placing portions of data in specific disk locations.

An Informix application developer or database administrator
will interact with the Informix database using the Informix
Structured Query Language (SQL). Understanding and using
Informix-SQL wisely can save tremendous amounts of development and administration effort. The most commonly used
Informix-SQL statements for both data manipulation and data definition are covered in this text complete with examples of usage.

One of the most enduring Fourth Generation Languages is
Informix-4GL. This development language represents a well-con-
ceived combination of procedural and non-procedural programming statements that allow a complete application to be
developed with ease. This tool is excellent for the development
of reports, database administration, and the transformation, conversion and filtering applications common in data warehouses
and data marts. This language is covered in detail in this text.

Despite the common maxim, it is generally not the computer
that fails but the human who programmed or administered it.
Careful, knowledgeable design, programming and administration are the base upon which computer applications are built.
These tasks require a solid knowledge foundation for the development tools being used. Using this book, you, the Informix
developer or administrator, can develop that solid foundation of
knowledge of the Informix product line for the products presented in this book.

Appreciation

Thanks to all those who helped in the development of this book.
Thanks especially for the great home support: Carolyn, Hannah
and Eric, and especially Carolyn. Their patience and understanding has been appreciated.

Thanks to all the technical editors including Harold Davis and
Seth Grimes. Most significantly thanks to the technical editors
Paul Gancz and Dave Kosenko who stayed with this effort to the
end and whose keen technical expertise kept me on the straight
and narrow.

Special thanks to the Informix Press member of this team, Judy
Bowman whose help and efforts are greatly appreciated.

And finally, thanks to the production team at Prentice-Hall:
Ralph Moore and Kerry Reardon who have helped make all this
information clear, clean and presentable.

Informix Product Overview

Since the company's founding in 1980 under the name
Relational Database Systems, the Informix software product line
has continued to grow and mature. From its initial product, C-
ISAM, a set of C language functions to provide indexed sequential access method (ISAM) access to data, the company has
continued to evolve. At its core is a powerful database server
designed to support the data management needs of the enterprise. A series of server options have recently been added to provide support for object-relational data access and extended data
types. Another option has added support for massively parallel
and clustered servers. And a rich set of development and expanded archive and recovery tools have helped to round out their
product line.

To understand where Informix software is going, it is helpful
to understand how it arrived where it is today. The following sections cover some of the history of the Informix product line,
detailing how the product line started and how it arrived at its
current product mix. The final sections describe the products
that make up the current product set.

History of Informix Products

As the computer industry has continued to grow and evolve in the years since the founding of Informix software, so too has the Informix product line. Starting in 1980 with a single product, Informix, under the name Relational Database Systems, developed a business model that involved selling software for the then-emerging market of Unix servers. At the time, many computer industry analysts felt open systems computers could not compete with the proprietary operating systems offered by IBM, Digital Computer, and others. But Informix founder Roger Sippl was firm in his commitment to the Unix operating system, a commitment that was to pay excellent dividends in the years to come.

The Informix product line, as Table 1-1 reveals, began with a series of products based on proprietary application programmer interfaces (APIs) and query languages. But a shift toward open standards soon emerged and remained a key corporate strategy for years to come.

Table 1-1 *Informix Product Line*

Product	Architecture	Release Date	Features
C-ISAM/RDS	Single-process architecture	1985	Proprietary query language
ISQL	Two-process architecture	1986	Open standards query language (SQL) and used Unix file system
Informix-4GL	Two-process architecture	1986	Fourth-generation development language
Turbo	Two-process architecture	1987	Internal file system (through raw disk), SQL
Online	Two-process architecture	1989	Same as Turbo
DSDA	Multi-threaded	1992	Parallel processing
IDS	Multi-threaded	1997	Replication, high-performance loader
IDS/XP	Multi-threaded	1996	Support and optimizations for MPP and clustered server environments
IDS/UD	Multi-threaded	1996	Support for object-relational features—data type extensions, user-defined functions, table and row-type inheritance

C-ISAM

Before online transaction processing (OLTP) database servers, rich data types, and 4GLs, there was C-ISAM, Informix's first product. C-ISAM was (and still is) a collection of C language routines to create and access data using ISAM. The functions that comprise C-ISAM access a database table like a file, using file descriptors and pointers to manipulate data in the file. Indexes are available to improve data search performance, but C-ISAM must access these indices explicitly; they are not available implicitly as with SQL database access. (Under the covers, Informix databases still use routines derived from these initial functions to read and access the tables in a database.)

The Relational Database and Informix-RDS

In the early 1980s, there were a number of database types available: heirarchical, network, relational, and various others. The relational database, storing data in a series of related tables, was just one of these. Though the theoretical concepts were considered solid and valid, there was an opinion offered by many who were more familiar with the legacy database, and that relational databases would never perform at the level of the legacy databases and that the extra disk access required to join two or more tables would be prohibitively expensive.

But Informix management believed in the concept of the relational database and developed the sequel to C-ISAM as a relational database product based on the C-ISAM function library. This product was named RDS (Relational Database System) and contained a relational database, a proprietary query language, a menu-driven tool for creating and accessing data in the database, and a report writing tool named ACE.

Informix-SQL Engine (SE)

While Informix-RDS met with some success, there was an increased interest in the relational database industry to move toward a standard query language. The Structured Query Language (SQL), originally developed by IBM, was in the process of becoming an industry standard. With all of these developments afoot, around 1985, Informix developed a portable database server program that used the industry standard SQL language for database queries. This product became the Informix-SQL Engine, sometimes called the Informix-Standard Engine (Informix-SE).

While previous products had used a single-process architecture, the Informix-SE product used a *two-process* architecture, with a **client** process that would access the data and a **server** process that would manage database access (see Figure 1-1). These processes were also referred to as the *front-end* and *back-end* processes. The client program could interface with the user and be developed in such a way as to make user access easy, and the server process could concentrate on the specifics of controlling access to the data, optimizing data retrieval, and providing for data integrity.

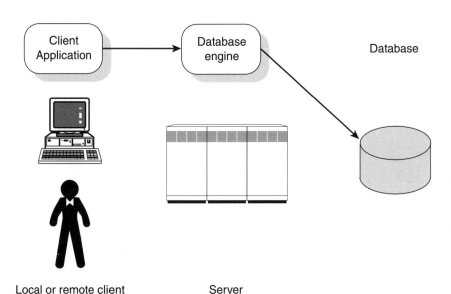

Local or remote client   Server

Figure 1-1 Informix-SE Two-Process Architecture

With a two-process architecture, the client programs, the *front-end*, communicate with the back-end program, the *server*, using *interprocess communication* (IPC). Unix sockets and shared memory connections are the most common methods of IPC access.

Using the two-process architecture provided a number of benefits for the development effort. The implementation of this architecture effectively decoupled the client and server portions of the application (which were tightly coupled using the single-process architecture of C-ISAM and RDS) and allowed the client and server applications to be developed and optimized separately. And significantly, the client and server programs did not have to reside on the same machine (though they often did in the early days of Unix computing).

The client program could be executed on a separate server or PC and, using Transmission Control Protocol/Internet Protocol (TCP/IP) sockets as an IPC mechanism, could communicate with the database server program running on a remote machine and remotely retrieve and manipulate the data in the database just as though the database were on the same machine. (This was the beginning of what has come to be known as *client-server* computing.)

Informix-Turbo

The initial Informix database product, Informix-SE, performed well up to the level of about 50 concurrent users and with fewer than 200 tables. Beyond that level, performance decreased rapidly. Data integrity was also an issue. Because all I/O was left to the Unix operating system, which was vulnerable to data loss during system failure, a system crash could lead to a loss or corruption of data in the database. These problems were addressed in a new product initially named Informix-Turbo, which was designed to address the performance, flexibility, and data integrity issues of the Informix-SE product.

The Informix-Turbo product managed all low-level disk I/O, treating the disk as a raw Unix device. This improved the performance of the product and also made the application code more portable. Database data was cached in shared memory, which was accessible to all Unix processes. These changes and others allowed the Informix-Turbo database to handle larger databases with more users and better performance.

Informix-Turbo was based in part on the Informix SE product but involved a significant rewrite of the code. A major difference between the products was the set of routines used to perform low-level disk I/O. The C-ISAM functions, which used Unix facilities to perform disk I/O, were replaced with relational storage access method (RSAM) functions. These functions provided some ISAM-type functionality but were aware of the new memory buffer cache and internal data structures.

A number of different programs were added to the server product to manage the additional components. These programs handled the buffer cache and logging and acted as a mediator between the front-end program and the back-end database server.

The creation of a memory buffer cache added a set of requirements to the system. All disk read and write operations would effectively use the buffer cache and did not read and write directly to disk. A great deal of code was required to manage the buffer cache. This code had to read pages of data from disk and put the data in the buffer cache. The code also had to synchronize the buffer cache with disk, so that periodically data pages that had been updated or created would be written to disk. This ultimately led to the creation of several additional programs, known as *daemons*, to manage the buffer cache and perform other housekeeping functions.

There also had to be contingencies to deal with the possible failure of the Unix machine. Should the machine fail, all data in the buffer cache (in machine RAM) would be lost. A facility was created to store the *before image* of a page (a unit of buffer cache) in a disk location. Should the machine fail, a recovery process could read these before images and write them to disk, thus restoring the database to a consistent state. This location for before images was named the *physical log*.

The Informix-Turbo front-end program started an **sqlturbo** process, which provided communication with the front-end program and the database engine. It was the job of this process to communicate with the database, access the shared memory buffer through IPC mechanisms, retrieve data, perform joins, sorts, and merges, and return the data to the front-end program. Every front-end application that attached to the database would start an **sqlturbo** process.

The Informix-Turbo product provided the foundation for future Informix database products. Upon this foundation, fragmentation, parallel processing, cluster support, and other features have been added in recent years as the following sections will detail.

Informix-Online Dynamic Server

In version 4.0 of Informix-Turbo, the product was renamed Informix-Online to reflect the significant changes made available in this release. Changes were made to support online backups, multiple instances on the same machine, communication between Informix-Online instances, an improved optimizer, and various performance optimizations.

With version 5.x (on the Sequent platform) and 6.0, the Informix-Online Dynamic Server was born. This product made use of internal multithreading and static fragmentation and provided some level of replication. Internal multithreading reduced the number of processes required to service the front-end, thus reducing the Unix resources needed to run the Informix server. Operating system calls that provided memory allocation and management were removed and code was created to assign these tasks to the engine, thus providing greater control and improved portability for the engine code.

Using internal multithreading allowed more control over when tasks would be performed and provided the means to reduce contention for engine resources. Most importantly, use of internal multi-threading allowed for finely grained control over parallel operations, the primary reason for the introduction of this feature.

Though Informix-Online Dynamic Server was a solid product, in the fast-paced world of database software, there has been no time to stand still. Informix has aggressively added features and functionality to its database engine products. Later releases of the server added support for additional parallel operations, query prioritization, and join operations. Additional data replication functionality, auditing features, and event alarms have also been added. Most importantly, several options have been added for object-relational and massively-parallel and cluster support, as discussed in the sections that follow.

Informix IDS/UD

One of the most significant features added to the Informix database server is the set of object-relational features in the Informix Dynamic Server with the universal data option (IDS/UD) engine. In 1995, Informix software purchased Illustra software, giving

Informix access to the Illustra object-relational database. While Illustra had a number of very good object-relational features such as user-defined data types, table and row type inheritance, and extensibility through Datablades, the database did not have good scalability and data integrity capabilities, features that Informix-Online had and were required for enterprise-class usage of the engine. The goal for Informix developers was to merge the Informix-Online Dynamic Server with the Illustra server to create a server with excellent object-relational functionality as well as scalability and data integrity features. The result of this effort is the IDS/UD.

The IDS/UD product provides a number of important object-relational features. The most important are as follows:

- Inheritance
- Data type extensibility
- User-defined functions

These components are explained in the following sections.

Data Type Extensibility

Data type extensibility enables the user to add data types to the database. No longer is the user limited to the ANSI SQL data types provided by most relational database vendors. Data type extensibility provides features such as row type definitions, which allow a database row to be defined and then used to create another table, effectively treating the row type as a data type.

User-defined data types can also be created, allowing *opaque* data objects (the engine knows nothing of the composition of the data object) to exist in the database. User-defined server functions are then written to operate on those data types.

Inheritance

Inheritance is one of the key components of code reuse. When applied to database tables and row definitions, it is the ability to indicate that a previously defined table or row type is the basis for a row or table being defined.

User-Defined Functions

The ability to create user-defined functions is one of the most powerful features of IDS/UD. Users can define functions in a variety of languages, from C to Java. These functions have the ability to manipulate the data in the engine buffer cache, avoiding the overhead of retrieving the data through an IPC, an overhead incurred by most middleware solutions.

Informix IDS/XP

The IDS/XP (extended parallel) server was designed to provide scalable performance on a massively parallel processing (MPP) machine—parallel systems connected by a single high speed network. (The data transfer speed of this high-speed network approaches machine bus speeds on many systems, so intercommunication between nodes is rarely a bottleneck.) This server shines where large amounts of data must be scanned quickly as in large decision support systems (DSS).

An MPP is a collection of nodes. With IDS/XP, an instance of IDS runs on a node; these instances are known as *coservers*. Each coserver manages its own set of resources. A request manager exists on each coserver and decides how each data request should be distributed across coservers. A *query optimizer, data dictionary manager,* and *scheduler* then work together on each node to process the request. The IDS/XP server expands the concept of static fragmentation (spreading data over multiple pieces of disk) to support fragmenting over disk on multiple coservers, thus allowing tables to be spread over multiple instances of IDS running on separate systems. The parallelism in this environment allows the resources of the coservers on the separate machines (the disk, CPU, and memory) to be used in parallel. Because there is nothing shared between the coservers, there is very little contention and the scalability of IDS/XP when adding coservers is near linear. This means that as additional coservers are added, performance increases in a near-linear fashion, so that using four coservers would be almost twice as fast as using two coservers for a given operation.

Informix Tools

To complement the core database product, Informix developed a suite of development tools that has been extended over the years. As a whole, Informix offers tools to manage data, from character-based development with Informix-4GL, to client-server GUI (graphical user interface) development with the Data Director product suite, to the creation of a Web site driven entirely from an Informix database using the Informix Web Integration option. These tools are an important adjunct to the Informix database server.

Informix Monitoring Tools

Informix provides a number of tools to maintain and monitor the Informix server. Because the Informix server has its roots firmly planted in Unix where character-based development was once commonplace, it is not a surprise that many of these tools are character-based. The `onmonitor` tool is used to create and maintain an Informix server instance, and the tried-and-true `dbaccess` is used to create databases and tables within a server instance, execute queries, and return results.

But in keeping with the industry trend toward GUI client-server tools, Informix has developed a complete set of GUI applications to provide the same functionality as the legacy character-based applications. The Informix Enterprise Command Center (IECC) is used to create and monitor multiple Informix server instances. And the Informix SQL Editor is used to execute queries and review results using a client-server GUI application. The Relational Object Manager (ROM) performs the same functions as the SQL Editor but has knowledge of the rich data types that are available with the IDS/UD engine. And the Schema Knowledge tool is used to create and maintain the components of relational databases.

Backup and recovery are managed through the `ontape` and `onbar` tools. The `ontape` tool provides a character-based user interface to backup Informix databases and server instances; it supports standard tape devices. The `onbar` utility provides support for both standard tape devices and storage managers.

Informix Language Tools

Informix provides a number of embedded language tools. One of the most commonly used is Informix Embedded SQL for C (ESQL/C). While Informix offers other embedded language tools, this continues to be the most commonly used. The ESQL/C product allows ANSI SQL statements and Informix extensions to be embedded directly into C-language programs.

At one point, Informix-4GL held approximately 40 percent of the 4GL market on Unix. This language has the structure and simplicity of the C language, but with safety and additional non-procedural syntax that make it an easy and accessible language. It contains a full set of procedural flow-of-control and conditional statements, nonprocedural statements for displaying a character-based input screen, and report-writing statements that provide control breaks and the ability to format output. Despite its age, this language continues to prove extremely useful for performing complex database updates, data cleansing and transformations, and character-based reporting.

Informix Internet Development Tools

One of the most important developments of the 1990s has been that of the World Wide Web and thin-client applications. With the thin-client paradigm, applications can be developed and deployed with virtually zero deployment cost; all that is required is that users have a compatible Web browser on their desktop. Deployment is immediate. This is a paradigm that has a great deal of appeal to the development community.

Informix software has responded to the significance of the Web with the introduction of several important tools. The Informix Web Integration option allows the creation of Hyper Text Markup Language (HTML) pages that use HTML extensions to retrieve data from an Informix database. Database-aware list boxes or check boxes and other HTML form elements can be created as part of the HTML page. Database-centered Web development provides the data integrity and transaction control of a relational database for the storage of Web pages, thus providing an added layer of security and control for site administrators.

Informix Product Architecture

The job of the Informix engine is, in short, to provide database services for multiple users. It accomplishes this task by allocating the available resources to the tasks at hand. But in the competitive industry of database servers, the object is not only to allocate resources effectively, but to do it in such a way as to optimize the performance of the database and use as little CPU resources as possible. This is accomplished by effective management of the resources available. In this vein, it is best to view the architecture of the Informix server from the perspective of resource management. The conceptual architecture of the server is therefore comprised of four basic components (see Figure 1-2), as follows.

- Disk I/O
- Memory (buffer)
- Thread (process)
- Communications

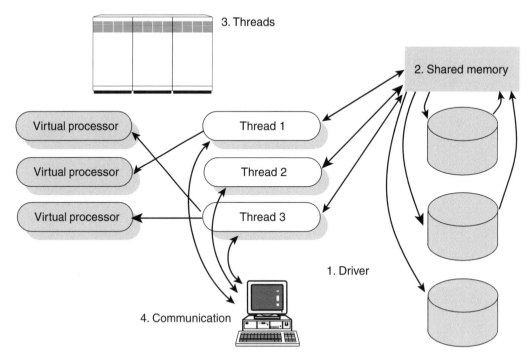

Figure 1-2 IDS Engine Architecture

These four components comprise all of the functions of the engine. When the engine receives a request, it allocates threads to service the request. These threads then request memory and disk I/O as needed. The front end or client uses the communication layer to communicate with the engine.

Disk I/O

The disk management component controls all interaction with the disk. This layer interacts with the memory management layer to buffer portions of the disk that have been requested by users. Portions of the physical disk are mapped to logical collections of disk space called dbspaces. Database tables and indices may optionally be mapped to multiple dbspaces, thus creating a *fragmented* table or index. Database logging is also controlled by this component.

Memory (Buffer)

The Informix server uses memory for a number of reasons: to buffer data from disk (cache), for sorting and merging data, for internal monitoring and control, and for managing communications. The management of this memory is a critical component of server operation. If the server does not have enough memory, sorts that could have been done in memory will be done on disk, thus degrading performance. Low memory could also lead to failed queries and, in severe cases, failure of the server.

In versions of the Informix server since the release of the Online Dynamic Server product, memory management has become an integral part of the engine allowing improved engine performance and code portability. Even low-level memory allocation (malloc()) is now performed by server code rather than using operating system calls.

Thread (Process)

Informix servers use their own internal threading mechanism to perform multithreading. Threads are lightweight (requiring very little resource to switch) and prioritized, but specific priorities cannot be altered by administrators. Threads allow requested database tasks to be distributed among multiple threads, thus allowing portions of a task to be performed in parallel.

The Informix server makes decisions on thread allocation based on the database activity being requested and the location of the data being processed. If the engine determines that a parallel operation will not cause contention, it generally spawns multiple threads to perform an operation. In this way, the fragmentation of the data being retrieved plays a big part in generating parallel database operations, because data that resides in multiple fragments can be retrieved using multiple threads, whereas data that has been placed in a single fragment will not use multiple threads.

Communications

The communications component of the architecture manages the communication between processes that connect to the engine and the database engine. As information is passed to and from the engine, it passes through this layer. Each process connected to the engine has a session control block that monitors the activity of the process and is under the control of the communications layer. The Informix database communications layer uses Unix IPC mechanisms such as sockets and shared memory to perform communications with the client applications.

Parallel Database Operations

A central aspect of the Informix product architecture is the ability to perform parallel database operations. The Informix database has the ability to perform these operations with the knowledge of physical data storage provided by static fragmentation.

When the Informix database server performs a database operation, it makes a decision about how to perform the operation in parallel. If possible, the engine performs database selects, inserts, and updates in parallel. Using an internal multithreading mechanism, database operations can be run in parallel across multiple CPUs (if available), thus improving performance.

This parallel operation capability is a key feature of the

Informix engine. The Informix database provides expression-based fragmentation, the ability to use expressions to fragment or disperse data across multiple disks. These expressions are then evaluated by the engine when data is retrieved, thus allowing intelligent decisions to be made concerning database access.

The database also uses multithreading to perform internal functions, so that functions such as logging and shared memory management benefit from internal multithreading. And data access operations that scan, sort, or merge data can also potentially benefit from the internal multithreading of the IDS engine. As later chapters reveal, the Parallel Data Query feature that triggers the optimizer to use multiple execution threads for queries takes the fragmentation of the data into consideration.

Chapter Summary

This chapter has offered a quick overview of the Informix product line, with some details about how the line started and how Informix arrived at its current product mix. From 1980, when the Informix software product line began under the name of Relational Database Systems, this powerful set of products has continued to evolve into a rich and complex product line that now extends to two variations of the database product and a range of monitoring, archive and recovery, and development tools. Understanding how these tools evolved is an important step to mastering them.

Next Chapter

You cannot begin to understand the dynamics of a database server without a grounding in its architecture. The next chapter covers the Informix server architecture and provides an explanation of its components. Concepts introduced in Chapter 2 are germane to later discussions on monitoring and performance tuning.

Informix Basic Concepts and Server Architecture

Any discussion of a database server technology requires an understanding of the server architecture. In this chapter, the architecture is used as a framework for a discussion of the basic concepts of the IDS server.

This chapter discusses the Informix engine architecture, the basic engine components, and concepts. The goal is to develop an understanding of the engine that will form the basis for the remaining chapters of this book. The discussion begins with the basic engine components.

IDS Basic Concepts

An understanding of several basic concepts is required to understand the Informix engine. These concepts involve the core of the Informix product: the memory location where it stores data, the name of the logical and physical components of the disk, and the internal multithreading it uses to perform its work. The following sections detail these and other core database concepts.

Shared Memory Buffer

The Informix server uses shared memory extensively to store and buffer data and to track and control the various threads that are running under its control. Controlling this shared memory buffer, synchronizing the buffer with the disk under its control, and providing for data integrity in the event the machine should fail are no small feats.

The buffer is logically divided into *pages* that are a fixed size (usually 2048 bytes, but it can vary depending on the hardware platform). These buffer pages contain some header information about the partition where the page exists on disk, the amount of data that has been written to the page, and the size and number of rows on the page, but they contain no specific information on the table or rows on the page. It is the partition number or page number that represents the key identifier for the data page. Index entries reference the page number and offset of a particular row within the page.

Multithreading and Virtual Processors

One of the more significant features of the IDS engine is internal *multithreading*. Internal multithreading is the ability to execute multiple tasks internally to the engine as multiple threads of execution that may be executed simultaneously.

Running multiple processes simultaneously is not a new concept; operating systems have been doing this for some time. But operating systems have usually performed multitasking, where each running program represents a separate operating system task or process. When the operating system switches from one task to another, it is known as a *context switch*, an operation that involves a somewhat expensive manipulation of the task's resources by the operating system. It is this context switch that internal application multithreading attempts to avoid.

Program *threads* can provide a lightweight and efficient method of a single process executing multiple internal threads of execution and moving between these threads with very little overhead. Multiple internal threads access the same program storage areas and thus avoid the need to use inter-process communication to exchange information between tasks (as separately executing programs would be required to do).

Informix implements threads using a proprietary package for lightweight (requiring very little overhead) threads. Threads are implemented to allow simple, fast switching of threads between CPU resources. They reduce operating system overhead, overall memory requirements, and contention for resources within the database management system (DBMS). These are benefits that are realized particularly well on hardware platforms that support multiple processors such as symmetrical multiprocessor (SMP) platforms.

Informix has two types of threads: *session* threads initiated for a user session, and *internal* threads initiated to manage the housekeeping operations of the database. The IDS engine usually runs a single-session thread for a client connection and internal threads to perform database I/O, logging, writing data pages to disk, and various administrative tasks.

In the Informix multithreading implementation, a *virtual processor* (VP) provides the logical capabilities that a CPU would provide in machine hardware. Multiple VPs can be configured. If a thread is running on a VP and requests a resource that is not currently available, it can release the VP and allow another thread to use it. When the resource the thread was waiting for becomes available, the thread can begin running on another VP, thus having migrated from one VP to another.
Informix divides CPU virtual processors into several classes as overviewed in Table 2-1.

The most common virtual processor is the CPU VP, which has the processor that has the most impact on system performance. The number of CPU VPs can be set using a configuration parameter and can be adjusted dynamically when the engine is online. This ability to dynamically add CPU VPs allows the CPU resource to be adjusted based on system load; as system load increases, additional CPUs can be added, and as system load decreases, the number of CPU VPs can be decreased.

There is not necessarily a one-to-one correspondence between VPs and physical CPUs, but the general rule of thumb is to leave one CPU to the operating system and allocate the remaining CPUs to a single VP. Using this strategy, a four-CPU system would have one CPU allocated to the operating system and three Informix virtual processors allocated to each of the remaining CPUs.

Table 2-1 *Classes of Virtual Processors*

Virtual Processor	Purpose
CPU	Runs session threads and some system threads
PIO	Writes to the physical log file if in an OS file
LIO	Writes to the logical log file if in an OS file
AIO	Performs nonlogging disk I/O
SHM	Shared memory communication
TLI	Network communication using TLI
SOC	Network communication using sockets
OPT	Performs I/O to optical disk
ADM	Administrative functions
ADT	Auditing functions
MSC	Miscellaneous; manages request for system calls that require a very large stack

By default, CPU VPs are not bound to a hardware CPU. The Informix CPU VP is implemented as a process that can migrate from one hardware CPU to another just as any other process would. Most operating systems running on SMP platforms have been optimized to manage process migration efficiently, thus correctly balancing the load on the system's CPU resource. But on some platforms, the task of migrating processes from one CPU to the next can be overridden using *processor affinity*. Processor affinity, where supported, can be used to bind a process to a specific CPU. The process that has been *affinitied* is attached to CPU and is given priority on that CPU. This behavior can be triggered using the PROCESSOR_AFFINITY configuration parameter. (If processor affinity is not provided on the platform, this configuration parameter is ignored by the engine.)

Thread Operation

Informix threads operate in a *cooperative multitasking* environment. Unlike the Unix operating system, which can preempt a running process, the Informix engine must wait for a thread to yield. Once a thread has yielded to the engine, the virtual processor loads another thread and begins processing for that thread, known as *context switching*. If a thread does not yield, the virtual processor must continue processing that thread. Most threads yield to the engine at several predetermined points in their processing and whenever they must wait for a shared resource.

Thread scheduling is conducted through control structures maintained in the virtual portion of shared memory. A session control block and a thread control block are maintained to record the state of the thread. These control structures are used when the thread stops processing to sleep and/or migrate to another VP.

Informix threads use *stacks* to store and retrieve private data. Because Informix threads may share a virtual processor, the data they use must be maintained in a location where other threads will not overwrite its contents. Stacks provide this private area. When the VP switches processing to a new thread (performs a context switch), the stack pointer (the address of the threads stack) is placed in the thread control block for that stack. When the thread begins processing again, it retrieves the stack pointer and begins using the stack for processing.

Processing *queues* are also used to control the processing of threads. In computer terminology, a queue is a list of items that a program needs to track. The IDS engine uses three queues: the *ready queue*, the *sleep queue,* and the *wait queue.*

The **ready** queue is a list of threads that are currently ready to run. When the VP performs a context switch, it retrieves the first thread of the appropriate priority from the ready queue and begins processing.

The **sleep** queue is used to track sleeping threads. Threads can either sleep for a specific period of time, in which case an administrative VP wakes them at a the specified time, or they can choose to sleep *forever*. With Informix threads, however, forever is a fixed period of time usually determined by the availability of resources; a thread that is attempting to use a busy resource often sleeps in the sleep queue until that resource becomes available.

The **wait** queue is used to track threads waiting for a particular event to occur. This queue is used to coordinate access to shared resources such as a buffer page in shared memory.

A **mutex** is a lock that makes use of an assembly language test-and-set mechanism. The mutex is used to coordinate thread access to shared resources. When a thread attempts to access a shared resource, it executes a mutex request that, if the resource is available, locks the resource for the thread. If the resource is not available, the call to the mutex indicates to the requesting thread that the resource is currently unavailable.

Informix Database Logging

The Informix server performs disk I/O operations **asynchronously**. Data is not written directly to disk, but disk I/O is instead performed against a *shared memory buffer*. This buffer is used to hold *pages* (fixed-size units of disk storage) read from or to be written to disk. All processes that read or write data to the database first interact with this shared memory buffer. (This interaction is transparent to the process, which simply believes it is doing a disk read or write operation.)

Maintaining the integrity of the data in the Informix database requires the ability to ensure the consistency of transactions. In order to provide this level of control, the Informix database provides for **database logging**. This logging activity is considered under the conceptual framework of the disk management layer of the Informix architecture.

The Informix server has two types of logs: the *logical log* and the *physical log* (see Figure 2-1). The **logical log** stores the transactions performed in the database and provides the ability to group a set of database updates together as a single transaction. This transaction can then be *committed* to the database or *rolled back*. By **committing** the transaction, the changes made to the data in the transaction become a permanent part of the database. By **rolling back** the transaction, all the work that has been performed in the transaction is removed from the database. Both commit and roll-back actions leave the database in a consistent state.

Physical Log

The **physical log** stores before images of the *pages* (units of shared memory containing, among other things, the rows of tables in the database) that are in the process of being updated. This physical log is used for failure recovery in a process known as fast recovery, and during the online backup process. The primary role of the physical log is to help maintain the integrity of the shared memory buffer. This log stores the before images of

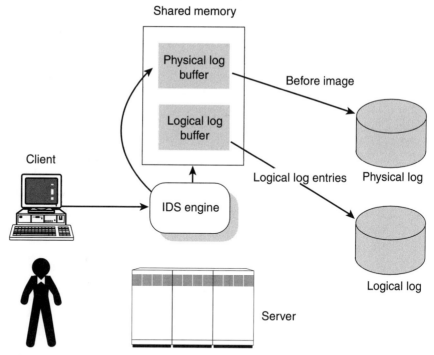

Shared memory

Physical log buffer

Before image

Logical log buffer

Client

IDS engine

Logical log entries   Physical log

Server

Logical log

Figure 2-1 *Logical and physical logging*

pages before the data on the buffer page is updated. (The term *physical log* is a bit of a misnomer; its role is largely to save roll-back pages in case they are needed by the system.) The steps involved in physical logging are as follows:

1. If the page is not already in the shared memory buffer, it is read from the disk to the shared memory buffer.
2. The unchanged page is copied to the physical log buffer.
3. The application modifies the page in the shared memory buffer.
4. The physical log buffer is flushed to the physical log on disk.
5. The shared memory buffer pages that have been modified are written to disk.
6. A checkpoint occurs. The shared memory updated pages are all written to disk, the physical log buffer is cleared, and the physical log on disk is *logically* emptied (the pointer is reset to the start of the file).

In the course of database updates, pages are written to the physical log and are cleared from the physical log only when a checkpoint occurs. The checkpoint synchronizes the physical log with the database. The *checkpoint* represents a point at which database integrity is guaranteed. All updated pages have been written to disk and the physical log is cleared. (Note that transactions may be open at this point, but could be rolled back if necessary using information in the logical log.) In the event of a *graceful shutdown*, the engine performs a checkpoint and clears the physical log just before bringing the engine into an offline state.

A *fast recovery* would be required if the engine were taken to an offline state without having the opportunity to perform a graceful shutdown. In this event, as the engine is brought online, the physical log is read and all pages in the physical log are written to the database, thus removing any updates that were not considered synchronized (by a checkpoint that would have cleared them from the log). A logical recovery is also conducted during fast recovery; this recovery is used to roll back transactions that were committed after the checkpoint and were incomplete when the engine went offline.

Logical Logs

The logical logs are used to provide the ability to roll back a transaction—that is, to remove all of the updates a transaction may have done. They provide the application programmer with the ability to begin a transaction, perform a series of updates to numerous tables, and then based on some system activity such as an error message, roll back the transaction and effectively undo all of the updates the transaction had performed with a single statement.

Logical log records contain all information needed to roll back a transaction. They contain a header with information about the record: the log record address, the record length, the record type, the transaction number, the logical log number, and a link to the previous record in the transaction. The log record type indicates the database action the log record records. Valid database actions can be virtually any database activity, both those initiated by a user and those conducted by the database as part of its housekeeping activities.

Logical logs are first buffered in memory and then written to disk, unless the option of *unbuffered* logging has been chosen, in which case they are written directly to disk synchronously, thus assuring transaction completeness and potentially degrading performance.

Logical log records are written for any database activity that updates data on disk. The most common user-initiated activity that would generate log activities would be the SQL update statement. An update statement would generate a log entry that would contain a record that indicates the table and row affected (though this would contain internal identifiers indicating the pages on disk that were affected). This could be written for each row affected, so the update statement directly impacts the size of the log entry. It is not uncommon for update or insert statements that affect a large number of rows to consume large portions of the logical log available. These entries would be written to multiple logical log files on disk. These log files are periodically written to tape and freed, but the logs that contain entries that are still part of an open transaction (the extensive update that has not yet updated all rows) cannot be written to tape and freed.

One possible consequence of this type of extensive update statement would be the dreaded *long transaction*. Such a transaction would fill nearly all available logs and then abort. In some instances, filling all available logs could halt system activity, because no logs would be available to start transactions. Two system configuration parameters can be set to minimize the possibility that a single long transaction could impact the function of the entire instance: LTXEHWM and LTXHWM. These two parameters are discussed in Chapter 3.

Checkpoints

As previously mentioned, checkpoints occur at predefined checkpoint intervals (set by a configuration parameter) or when the physical log buffer is 75 percent full. When a checkpoint occurs, the physical log is completely cleared by assuring that all the updated pages in the physical log have been written to disk.

When a checkpoint occurs, most system activity is halted because database sessions are not allowed to enter what are designated as critical sections of engine code. This is necessary to assure system integrity but places a performance constraint on checkpoint activity. Often, excessive checkpointing is a cause of system performance problems. If there are a large number of updated pages in the shared memory buffer, then writing these pages to disk could be a time-consuming task. Generally, a checkpoint takes a few seconds, though in systems where there is a problem, it could take a minute or more.

Chunks and dbspaces

A *chunk* can be considered the IDS physical representation of disk and the *dbspace* the logical representation of disk. A set of chunks is assigned to a dbspace—a dbspace is effectively a set of chunks. The IDS engine therefor recognizes physical disk as a series of chunks. These chunks are in turn related to dbspaces. Tables are created in dbspaces but can be written across several dbspaces using static fragmentation in what is referred to as *fragmenting* a table.

Chunks are usually limited to 2GB in size, so on installations where disk is greater than 2GB, the disk must be partitioned so that 2GB pieces are available to be mapped to IDS chunks. (Because the dbspace is a collection of one or more chunks, it is not limited to 2GB in size.)

Informix-SQL is not aware of individual chunks. All SQL statements interact with dbspaces in SQL DDL statements that specify disk storage.

Structure of Data Storage

A page is the physical unit of storage within chunks (similar to the page format used in shared memory storage). Within a chunk, there are various structures that track the pages within the dbspace. There is a *chunk-free list* page that contains a list of the free pages available in the chunk. This list makes it easier for the engine to determine which pages are free when it needs to add data to the dbspace.

The pages in a tblspace need not, and often are not, contiguous pages. A table is most likely composed of multiple sets of pages, known as *extents*. The IDS engine attempts to keep these extents contiguous, but there are cases where extents are not contiguous. The engine prefers to keep extents contiguous to make table scans easier.

Within the IDS engine, there is a logical concept of a *tblspace*. A tblspace contains all of the pages within a table or a table fragment. The tblspace also contains all pages allocated to indexes and bitmap pages (pages used to track page usage within table extents).

The initial chunk in a dbspace contains the redundantly named *tblspace tblspace*. The tblspace tblspace contains information on the tblspaces within the dbspace. It contains the location and structure of the tblspaces taking residence within the dbspace.

Informix Data Types

The Informix relational database stores data in a collection of related tables. These tables contain columns that, when created, are assigned data types. The Informix engine supports basic ANSI-SQL data types and a few additional database as shown in Table 2-2.

Table 2-2 Valid SQL Data Types

Data Type	Length	Minimum Value	Maximum Value
smallint	2	-32,767	+32,767
integer, int	4	-2,147,483,647	+2,147,483,647
smallfloat, real	4	platform dependent	platform dependent
float, double precision	8	platform dependent	platform dependent
decimal, dec, numeric	precision/2 + 1	-32 significant digits	+32 significant digits
money	precision/2 + 1	-32 significant digits	+32 significant digits
date	4	1/1/0001	12/31/9999
varchar	1 to a maximum 255	1 byte	255 bytes
char, character	programmer-defined	1 byte	32,767 bytes

Smallint

The Informix `smallint` is a 2-byte integer and corresponds to the C short integer. It is signed and supports a minimum/maximum value of +/-32,767. An integer overflow (trying to store a number greater than the maximum) is an error in Informix.

Integer

The Informix `integer` is a 4-byte integer that corresponds to the C `long` integer. It is also signed and supports a minimum/maximum value of +/-2,147,483,647. Integer overflow errors are trapped as they are with the `smallint` data type.

Unfortunately, there are no macro constants provided to test for maximum integer values; the programmer must store these values in variables and check them accordingly.

Smallfloat

The INFORMIX `smallfloat` is roughly equivalent to the C float or real. It has a minimum and maximum value that is officially machine dependent but is generally on the order of $+/-10^{16}$.

Decimal

Because of the difficulties and variations associated with using floating-point numbers on early Unix machines, Informix developed their own form of floating-point number representation: the `decimal` data type. This design move had the added advantage of making it easier to move data over the network, because the numeric data was stored in a consistent format from machine to machine.

The Informix `decimal` data type is stored internally, as shown in Table 2-3.

The `decimal` data type can be either fixed point in representation if a precision is specified during the declaration process, or floating point if no precision is specified. Its precision is very large, on the order of $+/-10^{32}$ or 32 significant digits. The decimal data type column is declared as follows:

Table 2-3 *Decimal Data Type Storage*

Component	Storage
Exponent	2-byte integer
Decimal position	2-byte integer
Number of digits	2-byte integer
Digits	Character with a length of declared precision/2

```
create table sales_rec ( sales_num integer,

                                 sales_amount decimal );
```

Because this declaration does not specify precision, this variable has the default of 16 digits of precision and the decimal point floats. If, however, the column had been declared as

```
create table sales_rec ( sales_num integer,
sales_amount decimal(10) );
```

it would create a decimal variable with a maximum number of 10 significant digits; or the column could have been defined as

```
create table sales_rec ( sales_num integer,
sales_amount decimal(10,2) );
```

This would create a `decimal` variable of 10 digits with a precision of 2 (2 digits to the right of the decimal place).

If m is the precision and n the scale, a column would be declared as follows:

. . .

```
decimal_column decimal(m,n)
```

The maximum value that could be stored in this column would be $10^{m-n} - 10^{-n}$. This means that a `decimal` could be declared

. . .

```
decimal_column decimal(2,0)
```

This column could then store a maximum of $10^{2-0} - 10^{-0}$ or 99(100-1). Any attempt to store a number larger than this would generate an expression error.

Money

The money data type is a special case of the decimal data type. It is, by default, a fixed decimal number with a scale of two. When the money data type is displayed, the default currency symbol is displayed to the left of the digits being displayed. The default output currency symbol may be changed by using the DBMONEY environment variable, which has the following format:

DBMONEY=scb

In this format, s is the symbol that precedes the money value, c is the symbol that separates the whole currency portion from the fractional portion, and b is the symbol that follows the money value. The valid values for c are "." or ",". The valid values for s or b are any series of characters that do not include a comma or a period.

Float

The float data type in Informix usually has the same precision as a C double on the machine platform. Once again, the precision is machine dependent but is usually limited to 10^{-32}. The language definition double precision is a synonym for float.

Date

The Informix date is represented internally as a 4-byte integer that represents the number of days since January 1, 1900, inclusive. The Informix engine automatically formats this value according to either its default format or the format specified by the DBDATE environment variable. The DBDATE environment variable is set as follows:

DBDATE=dmync

In this statement, d is the day being set, m is the month being set, y is the year, n is the number following the year position and represents the number of digits of the year to print. The number of year digits can be a two or a four. The final character c is the character used to separate the components of the date.

Datetime

The datetime data type is a means of representing an instant in time; it contains both date and time components. The datetime data type has a variable degree of precision. The user can define a datetime variable to be of a particular precision but then dynamically change the precision as needed. The datetime data type is composed of the fields year, month, day, hour, minute, second, and fraction of a second. This data type is very handy for applications that require a time stamp to be stored with a record. The datetime data type is declared as follows:

...

```
variable_name datetime first to last
```

In this example, the identifier *first* or *last* is one of the fields from Table 2-4, where the level for a *last* entry cannot precede a *first* entry from the list in the same datetime definition.

Table 2-4 Datetime Identifiers

Field	Valid Entries	Level
Year	Number from 1 to 9999	1
Month	Number from 1 to 12	2
Day	Number from 1 to 31, depending on month	3
Hour	Number from 0 to 23	4
Minute	Number from 0 to 59	5
Second	Number from 0 to 59	6
Fraction	5 decimal digits	7

Interval

The interval data type is used to represent a span of time. It represents the difference between two datetime values. It also supports a varying degree of resolution, which can be defined when the variable is defined or changed at runtime.

Because the interval data type is specifically designed to represent a span of time independent of dates, it must be represented by specific components that cannot mix dates and times.

Table 2-5 *Year/Month Intervals*

Field	Valid Entries	Level
Year	Number 1 to 9999 (default)	
	Number 1 to 999,999,999 (max)	1
Month	Number 1 to 99 (default)	
	Number 1 to 999,9999,9999 (max)	2

Table 2-6 *Day/Hour Intervals*

Field	Valid Entries	Level
Day	Number 1 to 99 (default)	
	Number 1 to 999,999,999 (max)	1
Hour	Number 1 to 99 (default)	
	Number 1 to 999,999,999 (max)	2
Minute	Number 1 to 99 (default)	
	Number 1 to 999,999,999 (max)	3
Second	Number 1 to 99 (default)	
	Number 1 to 999,999,999 (max)	4
Fraction	Number 1 to 999 (default)	
	Number 1 to 99,999 (maximum)	5

There are two interval types: those that represent a year/month
span of time and those that represent day/hours/minutes/sec-
onds. An interval would be declared with the following format:

. . .

```
interval_col interval first to last
```

In this example, the identifier *first* or *last* is one of the fields from
Tables 2-5 and 2-6, where the level for a *last* entry cannot precede a *first* entry from the list in the same `interval` definition.

The default entries are system defaults that can be overridden
during the declaration of the `interval` column. The following
declaration statement demonstrates this

. . .

```
interval_col interval year(5) to month ...
```

In this example, the interval column has been defined to allow five digits in the year, instead of the default value of four digits.

Character

The character data type is a fixed length string of characters of up to 32,767 characters in length. It is always blank padded to its defined length. Though it is usually null terminated, it does not depend on a null terminator to determine its length. Its length is fixed when the character variable is defined.

Varchar

The varchar data type is a variable length string of characters of up to 255 characters in length. The minimum and maximum sizes of the column are defined when the column is declared. The varchar can be used just as the character data type is used. The difference is that the varchar data type is not blank padded out to a defined length; the varchar uses only the storage required to store the character data that has been placed into the column.

Special Data Types

Some data types deserve special consideration from the engine. The standard data types supported by the engine are generally small data objects requiring storage of anywhere between 1 or 2 bytes to 32K bytes. But not all storage needs fit into the mold of standard data types. There has been a growing need to store rich data types in relational databases. Data such as audio and video clips and graphic images need to be stored with other data. This need led to the creation of the binary large object (BLOB).

The BLOB is a data type that stores a binary stream of data. The Informix engine knows nothing about the details of the data stored in a BLOB column; it knows only the size of the object. The database engine allows the data to be manipulated with standard SQL statements, though there are some limits on retrieval and update of the BLOB column.

It is not uncommon for BLOB data columns to be several megabytes in size. Storage and manipulation of such large objects present a problem. Informix provides two means of physical storage of BLOB data: either in the same physical space as a table or in its own dbspace. A BLOB stored in a table is referred to as a tblspace BLOB. A BLOB stored in its own dbspace is stored in what is known as a Blobspace and is referred to as a Blobspace BLOB.

A Blobspace is a special case of a dbspace designated to hold BLOBS of a certain size. A BLOB that is stored in a Blobspace never passes through the IDS shared memory buffer; it is written directly to the Blobspace (to disk). The structure of the Blobspace is designed to make this process more efficient.

When a Blobspace is created, the size of the page for the Blobspace, known as the Blobpage, is specified. The Blobpage size must be a multiple of the IDS page size. The Blobpage size can vary between Blobspaces and is best when the size of the BLOB to be stored is, on the average, close to or slightly smaller than the Blobpage size.

Rows that contain a Blobspace BLOB in a column do not contain the actual data for the BLOB. Instead, they contain a pointer to the BLOB data in the form of a 56-byte BLOB descriptor. This BLOB descriptor is a forward pointer to the location of the first segment of the BLOB. This segment could be a BLOB page in the dbspace, a BLOB page, or an optical platter (if the Online/Optical option is being used).

Mirroring

The Informix server provides the ability to *mirror* each dbspace created on the system. Mirroring provides a continuous backup for a logical portion of disk—in this case, a dbspace. This mirroring is provided through the Informix server software and is therefore distinct from **hardware** mirroring.

When mirroring is established with the Informix engine, there is a *primary* dbspace and a *secondary* or *mirror* dbspace. All disk I/O is directed at the primary dbspace, though disk writes are always made to both the primary and secondary (mirror) dbspace.

Disk reads are generally made against the primary chunk, but in the event there is an I/O wait in reading from the primary chunk, the engine reads from the secondary chunk. In the event a read fails on a primary dbspace, the dbspace is flagged as offline and a read is attempted on the secondary or mirror dbspace. All of this is done transparently to the user; the engine remains online and the query completes successfully.

Data Replication

Data replication in the Informix engine is the process of storing a database at more than one site. With Informix replication, the entire database, known as the *primary server*, is replicated from one site to another site, known as the secondary server. The primary server allows full read/write access, but the secondary server can be used only for read-only access.

Informix replication is designed to provide the high availability features of data replication with very little overhead and maintenance. It is not an add-on feature but is instead an integral part of the engine.

Data replication is implemented using a store-and-forward approach. Database records to be replicated are stored on the primary server and are then forwarded to the secondary server, where they are rolled forward against the replicated database. In this way, the secondary server remains current with the primary server. Log entries are stored in a *replication buffer* in shared memory on the primary server and then passed to a *reception buffer* on the secondary server. Once in the reception buffer on the secondary server, they are then rolled forward against the secondary server's database copy.

Data replication can be performed either *synchronously* or *asynchronously*. If performed **synchronously**, then transactions on the primary server are not completed until the secondary server has finished rolling forward the transactions. With this mode of replication, there is certainty that both the primary and secondary server are synchronized—they are both current to the same point in time. The downside to this approach is that performance on the primary is hindered by requiring that each transaction complete on the secondary before they can complete the transaction on the primary. Given that replication is being conducted over a network connection, all transaction data must be passed over the network from the primary to the secondary, a process that could be time-consuming even with high-speed network connections.

With **asynchronous replication**, the log entries on the primary are written to the logical log buffer and then copied to the replication buffer. The replication buffer on the primary is then periodically sent from the primary server to the secondary server. The secondary server receives the logical log entries in its reception buffer and then rolls forward the entries. The primary does not wait for the secondary server to complete the log roll-forward; it commits transactions and continues processing.

Tip

With asynchronous replication, log entries can be lost in the event of a system failure. When asynchronous replication is used and replication is restarted after a system failure, log entries that cannot be matched are written to a lost-and-found location, and any transactions that may have been committed on the primary but not the secondary are rolled back on the primary server.

To reduce the risk of lost transactions, the *unbuffered logging* option should be used for both the primary and secondary servers. This reduces the amount of time spent between the start of the transaction commit on the primary server and the time the log records are received by the secondary server.

System Reserved Pages

The IDS engine reserves a number of pages in shared memory for system use. These pages contain critical information about the system such as configuration parameters, a list of chunks and dbspaces, and backup and recovery information.

There are 12 reserved pages in IDS shared memory. Because of the critical nature of information kept in the system reserved pages and the requirements of system checkpoints, the Informix server keeps two copies of a number of these pages; in the event one copy is corrupt, the other copy could be used to provide the information. The IDS reserved pages are listed in Table 2-7 in the order in which they appear in shared memory.

Table 2-7 IDS Reserved Pages

System Reserved Page	Purpose
1 PAGE_PZERO	System Identification
2 PAGE_CONFIG	Copy of configuration file
3 PAGE_ICKPT	Checkpoint/logical-log tracking
4 PAGE_2CKPT	Alternate checkpoint page
5 PAGE_1DSP	Dbspace description
6 PAGE_2DSP	Alternate dbspace page
7 PAGE_1PCHUNK	Mirrored-chunk descriptions
8 PAGE_2PCHUNK	Alternate primary chunk page
9 PAGE_1MCHUNK	Mirrored-chunk descriptions
10 PAGE_2MCHUNK	Alternate mirror chunk page
11 PAGE_1ARCH	dbspace backup tracking
12 PAGE_2ARCH	Alternate archive page

The reserved pages are explained in more detail in the sections that follow.

PAGE_PZERO

This page contains IDS information—database system state, system flags, page size, date/time created, version number, and internal information.

PAGE_CONFIG

This is the system configuration reserved page and contains the configuration parameters for the IDS instance. This is effectively the contents of the `onconfig` file.

PAGE_CKPT

This page contains information to track the checkpoint and logical log files for the system. This tracks the time of the checkpoint, the physical log size and beginning address, the logical log identifier, the log position, the address of the dbspace descriptor page, and the mirrored-chunk descriptor page.

PAGE_DBSP

This page is the dbspace page and is used to store information on each dbspace and its current status, the number of the first chunk in the dbspace, the time the dbspace was created, the name of the dbspace, and the owner of the dbspace.

PAGE_PCHUNK

This is the primary chunk reserved page and is used to describe each chunk in the instance. The reserved page describes the chunk, the path name to the chunk, which dbspace or Blobspace it belongs to, and the status of the chunk. Chunk descriptive information indicates the chunk size, chunk offset, the number of free pages, and other relevant information.

PAGE_MCHUNK

The PAGE_MCHUNK reserved page is used to track each mirror chunk in the instance. It contains the information on the chunk such as its primary chunk number, the next chunk number in the dbspace, and other information on the chunk and its dbspace.

PAGE_ARCH

The PAGE_ARCH system reserved page is used to describe the most recent and second most recent archives performed on the database instance. This page also contains information on the logical log that records the backup and information on data replication.

Root dbspace

The root dbspace is the primary dbspace for the database instance. It contains the system reserved pages, which track critical information concerning the database instance. It also contains the default dbspace; if no specific dbspace is mentioned in an SQL statement, such as the create table or create database statement, the default root dbspace is used.

System Catalog

The system catalogs represent the entry point into a database. When a query is parsed by the database, the system catalogs are read to determine the location of the database tables referenced in the query. The optimizer also needs information on the indexes that exist for the tables in the query and the statistics on the data and indexes in the tables. All of this information is stored in the system catalogs.

If for some reason the system catalogs cannot be read, then access to the database is not possible. For this reason, the root dbspace should be mirrored; in the event the primary root dbspace fails, the mirror root dbspace takes over transparently. The tables listed in Table 2-8 are contained in the system catalogs.

The sysmaster Database

The IDS server instance maintains information on the databases within the instance. This information concerns the state of each of the databases, the sessions active, performance-related information, and archive and recovery statistics. This information is available in the sysmaster database. Some of the information is kept in conventional database tables within this database; other information is kept in shared memory tables and is merely mapped to SQL tables by the IDS engine. Table 2-9 lists the tables contained in the sysmaster database.

Table 2-8 *System Catalog Tables*

Table Name	Purpose
systables	Contains a list of all tables
syscolumns	Contains a list of all columns
sysindexes	Contains a list of all indexes for all tables
systabauth	Permissions by table
syscolauth	Permissions by table column
sysviews	SQL views that have been created
sysusers	Users that have been added to the database
sysdepend	Describes how each view or table depends on other views or tables
syssynonyms	Contains a list of the synonyms for each table or view
syssyntable	Outlines the mapping between each synonym and the object it represents
sysconstraints	Column constraints in place in the database
sysreferences	Referential constraints on columns in the database
syschecks	Check constraints defined for columns
sysdefaults	User-defined default values for columns
syscoldepend	Contains a list of columns specified as having check constraints
sysprocedures	Stored procedures created for the system
sysprocbody	Body of the stored procedure (compiled p-code)
sysprocplan	Query plan for data manipulation statements in stored procedures
sysprocauth	Privileges granted for stored procedures
sysblobs	Storage location of a BLOB column
sysopclstr	Describes the optical clusters in the database
systriggers	SQL triggers currently in use
systrigbody	Body of the SQL triggers currently in use
sysdistrib	Stores data distribution information for use by the optimizer
sysfragments	Stores fragmentation information for tables and indexes
sysobjstate	Stores information about the state of certain database objects (indexes, triggers and constraints)
sysviolations	Violations and diagnostics tables for a base table
sysfragauth	Privileges granted on table fragments
sysroleauth	User roles that have been granted on the system

Table 2-9 *sysmaster Tables*

Table Name	Information
sysadtinfo	Auditing configuration information
sysaudit	Auditing event masks
syschkio	Chunk I/O statistics
syschunks	Chunk information
sysconfig	Configuration information page
sysdatabases	Database information
sysdbslocale	Locale information
sysdbspaces	dbspace information
sysdri	Data-replication information
sysextents	Extent-allocation information
syslocks	Active locks information
syslogs	Logical log file information
sysprofile	System profile information
sysptprof	Table information
syssesprof	Counts of various user actions
syssessions	Description of each user connected
sysseswts	User's wait time on each of several objects
systabnames	Database, owner, and table name for the tblspace
sysvpprof	User and system CPU used by each virtual processor

Note

The database administrator should not make changes to any tables in the `sysmaster` database. The IDS engine depends on this information, and making changes could lead to unpredictable results.

Informix Server Architecture

As identified in Chapter 2, there are four main architectural components that constantly interact to perform the processing required of the Informix engine. These components manage the resources of the engine. They are as follows:

1. Disk I/O
2. Memory (buffer)
3. Thread (process)
4. Communication

Any activity of the server falls under the control of one of these components. A query that requests data requires work of several architectural entities. The communication component manages the memory connection; the memory component must allocate memory to process the data request; the disk I/O component must retrieve data from disk; and the process management component must allocate CPU resources (in the form of threads) to perform the work.

A central aspect of the Informix server architecture is the ability to perform tasks in parallel. Not only are the housekeeping functions of the engine performed in parallel, but individual queries can be broken down into parallel operations—individual threads of execution. The Informix engine architecture (see Figure 2-2) performs these parallel operations with decentralized control. None of the architectural components listed above

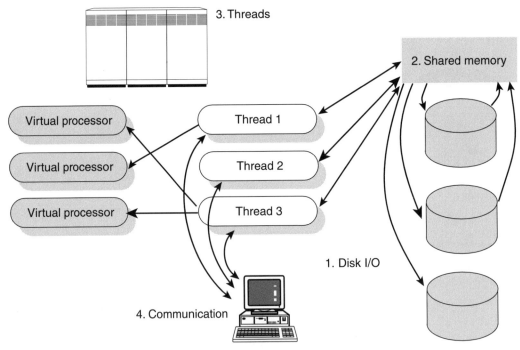

Figure 2-2 *Informix engine architecture*

retains control over the entire operation of a query. These components communicate and make requests of each other, but no component acts as a traffic cop and monitors and restricts the operations of another component; all are relatively equal.

This approach to processing reduces the contention that may occur during heavy processing and allows for better scalability. It also leads smoothly to the *shared nothing* approach to engine design used in the IDS/XP server option where the Informix architecture has paid excellent dividends, providing near linear scalability in the massively parallel processor (MPP) environment.

The following sections explain each of these architectural components.

The IDS Architecture: Disk I/O

The disk management component of the architecture controls all interaction with the disk. As mentioned previously, for Informix servers, the disk is effectively viewed in two layers: the *physical* layer, which involves a collection of chunks that relate to **physical** disk (in Unix, this is the device file) and the *logical* disk, which maps a collection of chunks to a dbspace. The database and its tables are in turn mapped to a dbspace or a set of dbspaces.

IDS Parallel Processing and Fragmentation

If a table is fragmented over five *dbspaces*, then it contains five separate *fragments*. If a query being processed requires the entire table to be scanned (every row in the table must be read), then the Informix server considers starting five separate *threads* (five internal processes) to scan each fragment of the table in a dbspace.

The Informix engine has the ability to perform multiple tasks or threads in parallel; as one task is being performed, another task that does not depend on its completion can also be performed.

But note that this parallelization in the Informix engine is dependent on a solid fragmentation scheme because it is the fragmentation of the data that triggers the parallel processing in the Informix engine.

An additional concept that is part of this architectural component is that of the fragment, a concept that is central to the
Informix server and its multithreaded engine. Fragmentation is
the mapping of the rows of a table to multiple dbspaces.
Known specifically as *horizontal fragmentation*, the Informix
engine provides the ability to place specific rows from a table
into specific dbspaces. The placement of the rows can be random or can be based on expressions that can optionally involve
table column values. When the Informix server makes decisions
on the amount of CPU resource (the number of processing
threads) to assign to a task, one of the criteria it evaluates is the
fragmentation of the tables being examined.

The IDS Architecture: Database Memory

For various reasons, not the least of which is performance, the
Informix engine performs virtually all memory management
operations required by the engine. If memory is allocated for a
task by the server, it is the server's responsibility to free that
memory when it is no longer needed. The memory management
layer is known as the *memory grant manager* (MGM).

This memory management task faced by the engine is further
complicated by the fact that IDS creates a shared memory buffer,
a shared portion of global program memory that is shared by a
number of users. So not only must memory be allocated and
released for the various tasks the engine must perform, but concurrency must be managed amongst the various users accessing
the global shared memory. This requires a sophisticated locking
mechanism to control memory efficiently. This is managed using
a "test and set" locking mechanism known as a *latch* (implemented as a *mutex* in IDS).

With early versions of Informix servers, low-level memory allocation was left to operating system calls to allocate and retrieve
memory from the global heap. Starting with Online Dynamic
Server, the engine took on the responsibility of low-level memory
allocation. This allowed for finely grained control of memory
allocation by the engine, allowing it to tightly control and priori-
tize these operations.

The Informix engine divides shared memory into several different portions: *resident, virtual,* and *communications*. The **resident**
portion contains the shared memory buffer and various other

tables and queues. The **virtual** portion contains control information on the processing that the engine is performing and various buffers and pools to support that processing. And if the engine is using shared memory interprocess communication, then the **communications** layer contains buffers and control structures to manage the communication between the engine and the processes using the engine's resources. These shared memory components are described in more detail in the following sections.

Resident Portion of Shared Memory

The resident portion of shared memory contains various buffers and tables that are relatively fixed in size. This portion of shared memory manages the buffering of data on disk and its movement between shared memory and disk. The process of asynchronously updating the disk is managed in part using this portion of shared memory.

The resident portion of shared memory stores fixed structures to track all of shared memory. Internal tables are created to track users, locks, transactions, tablespaces (tblspace), disk chunks, page-cleaners, and the buffer pool. Several internal tables track shared memory resources, as follows:

- Buffer table and hash table
- Chunk table
- dbspace table
- Lock table and hash table
- Page-cleaner table
- tblspace (table space) table and hash table
- Transaction table
- User table

Buffer Table

Hash tables are used to provide a rapid look-up mechanism. These tables use a common algorithm to map numbers or strings to a memory location. Hash tables are frequently used internally by the Informix engine and are specifically used for the buffer table, lock table, and the tablespace (tblspace) table.

The buffer table tracks the status of individual buffers. This status is either **empty, unmodified,** or **modified.** A modified or dirty buffer must be eventually written to disk; the strategy for

The portion of memory designated as **resident memory** should in fact be kept *resident* in memory. Unix and other operating systems allow portions of memory to be swapped to disk (*virtual* memory) to allow other programs to use the *physical* memory. Most but not all operating systems support the option of keeping portions of memory in RAM by making those memory segments resident. In order for IDS resident memory to remain resident, the operating system should support resident memory blocks and the IDS RESIDENT configuration parameter for the operating system should be set to 1. This is recommended for all but the most memory-constrained installations of IDS.

doing this is managed by the least recently used (LRU) queue mechanism. Because the buffers in shared memory are a shared resource, concurrency must be managed through buffer **locks**. Buffer locking provides a mechanism for allowing multiple users to access a buffer page without interfering with one another's work. The Informix engine supports two locks: *shared* and *exclusive*. The buffer table tracks the current lock level for each buffer.

Because the Informix engine supports concurrency, there may be situations where more than one user is waiting to access a buffer. The buffer table maintains an **access list**, which tracks the users (or threads) that are waiting to use the buffer and lock level of each thread.

Chunk Table

The chunk table tracks all of the chunks in the Informix server. If mirroring has been enabled, then a separate mirror chunk table is also created. This table contains the chunk number and the number of the next chunk for a given dbspace.

dbspace Table

The dbspace table is used to track all of the dbspaces in the system. This table tracks the dbspace number, the name of the dbspace (as named when the dbspace was created), date and time the dbspace was created ,and the status of the dbspace.

Lock Table

The lock table is the shared memory pool of the locks that have been created on the system. Each time a thread requests a lock, it writes an entry to the lock table. The table tracks the address of the transaction that owns the lock, the type of lock, the page or `rowid` (an identifier for the row) that is locked, and the `tblspace` where the lock is placed. Locks can be either *exclusive, update, shared, byte,* or *intent.*

Page-Cleaner Table

The page-cleaner table tracks the status of the page—cleaners—those threads that are responsible for having updated (dirty) pages in the buffer pool written to disk. This table tracks information on the status of the page cleaner and when it was last used.

`tblspace` *(table space) Table*

This table tracks `tblspaces` that are currently in use by an IDS session and are considered active by the engine. Active `tblspaces` could include tables, temporary tables, and internal control tables.

Transaction Table

The transaction table tracks all transactions currently active in the engine.

User Table

The user table tracks information on the user threads active on the system.

Shared Memory Buffer Pool

The shared memory buffer pool is contained within the resident portion of shared memory. This pool represents the largest portion of resident shared memory and contains database data pages that have been requested by a query. Any data that must be processed by the database must first be read into this buffer pool.

Buffer pages are the size of one IDS page with the exception of I/O that is performed in **big buffers** and I/O that is performed to

Blobspaces. Big buffers are 32 buffer pages in size. These buffers are used to improve performance of large disk reads and writes for reading and writing Blobs and performing sequential reads of data from disk. If the IDS engine determines that it must write multiple disk pages that are contiguous, then it will use big buffers. After a big buffer has been read into shared memory, the disk pages are allocated to regular buffers in the shared memory buffer pools.

Logical Log Buffers

The logical log stores a record of changes to data since the last backup. The logical log can be used to manage a transaction and provide a means of rolling back or undoing the transaction at the discretion of the user or application. The logical log can also be used to provide the ability to recover a database to a particular point in time.

To provide performance benefits, the IDS engine buffers log entries in shared memory before writing the entries to disk. The engine has three logical log buffers (see Figure 2-3), but only uses

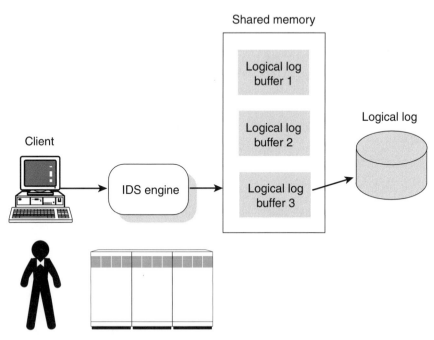

Figure 2-3 *Logical log buffers in IDS*

one of the buffers at a time. Before the engine writes the current log buffer to disk, it makes the second logical log the current logical log so that log entries can continue to be written while the first logical log is written to disk. Should the second logical log be filled before the first logical log has been written to disk, the third logical log would be used to allow the engine to continue writing log entries to a shared memory buffer while the first logical log is being written to disk.

Physical Log Buffers

The physical log is used to restore the database to consistency after a system failure. As stated previously, it stores *before images* of database pages that are in the process of being updated.

The physical log uses two buffers in shared memory (see Figure 2-4). As with the logical log buffer, as one buffer is being written to disk, the other buffer is used to allow the database to continue to write before images while the physical log is being written to disk.

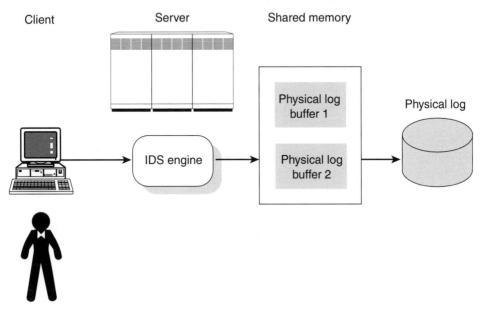

Figure 2-4 *Physical log buffers*

Data Replication Buffer

Data replication allows an IDS engine (the *primary* instance) to be replicated on another machine (the *secondary* instance). Should one instance go offline, the other instance would become the primary instance and could continue to run and process transactions for the database.

With IDS, data replication is implemented using logical logs. The primary instance holds logical log entries in a buffer in shared memory before forwarding them to the secondary instance. The secondary instance then uses the log entries to *roll forward* the database instance and bring it current with the primary instance. The data replication buffer is the same size as the logical log buffer.

LRU Management

Within shared memory, regular buffers are organized and managed through least recently used buffer queues. Because the size of the buffer pool is generally much smaller than the size of the database, there can be a great deal of interaction between the buffer pool and the data on disk. If a large table must be scanned and the size of the table exceeds the size of the buffer pool (a common occurrence), data must be moved in and out of the buffer pool. Deciding which pages to keep in memory and which pages to either remove from memory (if they have not been updated) or write to disk (if they have been updated) comes under the auspices of the LRU queue management.

The LRU queue is implemented as a pair of linked lists. One list is used to track the **free** or unmodified pages in the queue, referred to as the *Free LRU* (FLRU) queue. The other list is used to track the **modified** pages in the queue—the pages that must be written to disk referred to as the Modified LRU (MLRU) queue. The lists are *not* composed of the actual buffer pages, but are composed of pointers to the buffer pages.

As the IDS engine begins to move pages from disk into the shared memory buffer, if the buffer is filled with pages (as is often the case), it must decide which pages to move out of shared memory to make room for the pages that need to be read into shared memory. To move a page that is needed into memory that was previously in memory, the engine generates additional overhead to reread the page from disk. There is therefore a strong impetus to manage this process efficiently and remove only shared memory pages that will most likely not be needed. That is the purpose of the LRU queue (see Figure 2-5).

The linked list for the free LRU buffers is sorted in order of least recently used buffers. Page usage is considered the last time the page was accessed in the shared memory buffer. When the engine needs to place a page in the shared memory buffer and it needs to remove a page from the buffer, it selects an FLRU buffer list at random and finds the least recently used buffer in the queue. If it can latch the buffer, it is removed from memory and

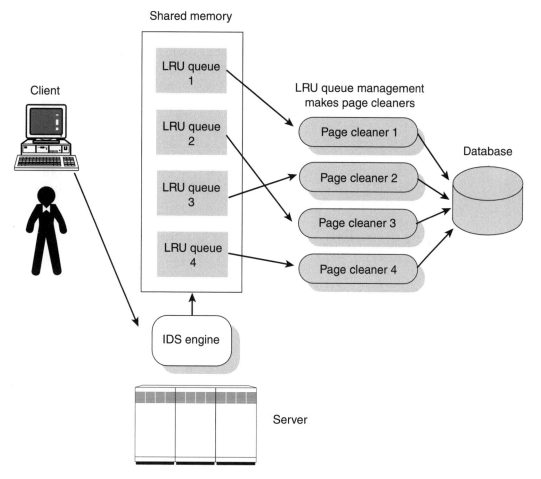

Figure 2-5 *LRU queue management*

the new buffer page is placed into memory. Should the FLRU queue be latched, the IDS engine randomly selects another queue and attempts to select a buffer from there.

Virtual Portion of Shared Memory

The virtual portion of shared memory contains various session-related structures and buffers. Because sessions constantly begin and end, this portion of shared memory is relatively fluid and can be expanded dynamically by the IDS engine. Session control blocks for sessions and memory to process queries for sessions are constantly allocated and deallocated.

Virtual shared memory buffers are allocated to perform in-memory sorts and for general use by sessions. If the engine cannot find a large enough segment in the virtual portion of memory, it attempts to add a virtual memory segment up to a limit set by IDS configuration parameters. When a user session terminates, the allocated memory is freed by the engine.

The virtual portion of shared memory is used to store the following:

- Big buffers
- Session data
- Thread data
- Dictionary cache
- Stored procedures cache
- Sorting pool
- Global pool

These components are explained in the sections that follow.

Big Buffers

Big buffers write large amounts of data to disk. These buffers are used to read tables sequentially and to read and write dbspace BLOBS. Once a big buffer has been read into shared memory, it is allocated to regular buffers.

Session Data

Session data is kept in *session control blocks* in the virtual portion of shared memory. These blocks contain a session id, the user id, the process id of the client process, the name of the host, and status flags on the status of the user session. Once the session has been terminated, the session control block is freed and the memory is returned to the virtual shared memory pool.

Thread Data

Once a client process has started a session, the session ultimately starts threads to perform its work. Threads are managed in a *thread control block*.

When the engine switches from one thread to another, the information on the current thread is kept in the thread control block. Information such as the program counter and global pointers is kept in this portion of shared memory.

The shared memory area used for threads also includes areas allocated for a program *stack* and *heap*. The size of the stack is configurable and defaults to 32 kilobytes. The STACKSIZE environment variable sets the stack size for *all* threads running in the engine. The INFORMIXSTACKSIZE environment variable can be used to set the stack size for a specific user session.

In programming terms, a *heap* is an area in memory for global storage. For a thread running in the IDS engine, this area serves the same purpose. It is a dynamically allocated area in memory used for storage by the thread. The size of the thread heap cannot be changed.

Dictionary Cache

The IDS engine stores data about the database in a series of system tables known as the *system catalog*. These catalog tables are actual tables in the database system, but to avoid the overhead of accessing a database table each time this information is needed, portions of the system catalog are read into shared memory, where they are accessed by user threads.

Stored Procedure Cache

When a stored procedure is first created, it is compiled into a form of optimized pseudo code. This psuedo code is stored in a system catalog table and then read when the stored procedure is run. To avoid the overhead of reading this table each time the stored procedure is executed, repeated calls to the stored procedure read the procedure from the system catalog into a stored procedure cache in virtual memory.

Sorting Pool

When the IDS engine must perform a sort, it attempts to do as much sorting as possible in the virtual portion of shared memory. How much memory is allocated for sorting is dependent on the number of rows to be sorted and the size of the row. The Informix Memory Grant Manager is responsible for allocating the memory used for sorting when the PDQPRIORITY is set to a value greater than 0. The limit on the total amount of memory to be allocated for sorts is set by the DS_TOTAL_MEMORY configuration parameter.

Global Pool

The global pool is used to store structures that are global to the IDS engine, such as the message queues used for communication poll threads. This area of memory is accessible by all IDS threads.

Communications Portion of Shared Memory

This discussion of database memory concludes with the communications portion of shared memory. The communications portion of shared memory is used to manage communications between processes attaching to memory and the engine. This portion of memory manages the message flow between the engine and processes that connect to the engine and request database resources. All interprocess communication is managed through this portion of shared memory.

IDS Architecture: Thread (Process)

Informix servers use their own internal threading mechanism to provide multithreading. Threads are lightweight (requiring little system resource to start and stop) and share the global memory area. Because threads are lightweight, transferring control from one thread to another is faster and more efficient than transferring control from one operating system process to another.

Internal multithreading of engine operations allows for parallelization of individual SQL operations. For a given SQL operation, threads can be spawned to execute portions of the query in parallel. The Informix engine makes intelligent decisions about which portions of the SQL statement should be processed in parallel. If it determines two tables being joined are on the same

The Informix optimizer takes a task and breaks it down into component subtasks. Not all of these tasks can be executed in parallel—In some cases, SQL subqueries and triggers cannot be executed in parallel. But there are a large number of queries that can enjoy the benefits of parallel processing, most noteably decision support queries.

The benefits of parallel processing are best realized on a multiprocessor platform such as an SMP machine. On these platforms, parallel scans and sort operations can be run on multiple CPUs, often dramatically reducing the processing time for long-running queries.

disk, it does not spawn two threads to read the tables in parallel because they would both be attempting to access the same disk and thus create contention. If two joined tables are **not** on the same disk, or the table is fragmented over multiple disks, then multiple scan threads are started to scan the disk. In this way, the fragmentation decisions made can directly affect the parallelization of queries run against the data.

IDS Architecture: Communication

The communication layer of the architecture manages the communication between the database engine and the user processes that connect to the database and request its services. Among other services, this layer listens for connections, tracks user processes, and buffers data transferred to and from the database.

The Informix database supports several different interprocess communication mechanisms and network protocols. This provides a great deal of flexibility in platforms and client connections. The interprocess communication mechanisms supported are as follows:

- Shared memory
- Stream-pipe communication
- TCP/IP network protocol
- IPX/SPX network protocol

Shared Memory Communication

This represents the fastest type of communication. This communication is performed via global memory that is visible to both the client process and the engine. Messages and data are written to a memory location by the client process. The server then reads and writes data to the same memory location. Because the memory is shared between multiple processes, locks are used to control concurrent access to the memory. This IPC mechanism requires the client process to operate on the same machine as the server.

Stream-Pipe Communication

This mechanism makes use of interprocess communication via streams and makes use of operating system calls to move data between the client and server. As with shared memory, this requires both the client and server to be on the same machine.

TCP/IP and IPX/SPX

Both of these communication mechanisms represent network communication protocols supported by IDS. These IPC mechanisms can be used on the same machine or via remote machines. Though not as fast as shared memory communication, this is the mechanism by which most PC-based client-server communication is conducted.

Tracing a Query Through the Engine

To develop a good understanding of the processing that occurs in the Informix engine, it is a useful exercise to trace the execution of a query through the engine. When a user connects to the Informix engine, a session control block is created in memory. This control block is a set of internal programmatic structures that is used to track the status of the connection. When the user executes an SQL statement, the query is tracked through structures in this control block.

The first step in the execution of a query is the *parsing* of the query. The parser examines the SQL statement being processed. It first determines whether or not the statement is syntactically correct. If it is, the parser then examines the database objects (usually database tables) and determines whether or not they exist and, if they exist, whether or not the user has permission to access the database objects.

The next step is the *optimization* of the query—that is, the process of choosing the most efficient query path to retrieve the data. This is a very important function that determines the most efficient method of processing the query. A great deal of effort has been made to make the Informix optimizer the best in the database business. As part of its evaluation process, the location of the database objects in the query is examined by the parser. If individual tables are located in separate dbspaces or tables are spread across multiple dbspaces (they are fragmented), then the optimizer may elect to launch multiple scan threads to retrieve this data. Because the data resides on separate portions of disk, these scan threads could potentially operate in parallel, scanning multiple disks simultaneously, and even processing the data retrieved in parallel.

Other factors are examined in determining a strategy for retrieving data. In some cases, the optimizer must determine whether or not to use an index and, if multiple indices exist for a table, which indices to use. This decision is based in part on the *selectivity* of the index. The selectivity of the index is the uniqueness of the index, which would range from completely unique to some degree of duplicates for an index key.

In many cases, an SQL statement may require tables in the relational database to be joined. The join key in most cases is specified in the where clause of the SQL statement. To complicate matters, there may be multiple tables that must be joined. The parser must determine how best to join these tables, which indices to use, and then how to bring all of the data together. In some cases, it may be better to retrieve the rows from two joined tables and use a hash table to determine which rows from the tables satisfy the join criteria (a *hash-join*). Another alternative is the *sort-merge—join,* where the rows from the two tables are sorted based on the join key, and then merged.

The optimizer must also examine whether or not the results must be sorted. If the results are sorted, then the optimizer could either perform a sort or use an index that satisfies the sort. This decision whether or not to use an index or perform a sort must be balanced with many of the other factors mentioned previously.

The Informix optimizer is a *cost-based optimizer*; its decisions are based on statistical costs for the various access path alternatives available. For instance, an index with low *selectivity* (numerous duplicates) would be assigned a higher weight than an index with high selectivity (unique index or an index with few duplicates). A number of alternative paths to the data are evaluated by totaling the statistical weights or costs for each of the choices in the path.

By default, the Informix optimizer does not try to rule out any specific path, but instead does an exhaustive search of all possibilities and chooses the option with the lowest cost. Though this may sound time-consuming, the elapsed time required is minimal and the benefit in improved path selection ultimately improves query performance.

This default optimizer behavior can be overridden using the SQL statement `set optimization low`. Using this optimization setting, the optimizer does not exhaustively search access path alternatives, but simply chooses the cheapest alternative on each branch of the decision tree and then evaluates the query access path based on those alternatives.

Processing the Query Results

Once the query path has been chosen by the optimizer, the SQL statement can then be processed. The resources are first allocated to process the query based on the access path chosen. Resources allocated are dependent on the resources available and the PDQ priority currently assigned to the user session. Resources assigned to the query are primarily the memory and threads required to process the query. A higher PDQ priority causes more memory and more threads to be assigned to processing the query and alternatively a lower PDQ priority causes fewer threads to be assigned.

Once the query has retrieved a certain number of rows from the tables to the engine buffer, the engine begins returning rows to the user session requesting the rows. This involves interaction between the front-end process that has connected to the engine and the back-end or server process. A synchronous protocol is used to perform this operation, sending rows to the front end, waiting for confirmation of receipt, and then sending additional rows as needed.

When the engine begins returning rows is dependent on the query. If the query is joining two tables and sorting the results, all rows must be retrieved and sorted before the engine can begin returning results. If, however, the engine is able to read an index to get the correct order for the data to be returned, then it can begin returning results immediately to the user.

Once all rows have been returned, many of the resources assigned to the process are deallocated (threads, memory). A certain portion of the session control block in the shared memory buffer remain until the user disconnects from the engine.

Parallel Data Query and PDQ Priority

The Informix database engine is *multithreaded*; processing is performed internally using multiple threads of execution. These threads can and usually do perform operations in parallel. If multiple CPUs are available to the engine for processing, then the engine can enjoy the benefits of internal parallel processing.

The Informix server performs various database operations in parallel by launching multiple processing threads to perform the operations required. These threads are launched to scan data tables and fragments, sort data, write log files to disk, and perform any other housekeeping or processing functions required of the engine.

The environment variable PDQPRIORITY has a direct impact on how the Informix server allocates resources to the processing of an SQL statement. The correct allocation of these resources can significantly improve the performance of query processing for many types of queries.

The PDQPRIORITY is an integer value that represents a percentage of resources to be allocated to query processing for a session. So a PDQ setting of 20 would allocate 20 percent of engine resources to query processing. The exception to this definition is when the PDQPRIORITY environment variable is set to a value less than 2. These values have special meaning as shown in Table 2-10.

Table 2-10 PDQPRIORITY Values

PDQPRIORITY	Result
PDQPRIORITY OFF	PDQ is **not** used.
1 or LOW	Perform only parallel scans.
100 or HIGH	Use all available system resources to process a PDQ query.

The PDQPRIORITY directly impacts the parallelization that a query receives. If set to 0, a query receives no parallel resources and is processed in serial. This is an appropriate setting for OLTP transactions that derive little or no benefit from parallel processing of a single query. (An OLTP system as a whole, however, does benefit from internal multithreading.)

A PDQPRIORITY setting of between 2 and 100 allocates some percentage of system resources based on the parameter setting to parallel processing for the query. This parameter affects parallelization by impacting the allocation of scan threads for the query. The parameter also impacts the allocation of memory, but it is the allocation of scan threads that addresses the parallel processing for the query. (PDQPRIORITY is covered in detail in the chapter on tuning the IDS engine, Chapter 5, "Monitoring and Tuning the IDS Engine").

IDS Options and Extensions

The previous sections have provided a description of the core Informix engine. Informix has continued to modify and improve the core engine in two strategic directions: object-relational and decision support. They have addressed the object-relational area with the Informix Dynamic Server Universal/Data option and they have addressed the decision support area with the Informix Dynamic Server/Extended Parallel option. These two variations of the Informix engine are explained in the sections that follow.

The IDS engine and its underlying code stream have continued to mature through the years. Growth for software products has generally meant the addition of features, functionality, and in the case of a product such as a database server, performance enhancements. This has been the case with the Informix Dynamic Server.

Most significantly for the Informix server has been the divergence of the server product in two directions. One direction was in the area of MPP support. In order to capitalize on the power of the MPP environment, some changes had to be made to the implementation of the IDS architecture. These changes resulted in the Informix Dynamic Server/Extended Parallel (IDS/XP) server. The other area of divergence was to provide an object-relational database based on the Informix Dynamic Server. The results of these efforts has led to the Informix Dynamic Server with the Universal Data (IDS/UD) option.

Architecture of IDS/XP

The Informix Extended Parallel server is designed to capitalize on the features of *massively parallel* machines. A massively parallel processing machine is composed of a series of distinct servers connected via a high-speed interconnect. These distinct servers are called *nodes*. The IDS/XP product runs a separate database instance known as a *coserver* on each nodes. The coservers communicate via the high-speed interconnect. These coservers achieve the best possible performance on the MPP architecture through some changes in the implementation of the Informix server architecture.

To capitalize on the features of the MPP architecture, the IDS/XP engine achieves maximum parallel performance by avoiding bottlenecks inherent in central coordination of query processing and dispersing query processing over the distinct IDS instances running on the coservers.

The IDS/XP architecture is a *shared-nothing* architecture no resources are shared among the coservers. The resources that are allocated in the Informix core server product are allocated slightly differently in the IDS/XP engine. In IDS/XP, a great deal of the allocation of resources to be devoted to the query is left to the individual coservers that process the query. While coservers communicate and coordinate, each coserver processing the query can still make decisions about how much memory and how many threads to assign to the retrieval of data.

Query Processing in IDS/XP

The IDS/XP server is a collection of coservers that act as one server. The user connects to a single coserver (which can optionally be any of the coservers in the IDS/XP instance). The coserver that the user connects to is known as the *connection coserver*. This connection coserver is then responsible for coordinating the processing for the query. Coordinating a query across multiple coservers could create a bottleneck on the initiating coserver. But this coordination role is reduced by the capability to split the query plan into subplans and leave it to the participating coservers to process the query. With this implementation, the connection coserver must initiate the query processing, perform any processing of its own, and then collect the results from the participating coservers.

Note

IDS/XP works very well in MPP environments with SMP clusters nodes because of the internal parallelization that can be realized by the IDS instance running on each node.

Note that given the implementation of IDS/XP, query processing is dependent on the performance of the individual coservers. A query processes only as fast as its slowest coserver. Likewise, if a single participating coserver does not have adequate resources to process its portion of the query, or a single node fails, the entire query fails.

The IDS/XP server is architecturally identical to the core IDS server. It is the implementation of resource allocation that is different. Memory allocation is left to the participating coservers. Each coserver receives a query subplan that it must then process. This processing is primarily done in isolation; the coserver can use only the resources available on its MPP node. At this point, memory allocation is performed as in the IDS engine. A processing thread requests memory, either receives or is denied the memory, and then acts accordingly.

Allocation of CPU resources is the same. The participating coserver receives a query subplan and then leaves it to its optimizer to determine how many threads to allocate to the retrieval and processing of the data.

Architecture of IDS/UD

The IDS/UD engine has the basic architecture of the IDS engine. It is in the implementation of the IDS/UD object-relational features of this server that the difference between these two products can be found.

The IDS/UD server is an object-relational database server that combines the time-tested features and performance of a relational database with the programmer productivity features of an object-oriented database.

The IDS/UD engine allows table and row-type inheritance, user-defined data types, and the ability to extend the features of the engine by creating server functions (user defined functions). IDS/UD server functions can be declared in the C language, Informix Stored Procedure Language, and the Java language (summer 1998). The combination of database table and row-type definitions, and functions that recognize these data type extensions, is a package referred to as a Datablade.

The IDS/UD engine executes server functions as direct extensions of the engine. The functions effectively execute as part of the engine code (they are loaded as shared library functions by the engine).

The ability to create data types from existing ANSI data types (row types) and to declare user-defined data types is significant. This concept of data type extensibility is central to that of object-oriented programming, where data is not considered a separate entity as such but is packaged or encapsulated with functions (also called methods) in what is known as an object. Data type extensibility also allows rich data types such as audio, video, or digital photos to be stored in a database and manipulated in a manner similar to standard SQL data types through server functions.

Table and row inheritance are handled through SQL statements that provide these object-oriented capabilities. These statements provide the ability to perform a number of object-relational functions such as create a row type, create a table that uses a row type, and create a table that is a superset of an inherited table.

Inheritance in IDS/UD

The functionality of inheritance is central to the notion of object-oriented code reuse. Inheritance allows all of the capabilities of an inherited object, data, and methods, to become part of the inheriting object. In the world of object-relational databases, the concept of inheritance is applied to table schemas. A table declaration can retrieve the schema of a named table or row type and use that schema effectively as its own. This can progress through a hierarchy, so that table A inherits from table B, which in turn inherits from table c.

Chapter Summary

This chapter began by covering the basics of the IDS engine. The shared memory buffer, the concepts of multithreading, and virtual processors were covered. These and other key concepts were discussed as required components for any discussion of the IDS engine.

The architecture of the IDS engine was then covered, including a discussion of the two Informix engine options: IDS/UD and IDS/XP.

Next Chapter

The next chapter covers the installation and configuration of the Informix server. This is one of the most critical aspects of IDS usage because a poorly configured server could easily lead to less-than-optimal performance and a disgruntled, unhappy set of users. The process of planning and executing a server configuration is covered along with the steps to take to validate the installation.

Chapter 3

Installation
and Configuration
of the Informix
Dynamic Server

The IDS engine is extremely flexible. This flexibility derives in large part from the configuration parameters available for the engine. The IDS server provides parameters to locate the message log, specify the number of locks, specify the size of the memory buffer, assign the number of logical log files for the server, and tune and direct a number of other engine operations. Chapter 4 details these engine configuration parameters and when possible, provides tips on initial settings for the parameter. (Additional coverage of parameters is covered in the chapter on monitoring and tuning the IDS engine.)

Each connection to the IDS engine represents a *user session*. The IDS engine also allows the operation of each user session to be controlled in part through a set of environment variables. These environment variables and their functions are detailed in this chapter.

IDS Configuration

The flexibility of the IDS engine, and the ability to install this engine on a variety of platforms and under a variety of user loads, is derived in part from the ability to configure the engine. Without the numerous configuration parameters available, the Informix server would not be nearly as flexible.

The Informix server stores configuration parameters in an ASCII file that by default is named onconfig. This file is read at system startup and contains parameters and corresponding values to control the engine. Comments can be included by entering a "#" on a line in the file; any characters after the "#" are ignored by the engine.

The name of the configuration file can be changed by setting the environment variable **ONCONFIG** to a value that specifies the name of the onconfig file for the server to use. For instance, a user who sets the ONCONFIG environment variable to onconfig.myfile and then runs Informix client software would have the client software read the onnconfig.myfile configuration file to determine how to connect to the database instance.

On startup, the Informix server reads the configuration file and attempts to make sense out of the entries. It runs several internal checks, and should some of the validations fail, the engine does not start.

Installation Preparation

Before installing the IDS engine, the hardware platform must be prepared. The database administrator must consider both the size of the database to be installed and the number of users who will be connecting to the database. The hardware platform should have adequate disk available to hold the data that will be stored in the database.

As discussed in Chapter 2, the Informix server recognizes disk as both *raw* disk, which it views as a collection of *chunks*, and *dbspaces* that map one or more chunks to logical representations of disk. When a database and tables are created in the Informix database, they are stored in dbspaces.

The Informix database uses *shared memory*, memory visible to multiple distinct operating system processes, to buffer the data retrieved and written to disk and to store status information and other system control structures. On Unix, shared memory must be configured as part of the operating system. This configuration includes the specific size of the shared memory available from the device. In order for performance to be optimal, there must be sufficient memory available in the shared memory buffer to handle the load on the engine. The number of locks and semaphores available on the system may also need to be adjusted. Review the product release notes for the product for specific information for the configuration parameters to alter (found in /release subdirectory of installation directory).

IDS Installation

The Informix Dynamic Server is usually installed via a tape or CD-ROM. A `tar` or `cpio` format file is extracted from the device, and an installation script is run.

A specific directory must be chosen as the **home** directory for the Informix files. A series of subdirectories are created under this directory depending on the product and product options being installed. The basic subdirectories are shown in Table 3-1.

Table 3-1 IDS Subdirectories

Subdirectory	Contents
etc	Software configuration files: `sqlhosts`, `onconfig`, and the like
msg	Error message files and help files
bin	Binaries, dlls, and shared object files (`oninit,onstat`, and the like)
lib	Library files for tools (ESQLC/4GL)

The software directory structure is, for the most part, rigid and should not be changed by users. Under the parent directory are a series of subdirectories that cannot be moved or renamed. The actual location of the parent directory, however, is flexible and is dependent on the setting of the **INFORMIXDIR** environment variable. The setting of this variable indicates the full path name for the parent directory for the software. For example, if this environment variable were set to /home/informix, then the full path to the Informix /etc directory would be /home/informix/etc.

In the ./etc directory are a number of configuration files used by the Informix server. One file located there is the sql-hosts file. The sqlhosts file stores values for Informix server names, the protocol to use to connect to those servers and other information as shown in Table 3-2.

Table 3-2 *SQLHOSTS File Entries*

Field	Description
dbservername	The name of the IDS server for the connection; this would match the DBSERVERNAME parameter in the onconfig configuration file.
nettype	The nettype parameter indicates the protocol to be used to connect to this database server.
hostname	Indicates the network host name of the machine host that contains the database instance for the connection; this entry must match an entry in the machine's /etc/hosts file.
servicename	The network service name of the service that will be used to connect to this database server; this does not apply to shared memory connections where this entry is not used.
options	This field contains additional options for the entry.

The sqlhosts file can contain multiple entries with each entry containing five fields, as shown in Table 3-2.

The nettype parameter identifies the protocol to use for the server instance. The choice of the protocol is very important, since not all protocols are supported on all platforms. Using the wrong protocol could preclude making a successful connection to the server instance. Each database release contains a set of release notes that are specific to that release; refer to these release notes (in the ./etc directory) for the protocol or protocols supported on the installation platform.

Running the Installation Program

Once the product has been installed from tape or CD-ROM, an installation program should be run to complete the install. At one point during the execution of the install program, a valid serial number and key (from the software packaging) must be entered. Once the serial number and key is entered, the installation program will *brand* the program binaries. Without this branding process, the programs cannot be run.

IDS Environment Variables

Informix uses a number of environment variables to provide flexibility and configurability. Because the variables are set in a user's environment, each user environment can be customized. A user can be given a specific, narrow view of the database instance, restricting the remote servers visible to the user (INFORMIXSQL-HOSTS, DBPATH), directing them to a specific server instance (INFORMIXSERVER, ONCONFIG) at a specific priority (PDQPRIORITY).

The environment variables provided by the Informix engine are extensive. The more important variables that apply directly to the engine are listed in Table 3-3.

Though they are numerous and sometimes complex, these environment variables add a great deal of flexibility and tunability to the Informix engine. Understanding the purpose of these variables is an essential part of using IDS. The following sections provide an explanation of these parameters.

ONCONFIG

The ONCONFIG environment variable identifies the name of the configuration file for the IDS instance to be used. When the server is started, the engine reads this file to determine the configuration of the engine; such information as the location of disk storage, the shared memory address and/or offset for the shared memory buffer, and other pertinent information contained within this file.

Table 3-3 *Environment Variables*

Environment Variable	Purpose
ONCONFIG	Informix configuration file to use for the IDS instance being run.
INFORMIXSERVER	Name of the Informix server instance to run (see DBSERVER environment variable and DBSERVERALIAS).
PATH	The PATH Unix uses to search for binaries to execute.
TERMINFO	terminfo file that contains the terminfo definition for the terminal to be used to access Informix applications.
DBANSIWARN	Set true if engine is to generate warnings when non-ANSI-standard SQL is used.
DBCENTURY	Allows the choice of the appropriate expansion when a two-digit year is given for a date or datetime value.
DBDELIMITER	Specifies the ASCII delimiter used with character load and unload facilities.
DBEDIT	Specifies the text editor to be used with Informix database utilities.
DBLANG	Specifies the directory for the message files used by the Informix product .
DBFLTMASK	Specifies the number of decimal digits Informix applications display.
DBMONEY	Specifies the display format of monetary values.
DBPATH	Indicates the network servers that contain Informix database instances (with SE product, specifies directories for the Informix-SE database).
DBPRINT	Specifies the print program the Informix product uses.
DBSPACETEMP	Indicates the dbspaces where temporary tables are built. Overrides the configuration parameter in the onconfig file.
DBTEMP	Specifies the full path name of the directory for temporary files generated by Informix gateway products and the Informix-SE engine.
DBTIME	Indicates the format to use for time display.
FET_BUF_SIZE	Specifies the size of the fetch return buffer (returning data from the server to the client) in bytes.
INFORMIXSERVER	Specifies the Informix server name (DBSERVERNAME) for the implicit client connection.
INFORMIXSHMBASE	Indicates where the base address is for the Informix server instance in shared memory.
INFORMIXSQLHOSTS	Specifies the full path name including the file name of the file containing server host information.
INFORMIXSTACKSIZE	Specifies the stack size used for a client session. Overrides the onconfig parameter setting.
INFORMIXTERM	The character terminal type to be used for Informix tools. Overrides the TERM environment variable.
ONCONFIG	Indicates the file for the onconfig file. Assumed to be in the $INFORMIXDIR/etc directory.
PATH	Search path for binary executables. This should contain $INFORMIXDIR/bin.
PDQPRIORITY	Priority setting (resource allocation percentage) used for decision support queries.
PSORT_DBTEMP	Directory where temporary files are written during a parallel sort operation.
PSORT_NPROCS	Specifies the number of threads to be allocated to sort a query; maximum value is 10.
TERM	Character terminal to use with all applications.
TERMCAP	The termcap file to use with character—based applications.

At sites where there is more than one instance of IDS running, there are usually multiple configuration files, one for each IDS instance. Users connect to specific instances of the engine by setting the ONCONFIG environment variable to the name of the configuration file for their instance. Note that the INFORMIXSERVER environment variable must contain a server name that matches the DBSERVER-NAME configuration parameter in the configuration file referenced by the ONCONFIG environment variable setting or a DBSERVER alias string in the DBSERVERALIASES parameter.

INFORMIXSERVER

This environment variable specifies the server name of the Informix server for implicit connections (connection attempts where the server name is not specified in the SQL statement or Call Level Interface [CLI] function call). This name must match either the DBSERVERNAME configuration parameter or one of the entries in DBSERVERALIASES list in the `onconfig` configuration file specified in the ONCONFIG environment variable. A corresponding entry must also be found in the `sqlhosts` host protocol configuration file to determine the connection protocol.

TERMINFO

The TERMINFO environment variable specifies the name of the terminal information file (sometimes referred to as the terminal information database). With some applications, this is used to define the character-based interface between the application and the terminal. (This is an alternative to the TERMCAP information file and is dependent on the application being used.)

PATH

The PATH environment variable specifies the search path for binary executables on the system. The only requirement for Informix software is that Informix binaries and, in some cases, shared libraries be in this search path. This is generally accomplished by specifying the Informix directory for binaries, the

./bin directory, relative to the Informix home directory in the search path.

Because the Informix home directory is specified in the INFORMIXDIR environment variable, the shell syntax `$INFORMIXDIR/bin` would resolve to the full path name for the Informix binaries. The following Bourne shell syntax would append the Informix binaries path to the PATH environment variable:

```
PATH=$INFORMIXDIR/bin:$PATH;export PATH
```

DBANSIWARN

The DBANSIWARN environment variable indicates that the engine should check for syntax that represents Informix extensions to ANSI SQL. If the engine finds syntax that is an Informix extension to ANSI SQL, it displays a warning message and continues processing. The variable does not need to be set to a specific value; it simply needs to be set to generate this warning.

This variable is useful at sites where programmers wish SQL usage to remain as close as possible to ANSI SQL. Setting this environment variable in the environment of database programmers would provide immediate feedback on the SQL statements that violate ANSI SQL standards. The following Bourne shell statement would set the DBANSIWARN variable:

```
DBANSIWARN=1
```

The following statement would unset the DBANSIWARN environment variable.

```
unsetenv DBANSIWARN
```

DBCENTURY

The DBCENTURY environment variable allows the user to choose the appropriate expansion for a two-digit date. The variable has a number of settings that allow a specific behavior to be used to expand a date or datetime setting. The current century can be chosen for expansion (the default behavior), the past century, the future century, or the closest century. The values listed in Table 3-4 are valid settings for this environment variable.

Table 3-4 *Settings for DBCENTURY*

Setting	Value
P	Past - use prior (past) date
F	Future - use future date
C	Closest - use closest century
R	Present - use present century for expansion

DBDELIMITER

The DBDELIMITER environment variable is used to set the delimiter character to be used when loading/unloading the data from the engine as ASCII data. The Informix SQL extension statements load and unload provide this capability as well as several Informix database utilities. By default, this value is the ASCII pipe character (|), but many utilities from other vendors prefer the comma or another character as a delimiter. (The value of the delimiter can also be specified in the SQL statement that initiates the load or unload operation.)

DBEDIT

The DBEDIT environment variable specifies the text editor to be used with Informix character applications. The default editor on Unix environments is the vi text editor. Another popular choice in the Unix environment is the GNU emacs editor.

DBLANG

The DBLANG environment variable indicates the directory where the message files are stored for the Informix product. Informix products read these message files at runtime and use them to display informational and error messages. If these message files cannot be located by an application that requires them (ESQL, Informix-4GL), these applications may not run.

DBFLTMASK

The DBFLTMASK environment variable specifies the number of decimal digits the Informix application displays. By default, Informix displays the decimal number with a maximum of 16 digits to the right of the decimal place. This environment variable can be used to override that default.

DBMONEY

The DBMONEY environment variable specifies the display format for monetary values. The format specifies an optional preceding character or characters, a character to separate the integral from the fractional part, and a trailing character or set of characters. Specifically, the format is as follows, and is explained in Table 3-5.

```
DBMONEY= <front> <separator> <back>
```

Table 3-5 DBMONEY Format

Character	Function
front	The symbol that precedes the monetary value. By default, this is the dollar sign '$'.
separator	The character that separates the integral from the fractional portion of the monetary value. By default, this is the period '.' character.
back	The symbol that follows the monetary value.

DBPATH

The DBPATH environment variable specifies the network servers that contain IDS instances. The `connect`, `database`, `start database`, and `drop database` statements use the DBPATH environment variable to determine where the database is located. This variable is used only if the location of the database is not explicitly stated or if the database cannot be located in the default server.

The DBPATH environment variable can contain up to 16 entries. Entries are in the format specified as follows, separated by a colon (:) delimiter:

```
DBPATH=//servername1://servername2
```

Using the Informix-SE engine, this setting has a different meaning. This variable indicates the full file system path name of the location of the Informix-SE database files. (The Informix-SE database uses the Unix file system for database files.)The DBPATH environment variable provides a certain degree of *location transparency,* making the actual location of the database relatively transparent to the application requesting access to the database.

The Informix client database connectivity layer first checks for the engine locally. If the engine cannot be found locally, the connection layer examines the DBPATH environment variable and, if it is set, checks the remote servers listed in the environment variable in a left-to-right fashion.

Using this approach, a user could have a DBPATH environment variable set to a remote server that contains a backup version of a database. As long as a local version of the database were available, the connection layer would continue to connect the user to the local database. In the event the local version was no longer available, the connection layer would transparently try to find the database on one of the remote servers listed in the DBPATH environment variable. If the database connection is made to the remote machine, the user has connected to a different database server transparently—no error messages or warnings are displayed to the user.

DBPRINT

The DBPRINT environment variable specifies the printer for Informix utilities to use for default printing. On Unix systems, this is usually set to the executable program that directs output to the printer device.

DBSPACETEMP

The DBSPACETEMP environment variable lists a set of dbspaces where temporary files will be written. The dbspaces listed are used in a round-robin fashion, writing temporary files first to one dbspace and then creating the next temporary file in the next dbspace in the list. Values in the list are delimited by either colons (:) or commas (,). This environment variable takes precedence over the onconfig parameter DBPSACETEMP, which serves the same function.

Using DBSPACETEMP environment variable, the distribution of temporary files could be accomplished on a user-by-user basis. If it is known that a certain user or application will generate a large number of temporary files, then the user or application could use an environment that sets the DBSPACETEMP environment variable to a set of dbspaces that reside on a different disk from that of the production OLTP system. Other users would continue to create their temporary files in the dbspaces listed in the onconfig parameter DBPSPACETEMP.

DBTEMP

The DBTEMP environment variable specifies the full path name of the directory used for temporary files. These temporary files may be generated by the Informix-SE engine or the Informix gateway products. (Note that IDS will *not* write temporary files to this directory.)

DBTIME

The DBTIME environment variable specifies a string that represents the format to use to display time. Only the output of datetime variables by certain Informix tools is affected by this setting.

FET_BUF_SIZE

The FET_BUF_SIZE environment variable sets the size of the return buffer for Informix front-end tools. When Informix tools retrieve data from the database, the data is stored in a return buffer [generally returned by a fetch cursor operation, thus FET(CH)_RET(URN)_BUF(FER)]. This buffer defaults to a size manageable for SQL select statements retrieving a small to medium number of rows (20–75).

When a front-end tool retrieves data from the database server, the server first reads rows from the database and places the rows in a buffer on the server. When the buffer on the server is full, it is sent to the front end. This process of sending the rows to the front end may involve sending the rows over the network and may therefore be time-consuming and expensive, so reducing the number of network operations is desirable.

If performance is sluggish, then setting the FET_BUF_SIZE to a larger number could improve performance. If set correctly, the number of network transfers could be drastically reduced and the overall speed of the transaction could be improved.

INFORMIXSHMBASE

The INFORMIXSHMBASE environment variable provides the base address in shared memory where the Informix instance shared memory buffer is located. This overrides the value of the SHM-BASE parameter in the `onconfig` configuration file.

INFORMIXSQLHOSTS

The INFORMIXSQLHOSTS environment variable provides the full path name (including the file name) of the `sqlhosts` file. By default, the system uses the file name `sqlhosts` in the $INFORMIXDIR/etc directory.

By using the INFORMIXSQLHOSTS environment variable, users can be given a restricted view of the Informix server environment. If there are one or more servers that a user should not be allowed to access, these servers can be omitted from the `sqlhosts` file designated for the user by the setting of the INFORMIXSQLHOSTS environment variable, thus prohibiting access to those servers through the IDS engine.

INFORMIXSTACKSIZE

The INFORMIXSTACKSIZE environment variable specifies the stack size for a client session in the Informix server. This environment variable overrides the `onconfig` STACKSIZE parameter in the `onconfig` configuration file.

INFORMIXTERM

The INFORMIXTERM environment variable specifies the character terminal to use with Informix applications. This effectively overrides the setting of the TERM environment variable.

PDQPRIORITY

The PDQPRIORITY environment variable provides a priority setting to the engine for decision support queries. This setting is active for the duration of the user session but can be overridden by an SQL 'set PDQPRIORITY' statement.

The value of PDQPRIORITY for a query can also be set using an SQL statement, a setting that would override the setting of the

Note The PDQPRIORITY is a very important setting; it controls the amount of resources the engine allocates for processing of the query. (In fact, it is more of a rough resource allocation percentage than a priority setting.) The value of this environment variable is one of the criteria used in determining the number of processing threads to allocate to the query; thus the PDQPRIORITY setting effectively controls the parallelization that a query receives during its processing. The PDQPRIORITY also impacts the amount of memory allocated to query processing.

The intention of engine designers was to limit the complexity of the configuration process by using a manageable set of configuration parameters where one parameter could impact multiple engine processes. This is a simpler approach than creating numerous parameters that adjusted separately would have had a limited impact on engine processing. The use of the PDQPRIORITY parameter is an example of this strategy.

environment variable. The default value for PDQPRIORITY is 0. The upper limit of the PDQPRIORITY variable is set by the MAX_PDQPRIORITY parameter in the `onconfig` file.

PSORT_DBTEMP

The PSORT_DBTEMP environment variable specifies the directory where temporary files will be written during a parallel sort operation.

PSORT_NPROCS

The PSORT_NPROCS environment variable specifies the number of threads to be allocated for a parallel sort operation. The maximum value is 10.

TERM

The TERM environment variable is set to indicate the character terminal to use with all applications, including Informix character applications. If the INFORMIXTERM environment variable is set, it takes precedence over the setting of this variable.

TERMCAP

The TERMCAP environment variable is used to indicate the file that contains the character terminal definitions to use. Informix uses the file referenced by this parameter unless the INFORMIX-TERM environment variable is set, in which case Informix applications will allow the setting of that environment variable to take precedence.

The `onconfig` File

The entries in the IDS configuration file dictate how the Informix server will operate. A number of these settings are *implementation specific*—their settings are dependent on the purpose of the database server and the resources available on the platform on which the server is being installed. The purpose of the database server is in turn dependent on the applications that access and use the server. Applications may fit the transaction profile of online transaction processing applications where a large number of users request a specific record or a small set of records. Or an application may fit the transaction profile of a decision support application where a large number of records is requested by a relatively small number of users. How an engine is tuned is very dependent on this usage profile. This section discusses appropriate initial settings for parameters. Chapter 5 discusses using these parameters to tune the engine based on its usage profile.

By default, the engine searches for the configuration file named `onconfig` in the `$INFORMIXDIR/etc` directory and, if found, uses the configuration parameters specified in that file. Because instance-specific configuration entries must be made for a new installation, it is good practice to leave the default configuration file intact and create a new configuration file for a new instance. The common practice is to name this file with an extension that contains the server name. For example, a server name of `myserver` would have a configuration file named 'onconfig.myserver'.

The user's view of the IDS engine instance is effectively controlled by the setting of both the ONCONFIG and INFORMIXSERVER environment variables. The INFORMIXSERVER environment variable must be set to connect to the engine but setting the ONCONFIG environment variable is optional because the engine defaults to `$INFORMIXSERVER/etc/onconfig` file. The configuration file contains all the parameters needed to connect to an Informix instance and the INFORMIXSERVER environment variable contains the name of the Informix server instance to use for the connection. The following section describes the configuration parameters available for the IDS engine (see Table 3-6).

ROOTNAME

The ROOTNAME is the unique name of the `dbspace` used to store the system reserved pages and `sysmonitor` database. These pages contain information such as the list of `dbspaces` in the database and their corresponding chunks.

Table 3-6 Configuration Parameters of *onconfig*

Parameter Name	Purpose
ROOTNAME	Root dbspace name
ROOTPATH	Path to the device that contains root dbspace
ROOTSIZE	Size of the initial chunk of the root dbspace
ROOTOFFSET	Offset into the root device for the root dbspace
MIRROR	Mirror flag; set to TRUE if dbspace mirroring will be used on the system
MIRRORPATH	Path for the device containing the root mirror
MIRROROFFSET	Offset into the mirror device for the root dbspace mirror
PHYSDBS	dbspace location of the physical log
PHYSFILE	Size of the physical log file in kilobytes
LOGFILES	Number of logical log files
LTAPESIZE	Size of the logical log tape output device
LTAPEBLK	Block size for the logical log tape device
LOGSIZE	Size of the logical log files
MSGPATH	Full path name for the system message log file
CONSOLE	Full path name for the system console device path
ALARMPROGRAM	Path for the alarm program
TAPEDEV	Path for the tape device
TAPEBLK	Block size for the tape device
TAPESIZE	Maximum amount of data for the tape device
LTAPEDEV	Tape device for the logical log tape device
LTAPESIZE	Maximum amount of data for the log tape device
STAGEBLOB	Staging device for the Online Optical
SERVERNUM	Unique id for the server instance
DBSERVERNAME	Name for the IDS instance
DBSERVERALIASES	List of alternate server instance names
NETTYPE	Network poll threads configuration information
DEADLOCK_TIMEOUT	Maximum time for network transaction
RESIDENT	Forced residency flag for shared memory
MULTIPROCESSOR	Multiple CPU machine flag
NUMCPUVPS	Number of CPU VPs at engine start
SINGLE_CPU_VP	Flag for single CPU VP
NOAGE	Processor aging flag
AFF_SPROC	Start processor affinity on this CPU number
AFF_NPROC	End processor affinity on this CPU number
LOCKS	Maximum number of locks for system

Table 3-6 Configuration Parameters of *onconfig (cont.)*

Parameter Name	Purpose
BUFFERS	Number of shared memory buffers
NUMAIOVPS	Number of asynchronous I/O virtual processors
PHYSBUFF	Size of physical log buffer in kilobytes
LOGBUFF	Logical log buffer size
LOGSMAX	Maximum number of logical logs allowed
CLEANERS	Number of buffer page cleaner processes
SHMBASE	Shared memory buffer address
SHMVIRTSIZE	Initial shared memory size for virtual shared memory
SHMADD	Size of shared memory segments added at runtime
SHMTOTAL	Total initial shared memory allowed
CKPTINTVL	Checkpoint interval in seconds
LRUS	Number of LRU buffer queues
LRU_MAX_DIRTY	Stop cleaning buffer at this percentage dirty LRU queues
LRU_MIN_DIRTY	Start cleaning percentage dirty LRU queues
LTXHWM	Long transaction high water mark as a percent of logs full
LTXEHWM	Long transaction exclusive high water mark as a percent of logs full
TXTIMEOUT	Transaction timeout
STACKSIZE	Size of process stack in kilobytes
OFF_RECVRY_THREADS	Number of offline worker threads during fast recovery or offline restore
ON_RECVRY_THREADS	Number of online worker threads started during an online restore
DRAUTO	Automatic data replication switchover flag
DRINTERVAL	Maximum time between data replication buffer flushes
DRTIMEOUT	Network timeout for data replication
DRLOSTFOUND	Path for data replication lost-and–found directory
CDR_LOGBUFFERS	Size of log buffer pool for CDR in kilobytes
CDR_EVALTHREADS	Number of CDR evaluator threads
CDR_DSLOCKWAIT	DS lock wait in seconds
CDR_QUEUEMEM	Maximum amount of memory for CDR queue in kilobytes
BAR_ACT_LOG	onbar activity log path name
BAR_MAX_BACKUP	Maximum parallel processes for each onbar session executed
BAR_RETRY	Number of times onbar retries an archive
BAR_NB_XPORT_COUNT	Number of database buffers used for data exchange
BAR_XFER_BUF_SIZE	Size of the onbar transfer buffer
RA_PAGES	The number of read–ahead pages to use during full table scans
BAR_BSALIB_PATH	Shared library path for the storage manager used by the onbar utility
RA_THRESHOLD	The read–ahead threshold

Table 3-6 Configuration Parameters of *onconfig (cont.)*

Parameter Name	Purpose
DBSPACETEMP	List of dbspaces for temporary files
DUMPDIR	Diagnostic data is dumped to this directory path
DUMPSHMEM	Shared memory dump flag
DUMPGCORE	gcore shared memory dump flag
DUMPCORE	Core shared memory dump flag
DUMPCNT	Number of shared memory gcore dumps
FILLFACTOR	Fill factor for index node creation
USEOSTIME	Flag for operating system time use
MAX_PDQPRIORITY	Maximum allowed PDQPRIORITY setting
DS_MAX_QUERIES	Maximum number of concurrent PDQ queries
DS_TOTAL_MEMORY	Total decision support memory to use in kilobytes
DS_MAX_SCANS	Maximum number of decision support scans to allow
DATASKIP	Flag for data skip (dbspace skip) feature
OPTCOMPIND	Flag for optimizer hints
ONDBSPACEDOWN	Flag for dbspace down option
LBU_PRESERVE	Set to TRUE to save the last logical log for administrative tasks.
OPCACHEMAX	Maximum size for optical cache size

ROOTPATH

The ROOTPATH is the full path name of the file or special device that contains the root dbspace. Within this device is the dbspace referenced by the ROOTNAME parameter.

The ownership on the device or file that stores any dbspace must be such that the user Informix can read and write to the device or file.

ROOTOFFSET

The offset in kilobytes into the root dbspace. On some hardware platforms, using a zero offset into a device (the default) does not work because device information is stored at this offset. On these platforms, this parameter must be set to some nonzero value to accommodate this anomaly.

ROOTSIZE

This parameter is used to set the size of the root dbspace. This value is only read during system initialization. Once the database instance has been initialized, this parameter is ignored. The size of the dbspace is then increased by adding chunks to the dbspace, not by altering this parameter.

MIRROR

In order to use Informix database mirroring with a dbspace, this parameter must be set to TRUE. This does not create a mirror for any particular dbspace; this just allows mirroring to be used in the database instance.

MIRRORPATH

This parameter is set to indicate the path to the device that is used to mirror the root dbspace. If this parameter is set, then the root dbspace *is* mirrored. If this parameter is not set, then the root dbspace *is not* mirrored.

Tip It is always a good idea to mirror the root dbspaces. Because of the critical nature of information in this dbspace, failure of the root dbspace would render the engine inaccessible—the engine would not be able to start. The only option in this case would be a cold (engine offline) restore.

Mirroring the root dbspace also provides a transparent failover in the event of a hardware failure on the root dbspace. Should the engine encounter an error on an I/O operation on the root dbspace, it would merely switch over to the mirror root dbspace and perform its I/O operation there.

MIRROROFFSET

This parameter represents the offset into the mirror device (referenced by MIRRORPATH) for the chunk referenced in the MIRRORPATH parameter, the chunk that will serve as the mirror for the root dbspace.

PHYSDBS

The PHYDBS parameter specifies the name of the dbspace that is used to store the physical log for the IDS instance.

PHYSFILE

The PHYSFILE parameter indicates the size of the physical log file in kilobytes.

> **Note** It is important that this file be sized appropriately; when this file fills (called a physical log overflow), it triggers a checkpoint and excessive checkpoints can degrade system performance. Chapter 5, "Monitoring and Tuning the IDS Engine," discusses this topic.

LOGFILES

The LOGFILES parameter specifies the number of logical log files. The size of each log file is set by the LOGSIZE parameter. This parameter is read only during system initialization. To add to the number of log files, use the onparams command or dbmonitor or some other appropriate utility.

> **Note** It is important to configure the engine with an appropriate number of logical log files. Too few log files and the database could execute a transaction that would exceed the available number of log files. When this happens, the database would try to roll back the transaction. If there are enough log files to roll back the transaction, then the impact on the entire system is minimal. If there are **not** enough log files available to roll back the transaction, then this situation could potentially lock the IDS engine.

LOGSIZE

This parameter is used to set the size of each logical log file that is created. This parameter is used when the database instance is initialized. Log files that are created after the engine has been initialized may use a new logical log size if a new value has been set since the initialization of the IDS instance.

The size of the logical log file is dependent on a number of factors. In a database that is relatively static—that is, it has very few updates—there will not be much activity logged (because database updates generate the most logging activity). On a system that sees more update activity, the logical log should initially be set using the following formula:

```
LOGSIZE = (users * maxrows) * 512
```

Where **users** is the maximum number of concurrent users expected on the system and **maxrows** is the maximum number of rows those users would expect to access at one time in a transaction.

Tip

Because each IDS instance is different with widely varying transaction profiles, it is difficult to predict exactly what system log activity will be. The database administrator should monitor system activity and watch for update activity that consumes large portions of the available logical logs (such as a data load of 100,000 rows that are 1000 bytes each). Logical logs number and size should either be tuned to handle this update activity, or the application itself should be altered to reduce the stress on the logical logs. Applications could be rewritten to perform more database commits (committing the rows written to the database and allowing the logical logs to be freed).

MSGPATH

This parameter is used to indicate the full path name of the system message file. The system message file stores the messages generated by the database server.

CONSOLE

This parameter is used to indicate the device for output of engine messages. This could be a terminal device or the full path name of an ASCII file. Engine status messages (log complete, checkpoint complete, and the like) are sent to this output device.

ALARMPROGRAM

The ALARMPROGRAM parameter stores the full path name of the alarm program executed by alarm events. When an alarm is triggered, this program is executed and passed parameters indicating the nature of the alarm.

The alarm program is not supplied by Informix; the administrator must make this available to the IDS engine.

TAPEDEV

This parameter indicates the path for the tape device to be used for backups. The Informix `ontape` backup utility uses this device as the output device for backups.

The `onbar` utility does not use the value of the TAPEDEV parameter for output. Instead, it uses the values in its own configuration file.

The logical logs are not output to this device but are output to the device specified in the LTAPEDEV parameter.

TAPEBLK

This parameter contains the block size for the tape device referenced by the TAPEDEV parameter. The value of this parameter is used by the `ontape` backup utility.

TAPESIZE

This parameter contains the maximum size of the tape device in blocks. The value of this parameter is used by the `ontape` backup utility.

Note If this parameter is set too low and the tape output process encounters an end-of-file error, the tape output process aborts. If the value is set correctly, then the `ontape` program stops and prompts for another tape when TAPESIZE bytes have been written to the tape device.

LTAPEDEV

The LTAPEDEV parameter contains the full path name for the device that is used for log tape output.

Note If the "continuous logging" log option is used, then this device should be a different device from the device used for backups, the TAPEDEV device.

Also, as logical log files become full on disk, they are written to this device. Once the logical log file is written to the tape device, the log file is freed on disk. If all log records in a log file are closed, then the log file can be scheduled to be written to tape.

Note that if a log file contains a log record that has not been committed because the log transaction spans multiple logical log files then the log file cannot be written to tape until the logical log transaction that spans the log files is committed.

LTAPEBLK

This parameter contains the block size for the logical log tape device specified by the LTAPEDEV parameter. The internal threads that write logical log files to tape use this device.

LTAPESIZE

This parameter stores the maximum size in kilobytes of the tapes that are written to the logical log tape device. When the the logical log output threads have written this amount of logical logs, it prompts for a new log tape on the console device.

STAGEBLOB

STAGEBLOB specifies the Blob device to be used as the online optical staging area, the area where optical data is stored before being written to the optical storage device.

SERVERNUM

The SERVERNUM parameter is used to select a unique number relating to this Informix server instance. In the case where there are more than one IDS instances running on the same machine, each SERVERNUM represents a relative position or offset within the shared memory allocated to Informix. This value must be unique for each instance within the local host computer; it need not be unique on the network.

DBSERVERNAME

The DBSERVERNAME parameter is a unique name assigned to this database instance. This entry must have a corresponding entry with a corresponding protocol in the sqlhosts file. If there is to be more than one protocol used to connect to the database server, then additional protocols and server names must be entered in the sqlhosts file and the DBSERVERALIASES configuration parameter must list the additional server names assigned.

DBSERVERALIASES

The DBSERVERALIASES is used to provide one or more alternative names for this database instance. These alternative names are used to assign additional connection protocols (such as TCP/IP) for connecting to the engine. These server names must have a corresponding entry and protocol in the sqlhosts file.

NETTYPE

The NETTYPE parameter entries provide information on the connection protocols that are used to connect to the Informix server. Each connection protocol that is used to connect to the Informix engine has a corresponding set of *poll threads* that listen for a connection of that type.

These NETTYPE entries must have a corresponding entry in the `sqlhosts` file. The entry in the `sqlhosts` file specifies where and how the poll threads listen for a connection. For instance, if a poll thread is being started to listen for TCP/IP connections, an entry in the `sqlhosts` file would specify network services (relating to TCP/IP ports) where the threads would listen for a TCP/IP connection.

The NETTYPE configuration entries provide information on the type of network connection, the number of threads assigned to manage the memory connection, the number of concurrent connections for that network type, and the class of virtual processor that runs the poll threads for that connection.

The NETTYPE parameter specifies this information for each protocol type the server uses. The entries use the format

```
NETTYPE  protocol, poll threads, connections, VP class
```

In this configuration file entry, the *NETTYPE* indicates the configuration parameter being specified, *protocol* is the connection protocol being specified, *poll threads* are the number of poll threads that are started to manage this protocol, *connections* is the maximum number of connections that are allowed for this protocol, and *VP class* is the virtual processor class where these poll threads are run.

 When the maximum number of connections is reached for a specified protocol, the database engine does not allow any additional connections for that protocol.

DEADLOCK_TIMEOUT

The DEADLOCK_TIMEOUT parameter is used to set the time in seconds that the system waits for a remote lock. Note that this only applies to distributed transactions, not to the other locks used by the system.

RESIDENT

This parameter represents a flag with two settings: TRUE or FALSE. Setting this flag to FALSE (or 0) would allow the Informix portion of shared memory to be swapped out to disk. Setting this parameter to TRUE would enforce **forced residency** and the operating system would not be allowed to swap the shared memory to disk.

Generally, setting RESIDENT to TRUE is considered the optimal setting. Having memory swapped to and from disk can be a time-consuming task that could seriously impact system performance.

MULTIPROCESSOR

The MULTIPROCESSOR parameter is used to indicate whether or not the machine platform is a multiprocessor (SMP—symmetrical multiprocessor) machine or not. It is set to 1 for TRUE if this is a multiprocessor machine, or set to 0 for FALSE if it is not.

This code is used internally by the engine to assign processing to the tasks that it must perform. If the IDS engine is aware that there is only a single CPU available, it manages these tasks differently.

NUMCPUVPS

The NUMCPUVPS is set to the number of virtual processors of the CPU class for the engine to create when the engine starts. This value can be changed dynamically at runtime using the onmode utility.

SINGLE_CPU_VP

The SINGLE_CPU_VP parameter is set to 1 for TRUE if the engine is to allocate a SINGLE_CPU_VP for this database instance.

NOAGE

If this parameter is set to 1 for TRUE, then the engine does not allow the operating system to age the processes that represent its virtual processors. By default, the Unix operating system ages or lowers the process priority of any long-running task. If this parameter is set to TRUE, the engine attempts not to allow this processor aging.

AFF_SPROC

The AFF_SPROC parameter allows the use of *processor affinity* on multiprocessor platforms. Processor affinity is an operating system feature that allows a particular process to be bound to a CPU on a multiprocessor machine. This feature is not available on all operating systems; if this feature is not available then, setting this parameter is ignored by the engine.

The AFF_SPROC parameter is set to the starting CPU for processor affinity.

> **Note** Processor affinity removes the responsibility of migrating the running processes from one CPU to another from the operating system. It binds a process to a CPU, giving that process priority on the CPU. This theoretically would allow that process more access to CPU cycles, but in practice, altering this parameter does not always have a significant impact on performance. Most SMP versions of Unix do a good job of migrating processes among CPUs and allocating CPU cycles efficiently, thus precluding the need to set this parameter.

AFF_NPROC

The AFF_NPROC parameter is used to indicate the end processor for processor affinity. For example, if processor affinity is to be assigned to five CPUs on a six CPU system (leaving one CPU to the operating system), then AFF_SPROC would be set to 0 for CPU 1 and AFF_NPROC would be set to 4 for CPU 4.

LOCKS

This parameter is used to set number of locks used on the system. Locks are used by IDS to lock rows or buffer pages during certain operations. Should the IDS engine run out of locks during a query, the query would fail and engine operation would continue. Locks consume 44 bytes of space, so configuring an adequate number of locks does not remove a significant amount of memory resource from the system.

BUFFERS

This parameter is used to set the number of shared memory buffers allocated for the system. This parameter identifies the bytes allocated for the shared memory buffer.

The number of BUFFERS allocated is dependent on the application being run and the amount of memory resource available on the system. In general, the number of buffers allocated should be from 20 to 25 percent of the system memory available.

NUMAIOVPS

This parameter is used to set the number of AIO VPs (virtual processors) allocated to perform asynchronous I/O for the engine.

PHYSBUFF

This parameter indicates the number of kilobytes to allocate for each of the two physical log buffers for the system. Physical log pages are buffered at this location in memory before being written to the physical log on disk. Two buffers are used to allow writes to continue to one buffer while the other log buffer is being written to disk.

LOGBUFF

This parameter indicates the number of kilobytes to be allocated for each of the three logical log buffers used by IDS. If the *buffered logging* option is used, then logical log pages are buffered at this location in memory before being written to the logical log file on disk.

LOGSMAX

This parameter indicates the maximum number of logical logs that can be added to the system. If an attempt to add a logical log leads to a total number of logical logs that exceeds this number, then an error is returned and the add logical log process will fail. This number may be changed after the database instance has been initialized, but the engine must be restarted before the value will be recognized.

CLEANERS

This parameter indicates the number of page-cleaner threads that are allocated to manage the LRU queue. Page cleaner threads are used to write updated (dirty) buffer pages to disk.

SHMBASE

This is a hexadecimal value that represents the base or starting address of the shared memory buffer used by the Informix engine. On some systems, the default SHMBASE address is in use for some other application and the Informix engine must be directed to use another base address. This parameter is overridden by the INFORMIXSHMBASE environment variable.

SHMVIRTSIZE

This parameter is used to set the initial size of the virtual shared memory segment. Virtual shared memory is defined as those portions of shared memory that are used for fixed overhead, shared structures, and private structures. The formula for estimating this parameter is as follows:

```
fixed overhead = shared structures + ( max concurrent sessions

                                      *   private structures)
```

These values are defined as follows:

Fixed overhead	Global pool + thread pool
Shared structures	AIO vectors + sort memory + dbspace backup buffers + dictionary size + size of stored procedure cache + histogram pool + other pools
Private structures	Session stack + session heap + session control block structures

SHMADD

The SHMADD parameter is used to set the value for shared memory segments that are added to the system as they are needed during the processing of DSS queries. Memory is added up to the SHMTOTAL parameter value if it is nonzero, or up to the point at which the operating system no longer provides more memory for the server.

Tip

Memory is added more efficiently if it is added in large portions, so setting SHMADD to a high but manageable number is considered optimal. The downside to this strategy would be that memory has been allocated to a query and is no longer needed and has yet to be freed by the IDS engine.

SHMTOTAL

The SHMTOTAL parameter is set to the total amount of DSS memory the engine allocates. If this value is zero, the engine attempts to allocate memory until the operating system prohibits allocation of additional memory.

CKPTINTVL

The CKPTINTVL parameter is used to set the interval for the Informix server checkpoint in seconds. This is a very important parameter because the checkpoint halts most system activity while the buffer cache is synchronized with the disk; excessive checkpointing can impact system performance. Setting the checkpoint interval too high, however, can create a situation where the checkpoint takes too long to conduct and thus impacts system throughput.

LRUS

The LRUS parameter is used to set the number of least recently used queues for the engine. The LRU is used to track updated (or *dirty*) pages in the system buffer; these are pages that must be written to disk at some point in time. The decision on when to write these pages to disk is important and can have a significant impact on system performance for update-intensive systems. The Informix server uses this parameter combined with the LRU_MIN_DIRTY and LRU_MAX_DIRTY parameters to determine when and how to flush or write pages to disk, also known as cleaning the LRU buffers. Tuning the LRU queue is covered in more detail in Chapter 5.

LRU_MAX_DIRTY

The LRU_MAX_DIRTY parameter is used to indicate the maximum number of pages that a LRU queue is allowed to have before a cleaner thread is wakened to clean the LRU queue. The queue is cleaned down to the percentage specified in LRU_MIN_DIRTY.

LRU_MIN_DIRTY

The LRU_MIN_DIRTY parameter specifies the minimum dirty pages to be left in a LRU queue as a percentage of the total number of buffers in the queue. When a page cleaner is wakened to clean a queue, it starts cleaning at LRU_MAX_DIRTY percent and continues cleaning (writing updated pages to disk) until the queue reaches LRU_MIN_DIRTY percent dirty pages.

LTXHWM

The LTXHWM parameter is used to indicate the long transaction high water mark. The long transaction high water mark (LTXH-WM) represents a percentage of the total number of logs allocated in the Informix server. When the number of filled logs reaches this percentage, a thread is assigned to perform a logical log rollback.

A *long transaction* occurs when a transaction that spans multiple transaction logs does not have enough logs to complete and must be rolled back. To avoid situations where there are not enough logs left to complete the rollback, which would effectively freeze the database instance, the LTXHWM parameter should be set to an adequate percentage to allow enough free logical logs to remain in the log file to complete a rollback.

LTXEHWM

The LTXEHWM parameter is used to indicate the long transaction exclusive high water mark. This value represents a percentage of the total number of logs allocated in the Informix server. When the number of filled logical logs reaches this percentage, a logical log rollback begins and the thread performing that rollback is given exclusive access to the logical logs.

TXTIMEOUT

The TXTIMEOUT parameter is set to the transaction timeout for distributed transactions in seconds. When the server is involved in a distributed transaction and asks a remote server to perform an action, it waits the number of seconds specified in TXTIMEOUT for a response; if it does not receive a response in the specified number of seconds, the transaction is aborted.

Note that TXTIMEOUT only applies to distributed transactions—transactions between multiple instances of IDS regardless of whether or not the instance resides on another machine. The TXTIMEOUT does not apply to transactions local to the Informix instance.

STACKSIZE

The STACKSIZE parameter is set to the size of the stack for IDS threads in kilobytes. This value does not have an upper limit. Generally, the stack is set to 32 kilobytes, but recursive operations such as those performed by stored procedures would require more stack space. If the stack space is not available, the Informix engine allows the stack to grow. If there are to be a large number of recursive or other operations that would require large amounts of stack space, then this number should be set higher than 32 kilobytes to avoid the overhead of allocating additional stack space at runtime.

OFF_RECVRY_THREADS

The OFF_RECVRY_THREADS parameter is used to indicate the number of offline recovery threads that are allocated to perform a logical recovery of a database. When the Informix server determines that the server was not shut down gracefully (this would be indicated by pages in the physical log), then it initiates the number of offline recovery threads specified in the OFF_RECVRY_THREADS parameter to bring the server back to a consistent state and bringing it back online.

ON_RECVRY_THREADS

The ON_RECVRY_THREADS parameter is set to the number of online recovery threads that the engine initiates during an online recovery (a warm restore). Online recovery threads would be needed in the event an online restore required a log rollforward.

DRAUTO

The DRAUTO specifies an integer value of 0, 1, or 2 to indicate the type of data replication switchover used in the event a replicated instance of the database fails. These values are explained in Table 3-7.

Table 3-7 DRAUTO Values

Value	Data Replication Type
0	Manual
1	Retain
2	Reverse

A **manual** switchover indicates that the engine does not automatically switch over in the event of a failure; the switchover must be performed manually.

A **retain** parameter indicates that the IDS instance automatically switches the secondary instance to standard mode on a data replication failure, and automatically switches the primary back to secondary when restarting data replication.

A **reverse** parameter indicates the engine automatically switches secondary to standard on a data replication failure, and then switches the original primary to secondary when restarting data replication.

DRINTERVAL

The DRINTERVAL parameter is set to indicate the interval in seconds between buffer flushes between two replicated instances of the Informix server. The engine waits this number of seconds before performing a buffer flush from one database instance to the other.

DRTIMEOUT

The DRTIMEOUT parameter indicates the network timeout in seconds between the replicated instances. This is the number of seconds the engine waits for a response from a replicated instance before determining that the replicated instance is no longer available.

DRLOSTANDFOUND

The DRLOSTANDFOUND parameter is set to the directory path for storage of log transactions that could be lost in certain types of data replication situations. Lost transactions are those transactions that contain transactions committed on the primary database server but not committed on the secondary server.

CDR_LOGBUFFERS

This parameter is used to identify the memory to be used for log buffers for enterprise replication.

CDR_EVALTHREADS

This parameter is used to set the number of evaluation threads to be allocated for enterprise replication.

CDR_DSLOCKWAIT

This parameter indicates the time in seconds that enterprise replication waits for a lock.

CDR_QUEMEM

This indicates maximum amount of memory used for the send/receive queue with enterprise replication.

BAR_ACT_LOG

This parameter specifies the location of the onbar activity log. The onbar backup and recovery utility writes messages to this log file.

BAR_MAX_BACKUP

This parameter is used to set the maximum number of parallel processes that are allowed for each onbar command that is being executed. This parameter is ignored for a whole-system backup or restore.

BAR_RETRY

This parameter specifies the number of times onbar retries a backup or restore operation. The possible settings are shown in Table 3-8.

Table 3-8 BAR_RETRY Settings

Setting	Description
BAR_ABORT	When an error is encountered, the backup is aborted and an error message is returned.
BAR_CONT	When an error is encountered on a database object, an error message is returned and that backup is aborted, but any other database objects remaining are archived or restored.
(n)	If set to a specific number, attempts this number of retries before aborting the backup of that database object and moving to the next object.

In the event the archive of a logical log file fails, the onbar utility aborts the attempt regardless of the setting of BAR_RETRY.

BAR_NB_XPORT_COUNT

This parameter specifies the number of data buffers used by each onbar process to exchange data with the engine. This value can affect the performance of onbar with more buffers, providing faster throughput for the archive/recovery process.

BAR_XFER_BUF_SIZE

This parameter specifies the size of the transfer buffer in pages. The transfer buffer is used to move data between the engine and the onbar utility.

BAR_BSALIB_PATH

This parameter indicates the path name of the library for the storage manager used by the onbar utility. The default path name is /usr/lib/libsad001.*xx*, where *xx* is the shared library file name.

RA_PAGES

The RA_PAGES parameter is set to the number of read-ahead pages the engine uses when scanning a table. This feature is implemented only in cases where the engine is scanning a table or index and reading a large number of contiguous pages.

RA_THRESHOLD

The RA_THRESHOLD is set to the number of read-ahead pages for IDS read-ahead. This specifies the number of unprocessed pages in the buffer page that signals the engine to perform the next read-ahead operation.

DBSPACETEMP

The DBSPACETEMP parameter specifies a list of dbspaces used for temporary storage. The list is separated by semicolons or commas. The dbspaces in this list are used in a round-robin fashion in the sequence in which they appear in the list.

DUMPDIR

The DUMPDIR parameter is set to the directory where engine diagnostics are dumped in the event the system must shut down unexpectedly.

DUMPSHMEM

This parameter is set to indicate whether or not shared memory is to be written to a file (*dumped*) in the event of a system failure. This parameter is set to 0 if shared memory is not to be dumped, and the value of 1 if shared memory is to be dumped.

Dumping shared memory is sometimes useful for debugging purposes, when there is a problem with the engine at a certain point in time. When this occurs, shared memory can be dumped during a system failure and then later analyzed using the onstat command.

DUMPGCORE

If the DUMPGCORE parameter indicates whether or not the engine will write (*dump*) a core image using the gcore utility in the event of an assertion failure. If the parameter is set to 0, the engine will not write shared memory using gcore. If the parameter is set to 1, then the engine will write shared memory using the gcore utility.

DUMPCORE

This parameter is set to indicate whether or not the engine should write (*dump*) a core image in the event of an assertion failure. If the parameter is set to 0, a core image is not written. If the parameter is set to 1, a core image is written in the event of an assertion failure.

DUMPCNT

The DUMPCNT parameter specifies the number of times a thread performs a dump due to assertion failures. Either the shared memory is dumped or a core file is generated using the `gcore` utility. It should be set to a positive integer value.

FILLFACTOR

The FILLFACTOR parameter is used to indicate the percentage of an index node that should be left free for additional index entries. By leaving additional space in an index node, as additional entries are added, there is no need to split the node in the event new entries need to be made to the index node. A high value would compact most of the index node, so that with an entry of 100 percent, any new entry would require the node to be split.

Note The FILLFACTOR for the instance can be overriden by specific syntax when the index is created, which allows a fill factor to be defined for an index using the SQL `create index` statement.

USEOSTIME

The USEOSTIME flag is used to indicate whether or not the operating system facilities are used for engine process timing. If this flag is set to 1 for TRUE, it specifies that the engine uses subsecond granularity (for datetime and interval values) by requesting the time from the operating system. If this FLAG is set to 0 for FALSE, then the engine retrieves the time from the operating system once per second.

MAX_PDQPRIORITY

The MAXPDQPRIORITY indicates the maximum PDQPRIORITY value allowed by the engine. Because a PDQPRIORITY setting for a process controls how much engine resource it can use to process a query, this engine configuration parameter allows the database administrator to limit the DSS load on the engine by limiting the amount of resources any particular user can access.

DS_MAX_QUERIES

The DS_MAXQUERIES parameter limits the number of concurrent DSS queries that can be run. The `onmode` utility can be used to override setting this at runtime.

DS_TOTAL_MEMORY

The DS_TOTAL_MEMORY parameter specifies the total amount of memory made available for decision support queries. This number should be smaller than physical memory less the memory required by the operating system and the Informix buffer pool. Note that this parameter is exclusive of the SHMTOTAL parameter as in the following formula:

```
DS_TOTAL_MEMORY = SHMTOTAL - non decision support memory
```

DS_MAX_SCANS

The DS_MAX_SCANS parameter is used to set a limit on the total number of scan threads that can be executed concurrently. The engine determines how many scan threads are started for a query based on the following criteria:

- Value of PDQPRIORITY for the session
- Limit on scan threads set by DS_MAX_SCANS
- Limit on PDQ priority set by the MAX_PDQPRIORITY configuration parameter
- Number of fragments in the table being scanned

Threads are reserved for a process based on the following formula:

```
threads = min ( nfrags, (DS_MAX_SCANS * PDQPRIORITY / 100 *
MAXPDQPRIORITY / 100 )
```

The `onmode` utility allows this configuration parameter to be overridden at runtime.

DATASKIP

The DATASKIP parameter provides a flag that indicates whether or not the IDS Data Skip feature is to be activated in this IDS instance. If the data skip feature is active, then the server allows a query to continue if a `dbspace` is down. The IDS engine would generally abort a query if it required data from a `dbspace` that was offline.

OPTCOMPIND

The OPTCOMPIND configuration parameter is a flag that is used to help the server decide the optimal join method to use for queries. Acceptable values are shown in Table 3-9.

Table 3-9 *OPTCOMPIND Values*

Value	Description
0	When indices are available on two joined tables, use the appropriate index to join the two tables.
1	If the transaction mode is not repeatable read, the optimizer behaves as it does for OPTCOMPIND=2.
2	The optimizer uses costs to determine the access bath. Index scans are not given preference. This is the default value.

ONDBSPACEDOWN

This parameter indicates the action taken during query processing if a `dbspace` accessed in the query is taken offline. The actions and the appropriate flag setting are shown in Table 3-10.

Table 3-10 *ONDBSPACEDOWN Actions and Flag Settings*

Setting	Action	Description
0	Continue	Continue processing after marking the `dbspace` offline.
1	Abort	Abort query and bring engine offline.
2	Wait	After disabling the `dbspace`, the Informix server hangs all updating threads as soon as the next checkpoint occurs.

The impact of having a dbspace offline must be considered when setting this configuration parameter. If the system can manage having a single dbspace (a single part of the database) offline but yet continue to operate and return meaningful results, then a setting of 0 may be appropriate. But if a system cannot return meaningful results with a dbspace offline, then a setting of 1 or 2 may be more appropriate.

LBU_PRESERVE

The LBU_PRESERVE parameter indicates to the server that the last logical log should be reserved for administrative tasks. The IDS engine blocks further log update activity when the next to the last log is filled (rather than the last log). (This effectively helps provide the ability to use a log backup to free logical logs in the event the logical log high water mark has been reached.)

OPCACHEMAX

The OPCACHEMAX parameter specifies the size of the memory cache for the IDS optical subsystem. The IDS Blobs are stored in the memory cache before being written to the optical subsystem (and then, ultimately, to the optical device).

Summary

This chapter has covered the installation and configuration of the IDS engine. Installing the IDS engine is a fairly straightforward process; this process merely writes the software binaries and configuration files onto the disk. Within the configuration files are a series of parameters that must be set correctly in order to run the software.

The configuration parameters for the Informix engine enable the extensive flexibility of the product. Using these parameters, the Informix engine can be tuned and adjusted for the environment and purpose for which it was purchased. But with this flexibility comes responsibility; the database administrator must know and understand the parameters used to configure the engine.

Setting some configuration parameters is often a repetitive process. Initial settings may work well in a test environment, but as the user load is increased or more data is added to the system, the performance of the engine may suffer and parameters may need to be adjusted. This process of tuning the engine by adjusting these parameters is discussed in Chapter 5.

Next Chapter

The next chapter covers the process of managing the disk using the Informix engine. As Chapter 1 indicated, the early releases of the Informix engine removed the management of the disk from operating system administration and absorbed large portions of this into the engine. This enhanced performance, provided greater data integrity, and added flexibility to database operations. The next chapter explains how to make optimal use of this capability using the IDS engine.

Managing the IDS Disk

The IDS engine manages disk through both a logical and physical view. This chapter describes the process of mapping and configuring disk with the IDS engine. The basic concepts and terms are introduced first, and then the tasks of configuring disk space within the engine are presented thereafter. This chapter ends with a discussion of the process of adding and dropping disk space and databases and monitoring disk space usage.

The IDS View of Disk

The Informix engine views disk on the *physical* and *logical* levels (see Figure 4-1). On the physical level, the engine references disk as *chunks*. These chunks relate to either device special files or operating system files. A chunk can comprise all or part of the device referenced. If a chunk comprises only a part of a device,

Physical view   Logical view

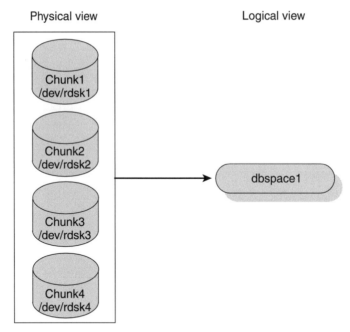

Figure 4-1 *Physical and Logical View of Disk*

then an offset is required to determine the location of the chunk within the physical device. (Chunk declarations always require an offset even if the offset is 0.) Chunks are in turn related to logical representations of disk called a *dbspace*. When Informix SQL statements reference disk, it is always as a dbspace.

Defining Physical Disk Layout

A chunk in the Informix database can reference a *character special device*, a file usually located in the /dev/rdsk directory on a Unix system. When the IDS engine uses this method of interacting with disk, it is known as using *raw disk*. This method provides the best performance and most reliable method of disk i/o for the engine. When using raw disk, the Informix engine maintains complete control over disk I/O, deciding when and where disk reads and writes take place.

Another alternative for disk I/O is to use a file on the file system for disk; this is known as using *cooked files*. These files are simple operating system files, and it is the responsibility of the operating system to perform I/O on these files.

When using raw disk, the IDS engine has the capability of performing asynchronous I/O for disk operations thus improving overall throughput. When using cooked files, this is not a possibility.

Logical Disk Layout

With the IDS engine, multiple chunks are mapped into a logical representation of disk known as a dbspace. Each unit of disk within the dbspace is known as a *page*. The physical layout of the dbspace contains a set of informational structures that describe the chunks and tables within the dbspace. A *chunk-free list* is used to track the free pages within the chunk, and a tbl- space tblspace is used to track the tables within the dbspace.

The *chunk-free list* contains the starting page as a page offset into the chunk for each section of free space, and the length of the free space in pages. The chunk-free list is essentially a linked list with pointers to the free sections of disk within a chunk. As additional chunk-free list pages are needed to track free space within the chunk, a new page is created and is linked to the existing chunk-free list pages. As pages in a chunk are allocated to tables, the offset of the free list and the size of the free space are altered to recognize the change. When pages are freed, entries are added to the chunk-free list to identify the offset and size of the free space. If the space that has been freed is contiguous with existing free space, then the size of the free space is updated to recognize the newly freed space.

A tblspace is a collection of pages that comprise a table in the database. The redundantly named tblspace tblspace is used to track the location and structure of all tblspaces within a dbspace—a tblspace (or structure) to track tblspaces. The tblspace tblspace contains a bit map of the pages in the tblspace, and then a series of pages describing the tblspaces in the dbspace. Each tblspace page in this table contains information about the table including columns, indexes, and the extents for the table including the first page of the tblspace tblspace, which is used to track itself.

Maintaining dbspaces

As discussed previously, a chunk represents physical disk space and a dbspace represents a set of chunks. A dbspace is effectively a *logical* representation of disk space and a chunk is a *physical* representation of disk space. Using the IDS engine, you would create a dbspace with an initial chunk and then add additional chunks to the dbspace. The process of adding chunks is the same both with raw disk and cooked files.

The onspaces command can be used to maintain dbspaces and their constituent chunks from the command line. Using a command line program provides a convenient way to produce a shell script for disk maintenance that has the added benefit of maintaining a running record of the disk space added or dropped from the system. The format of the onspaces command is as follows:

```
onspaces -d <dbspacename> |
          -c <dbspacename> |
          -a <dbspacename>
     -p <pathname> -o <offset> -s <size> [-m path offset]
```

The '–a' parameter is used to add a dbspace, Blobspace, or chunk, the '–c' parameter is used to create a new dbspace or Blobspace, and the '–d' parameter is used to drop a dbspace, Blobspace, or chunk. The parameter values passed to the onspaces utility are explained in Table 4-1.

Creating and Dropping a dbspace

One method of adding a dbspace to the IDS instance is to use the onspaces command. The onspaces command can be used to create a dbspace as follows:

```
onspaces -c dbspace1 -p /dev/rdsk0 -o 0 -s 12000
```

Table 4-1 *Parameter Values for the* `onspaces` *Utility*

Parameter	Description
dbspacename	The `dbspace` or Blobspace to be created when this is an argument to the -d or –a parameter; the `dbspace` to which the chunk will be added when this is an argument to the -a parameter
pathname	Path name to the device special file or the operating system file to use
offset	Offset into the device or file referenced
size	Size of the file or device in kilobytes

This command would create a new `dbspace` named `dbspace1` using a first chunk of `/dev/rdsk0` with a zero offset and a size of 12,000 kilobytes.

Alternatively, the `onmonitor` utility can be used to create a `dbspace` using a menu-driven, character-based interface. Using `onmonitor`, the user would select the "Dbspaces" menu and choose the option to "Create a dbspace." This displays a screen with fields for the name of the `dbspace`, the path name for the primary chunk (the first chunk) for the `dbspace`, and information on whether or not the `dbspace` will use mirroring or whether or not the `dbspace` is a temporary `dbspace` the user would enter the appropriate information and then press the Esc key to save the information and create the `dbspace`. Information entered is checked on exit from the field, thus providing immediate feedback on offending values (as opposed to using the `onspaces` command, which does not always identify which value or parameter was incorrect).

Occasionally it is necessary to drop a `dbspace` and use the disk space for some other purpose. The Informix engine will *not* allow a `dbspace` to be dropped if there is data currently in the `dbspace`. (Note that the data in the `dbspace` need not be data records in a table but could simply be an empty database that would still contain a number of system catalog tables with records containing information on the database.) The user dropping the database must be user `informix` or have database administrator (DBA) privileges to drop a `dbspace`. The syntax for the `onspaces` command to drop a database is as follows:

```
onspaces -d <dbspacename> [-p <pathname> -o <offset>] [-y]
```

The optional path name syntax is required only if a chunk is being dropped. To drop an empty database named `mydbspace`, the following command would be used:

```
onspaces -d mydbspace
```

This command prompts the user executing the command before actually dropping the `dbspace`, unless the '–y' flag has been passed to the command, in which case the user is not prompted and `dbspace` is dropped without comment.

The `onmonitor` command can also be used to drop a `dbspace` or `Blobspace`. The user would first select the "Dbspaces" menu and then choose the option to "Drop" a dbspace. This displays a list of `dbspaces` currently on the system. The user would use the arrow keys to highlight the `dbspace` to be dropped and then press the Ctrl-B or F3 key (function key 3) to drop the `dbspace`.

Adding Chunks to a dbspace

As data is continually added to a `dbspace`, it eventually requires the allocation of additional disk space. To add space to a `dbspace`, additional chunks must be added. The onspaces command provides a set of options to add chunks to an existing dbspace. The following command adds a chunk to `dbspace1` from the raw device `/dev/dsk1` at an offset of 0. The size of the chunk added was 12,000 kilobytes:

```
onspaces -a dbspace1 -p /dev/rdsk/dsk1 -o 0 -s 12000
```

The following command is identical to the previous command with the exception of the argument to the -p parameter. In this case, a Unix operating system flat file is used to reference the device for the chunk being added to the `dbspace`. If this file is a Unix system file, the IDS engine would open the file and extend it to the specified size by writing binary zeroes to the file.

```
onspaces -a dbspace1 -p /mydata/myfile -o 0 -s 12000
```

Alternatively, the `onmonitor` program can be used to add chunks to a `dbspace`. To add a chunk using the `onmonitor` program, the user would choose the "Dbspace" menu option, and then choose the "Add chunk" option. A list of the current dbspaces in the system is displayed as shown in Figure 4-2.

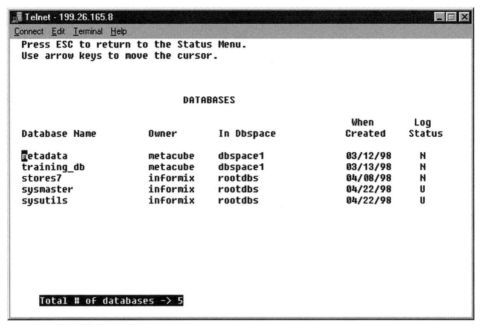

Figure 4-2 Adding Chunks using Onmonitor

Using the arrow keys, the user would highlight the dbspace to which a chunk will be added and then press Ctrl-B or the F3 key (function key 3). The "add chunk" screen is then displayed containing input fields for the parameters described previously for the onspaces command: the dbspace name to which the chunk will be added, the full path name of the chunk being added, the offset into the chunk, the size of the chunk, and mirror chunk information if applicable. The onmonitor program validates input for each field as data is entered.

Using dbspace Mirroring

If dbspace mirroring is being used, then mirror information must be entered for each chunk added to the dbspace using the '–m' parameter. Using dbspace mirroring, all data written to a dbspace is mirrored using the IDS engine by being written to another dbspace. Data read operations can optionally read from a mirror dbspace if the primary dbspace is busy. Once mirroring has been started, it runs without intervention until it is turned off using the `onspaces` command. The following example adds a primary chunk and mirror chunk to `dbspace1`:

```
onspaces -a dbspace1 -p /dev/rdsk1 -o 0 -s 12000 -m /dev/rdsk2 0
```

Executing this statement adds a chunk to `dbspace1` along with its corresponding mirror chunk. This asserts that the `dbspace` was created with mirroring; if that is not the case, then this command would fail.

Dropping a Chunk

If there is no space currently being used in a chunk, the chunk may be dropped. Only a user with database administrator privilege may drop a chunk using the following `onspaces` syntax:

```
onspaces -d <dbspacename> [-p <path name> -o <offset>] [-y]
```

To drop a chunk in `dbspace1`, the following statement could be used:

```
onspaces -d dbspace1 -p /dev/rdska01 -y
```

This command drops the chunk `/dev/rdska01` from the `dbspace` named `dbspace1`. Because the '–y' flag has been passed to the `onspaces` command, the chunk is dropped without prompting the user.

Only empty chunks can be dropped from a `dbspace`. Given the manner in which IDS writes data to chunks, there is a possibility that a chunk that has been a part of the system for some time could have data from several different tables on pages in the chunk. To free the chunk, the tables would have to be dropped or moved (through a process of unloading data, dropping the table, and then reloading the data) in order to remove the pages from a given chunk. This has the potential of being a tricky process.

In practice, it is uncommon to drop a single chunk from a `dbspace`. The more common approach is to remove data completely from a `dbspace` and then drop the `dbspace`, thus freeing the chunks within the `dbspace`.

Using Soft Links to Assign Chunks

Often it is useful to create a level of indirection between the chunk name and the device files. The reason for this is that once a chunk has been added to the IDS engine, the name and size cannot be modified. In the event the device files must be moved or the disks renamed, the capability to effectively rename chunk references could prove valuable. This level of indirection is created using a Unix *file link*. A link can be either a *soft* link where the link is across file systems, or a *hard* link where the link is in the same file system as the file itself.

The soft link is created using the Unix `ln` command. The syntax for creating a soft link is as follows:

```
ln -s <existing file> <link file>
```

To create a soft link from a device file to a Unix file, the following command would be executed:

```
ln -s/dev/rdsk0 /data/myrawfile
```

This command would create a soft link between the Unix file and the raw device file. In the event the name of the raw device file were changed (the data was moved to a new disk, a new controller, or a new device driver were obtained) the raw device file name could be *changed* as follows:

```
rm /data/myrawfile
ln -s /dev/rsk0a1 /dev/rsk0a1
```

Creating Database Tables

Informix-SQL statements reference `dbspace`s when databases and tables and indexes are created. When a database is created, by default the database and its system tables are placed in the root `dbspace`. Using the in `<dbspace>` statement, this default can be overridden as follows:

```
create database db1 in dbspace1;
```

Note that when links are used to map raw devices into IDS, IDS has no knowledge of the actual physical disk being used. There is the potential that links could become crossed and two chunks could be directed at the same portion of disk. The following provides an example.

A dbspace is created with a single chunk mapped to raw device /dev/rdsk1a through a link named chunk1, as follows:

```
ln -s /ids_chunk/chunk1 /dev/rsk0a1
onspaces -c -d dbspace1 -p /ids_disk/chunk1
```

A second dbspace is created with a single chunk inadvertently mapped to the same raw device used for the first dbspace as shown below:

```
ln -s /ids_chunk/chunk2 /dev/rsk0a1
onspaces -c -d dbspace2 -p /ids_disk/chunk2
```

The IDS engine would not be aware of this error. Internally, the engine does perform a validation on the path name (specified in the -p parameter passed to the onspaces command), but in this case, the validation would pass because the engine would perceive /ids_disk/chunk1 and /ids_disk/chunk2 as two separate portions of disk.

Were this to occur, the dbspaces would be created, but disk write failures would soon occur and data would be corrupted. The only recovery option in this case would be dropping both dbspaces (if possible), correcting the problem, and restoring from tape.

As the saying goes, "An ounce of prevention is worth a pound of cure." It is best to closely track the linking of chunks to raw disk to avoid the problem identified previously. Placing all link statements within a single shell script file would provide a consistent location for validating links. Future attempts to add additional links would then start by referencing this shell script to determine the physical disk the links are mapped to.

This statement would create a database named db1 in dbspace1. This would place all of the system tables for the database in that dbspace and any table created in the database would, by default, be placed in that dbspace. Once a database has been created in dbspace, it cannot be moved. If the in dbspace clause had been eliminated, as follows, then the database would have been created in the root dbspace:

```
create database db1;
```

When a table is created in the Informix database, it is put by default in the dbspace in which the database is located. The following create table statement demonstrates this default:

```
create database db1 in dbspace1;
create tabl t1 (col1 int, col2 char(20));
```

This table would be created in dbspace1, the dbspace in which the database has been created. This default could be overridden as follows:

```
create database db1 in dbspace1;
create tabl t1 (col1 int, col2 char(20)) in dbspace5;
```

This create table statement would create the table t1 in the dbspace dbspace5. Tables can be further spread over disks via the fragmentation statement as demonstrated in the next section.

Note that as the IDS engine uses chunks in a dbspace, they are used in the order that chunks were added. The engine makes valiant attempts to keep the pages in a table contiguous. When a table is created, it is *pre-extended* with what is referred to as a table *extent*. An extent is a contiguous collection of pages for a table and a table is a set of one or more extents (see Figure 4-3). While the pages in an extent are contiguous, the extents that comprise a table are not contiguous (because two contiguous extents would be merged into a single extent by IDS). An extent resides in a single chunk and cannot span chunks.

A table is created with an initial extent that has a default of eight system pages, so on a system with a 2-kilobyte page size, the default extent size would be 16K. If the table is created with a next extent size value, the default for this is also 16K. The initial

Dbspace dbspace1

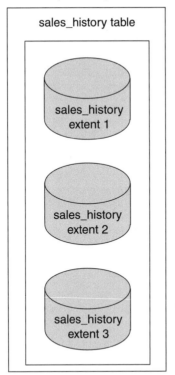

sales_history table

sales_history
extent 1

sales_history
extent 2

sales_history
extent 3

Figure 4-3 *Table with Extents*

extent and next extent can be specified in the `create table` statement as follows:

```
create table testit ( col1 int,
                       col2 int,
                       col3 char(10))
       extent size 50
       next size   10 ;
```

This table is created with an initial extent size of 50K as specified by the `extent size` clause and a next extent size of 10K as specified by the `next size` clause.

As the pages in a table are filled with rows, the first extent for the table fills. The IDS engine then begins looking for space based on the amount of contiguous space needed (as defined by the"'next extent" size for the table). It does this by searching the chunk-free list for the dbspace in the order in which chunks were added to the dbspace. When it finds adequate contiguous space in a chunk (space found >= next extent size), it allocates the next extent for the table in that chunk. If the next extent allocated happens to be contiguous with the last extent of the table, the two extents are merged into a single extent.

A table that has a few extents is easier to scan. If a table is found to have a large number of extents (as revealed by the output of the oncheck -pe command), table scan performance could be improved by making the data in the table contiguous. To make the data in the table contiguous, it is necessary to create a new table with a large enough initial extent to hold the data currently in the table. It would then be necessary to move the data from the old table to the new table. The following SQL could accomplish this task without unloading the data to disk:

```
create table newtable (col1 int, col2 int, col3 char(10))
    extent size 100
    next size 50;

insert into newtable select * from testit;
rename table testit to x;
rename table newtable to testit;

-- validate that operation was successful
drop table x; — drop the old table
```

This SQL script creates a new table with a larger extent size and then copies the data from the old table to the new table. The old table is then renamed to a temporary name, and the new table is renamed the correct name for the table. When the copy operation is completed, the old table with the temporary name can then be deleted. Note that though this operation avoids having to unload the data to disk, it does require double the space required for the table to complete the operation. The other option would be to unload the data in the table to disk, drop the old table, re-create it with a larger initial extent size, and then load the data back into the table.

If a table has too many extents but the administrator does not wish to reload the table, the next extent size could be altered to reduce the need for IDS to create new extents for the table. This can be accomplished with the alter table statement as follows:

```
alter table testit
      modify next size 20;
```

In this example, the table `testit` is altered from having a next extent size of 10K to having a next extent size of 20K .

Locking Granularity for a Table

When a table is created, locking granularity can be expressed in two ways: with *page-level* locking or *row-level* locking. The default locking granularity is page-level locking.

With page-level locking, when a user reading the table requires a lock for a single row, the entire page is locked. When the user needs to read the next row on that page, the engine does not need to acquire another lock for the user, because the user is already holding a lock for that page.

Page-level locking is an efficient form of locking if a process must read a large number of contiguous rows in a table, such as a scan of the entire table. Only one lock must be acquired for the entire page, so there is less locking overhead. And fewer locks are required to read the table, so there are fewer system resources used.

The downside of page-level locking is the loss of concurrency. A process that is reading a small number of rows on a page is nevertheless locking all of the rows on the page and so is limiting access to rows that are not being used.

With **row-level locking**, only the row being accessed is locked, not the entire page. This allows much greater concurrency, but has a higher system overhead and uses more system resources.

For a system such as an OLTP system, where concurrency is important and locks are generally not held for a long period of time, row-level locking may be the best choice. For a batch system where it would not be uncommon to read a large number of contiguous rows from a table and where concurrency may be limited, page-level locking may be suitable. Page-level locking would also be suitable for data warehouse or decision support access where full table scans are not uncommon.

The following create table statement overrides the system default of page-level locking:

```
create table regions (region int,
             region_name char(10),
```

```
                    region_description char(25))
            lock mode row;
```

In this SQL statement, a table is created using a lock mode of row. This establishes row-level locking for that table.

The `alter table` statement can be used to alter the lock mode for a table. The following statement changes the lock mode for a table from the default of page-level locking to row-level locking:

```
            alter table regions lock mode (row);
```

(Note that a number of factors affect the locking and concurrency for data access, including the isolation mode for the transaction and the transaction mode of the database. These issues are discussed in more detail in Chapter 5.)

Fragmentation

One of the most significant capabilities of the Informix Dynamic Server is the ability to statically fragment data across multiple portions of disk. The Informix parser understands this table fragmentation and can use it to develop a query plan that manipulates data in parallel. (See Figure 4-4.)

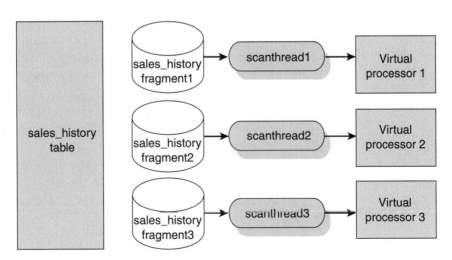

Figure 4-4 *Fragmentation and Parallel Access.*

This capability is provided in the Informix engine by distributing data across dbspaces using the Informix-SQL 'fragment by' clause. This clause is used with the 'create table' statement to specify a fragmentation strategy (also referred to as a distribution strategy) for a table. The fragmentation strategy indicates how the data is distributed either specifying a round-robin distribution or with an expression-based distribution strategy.

The following statement distributes data across four dbspaces using a **round-robin** distribution method:

```
create table t1 (col1 int,
            col2 char(20),
            col3 int )
      fragment by round robin in dbs1,dbs2,dbs3,dbs4;
```

This statement distributes data in a serial fashion across the dbspaces dbs1,dbs2, dbs3, and dbs4; that is, as data is written to a table a row is written to dbs1 and the next row to dbs2 and so on.

When an expression-based fragmentation strategy is combined with the IDS engine's ability to perform parallel processing, a powerful query capability is enabled. When a query is processed by the IDS engine, it may be necessary to *scan* a table or index to satisfy the query. Scan threads are initiated to perform this processing and, if possible, multiple scan threads may be started to read each separate fragment that is to be read during the query. If a table is spread across multiple fragments, then depending on certain conditions, it may be possible to start multiple scan threads to read those fragments. If a table has been fragmented by an expression and the where clause for the query references a column value in that expression, then it may be possible to eliminate one or more fragments from the table scan operation, a process known as *fragment elimination*. This is beneficial to query processing, since it reduces the amount of work necessary to process the query.

Tables can be fragmented using virtually any expression that involves constants and columns within the table. The following demonstrates a fragmentation strategy for a table containing sales data:

```
create table sales_facts (
        salesman   int,
        region     char(5),
```

```
        sales_date    date,
        sales_amount decimal(12,2))

fragment by expression
        region in ("NW", "NE", "MA" ) in dbspace1,
        region in ("SE","SN" ) in dbspace2,
        region in ("SW", "MW" ) in dbspace3;
```

This fragmentation strategy distributes the rows for the table into three dbspaces. The distribution is based on an equality expression for the region key (a *dimension* in multidimensional modeling terms). Data from specific regions is placed in specific dbspaces depending on the region column of the record being written to disk.

The IDS engine uses an optimizer that can interpret a query and discern whether or not the table that contains the data is fragmented on any of the filter criteria. If the data is fragmented on the filter criteria, then it may be possible to eliminate some of the fragments from the query plan based on the filter criteria. The following query demonstrates this capability:

```
select *
from sales_facts
where region in ("NW", "SE" );
```

The optimizer reviews this query and determines that the data in the table is fragmented on the region column. Because the query requests only regions "NW" (in dbspace1) and "SE" (in dbspace2), no scan thread is required for dbspace3. Two scan threads are started for the two table fragments in dbspace1 and dbspace2; the fragment in dbspace3 is *eliminated* from the search path—it is not searched.

Developing a Fragmentation Strategy

Fragmentation provides control over the physical layout of the data in a table. As discussed in the previous chapter, the IDS engine uses the fragmentation of data in a table to determine how many scan threads to use to scan the table. Each scan thread can be run on a separate CPU VP. The IDS engine uses parallel processing to retrieve data from the database so the fragmentation of data directly impacts the parallel processing of the

IDS engine. By locating the data fragments in a table in such a way that parallelization can be achieved, the performance of certain queries (primarily decision support queries that scan large amounts of data) can be improved.

Fragmentation for Archiving

The most common use of fragmentation is to enhance the performance of the engine through parallel processing. But fragmentation can also be used to segment data for backup and recovery purposes. An example of this would be when a portion of the data in a table is legacy data that is updated infrequently. The backup and recovery schedule for this legacy data may have the data archived only once a month, but the remaining current data in the table should be archived daily. By fragmenting in such a way that the legacy data is in a separate dbspace from the current data, the legacy data and current data could be on separate backup schedules. This is possible because certain IDS archive/restore utilities can optionally reference a dbspace, allowing dbspaces to be archived alone or in groups.

Fragmentation for Performance

To allow a query to achieve parallelization, data should be arranged on disk using a fragmentation strategy that reflects the way data in the table is accessed. Most significantly, data access is different for the two main types of database systems: decision support systems and online transaction processing. These two database types retrieve data very differently and, as with any fragmentation strategy, require some consideration of the queries to be directed at the data and the expected response times in determining the appropriate strategy.

OLTP Fragmentation Strategies

OLTP systems generally require fast access to a small number of records with a large number of concurrent users. There are several fragmentation strategies that can be used for OLTP systems with benefits and costs associated with each approach.

When accessing data in an OLTP application, data must be retrieved quickly; there isn't any time for scanning large portions of the table. For this reason, an index is usually used to provide rapid access to the data. The transaction profile generally involves a quick read through a b-tree index, reading a small number of records to arrive at the correct index entry. The index entry contains a reference to the page in the table and corresponding row on that page where the data is stored. This page/row reference is then used to retrieve the row from the table. In all, this entire operation usually takes less than a second. On a busy, well-tuned system, an IDS engine can process hundreds of OLTP transactions in a second.

It is possible that with an OLTP system, fragmentation and its corresponding parallel processing may have little impact on system performance. In the case of an application with a heavy OLTP transaction processing load, distributing the actual data records (not the index) across several disks and/or controllers may help balance the disk I/O load and reduce disk contention. Using this strategy, the index would be placed in a single dbspace (a *detached* index) with the presumption being that given the level of access for the index pages, they would remain constantly in the buffer pool. The data in the table would be fragmented by round robin to provide even distribution over an available set of disks and/or controllers. (This is similar to a *disk striping* strategy, placing data evenly over a number of disks.)

An argument could be made that on a system with a large amount of data to be applied to the buffer pool, a large portion of the pages from the data table would be in memory and OLTP disk I/O could in fact be negligible. The onstat command with the -g iof option can be used to determine whether or not the I/O for a portion of disk is suffering from contention problems. This command prints I/O statistics for each chunk/file, including information about temporary files and sort-work files. (Using the onstat command to monitor disk is discussed in more detail in Chapter 5.)

If it is determined that there is no significant disk I/O contention problems, then a fragmentation strategy based on backup and recovery needs for the data in the table should be used as long as it does not interfere with the OLTP transaction processing performance. This means that the index should remain detached and just the table data distributed across multiple fragments.

Fragmentation can also benefit indexes. As the size of the index grows, the b-tree index could become deeper and index access could be slowed by the depth of the index. The smaller the index, the shallower the internal b-tree and the quicker the access. For this reason, on a large table with a corresponding large index, using an expression fragmentation scheme with an attached index could be beneficial. By using an expression fragmentation scheme, the large table can be divided into several smaller portions with the corresponding attached index for each portion being smaller (and thus shallower). Indexing, fragmentation, and other tuning topics are discussed in more detail in Chapter 5.

DSS Fragmentation Strategies

The transaction profile of a DSS query is a query that reads a large number of records in a table and performs some sort of aggregation operation on the data. The query generally runs a long time (compared to OLTP queries) and scans a large number of the records in the data table or tables. Because it is reading a large number of records, there is usually no reason to use an index to access data in the data table. Instead, the query attempts to scan the entire table. This is a query that would benefit from parallelization, that would avoid having to scan the table in a serial fashion.

In order to generate a parallel query, the data must be fragmented. The fragmentation scheme chosen should be one that involves an expression, thus allowing for the possibility that some set of fragments could be eliminated for a given query, thus reducing the amount of work required to perform the query. The fragmentation expression should involve a column that is consistently used in queries directed at the table. Using the sales_facts table from the previous example, a fragmentation strategy could be developed, as follows:

```
create table sales_facts (
        salesman   int,
        region     char(5),
        sales_date   date,
        sales_amount decimal(12,2))

fragment by expression
        region in ("NW", "NE", "MA" ) in dbspace1,
        region in ("SE","SN" ) in dbspace2,
        region in ("SW", "MW" ) in dbspace3;
```

```
— query to run against the sales fact table

select *
from sales_facts
where region in ("NW","SW") and
      (sales_date > "01/01/1998" and
            sales_date < "03/31/1998");
```

In this example, the data table has been fragmented by the region column. The query that selects data from the table uses region in the filter criteria, but also uses the sales_date in the filter criteria. The engine is still able to use fragment elimination because the sales_date is part of a boolean and operation so both the region filter criteria and the sales_date filter criteria must be satisfied. If the query had used an or condition in the query statement, then there would have been no fragment elimination, as follows:

```
select *
from sales_facts
where region in ("NW","SW")   or
      (sales_date > "01/01/1998" and
            sales_date < "03/31/1998");
```

In this example, both query filter conditions must be satisfied for each row retrieved from the table. Since the data has been fragmented based on the region and fragments cannot be eliminated based on the sales_date , all fragments must be read.

The downside of fragmentation by expression is that it can be difficult to find a method of evenly distributing data over a number of fragments. What often occurs is an uneven distribution of data so that one fragment could have significantly more data than another fragment. If a query is run in parallel and multiple fragments are scanned, the scan operation will take as long as the longest-running scan thread, so the scan thread that must read the largest fragment is the bottleneck of the operation.

Another consideration in the fragmentation scheme is the number of CPUs available to the IDS engine. If there are only four CPUs available to the engine, then at most four scan threads are able to run in parallel. Using a fragmentation scheme that fragments data across nine fragments where one or two fragments will be eliminated would create a situation where seven scan threads would be needed. Because only four scan threads can run in parallel, a fragmentation scheme that yields seven scan threads may not necessarily be any better than a scheme that yielded four scan threads (equal to the number of CPUs available to the engine). At issue in this case is not only the number of CPUs available to the engine but the physical disks available and the I/O throughput on those disks. Because scan threads are often waiting for I/O, exceeding the number of physical CPUs could in fact improve throughput. Experimentation through various benchmark iterations is necessary to determine the optimum fragmentation scheme in balance with the maximum number of CPUs to be allocated to the database instance. (These issues and other performance tuning issues are covered in more detail in Chapter 5.)

Fragmentation Strategies for Archive/Recovery

By fragmenting data in a specific table into specific dbspaces on disk, the table data can be arranged in a way that makes sense for backup and recovery purposes. But such a strategy may not make sense for performance optimization. The database administrator must somehow balance the two approaches to achieve a strategy that achieves optimization and provides a useful backup and recovery mechanism.

Using the sales_fact table from the previous example, if only the current month data contains volatile data and the previous months represent relatively static information, the administrator may want to back up the prior month's data on a weekly or monthly basis and back up the current month's data on a daily basis. Because the Informix backup and restore utilities use the dbspace as the smallest restore *object*, data must be fragmented using a strategy that places current month data in one dbspace and prior month data in one or more other dbspaces. The following provides an example:

```
create table sales_facts (
        salesman    int,
        region      char(5),
        sales_date  date,
        sales_amount decimal(12,2))

fragment by expression
        sales_date > "03/01/1998" in dbspace1, - current month
```

```
sales_date < "02/01/1998" and sales_date > "01/31/1998" in dbspace2,
  — prior months ...
sales_date < "01/01/1998" and sales_date < "02/01/1998" in dbspace3,
sales_date < "01/01/1998" in dbspace4; — prior year
```

This strategy places the current month and all prior months in distinct dbspaces, with the exception of prior year data, which is placed in a single dbspace. This would allow three different backup plans to be implemented, with the current month's data being backed up nightly, the previous month's data being backed up weekly, and the prior year's data being backed up monthly.

This strategy does not necessarily run counter to the goal of optimizing performance. If queries retrieve data based on sales_date, then fragment elimination is still possible.

Other Fragmentation Considerations

In some cases, the distribution of the data is dependent on factors other than performance. As mentioned previously, archiving is one of these considerations. Another consideration could be the efficient allocation of data space. If it is not possible to develop a useful fragmentation scheme based on the queries being run against the data, then the fragmentation scheme would not be an important consideration. For instance, an expression-based fragmentation scheme that eliminated at best one fragment out of 15 would not be much of an improvement over a round-robin fragmentation scheme on the same table. In this case, a round-robin fragmentation scheme might be better, providing an even distribution of data across fragments and avoiding the additional query-processing time required to scan an uneven fragment.

Using Data Distributions

The Informix engine provides a useful method for determining the nature of the data stored in database tables. This information is available in the form of *data distributions*, a statistical method for sampling data. Data distributions contain information on the values stored in the columns of the table across rows. So if a column contains an integer, then a sampling of the integer values in the column and the number of occurrences for specific values would be provided in a data distribution of that table. The same would hold true for character string data; a sampling of character string values and a corresponding number of occurrences would be indicated in the output for that table.

Data distributions use information compiled and stored by the update statistics command using the medium or high parameter. The "update statistics" command must therefore have been run previous to any attempt to display this information.

The dbschema command is used to print the information generated by the "update statistics" command. When the update statistics medium command is used to generate statistics, only a sampling of the data is used, as opposed to the update statistics high command, which will work with all of the data in a table. Given the purpose for which this information is used—to determine the proper query access path—a statistical sampling is every bit as useful as reading and sorting data from the entire table, and the decrease in accuracy is worth the time saved using this method of generating statistics. The dbschema command is used to display the data distribution information for a table or column using the following format:

```
dbschema -d <database name> -hd <table name>/ 'all' |
                <table name:column name>
```

The database name is the name of the database that contains the table. Optionally, either the table name or table name and column name can be used to indicate the name of the table and column to use, or "all" can be used as an argument to indicate that data distribution information should be generated for all of the tables in the database.

The following example expands upon the sales_facts table example shown previously to add additional dimensional attributes for product ID and sales code. The schema for this expanded fact table is as follows:

```
create table sales_facts (
        salesman_id     integer,
        Prod_id         char(5),
        sales_code      char(5),
        region          char(5)
sales_amt       decimal(12,2));
```

The salesman_id represents a unique identifier for the sales-man who made the sale. The prod_id identifies the product that has been sold and is a foreign key for the product dimension table. The sales_code represents an informational code about the sale; it is additional information that is tracked concerning the sale, possibly for a promotion that was used to generate the sale or some other purpose. And the sales_amt represents the dollar amount of the sale. The following is sample output from this fact table:

salesman_id	prod_id	sales_code	region	sales_amt
0	AA-331	A-OK	NW	1023.331
1	AB-931	B-1	SW	1605.28

The next example is sample output of data distributions for this fact table. Distributions are prepared for each column in a table. For the following example, the first distribution is for the sales_facts table column salesman_id.

The date the distribution was created is listed and the level of update statistics is identified on the next line; in this case, medium mode is identified with a 2.5 resolution and 95 percent level of confidence. The resolution represents the percentage of the total sample that will be placed in each bin or grouping listed in the output. So if a sample is 100 rows, then a resolution of .1, or 10 percent, produces output with 10 bins. The following is the output from the distribution:

```
Distribution for informix.sales_facts.salesman_id
Constructed on 03/14/1998
Medium Mode, 2.500000 Resolution, 0.950000 Confidence

— DISTRIBUTION —
          (                          0)
— OVERFLOW —
    1: (   30,                       0)
    2: (   30,                       1)
    3: (   30,                       2)
    4: (   30,                       3)
    5: (   30,                       4)
    6: (   30,                       5)
    7: (   30,                       6)
    8: (   30,                       7)
    9: (   30,                       8)
   10: (   30,                       9)
```

The next section lists the distribution for the sales regions (dimensions) in the fact table. In scanning the information in this column, the update statistics routine did not find distinct values, but instead found a large number of duplicates. This information is therefore placed in the **overflow** section of the distribution output.

There are five distinct sales regions in the fact table. These values are listed in the output that follows. Each row contains statistics about the values appearing in the table column. The output column on the left contains the bin number, which in this case numbers 1 through 5. The first column in the parentheses contains the number of times the value in that row appeared in the sampling. On the far right is the value that the information in the row references. For example, the first row in the output contains the following information:

```
1: (   28,          AL    )
```

This indicates that in bin number 1, the update statistics routine found 28 occurrences of the value "AL." Additional rows in the output indicate there were 48 occurrences of the value "MW," 48 occurrences of the value "NE," 128 occurrences of the value "SE," and 48 occurrences of the value "SW."

```
Distribution for informix.sales_facts.region
Constructed on 03/14/1998
Medium Mode, 2.500000 Resolution, 0.950000 Confidence
— DISTRIBUTION —

        (                AL    )

— OVERFLOW —

    1: (   28,          AL    )
    2: (   48,          MW    )
    3: (   48,          NE    )
    4: ( 128,           SE    )
    5: (   48,          SW    )

Distribution for informix.sales_facts.prod_id

Constructed on 03/14/1998

Medium Mode, 2.500000 Resolution, 0.950000 Confidence
```

```
— DISTRIBUTION —

        (                    AA-123          )


— OVERFLOW —

    1: ( 156,         AA-123        )
    2: (  24,         AA-331        )
    3: (  24,         AB-931        )
    4: (  48,         BB-321        )
    5: (  48,         XX-323        )

Distribution for informix.sales_facts.sales_code

Constructed on 03/14/1998

Medium Mode, 2.500000 Resolution, 0.950000 Confidence


— DISTRIBUTION —

        (                    A-OK           )

— OVERFLOW —
    1: (  28,         A-OK          )
    2: ( 100,         A1            )
    3: (  48,         B-1           )
    4: (  28,         B-OH          )
    5: (  48,         H-1           )
    6: (  24,         Z-5           )
    7: (  24,         Z-6           )
```

The following section reveals the wide dispersion of values for the sales_amt column. The total for sales varies widely from sale to sale. In a total of 300 sales records, the update statistics routine identified 70 distinct values for the sales_amt column. [In this case, the repetition is probably due to the formula used to generate the column value, $n*100.33* \bmod(n,5)$ where n is an iteration counter].

```
Distribution for informix.sales_facts.sales_amt

Constructed on 03/14/1998
```

```
Medium Mode, 2.500000 Resolution, 0.950000 Confidence


   — DISTRIBUTION —

            (                              0.00)


   — OVERFLOW —

        1: (   60,              0.00)
        2: (    3,            100.33)
        3: (    3,            401.32)
        4: (    3,            601.98)
        5: (    3,            902.97)
        6: (    3,           1103.63)
        7: (    3,           1404.62)
        8: (    6,           1605.28)
        9: (    3,           2106.93)
       10: (    6,           2407.92)
      ...
       59: (    3,          24982.17)
       60: (    3,          25684.48)
       61: (    3,          26487.12)
       62: (    3,          27691.08)
       63: (    3,          27992.07)
       64: (    3,          29497.02)
       65: (    3,          29697.68)
       66: (    3,          31704.28)
       67: (    3,          33710.88)
       68: (    3,          35717.48)
       69: (    3,          37724.08)
       70: (    3,          39730.68)
      }
```

Using Distribution Information to Determine Fragmentation Strategies

The distribution information produced by the 'dbschema -hd' option produces information that is invaluable in developing expression-based fragmentation strategies. If the goal is to distribute information evenly across disks and/or disk controllers, then understanding the distribution of data values is crucial.

Using the previous example, if the region key were being considered as a column to use for a fragmentation expression, then the information provided by the distribution output would confirm the appropriateness of this strategy.

As the distribution output indicated, there are five distinct values for the region column, so up to five fragments could be used to fragment data on this column alone. The number of values to be placed in each fragment would be as follows:

Count	Region Value
28	AL
48	MW
48	NE
128	SE
48	SW

Unfortunately, using a strategy based solely on the value of the region column would not produce a completely even distribution of data. The fragment holding the region values that matched "SE" would hold 128 rows, more than double that of any other fragment. This may not be a problem if it is determined that the access for the data is evenly distributed across all five regions; in this case, it is only data storage that is uneven and that can be managed by adding additional disk to the fragment holding region "SE." The fragmentation scheme for this strategy would be as follows:

```
... fragment by expression

        region = "AL" in dbspace1,
        region = "MW" in dbspace2,
        region = "NE" in dbspace3,
        region = "SE" in dbspace4,
        region = "SW" in dbspace5;
```

Should disk space be constrained, then it may be best to spread the data over fewer disks by combining more than one region into a single dbspace. Using the distribution information, the regions with fewer values would be combined together as follows:

```
.... fragment by expression

        region in ("AL","MW") in dbspace1,
        region in ("NE","SW") in dbspace2,
        region = "SE" in dbspace3;
```

This strategy places 76 (28+48) rows in dbspace1, 96 (48+48) rows in dbspace2, and 128 rows in dbspace3. While this strategy still does not achieve a completely even distribution of the data, it provides a more even distribution than the first strategy shown and reduces the number of dbspaces (fragments) required to three.

Data Distributions that Vary with Time

Note that the statistics generated by the 'update statistics' command is a snapshot; it represents a point in time, the point in time identified in the distribution output. As data is continually added to the database, distributions will change. In some cases it is probable that the distribution of data will remain fairly constant, so a distribution generated in March should still be valid in June. But database administrators should continue to generate distributions and review them to determine whether or not new fragmentation strategies are needed.

The Chicken or the Egg?

In a twist on "Which came first, the chicken or the egg?" a table must be created and loaded before distributions can be run to determine how to fragment the data in the table. This leaves the administrator with the option of performing a two-part operation. First the administrator would load the table and run distributions on the data in the table. Once a fragmentation scheme had been determined, the data would be unloaded, the table re-created with a fragmentation scheme, and then the data would be reloaded. An alternative is to leave the data in the table and use the "alter fragment" statement, but this could require a significant amount of disk space or log space to complete.

If, based on a review of data distributions, a new fragmentation strategy should be needed, the `alter fragment` statement can be used to change the fragmentation strategy for the data. Note that this statement requires data to be written to the new fragment (`dbspace`) while the old fragment remains in place. With a large table, this operation could require a significant amount of disk space to complete the modification.

Monitoring Disk Usage

The IDS database engine will continue to add space to a table as needed through a process known as adding extents. It continues to do this up to the point there is no more space left in the `dbspace` to add extents. At that point, any writes to the table will fail and the corresponding SQL statements will abort; the system remains online and the database administrator needs to address the problem either by adding space to the `dbspace` (by adding additional chunks) or removing data currently in the `dbspace` and freeing space. (Note that data can only be removed by dropping tables that are currently in the `dbspace`; simply deleting data from an existing table will not add free space to the `dbspace`.)

The `onstat` command with the -d option lists the `dbspaces` in the database and the space remaining in them. The output from this command is shown as follows:

```
*INFORMIX-OnLine Version 7.22.WC1      — On-Line — Up 00:01:07 — 9024 Kbytes

Dbspaces
address   number    flags    fchunk    nchunks  flags     owner     name
831980ec  1         1        1         1        N         informix  rootdbs
 1 active, 2047 maximum

Chunks
address   chk/dbs offset    size      free     bpages    flags path name
83198158  1   1    0        2120      33                 -PO   rootdbs_dat.000
 1 active, 2047 maximum
```

The output from this command is in two parts. The first section of the command lists information about the `dbspaces` that are present on the system. In the output for this section, the first column displays the *address* of the dbspace, an internal number that represents the location of the dbspace information in shared memory. The next column displays the *number* of the dbspace; this number is used to reference the dbspace in the next section of output. The next column displays the *flags* for this dbspace. These flags are a hexadecimal number and have the following meanings:

Value	Description
0x0001	No mirror
0x0002	Mirror
0x0004	Down
0x0008	Newly mirrored
0x0010	Blobspace

The next column titled fchunk indicates the chunk number of the first chunk in the dbspace. In this example, this is the initial chunk of the dbspace and cannot be dropped from the dbspace. The next column provides a set of flags that concern the dbspace; their meaning is as follows.

Position	Description
Position 1	M—Mirrored
	N—Not mirrored
Position 2	X—Newly mirrored
	P—Physically recovered, waiting for logical recovery
	L—Being logically recovered
	R—Being recovered
Position 3	B—Blobspace

The final two columns indicate the *owner* of the dbspace (the user who created the dbspace) and the *name* assigned to the dbspace.

```
...
Chunks
address    chk/dbs offset    size       free       bpages    flags path name
83198158 1    1    0         2120       33                   -PO   rootdbs_dat.000
 1 active, 2047 maximum
```

The final section in this output as shown above displays information about the chunks that comprise the dbspaces in the system. This information relates to the space used in the existing chunks. The first column is the address of the chunk information in shared memory. The following column contains the chunk number and the dbspace number displayed on the row; the dbspace number references the dbspace number in the first section. The next column is the offset of the chunk into the device (referenced in the path name output on the same line). The size of the chunk is displayed in the following column, followed by the bytes free in the chunk. The next column displays the Blobpages in the chunk, followed by a column with hexadecimal flags indicating the status of the chunk. These flags are as follows:

Position	Description
Position1	Description
	P—Primary
	M—Mirror
Position 2	O—Online
	D—Down
	X—Newly mirrored
	I—Inconsistent
Position 3	B—Blobspace
	- —Dbspace
	T—Temporary dbspace

The final column displays the path name of the device that represents the chunk. In the output displayed previously, the size of the chunk is 2120K with 33K free and it is a *primary* chunk that is currently *online*

The database administrator should closely monitor disk usage for a table. Note that the onstat command does not report space usage for a table but instead reports space usage by the chunk. So the best path to discerning space usage for a table is to identify the chunks where the table resides and track space usage for those chunks. The `oncheck` command can be used to supply this information using the following syntax:

```
oncheck -pt <database_name:table_name>
```

The following command would produce a listing for the table orders in the stores7 database.

```
oncheck -pt stores7:orders
```

Part of the output generated by this command identifies the `dbspaces` where the fragments for the table are located. The output also provides useful information on the number of rows allocated for the table and the number of rows currently used. (Though the number of rows used is useful to know, note that the size of the last fragment and the space available for a next extent has the potential to limit writes to the table, not the number of rows remaining in the final extent.)

Once these chunks are identified, the space available in final chunk of the table should be determined.

The size of a table in a `dbspace` does not always reflect the number of rows in the table. Because a table is created with a series of extents, the physical space taken by a table either exceeds or is equal to the space taken by the number of rows in the table. Deleting records in a table would therefore not reduce the space taken by the table in a `dbspace` because the table continues to consume its allocated (the size of its extent) space.

To add space to a `dbspace`, the `onspaces` `-a` command can be used. This command adds a chunk to an existing `dbspace`, as follows:

```
onspaces -a dbspace1 -p /dev/rdsk1 -o 0 -s 5000
```

This command adds a 5MB chunk from the raw disk device `/dev/rdsk1` to the `dbspace dbspace1`.

It is important to monitor the disk I/O in the `dbspaces`. To avoid I/O contention, read and write operations should be distributed as much as possible. Executing the `onstat` command with a -D (uppercase letter D) option lists the `dbspaces` in the database instance, their corresponding chunks, and the I/O operations on those chunks. The following is sample output from this command:

```
INFORMIX-OnLine Version 7.22.WC1      — On-Line — Up 00:05:24 — 9024 Kbytes

Dbspaces
address   number    flags    fchunk   nchunks  flags     owner     name
82efa0ec 1         1        1        1        N         informix  rootdbs
 1 active, 2047 maximum

Chunks
address   chk/dbs offset    page Rd  page Wr  path name
82efa158 1   1   0         276      705
D:\IFMXDATA\ol_ataylor_homepc\rootdbs_dat.000
 1 active, 2047 maximum
```

This output displays information on the pages read and written to the various chunks on the system. Unfortunately, this information is on a per-chunk basis, not on the dbspace level. The first portion of the output displays the dbspaces on the system, a number that indicates the internal number used to reference the dbspace, and columns indicating the number of chunks in the dbspace and flags that indicate the status of the chunks. Finally, the last two columns indicate the owner of the dbspace and the name assigned to the dbspace.

The second portion of the display provides information on the chunks that comprise the dbspaces listed in the previous section. The internal address of the chunk is provided and a column that indicates the chunk number and the dbspace number for the chunk. Another column indicates the offset of the chunk into the device. The columns for page Rd and page Wr provide crucial information on the page read and write operations for that chunk. These counts are relative to the last time the counts were set to 0 using either the onstat -z command or having initialized shared memory with engine startup.

Additionally, the onstat command with the -g iof parameters can be used to output the I/O per chunk and also lists the I/O for temporary files and sort-work files. The following is a sample of the output of this command:

```
INFORMIX-OnLine Version 7.22.WC1     -- On-Line -- Up 00:02:50 -- 9024 Kbytes
AIO global files:gfd path name       totalops  dskread dskwrite  io/s
 3 *D:\data\rootdbs_dat.000  25        19        6        0.1
```

This command lists the path name for each chunk and lists I/O statistics for that chunk. It lists the total operations for the chunk in the `totalops` column, the number of disk read operations in the `dskread` column, and the number of write operations in the `dskwrite` column. The final column lists the I/O per second for the chunk, a very good indication of the efficiency of I/O on that chunk.

One possible goal for the physical/logical disk layout is the even distribution of disk I/O across the disks that comprise the system. If one portion of disk is receiving the bulk of disk I/O, then during periods of high system activity, there could be I/O contention on this disk.

Note that while even distribution of I/O is a worthy goal, it is not the only consideration in establishing or tuning the system. Other factors can affect performance of the system. Uneven distribution of I/O could be caused by physical or logical logs on the disk, or a report run once a day that performs a serial scan of data on a specific disk. These are problems that can be fixed by solutions other than the distribution of data in a specific table. For instance, problems with excessive log activity could be addressed by moving logical log files to another `dbspace`. And problems with excessive report activity could be managed by running the report overnight when OLTP activity is minimal.

Tuning a system involves looking at a number of factors: the applications being run against the system, the hardware resource available, the user load, whether or not access is online or batch or a combination of both. All of these factors must be weighed in determining how to tune the system. This chapter presented a brief introduction to some of these topics; tuning is discussed in more detail in Chapter 5

Summary

This chapter discussed how the IDS engine interacts with the disk, both on a logical and physical level. On the physical level, the IDS engine is allocated disk in chunks, which map directly to disk devices and/or files. On the logical level, the engine views collections of chunks as `dbspaces`. Within `dbspaces`, databases are created and within the databases, tables are created and manipulated.

A number of tools are available for managing disk with the IDS engine. Command line tools can be used to perform all administrative functions, making it possible to create shell scripts for virtually all database maintenance tasks. Additionally, menu-driven, character-based tools such as `onmonitor` and GUI tools such as the Space Explorer and Informix Enterprise Command Center can be used to maintain and monitor the database.

Using the IDS engine, data in tables can be distributed over multiple dbspaces, a process known as fragmentation. The IDS optimizer understands the fragmentation of the data and can use it to perform parallel scans of multiple fragments during query processing. Fragmentation can also be used to distribute data across `dbspaces` for backup and restore purposes.

Various facilities can be used to monitor the disk, including the `onstat` command and data distributions. The `onstat` command can provide the disk usage for a `dbspace` and the chunks that comprise the `dbspace`. The `dbschema` command can be used to output the data distributions for the data stored in a table. These tools can be used to make informed decisions concerning fragmentation schemes for a table.

Next Chapter

The next chapter expands on the information provided in this chapter to discuss the monitoring and tuning of IDS databases. The `onstat` command and its extensive output options are discussed, and tips are provided on using this information to tune an Informix database. The `onmode` command can be used to manipulate a number of engine tunables while the engine is online allowing parameter changes to be made quickly during iterative benchmark runs.

By reviewing the output from the `onstat` command and altering appropriate configuration parameters various tuning strategies can be implemented to improve the overall performance and efficiency of the IDS engine. Several potential tuning strategies are discussed in the next chapter.

Monitoring and Tuning the IDS Engine

Informix provides a number of tools to monitor and tune the database IDS engine. Monitoring tools allow numerous facets of database operation to be monitored and controlled. The progress of an individual query can be tracked through the entire system, or the operation of the system as a whole can be monitored.

This chapter discusses how to identify and isolate performance problems in the IDS database. Using the configuration parameters presented in Chapter 4, the process of monitoring and tuning the IDS engine is explained.

Tuning Strategies for IDS

Tuning an IDS engine is not a simple, straightforward process. There is no magic bullet, no single, simple solution to tuning that applies to all applications on all platforms. Instead, there is an array of strategies that must be applied depending on the needs of the application and the availability of resources on the platform. Administrators tuning the database must evaluate the application being run, the platform and resources available, the load upon the machine, as well as other factors that may impact the system.

A number of factors can impact system performance. Poor performance can often be traced back to some resource limitation, either CPU or disk. But poor performance could also be related directly to the nature of the query or queries being run. A particular query could attempt to retrieve data from disk tables in a way that requires all records in the table to be retrieved, a serial scan of the table; a solution to this problem could be to create an index that would preclude scanning the entire table.

Generally speaking, an attempt to tune a system should first determine whether or not available resources are being stressed. Is disk I/O excessive on any particular disk? Is it approaching the limitations of the I/O channel? Is CPU resource constrained?

A common restraint on engine resources is CPU. The IDS engine requires sufficient CPU resources to operate efficiently, and the availability of these resources should be evaluated in any effort to tune the engine.

Is CPU usage approaching 100 percent? If there are multiple CPUs available (as on an SMP platform), is the system load being evenly balanced across all CPUs? Are all CPUs available to the engine being used? Inadequate CPU resources can have a significant impact on IDS engine performance and very often represents the performance bottleneck in a system.

The first step in tuning should be to evaluate the performance of the IDS database in relation to available machine resources: CPU and disk throughput. A number of `onstat` commands and several operating system commands can be used to determine resource usage and identify potential bottlenecks. These commands should be run during system idle time (when the IDS system is online but there are no users using the system) and when the system is operational and running a full load of user activity.

Tuning a system should also involve evaluating the application or applications being run against the database. Frequently the source of a slow-running query is not the resources constraining the system but the query being run. A query may be written incorrectly, forcing a scan of a large table, or an index may be needed to reduce the number of records that must be scanned.

Occasionally, the structure of the relational tables must be altered to provide a faster access path for the data.

In short, a balanced approach that looks at all potential problem areas for poor performance is the best approach to tuning a database. Potential problem areas are machine resource bottlenecks, IDS configuration parameters, database logical and physical structure, the queries and application being run against the database, and the user load on the database. The following sections will examine these problem areas and suggest solutions to any problems that may exist.

Monitoring IDS Using the onstat Utility

The onstat utility is used to retrieve statistical information on various operations of an IDS database. The onstat command is character-based and is executed from the command line. Numerous options are available and many date back to early product releases, but are still valid today. With the addition of the multi-threaded features of the 6.x and 7.x engine product, a set of sub-options was created under the -g parameter to accommodate the increasing complexity of the engine and the information available to monitor the engine. The full set of onstat options available is listed in Table 5-1. Several of these options are obscure, containing information that is only useful for very specific monitoring tasks (tracing a performance problem or debugging the engine). Only those options that are useful in monitoring and tuning the database will be discussed in this chapter.

Beginning with and following the release of version 6.0 of the Informix server, a number of important features were added to the engine, features such as multithreading and internal management of memory. A –g option and corresponding parameters were added to the onstat utility primarily to provide the capability to monitor these features. Table 5-2 lists the parameters for the –g option.

Table 5-1 *Options and Parameters for the onstat Utility*

Option	Purpose
C	B-tree cleaner requests
B	All buffers currently allocated whether or not in use
b	All buffers currently in use
X	Buffers including addresses of threads waiting <for buffers>
h	Buffer hash chain information
c	Displays configuration file information
f	Information on dataskip option
d	Displays information on chunks and dbspaces
D	Displays information on dbspace chunks and page reads and writes per chunk
i	Puts **onstat** into interactive mode
s	Displays latch information
k	Displays locks held
l	Displays logging information for both physical and logical logs including page addresses
R	Displays LRU queues
g	Displays monitoring information
m	Displays IDS message logs
p	Displays system statistical information
O	Displays information on IDS or online optical memory cache and staging area `Blobspace` information
r <seconds>	Repeats an **onstat** command(s) a specified number of seconds
o <file name>	Outputs shared memory segment to the specified file
a	Displays a summary of user-oriented options
t	Output of active `Tablespaces`
x	Output of transaction information
u	Displays user threads and transactions
F	Displays page write statistics—gathered when pages are flushed
i	Puts `onstat` into interactive mode
z	Zeroes all statistical counters

Table 5-2 *onstat -g Parameters*

Option	Purpose
act	Prints active threads
afr <pool name> I <session id>	Allocated memory fragments for a session or specified memory pool
all	Displays multithreading information
ath	Displays all threads
con	Prints conditions and waiters
dic <table>	Without parameter, prints one line of information for each table cached in shared memory. When used with the table parameter, displays information only for the specified table
dri	Data replication information
dsc	Data distribution cache
ffr <pool name> I <session id>	Displays free fragments for a pool of shared memory or specified session
glo	Displays global multithreading information
iob	Prints big-buffer use by I/O virtual processor class
iog	Asynchronous I/O global information
ioq	Asynchcronous I/O queuing statistics
iov	Asynchcronous I/O by virtual processor
lmx	Displays all locked mutexes
mem <pool name> I <session id>	Prints memory statistics for a pool or specified session
mgm	Displays MGM (Memory Grant Manager) resource information
nbm	Displays block bitmap for nonresident segments
nsc <client id>	Displays shared memory status by client ID
nsd	Displays network shared memory data for poll threads
nss <session id>	Displays shared memory status by session ID
ntd	Network statistics by service
ntm	Network mail statistics
ntt	Network user times
ntu	Network user statistics
pos	Prints `infos` and DBSERVERNAME file
ppf <partition> I 0	Prints partition profile for partition number; 0 prints profiles for all partitions
prc	Prints stored procedure information

Table 5-2 *onstat -g Parameters (continued)*

Option	Purpose
qst	Prints queue statistics
rbm	Prints block bitmap for the resident segment
rea	Prints ready threads
sch	Prints the number of semaphore operations
seg	Prints shared memory segment statistics
ses <session id>	Session information by session ID
sle	Prints sleeping threads
spi	Prints spin locks
sql <session id>	Prints SQL information by session ID
stk <tid>	Dumps stack of specific thread
sts	Displays maximum and current stack use per thread
tpf <tid>	Displays thread profile for tid; 0 prints profiles for all threads
ufr <pool name> I <session id>	Displays allocated fragments by use
wai	Prints waiting threads; waiting on condition, mutex, or condition
wmx	Prints all mutexes and waiters
wst	Prints wait statistics

The `onstat` command is executed from the command line. The command is executed, and the results are returned to the terminal device where the command was executed (`stdout`).

If the `onstat` command is executed with no parameters, the `onstat` command will display the output from the `onstat -up` command, listing all user threads and profile statistics. If executed with a specific set of parameters shown above, the `onstat` command will produce output for those parameters. The following command would display profile statistics for the current server:

```
onstat -p
```

To display information on chunks and `dbspaces`, the following command would be executed:

```
onstat -d
```

The `onstat` command allows multiple options to be executed together by placing them together as input parameters. The following command would display user threads (-u) and the table information (-t) for the current database instance:

```
onstat -ut
```

Informix monitoring tools provide a wealth of information on the activities of the engine and user threads. But making sense of this output is no trivial matter. The following section suggests strategies for evaluating and interpreting `onstat` output to monitor and tune the engine.

Using the onstat Utility to Identify Resource Bottlenecks

The engine needs two primary resources from the machine on which it is operating: disk and memory. The `onstat` utility and several operating system utilities provide a means to monitor the resources being applied to the database engine. The `onstat` utility can be used to display the disk activity of the engine, the number of disk reads and writes, and the log activity for both the logical and physical logs. The `onstat` utility would also be used to look for contention with shared resources, the number of locks being held, whether or not threads are waiting for locks, the activity of the LRU queue, and other indications of contention. The engine resources to examine and the `onstat` commands used to examine them are listed in Table 5-3. The process of using the commands to then tune the engine is covered in the following sections.

Monitoring CPU Usage with onstat –g glo

The IDS engine depends on CPU to perform its tasks. This is especially true of parallel processing, which requires sufficient CPU resources to be effective. The `onstat -g glo` command can be used to list the CPU resources used by the engine as a

Table 5-3 *Examining Engine Resources with onstat*

Resource	onstat Command
Buffers/memory	-p,-P
CPU	-g glo
Disk activity	-P, -g iof
Log activity	-l, -L
Lock activity	k
LRU queue	-R, -F
Checkpoints	-m
Physical logging	-l

whole (globally). This command lists information about the multi-threading operations of the engine and thus provides valuable information on the CPU utilization of the engine. The following is sample output from that command:

```
INFORMIX-OnLine Version 7.22.WC1      — On-Line — Up 00:02:15 — 9024 Kbytes

MT global info:
sessions threads  vps      lngspins
0        10       7        0

               sched calls      thread switches  yield 0   yield n    yield forever
total:         318751           598              312823    225        84
per sec:   0                    0                0         0          0

Virtual processor summary:
class    vps    usercpu       syscpu         total
  cpu    1      0.00          0.00           0.00
  aio    1      0.00          0.00           0.00
  lio    1      0.00          0.00           0.00
  pio    1      0.00          0.00           0.00
  adm    1      0.00          0.00           0.00
  soc    1      0.00          0.00           0.00
  msc    1      0.00          0.00           0.00
  total  7      0.00          0.00           0.00
```

```
Individual virtual processors:
    vp        pid      class    usercpu       syscpu         total
     1     fff80c29      cpu      0.00         0.00          0.00
     2     fff91265      adm      0.00         0.00          0.00
     3     fff910cd      lio      0.00         0.00          0.00
     4     fff90f55      pio      0.00         0.00          0.00
     5     fff90a3d      aio      0.00         0.00          0.00
     6     fff90885      msc      0.00         0.00          0.00
     7     fff9076d      soc      0.00         0.00          0.00
                         tot      0.00         0.00          0.00
```

The first two sections of output identify information about the operations of all virtual processors in the engine. The **MT global info** section identifies the number of active **sessions** running on VPs and the total number of **threads** in the engine. The **vps** column in this output indicates the number of VPs in use in the engine (including administrative VPs, which cannot be adjusted with configuration parameters). The **lngspins** column indicates the number of long spins by a thread waiting to use a VP.

```
           sched calls    thread switches   yield 0   yield n   yield forever
total:     318751         598               312823    225       84
per sec:   0              0                 0         0         0
```

The next section of output lists sum totals (because the last time counts were cleared) and per-second counts about thread management by the VPs. The **sched calls** column in this output lists the scheduled thread calls. The **thread switches** column lists the switches between threads. Several columns are then used to list the number of times a thread has yielded.

The final section of output lists a summary of virtual processor activity by class, listed as follows:

```
Virtual processor summary:
    class    vps    usercpu       syscpu         total
     cpu      1      0.00         0.00          0.00
     aio      1      0.00         0.00          0.00
     lio      1      0.00         0.00          0.00
     pio      1      0.00         0.00          0.00
     adm      1      0.00         0.00          0.00
     soc      1      0.00         0.00          0.00
     msc      1      0.00         0.00          0.00
     total    7      0.00         0.00          0.00
```

For each class of VP, this output lists the number of VPs running for that class under the **vps** column, the amount of user CPU time for that VP under the **usercpu** column, and the amount of system CPU time for that VP under the **syscpu** column. The final column lists the total for both 'usercpu' and 'syscpu' for each class. The last line in the output lists the totals for all VPs.

This output is similar to the output of Unix utilities such as sar and vmstat. The user CPU seconds output indicates the CPU seconds that were used to execute program instructions for the IDS engine. The system CPU seconds output indicates the time the CPU was executing system calls to carry out the work of the IDS program. Expectations with IDS are that user CPU seconds should be higher than system CPU seconds because IDS does not use a large number of system calls. The CPU classes displayed in the output are as listed in Table 5-4.

Table 5-4 CPU Classes

CPU Class	Description
cpu	General-purpose CPU VP;. most user threads run on this VP
aio	Performs asynchronous I/O operations
lio	Logical log VP
pio	Performs physical logging
adm	Performs administrative functions
shm	Executes SHM listener threads
tli	Executes TLI listener threads
soc	Executes listener threads
msc	Executes miscellaneous threads

Interpreting onstat VP Output

The CPU VP class is the general-purpose VP used to execute user threads. So a thread that is scanning a section of disk would run on a **cpu** class VP. A VP of class **aio** runs threads that are performing asynchronous I/O. If kernel aio is enabled (kaio), then I/O to raw devices will be handled by kaio threads, which ultimately pass the I/O off to a system call to perform the asynchronous read/write operation.

The `lio` and `pio` VPs perform logical logging and physical logging, respectively. These threads are not under the control of the administrator but provide useful information nevertheless. For a given session, if it appears that a significant number of CPU seconds have been applied to `lio` and `pio`—more than has been used by the CPU VPs—then CPU resources could be constrained by excessive logging.

The `adm` and the `msc` VP class is used to execute administrative functions and miscellaneous threads, respectively. The operation of these VP classes is not under the control of the system administrator. The `soc` VP class is used to listen on Unix sockets for connections.

Using Operating System Resource Monitors

Executing the `sar` or `vmstat` commands can reveal the CPU usage for the system as a whole. The output of these commands indicates how much resource is available for the VPs.

On a *symmetrical multiprocessor* platform platform, `sar` output that revealed 80 to 100 percent CPU usage for all CPUs would indicate that virtually all CPU on the platform is being used. If this output was generated when the engine was not being stressed (during a period of slow system activity), this would indicate that there is little or no CPU resource available for the engine when IDS experiences a peak system load; the engine is constrained by CPU resource. Without CPU resource, processing will be forced to wait to run on a CPU VP slowing the processing of the IDS engine.

If running `sar` or `vmstat` reveals that CPU usage for the system as a whole is running at 30 to 50 percent, then there is additional CPU resource available for the engine. This resource can be made available to the engine by adding CPU VPs. CPU VPs can be added dynamically using the `onmode` command, a very useful capability. By dynamically adding and dropping CPU VPs, CPU resource can be applied to peak system loads and then later returned to the operating system for other purposes. CPU VPs can also be added for benchmark runs to determine the impact of additional CPU resource to engine execution of a certain query.

Addressing CPU Resource Problems

If system performance is below what is expected and there are CPU resources available on the machine, the onmode utility can be used to add CPU VPs and thus increase the amount of CPU resource available to the engine. On an SMP machine, where there are multiple CPUs available for application use, adding additional CPU VPs can absorb available CPU resource and allow the IDS engine to scale as needed. The onmode command can be used to dynamically add CPU VPs as follows:

```
onmode -p +/-<number of VPs to add> <VP class>
```

The VP class can be one of the classes listed in Table 5-4. This command can be used to add VPs so that the IDS engine has more VPs than are available for processing by the engine. The number of VPs can be reduced down to the number of VPs that were allocated when the engine was started, not below that number. So if the engine were started with five CPU VPs and two VPs were added, the most that could be reduced using the onmode command would be two VPs. The following command adds two CPU VPs to the IDS engine:

```
onmode -p +2 CPU
```

The following command could be used to reduce the number of CPU VPs by two:

```
onmode -p -2 CPU
```

If it appears from the onstat -g glo output that a large number of CPU seconds are being devoted to logical logging or if it is known that several batch processes will be running that will generate a great deal of logging activity, additional logging VPs could be added to help manage the load. Then when system logging activity is reduced, the number of logging VPs could be lowered. The following command would be used to add two lio VPs to the IDS engine:

```
onmode -p -2 LIO
```

Monitoring IDS Memory Usage

Tuning the memory buffer of the IDS engine has some overlap with the tuning of the disk, because what is desired is to reduce the expensive disk I/O operation as much as possible. Tuning both operations is essential to good disk performance.

The IDS engine arranges a portion of its shared memory in what is known as a buffer cache or *shared memory buffer cache*. This buffer cache is used to cache the data that is retrieved from disk. Every IDS read operation reads data from a buffer cache page, never directly from disk if a page is not in memory, a read command is issued to get the page from disk. So all data on disk must be read into shared memory before any IDS operation can operate on it.

If possible, IDS would like to reduce the number of times disk operations occur. Once a page is read into memory, the IDS engine reads it from memory unless some other resource is using the page (which would create a *resource contention*). If IDS finds the page in memory, this is known as a *cache hit*. A high number or percentage of cache hits (as indicated by the 'onstat' -p output) indicates the engine is performing data read operations efficiently.

Using the 'onstat -p' option lists the profile counts for the engine. The output of this command is as follows:

```
INFORMIX-OnLine Version 7.22.WC1     — On-Line — Up 00:04:55 — 9024 Kbytes

Profile
dskreads  pagreads  bufreads  %cached  dskwrits  pagwrits  bufwrits  %cached
258       276       28280     99.09    608       705       5302      88.53

isamtot   open      start     read     write     rewrite   delete    commit   rollbk
20056     3014      3213      5950     2739      105       51        230      0
```

```
ovlock     ovuserthread        ovbuff   usercpu   syscpu    numckpts  flushes
0          0                   0        0.00      0.00      2         4

bufwaits   lokwaits  lockreqs  deadlks  dltouts   ckpwaits  compress  seqscans
23         0         6203      0        0         1         2         172

ixda-RA    idx-RA    da-RA     RA-pgsused         lchwaits
25         0         1         22                 1
```

An explanation of the this output is as shown in **Table 5-5**.

Table 5-5 Engine Profile Counts Explained

Count	Explanation
dskreads	Number of actual reads from disk
pagreads	Number of pages read
bufreads	Number of reads from shared memory (cache hits)
%cached	Percentage of reads cached. 100 * (bufreads-dskreads)/bufreads
dkswrits	Number of writes to disk (including physical and logical logs)
pagwrits	Number of pages written
bufwrits	Number of writes to shared memory (creating dirty pages)
%cached	Percentage of writes cached. 100 *(bufwrits-dskwrits)/dskwrits

The general rule of thumb is that if the percentage of cache hits (%cached) is less than 80, then the engine can probably be tuned by adding more memory to get a higher cache hit ratio. But this is just a rule of thumb; on platforms where memory is limited and/or applications read vast amounts of data that will not fit into shared memory (common in data warehouse/DSS applications), then this rule of thumb does not apply. Administrators must determine what is appropriate for their system. Note that in general, a better cache hit ratio generally improves data retrieval.

Because of the variable nature of access in an open environment where users are allowed to run any application option at any time, it is difficult to determine the exact memory required by an IDS server. Administrators should monitor system activity and attempt to determine the peak activity load on the system.

Repeating onstat Options to Monitor IDS

The system could be monitored using the `onstat` command to repeat a set of options and output the options to a file. The file would effectively be a log of system activity over a period of time. This log could then be reviewed to determine the peak activity for the system.

The `onstat` utility repeats a set of options using the `-r` option. The argument supplied to the `-r` option is the number of seconds to wait before executing the command again. When `onstat` is run in this fashion, it executes in a perpetual loop and continues this loop until the utility is aborted, either with a control-C keystroke from the interactive command line, or using the Unix `kill` command to kill the process running the `onstat` command. A script could be created to repeat commands as follows:

```
onstat -p -r 300 -z >> output.log
```

This script would execute the `onstat` command with the -p option repeatedly every 300 seconds (5 minutes). The '-z' option would be executed *after* the '-p' option, zeroing or clearing the statistical counts and allowing a five-minute snapshot of system activity to be accumulated in the `output.log` file.

A certain portion of memory is set aside for the processing of what the engine considers *decision support queries*. These are queries that will scan large tables and require memory for processing the sorts and joins between the tables in the query. The total amount of decision support memory is set with the DS_TOTAL_MEMORY configuration parameter, which can be adjusted with the engine online using the `onmode` command with the –M parameter.

Addressing Memory Problems

The obvious solution to a problem of poor buffer cache hit ratios is to allocate memory to the IDS instance. But this must be balanced against the needs of other applications on the platform that require shared memory.

In the event that physical memory is available, it must be verified that the physical memory has been allocated as shared memory on the platform. If the physical memory is available and has been allocated as shared memory, then the IDS configuration file parameters for shared memory can be adjusted to recognize the change.

Monitoring Disk Activity

The IDS server is extremely flexible in allowing data to be distributed physically across multiple disks. And proper distribution of data can alleviate the disk I/O bottleneck. But determining the proper distribution of data in an IDS database, known as the *fragmentation* of data, can be a tricky task.

To determine whether or not there is a data I/O bottleneck, the reads and writes per dbspace or chunk must be monitored. This can be determined using the onstat command with the -D parameter; this command reveals the reads and writes per chunk, shown as follows:

```
INFORMIX-OnLine Version 7.22.WC1     — On-Line — Up 00:05:24 — 9024 Kbytes
Dbspaces
address   number   flags    fchunk   nchunks   flags     owner      name
82efa0ec 1        1        1        1         N         informix   rootdbs
 1 active, 2047 maximum
Chunks
address   chk/dbs offset   page Rd   page Wr   pathname
82efa158 1   1    0        276       705       D:\IFMXDATA\ol_ataylor_homepc\
                                               rootdbs_dat.000
 1 active, 2047 maximum
```

The first part of the output of this command lists information about the dbspaces on the system. In the output for this section, the first column displays the address of the dbspace, an internal number that represents the location of the dbspace information in shared memory. The next column displays the number of the dbspace; this number is used to reference the dbspace in the next section of output. The next column displays the flags for this dbspace, a hexadecimal number the meaning of which can be seen in Table 5-6.

Table 5-6 *The dbspace Flag Values*

Value	Description
0x0001	No mirror
0x0002	Mirror
0x0004	Down
0x0008	Newly mirrored
0x0010	Blobspace

The fchunk column indicates the chunk number of the first chunk in the dbspace. This is the initial chunk of the dbspace and cannot be dropped from the dbspace. The next column provides a set of flags that indicate the status of the dbspace; their meanings are shown in Table 5-7.

Table 5-7 *The dbspace Status Flag Values*

Position	Description
	M—Mirrored
1	N—Not Mirrored
2	X—Newly Mirrored
	P—Physically recovered, waiting for logical recovery
	L—Being logically recovered
	R—Being recovered
3	B—Blobspace

The final two columns indicate the owner of the dbspace (the user who created the dbspace) and the name assigned to the dbspace.

The final section of this onstat output is shown as follows. This section displays information about the chunks that comprise the dbspaces in the system. This information relates to the space used in the existing chunks.

```
...
Chunks
address   chk/dbs offset   size      free      bpages    flags pathname
83198158 1   1    0        2120      33                  -PO   rootdbs_dat.000
 1 active, 2047 maximum
```

The first column in this output is the address of the chunk information in shared memory. The column number and the dbspace number are also displayed on the row; the dbspace number references the dbspace number in the first section.

The next column on this row is the offset of the chunk into the device (referenced in the path name output on the same line). The size of the chunk is displayed in the following column followed by the bytes free in the chunk.

The next column is named bpages and displays the Blobpages in the chunk followed by a column with hexadecimal flags indicating the status of the chunk, which are shown in Table 5-8.

Table 5-8 Chunk Status Flags

Flag	Description
0x0001	No mirror
0x0002	Mirror
0x0004	Down
0x0008	Newly mirrored
0x0010	Blobspace

The final column displays the pathname of the device that holds the chunk. In the output displayed previously, the size of the chunk is 2120 kilobytes with 33 kilobytes free.

Addressing Disk Problems

The goal of disk management with the IDS engine is to distribute data access as evenly as possible. A common-sense approach that does not situate logical logs, physical logs, and all volatile data on the same physical disk is a good approach. High-access data tables and logs should be distributed over multiple disks as much as possible. The database administrator must be aware of the physical location of the disk being mapped to dbspaces. If possible, the fragments for a large table should be spread over multiple disks by assigning those fragments to multiple dbspaces. But if in fact those dbspaces have chunks on the same disk, the goal of distributing disk I/O load has not been met.

Reviewing the output onstat -D displays the reads and writes (Page Rd and Page Wr). If the output of this command indicates that a large percentage of the disk I/O is directed to a small set of dbspaces, then portions of a table could be relocated to another dbspace with the alter fragment command. A discussion of fragmentation schemes for distributing data across multiple dbspaces, an important part of proper data distribution with the IDS engine, is provided later in this chapter.

Log Activity in the IDS Engine

As discussed previously, Informix provides facilities to buffer both the *physical* and *logical* log output in shared memory before it is written to disk. Determining the correct size of these buffers can help reduce the number of disk writes required to write logs to disk and thus improve performance.

The onstat command with the "-l" parameter prints information about physical and logical logs. The first section of the display output displays the information about the physical log that is shown in Table 5-9.

The second section of the output displays the information about the logical log shown in Table 5-10.

Additional output is provided to describe the state of each log file, but tuning log I/O is not concerned with the state of each log.

Table 5-9 *onstat Physical Log Output*

Item	Description
buffer	Number of physical log buffers
bufused	Number of pages in a physical log buffer
bufsize	Size of each physical log buffer
numpages	Number of pages written to the physical log
numwrits	Number of writes to the disk
pages/io	Number of physical log pages per write (numpages/numwrits)
phybegin	Physical page number of the beginning of the log
physize	Size of the physical log in pages
phypos	Current position in the physical log where the next log record write will occur
phyused	Number of pagers used in the log
%used	Percentage of pages used

Table 5-10 *onstat Logical Log Output*

Item	Description
buffer	Number of the logical-log buffer
bufused	Number of pages used in the logical log buffer
bufsize	Size of each logical log buffer
numrecs	Number of records written
numpages	Number of pages written
numwrits	Number of writes to the logical log
recs/pages	Number of records per page (numrecs/numpages)
pages/io	Number of pages/io (numpages/numwrits)

Addressing Log Performance Problems

To tune the logical log, what is desired is to maximize the pages per log write I/O and thus reduce the amount of disk I/O the engine must do to get the log files (both physical and logical) to disk. This can be accomplished by altering the size of the buffer used to store the log files. To accomplish this task, the configuration parameters LOGBUFF and PHYBUFF would be altered until the buffer size was as close as possible to the pages per I/O reported in the `onstat -l` output.

If large portions of the logical log were being kept on the disk that was being saturated with I/O requests (as revealed by executing the `onstat -D` and `onstat -g iof` command) , then it may be necessary to move some or all of the logical log files to a less contentious portion of disk. This can be accomplished using the `onparams` command.

Evaluating and Tuning Physical Log Activity

As discussed previously, the physical log is used to store *before images* of pages that are to be updated. This copy is written to the physical log on disk and used in the event a system recovery requires the updated page to be restored to its previous state (as in a *fast recovery*). But before the 'before image' is written to the physical log on disk, it is first written to the physical log in memory. This buffer location in memory is written to disk at certain intervals.

There are two physical log buffers in memory. When the first physical log buffer is filled, a second physical log buffer in memory is used, thus allowing writes to the physical log buffer to continue and not hindering system performance. When the physical log reaches 75 percent full, a checkpoint is triggered and the contents of the physical log are written to disk.

The physical log can impact performance in two ways. First, the IDS engine constantly writes to the physical log so the disk containing the physical log will experience a large amount of disk I/O. The second is that when the physical log fills to 75 percent, it forces a checkpoint that, as discussed in the previous section, can hinder system performance.

The Physical Log Location

To avoid the excessive disk I/O of physical logging on a section of disk, the location of the physical log can be changed. When the engine is created, the physical log is placed in the root `dbspace`, a `dbspace` where a large amount of disk activity can occur. The physical log can be moved by altering the PHYDBS configuration parameter and restarting the engine.

The PHYDBS parameter indicates the `dbspace` where the physical log is to be located. The physical log can be located in any `dbspace` large enough to hold the physical log as contiguous space. It is recommended that the log be placed in a `dbspace` that will not be impacted by the large amount of disk I/O performed on the log. (Alternatively, the `onparams` command or the `onmonitor` utility can be used to move the physical log.) Once the PHYDBS parameter has been changed, the engine must be restarted to recognize the parameter change.

The Physical Log Size

If the physical log continually fills to 75 percent and forces checkpoints in between the set checkpoint intervals, then the size of the physical log can be made larger to reduce the number of checkpoints. This would lengthen the time between checkpoints, but it could also increase the length of the checkpoint because there would be more pages in the physical log to flush to disk.

A shorter checkpoint interval, however, would allow for a smaller physical log and faster checkpoint processing. So ultimately what is needed is a balance between physical log size and the checkpoint interval; a balance that yields minimal checkpoint overhead and provides for minimal data loss in the event of a system failure.

Blobs that are stored in a `blobspace` are not written to the physical log. (The data integrity of Blobspace blobs is managed through another mechanism.) But `tblspace` Blobs, Blobs stored with the data records in a table, are written to the physical log. The `tblspace` Blob should therefore be used judiciously to avoid table updates that lead to heavy physical log activity.

It is recommended that the physical log initially be set to a size estimated by the number of concurrent users on a system and an approximation of the size of the pages that these users may be updating at a given point in time. Given that it may be difficult to approximate the number of pages held by a set number of concurrent users, a different approach would be to begin with a certain physical log size and then monitor the physical log during system activity. If the physical log becomes full and forces checkpoints between checkpoint intervals, the size of the physical log should be increased.

The physical log size can be changed using the PHYSFILE parameter. Once this parameter has been changed, the engine must be restarted to recognize the change. Additionally, the `onparams` command or `onmonitor` program can be used to change this parameter.

Evaluating the LRU Queue

As previously mentioned, the IDS engine buffers all I/O in shared memory. Any writes to database tables are first *written* to pages in the shared memory buffer. Periodically the pages that have been updated in shared memory (referred to as *dirty pages*) must be written to disk, a process sometimes referred to as *flushing* the buffer to disk. The pages are written to disk by a thread known as a *page flusher* thread.

The updated LRU buffers are managed through a mapping mechanism known as the *least recently used* buffer. This mechanism maps to pages in the shared memory buffer.

The LRU queue is designed to provide maximum throughput on an update intensive system. Using a properly tuned LRU queue, pages that are expected to be used soon will be kept in memory, thus avoiding having to read the page back from disk to populate shared memory.

Evaluating LRU Performance

Two `onstat` commands can be used to evaluate the performance of the LRU management system, the '-F' command can be used to display page flusher commands; the '-R' command outputs information on the LRU queues. The '-F' option produces the following output:

```
INFORMIX-OnLine Version 7.22.WC1     — On-Line — Up 07:00:59 — 9024 Kbytes

Fg Writes      LRU Writes     Chunk Writes
0              0              31
```

```
address   flusher   state     data
82efc448  0         I         0            = 0X0

states:  Exit Idle Chunk Lru
```

The first part of the command displays cumulative information for the LRU queues, as shown in **Table 5-11**.

Table 5-11 *LRU Queues*

Fg writes	Number of foreground writes
LRU writes	Number of LRU writes
Chunk writes	Number of chunk writes

The information in each of these columns explains why page
cleaners have been wakened to clean dirty buffers. The output of
the *foreground writes* column represents writes that have been
triggered by operations that needed to write to the queue but
couldn't because of the dirty buffers, and therefore had to wake
a page cleaner to clean the buffer.

The output of the *LRU write* column indicates the number of
times that a cleaner was wakened by the LRU mechanism when
it determined that the LRU_MAX_DIRTY percentage has been
reached for a given queue.

The output of the *chunk writes* column indicates the number
of times a cleaner was wakened to clean a buffer during a checkpoint. At this time, the buffers are sorted by the chunk to which
they belong and a page cleaner is assigned a chunk and a sorted
queue for output (thus the term *chunk write*).

The second part of the command output displays information
about the page cleaners (flushers) on the system, as follows:

```
address   flusher   state     data
82efc448  0         I         0            = 0X0

states:  Exit Idle Chunk Lru
```

The **address** column displays the address (in shared memory)
for the page cleaner being referenced on that row of output. The
flusher column displays the flusher (cleaner) number for the

flusher being referenced. The **state** column displays the state of the page cleaner where state is one of *Exit, Idle, Chunk,* or *LRU*. If the state indicates *Exit,* then the page cleaner has exited and is no longer running. If the state indicates *Idle*, the page cleaner is waiting (sleeping) to be wakened and assigned a queue to clean. If the page cleaner is in a *Chunk* state, then it has been wakened at checkpoint time is performing a **chunk write**. If the page cleaners state is in an *LRU* state, then it has been wakened by the LRU queue, assigned an LRU to clean and is performing an **LRU write**.

To properly tune the LRU queue, the goal is to reduce the amount of chunk writes that are occurring because these occur at checkpoint time and, if they take too long, can increase the length of the checkpoint. What is desired is to have the buffers cleared by the LRU mechanism as would be indicated by the LRU writes column in the output shown previously. The '-R' command displays the information about the LRU queues shown in Table 5-12.

Table 5-12 -R LRU Queue output

#	Queue number f/m queue type
f	Free LRU queue
F	Free queue with fewest elements
m	MLRU queue
M	MLRU queue that is being flushed
length	Length of the queue measured in buffers
% of	Percentage of queue in subqueue
pair total	Total number of buffers in the LRU queue

This section of the output displays information about the status of each individual queue. The pair total display in the output contains information on the total number of buffers in the queue. This is useful in determining whether or not the queue is too large to be written easily during a page flush operation. The output of the % of column can give some idea of how quickly the queues are filling.

The next section of the output displays summary information for the queues as shown in Table 5-13.

Table 5-13 – LRU Queue Summary Information

dirty	Total number of buffers that have been modified in all LRU queues
queued	Total number of buffers in LRU queues
hash buckets	Number of hash buckets
buffer size	Size of each buffer
start clean	Value of LRU_MAX_DIRTY
stop at	Value of LRU_MIN_DIRTY

The final section of output represents totals for the LRU activity. The total number of dirty or modified pages is listed along with the total number of LRU queues and the size of each buffer. The number of hash buckets is listed, and finally the value of the configuration parameters LRU_MAX_DIRTY and LRU_MIN_DIRTY.

The LRU queues should be monitored during system activity using the onstat command with the -r option to repeat the command at specific intervals. Administrators should look for queues that are filling so fast the page cleaners do not have time to flush the dirty pages before the checkpoint. The following section discusses tuning strategies for the LRU queue.

Tuning LRU Management

The management of LRU queues can have a significant impact on system performance, though its impact is indirect. If modified pages (dirty pages) are not written to disk by page flushers when the LRU management signals them to do so, then they are written at checkpoint time. The problem with writing the pages at checkpoint time is that checkpoints effectively halt all critical system activity (which has the effect of halting most system activity) while the checkpoint does its work. If a large number of dirty pages must be written during the checkpoint interval, then the checkpoint could take some time. (Halting system activity for 60 seconds while the checkpoint writes a large volume of dirty pages to disk is almost sure to bring the wrath of the user community.)

So the basic task in tuning the LRU queue management is to maximize the amount of work performed to manage the LRU queue during normal system processing and minimize the work performed at checkpoint. This can be accomplished by having the LRU queue management facility trigger more page writes before the checkpoint occurs. Four parameters are available to help trigger these page writes: LRU_MIN_DIRTY, LRU_MAX_DIRTY, LRUS and CLEANERS. These parameters are explained in Table 5-14.

Table 5-14 – LRU Configuration Parameters

Parameter	Description
LRUS	Number of shared memory LRU queues to create
LRU_MIN_DIRTY	Quit cleaning LRUs at this percentage dirty pages
LRU_MAX_DIRTY	Start cleaning LRU queue at this percentage dirty
CLEANERS	Number of page cleaner threads assigned

The LRUS parameter indicates the number of LRU queues to create. The number of queues chosen impacts the size of the queue and the size of the queue impacts how long it will take to write the queue to disk. The LRU parameter must therefore be balanced with the CLEANERS parameter, which sets the number of cleaner threads that are assigned to write the dirty pages to disk by the LRU mechanism. The general rule of thumb is that the number of LRUs should be set equal to the number of CPU VPs and the number of CLEANERS should be set to the number of chunks.

The IDS engine monitors the pages in the LRU buffer in each queue. When a queue reaches the LRU_MAX_DIRTY percentage of dirty pages, a cleaner thread is assigned to write the dirty pages in that queue to disk. The cleaner thread will continue to write pages to disk until the percentage of dirty pages in that queue is the LRU_MIN_DIRTY percentage; at that point it will stop writing pages.

As stated previously, the goal in tuning the LRU queue is to minimize the number of pages that are written at checkpoint. The requirement is therefore to write as many pages as possible between checkpoints. The page writes written between check-points are primarily triggered by the LRU mechanism. So the goal is therefore to maximize the number of pages written by the LRU mechanism.

To get the LRU queue to trigger more page writes, the LRU_MAX_DIRTY parameters should be set lower. By setting this parameter lower, the LRU mechanism will trigger page writes sooner.

When the page cleaner thread is wakened and assigned an LRU queue to clean, it will clean the queue (write updated pages to disk) until it reaches the LRU_MIN_DIRTY percentage. To force the cleaner thread to write more pages to disk in between check-points, the LRU_MIN_DIRTY percentage should be set lower, thus more pages will be written when the page cleaner is wakened by LRU management.

In setting the LRU parameters, the *delta* or difference between the LRU_MIN_DIRTY and LRU_MAX_DIRTY settings have a direct impact on the amount of work that must be performed by the page cleaners. For example, if a system has 1 GB of memory available for the shared memory buffer and has been assigned 20 LRU queues, each LRU queue will be assigned to a queue of 50,000,000 bytes (1,000,000,000/20). If the LRU parameter settings were LRU_MIN_DIRTY=10 and LRU_MAX_DIRTY=30, then the delta is 20 and the page cleaners would be expected to write 20 percent of the 50 MB buffer, or 10 MB (.2 * 50,000,000) when it is wakened to clean a buffer. In practice, when IDS is in production and updates are being performed at a steady rate, it is highly likely that once one page cleaner is wakened to clean a dirty buffer, others will soon be wakened. Whether or not LRU settings are optimal would be dependent to a large extent on the machine resources available to IDS, such as the number and speed of the disk drives (I/O throughput) and the amount of CPU resource available (some CPU cycles are required to perform the writes). If some review determined that the 10 MB per cleaner number were too large (as set by the delta between LRU_MIN_DIRTY and LRU_MAX_DIRTY), then the number could be made smaller by increasing the number of page cleaners using the CLEANERS configuration parameter.

Review and experimentation are the key to determining the correct LRU settings for an IDS system. The profile of the IDS system, whether it has a heavy or light update load or some periodic combination of the two, is the primary consideration when setting these parameters. The following sections discuss these considerations and their impact on tuning the LRU queues.

LRU Parameter Settings for a Heavy Update Load

A system with a heavy, constant update load and a great deal of concurrency, a common transaction profile for an OLTP system, must try to minimize checkpoint time and maximize the amount of dirty buffer pages written between checkpoints.

For a system such as this, setting LRU_MAX_DIRTY to 10 and LRU_MIN_DIRTY to 2 could be an effective setting. This tight delta would force a large number of pages to be written between checkpoints and leave minimal disk write work to be performed at checkpoint time. Asserting that machine resources can manage the disk write load between checkpoints, the checkpoints would be required only to write between 2 and 10 percent of the each LRU queue to disk, making quick work of the concurrency inhibiting tasks that the engine must perform at checkpoint time.

LRU Parameter Settings for a Light Update Load

What may be a good setting for a system with a heavy update load may not be a good setting for a system with a light update load and a heavy query load. With a light update load and ample disk and CPU resource, setting LRU_MAX_DIRTY to 40 percent and LRU_MIN_DIRTY to 15 percent may be an adequate setting. This would mean that in most cases, the system would be writing a queue only 15 percent full at checkpoint time and cleaning 25 percent of some of the queues in between checkpoints.
In this case we assert that since the update load is light, the LRU algorithm is effectively spreading the update load across buffer queues, and that only a few queues need to be cleaned in between checkpoints. When checkpoint occurs, there would be some number of queues to clean between 15 and 40 percent full; with ample system resource available, this could be managed during checkpoint. (If it appeared checkpoints were taking too long, a tighter delta could be created by lowering the LRU_MAX_DIRTY setting to 30 or 25.)

LRU Settings for a Decision Support System

The decision support system has a different transaction profile from an OLTP system. A decision support system has very large update transactions for the data load operations followed by periods in which long running queries are run with no updates taking place. In many such systems, the updates may occur when users are not on the system, a time when a long checkpoint may be of little consequence. Even though a long checkpoint during the data load process would not impact users (who would not be on the system), it is still important to tune the LRU buffer management to effectively perform its duty, since such tuning will improve throughput and minimize load time.

The object is to provide the best possible throughput without detracting from the overall performance of the system. An LRU_MAX_DIRTY setting of 60 percent and an LRU_MIN_DIRTY setting of 20 percent may be adequate for a DSS system. This would potentially, during a heavy update, leave a number of queues to be cleaned at checkpoint time at between 20 and 60 percent dirty. This could periodically create a lengthy but manageable checkpoint, but with little competition for resources, it would most likely not impact throughput.

Should throughput be compromised by these settings, then setting LRU_MAX_DIRTY to a lower number would force more buffer pages to be written between checkpoints. An LRU_MAX_DIRTY setting of 40 percent would force more cleaner thread activity and potentially provide shorter checkpoints.

Iterative Benchmarking for LRU Tuning

As with many other system configuration parameters, there is no simple formula for the setting of LRU parameters. The LRU settings are dependent on platform-specific variables (the number of disks, the speed of disks, the amount of memory available) that are difficult to quantify. The variability of platform factors require an approach to tuning that attempts to discover the capabilities of a platform through iterative benchmarking. Benchmark programs must be developed that stress the engine resources impacted by the LRU parameters. Because the LRU parameters affect the way in which updates are performed, the benchmark programs must update the engine in such a way as to stress the engine. The benchmark process should be an iterative one, with a benchmark being run and then followed by an evaluation of the results. If necessary, the engine parameters are then adjusted and the benchmark is re-run and results are evaluated once again. This process is repeated until performance is considered optimal.

This benchmark process is important. Engine parameters should not be changed without some evaluation of the impact of the change. Iterative benchmark runs will yield the best results, making small, subtle changes in parameters, performing a benchmark, and then evaluating the results.

Evaluating and Tuning Checkpoints

As mentioned previously, the IDS engine performs checkpointing to synchronize the shared memory buffer with disk and provide a fixed recovery point. Checkpointing is necessary to provide for system integrity. But a checkpoint does not allow engine code to enter critical areas while checkpoints are occurring. This virtually halts updates during checkpoints, and a long checkpoint can make the engine appear to hang. Excessive checkpointing activity can slow system processing and hinder performance.

In practice, checkpoint intervals are usually set between 5 and 30 minutes on OLTP systems (as set by the CKPTINTVL configuration parameter), but these are not firm values. The value set for a specific system should be based on the needs of that system.

The checkpoint represents a point where, in the event of machine failure, it is possible to restore the system to a consistent state. A short checkpoint interval would preserve more work than a longer checkpoint interval in the event the system were brought down unexpectedly. If a system provided a checkpoint interval of 5 minutes and failed 1 minute before checkpoint time, only 4 minutes of system activity would potentially be lost. If, however, a system had a checkpoint interval of 30 minutes and failed 1 minute before checkpoint, 29 minutes of system activity would potentially be lost. (System activity would be lost completely in a nonlogged database. In a database with transaction logging, only transactions that had not been committed would be lost.) A longer checkpoint interval would also have the impact of lengthening the time required for fast recovery because fast recovery recovers from the point of the last checkpoint.

But a system that experienced a checkpoint every 5 minutes would have potential system degradation every 5 minutes when the checkpoint occurred. (Note that proper LRU management could reduce the overhead of the checkpoint significantly, but some degradation would be experienced.)

A batch system would have a significantly different transaction profile from that of an OLTP system and would thus not have the same recovery issues as an online system. A batch process can often be recovered by simply rerunning the batch process. A checkpoint interval of 30 minutes or more may be appropriate on this type of system.

Any system that is update intensive will stress IDS by forcing before images to be written to the physical log. Because filling the physical log to 75 percent will force a checkpoint, a long checkpoint interval in tandem with a heavy update load will force a large number of checkpoints making the long checkpoint interval (as set in the configuration parameter CKPTINTVL) moot. (A checkpoint interval of 30 minutes would never be reached if the heavy update load forced checkpoints every 5 minutes by filling the physical log 75 percent full.)

Tuning Queries and Applications

Tracking the performance of specific queries is a very effective way to find performance bottlenecks in an application. Tracking query performance involves running the query and then using the onstat utility to track the execution of the query (identified as a *session* in onstat output).

Tracking the execution of a query using the onstat command will identify the tables accessed by the query, the number of scan threads used to read .data from the tables and/or indices, the temporary tables used, and the amount of memory allocated. This information can then be used to determine how to optimize the query as discussed in the following sections.

Tracking the Query Session with 'onstat –g ses'

Two `onstat` parameters can be used to track the activity of a query session. The `onstat` command with the '`-g ses <session id>`' parameter will list information about the specific session, and the `onstat` '`-g sql <session id>`' will provide information about the SQL statement being processed.

Viewing Session Activity with the 'onstat -g ses' Command

The `onstat` command with the `-g ses` option displays information about the sessions or a specific session being run. The output for this command is as follows:

```
INFORMIX-OnLine Version 7.22.WC1      — On-Line — Up 00:05:07 — 9024 Kbytes

session                                      #RSAM    total      used
id       user      tty      pid    hostname threads  memory    memory
13       informix  -        0      -         0        8192      4628
3        informix  -        0      -         0        16384     12256
2        informix  -        0      -         0        8192      4628
```

The output from the command displays session information for all sessions, whether or not the sessions are active. Each line displays the session ID, the user who initiated the session, where the user accessed the system, the `tty` (terminal ID), the process ID of the connecting process, the host name of the machine for the host process, the number of threads being used by the user, the total memory allocated for the user, and the total memory currently being used. The columns displayed for this command are listed in Table 5-15.

The session output generated by this command provides information on the status of the query and the amount of resources currently used. Any query referencing an inordinate amount of memory should be examined more closely. Additional informationcan be obtained about a session by passing the session ID into the `onstat` command as a parameter (`onstat -g ses <session id>`); the following is sample output from this command.

```
INFORMIX-OnLine Version 7.22.WC1      — On-Line — Up 00:08:03 — 9024 Kbytes

session                                      #RSAM    total      used
```

Table 5-15 *onstat -g ses Command Output*

Column	Purpose
Session	Internal IDS session ID for the user session
user	Operating system user name for the connection
tty	Operating system terminal ID of the user's terminal (if any)
pid	Operating system process ID of the user's client session
hostname	Host name from which the user session originated
#RSAM threads	Number of threads currently operating for the user session
total memory	Memory allocated for the user session
used memory	Memory currently being used by the user session

```
id          user       tty      pid     hostname threads  memory      memory
14          informix ATAYLOR_   fff9b3c7 ataylor_ 1          49152        30432


tid         name      rstcb     flags    curstk     status
27          sqlexec  82efd0e4  Y—P—      756        82efd0e4 cond wait(netnorm)


Memory pools      count 1
name              class addr      totalsize freesize #allocfrag #freefrag
14                V      82ffa014 49152     18720     276          12


name            free        used          name          free        used
overhead        0           108           scb           0           80
opentable       0           3508          filetable     0           628
log             0           4180          temprec       0           1596
gentcb          0           7660          ostcb         0           2008
sort            0           52            sqscb         0           7520
rdahead         0           116           hashfiletab   0           276
osenv           0           1192          sqtcb         0           1348
fragman         0           160


Sess   SQL                Current          Iso Lock       SQL    ISAM  F.E.
Id     Stmt type          Database         Lvl Mode       ERR    ERR   Vers
14     -                  testit           NL  Not Wait   0      0     7.22


Last parsed SQL statement :
  select * from t1
```

The first part of the output of the -g ses <session_id> command is the same as the -g ses command. It displays information on the session, the connection terminal, the process ID of operating system, the amount of memory allocated, and the amount of memory used by the session.

The next part of the output displays information on the threads currently running for that session. The thread ID is listed in the *tid* column followed by the name of the thread (e.g., sqlexec). The *restcb* column lists the address for the *control block* of the thread. The next four columns provide information on the amount of memory being used by the thread.

The next section of the output is shown as follows. This section displays information on the memory being used for the session. The various names listed are internal names for IDS memory structures.

```
Memory pools      count 1
name           class addr      totalsize freesize #allocfrag #freefrag
14              V      82ffa014 49152     18720    276         12

name             free        used          name             free        used
overhead         0           108           scb              0           80
opentable        0           3508          filetable        0           628
log              0           4180          temprec          0           1596
gentcb           0           7660          ostcb            0           2008
sort             0           52            sqscb            0           7520
rdahead          0           116           hashfiletab      0           276
osenv            0           1192          sqtcb            0           1348
fragman          0           160

Sess   SQL                 Current        Iso  Lock      SQL    ISAM  F.E.
Id     Stmt type           Database       Lvl  Mode      ERR    ERR   Vers
14     -                   testit         NL   Not Wait  0      0     7.22

Last parsed SQL statement :
   select * from t1
```

The final section of the output displays information on the SQL statement being executed. The output contains columns for SQL statement type, the current database, the isolation level (Iso Lvl), the lock mode, and the error generated for the SQL statement (if any). The final column identifies the version of the Informix front-end client software component (ESQL/C, Informix-4GL) that established the connection.

This command output is useful in determining the amount of IDS resources being used by a session, information that can be used to monitor the IDS system for problem queries and general resource usage. The first sections of output of this command indicate the number of threads and memory that have been allocated to a session. A session that is using a large amount of system resource such as memory, could be a runaway session (the query from hell) that is beginning to limit overall engine performance. Running the `onstat -g ses` command would identify the session and the memory and threads being used for the session. Then running the `onstat -g ses <session id>` command would indicate the query being run.

The administrator could then review this query to determine whether or not it was appropriate. For instance, a query that was selecting all rows in a 6-million-row table would be suspect. It may be a necessary query, but running the query would raise a number of tuning issues, such as whether or not there are adequate resources to run the query, when the query should be run, and whether or not to limit the resources to allocate to the query using various facilities available. The following sections will cover these topics.

The 'onstat -g sql' Command

Executing the `onstat` command with the `-g sql <session id>` parameters displays information on the SQL statements currently running. This command provides additional information on SQL statements being run on the system. The following is sample output from this command:

```
INFORMIX-OnLine Version 7.22.WC1      — On-Line — Up 00:07:19 — 9024 Kbytes

Sess  SQL             Current          Iso Lock        SQL    ISAM  F.E.
Id    Stmt type       Database         Lvl Mode        ERR    ERR   Vers
14    -               testit           NL  Not Wait    0      0     7.22

Last parsed SQL statement :
  select * from t1
```

The output for this command is described in Table 5-16.

As with the `onstat -g ses` command, this command provides a means of monitoring queries being run on the system and the current state of those queries, most importantly whether or not the query has encountered an error. An administrator may

Table 5-16 *onstat -g sql Command Output*

Session id	Internal IDS session ID
SQL stmt type	SQL statement type
current database	Current database on which the statement is executing
Iso Lvl	Logging isolation level for the SQL statement
Lock Mode	Lock mode for the statement
SQL Err	Last SQL error generated by the statement
ISAM Err	Last ISAM error generated by the statement
F.E. Vers	Front-end (client) version for the session

use this command to determine whether or not a query being run by a user has failed and, if so, the reason for the failure.

Monitoring Active Threads with 'onstat –g act'

The onstat command executed with the '-g act' option displays useful information about the active threads for a query. This is important information when trying to determine the amount of parallelization being experienced by the query. The following is the output for this command:

```
INFORMIX-OnLine Version 7.22.WC1      — On-Line — Up 07:00:38 — 9024 Kbytes

Running threads:
tid     tcb       rstcb     prty      status      vp-class    name
7       82f7d944  0         2         running     7soc        soctcppoll
35      8305a764  82efccb0  2         running     1cpu        sqlexec
```

In this example, the engine is managing two active threads, a soctcpoll thread that listens or polls a TCP/IP socket for a connection, and an sqlexec thread that performs the work of executing the query. Each row in this output displays information about a specific thread. The columns displayed on each row are shown in Table 5-17.

The VP class information indicates the virtual processor on which the thread is running. This command is useful in determining how the CPU resource is being used by the IDS system

TTable 5-17 onstat *-g act Command Output*

tid	Internal IDS thread ID number
tcb	Address of the thread control block
status	Satus of the thread (the -g act option will only display *running* threads)
vp-class	VP class on which the thread is running
name	Name of the thread type

overall. Running this command during the execution of a query would indicate the active threads (the threads currently being run by IDS) used to process a query (and any other system activity being run at the time). For instance, if a query were run that made use of parallel processing, executing this command would display the active scan threads used by the query.

Monitoring Asynchronous I/O with 'onstat –g iof'

Executing the onstat command with the -g   iof option will display information about the asynchronous I/O (AIO) threads running on the system. The following is an example of this output:

```
INFORMIX-OnLine Version 7.22.WC1      — On-Line — Up 00:01:24 — 9024 Kbytes

AIO global files:
gfd pathname          totalops  dskread dskwrite   io/s
3 *D:\rootdbs_dat.000     23        17       6      0.3
4 *d:\chunk1               5        5        0      0.1
```

This command displays information on the read and write operations per chunk (similar to the onstat –D output), including a very useful I/O per second output (io/s). The io/s column is a good indicator of the amount of throughput for a particular portion of disk. If it appears that certain chunks are experiencing an inordinate amount of throughput, then the contents of the disk (chunk/dbspace) should be reviewed. There may be a valid reason for the large amount of I/O, for instance physical or logical logging is being performed on the chunk, or a table that is constantly accessed is located on the chunk. But a high level of I/O could also reveal a problem that could be addressed by moving or fragmenting tables, moving logical log files, or relocating the physical log.

Excessive I/O could also reveal a portion of disk that is saturated beyond the point at which the I/O subsystem can handle throughput efficiently. Whether or not this is the case is dependent on the I/O subsystem being used and, if it appears this could be the case, should be reviewed with the system administrator for the IDS hardware platform.

Addressing System Resource Problems

The most obvious method of addressing a system resource problem that leads to diminished performance is to add an additional machine resource. This does not necessarily mean adding additional disk or CPU to the machine. It may just mean that if this resource is available on the system, then this resource should be made available to the IDS instance with performance problems.

Database engines can require significant CPU resource to accomplish their work. The CPU resource available to the engine is equally as important as the disk resource available. In fact, in many cases the engine is CPU bound, meaning the available CPU resource is more important than the disk resource available. The machine CPU resource can be in significant demand if parallelization is achieved through proper fragmentation of tables.

One of the most common hardware platforms available today is the symmetrical multiple processor platform which uses multiple CPUs to provide processing power to applications. The number of CPUs used is flexible, allowing users to add additional CPUs as needed up to a specified limit.

If a query requires five scan threads on a machine with only four CPUs, it will not be able to achieve full parallelization of the query. In this case, adding an additional CPU to the machine and making the CPU available to the database engine could improve performance.

The IDS engine recognizes CPU resource through the CPU virtual processor (VP). The CPU VP can either be added in the `onconfig` configuration file or it can be added dynamically through the `onmode` utility. CPU VPs can be added in the `onconfig` file by altering the NUMCPUVPS configuration parameter. This parameter is read only during system startup, so changing it after the engine is running will *not* add CPU VPs. The NUMCPUVPS has a numeric parameter that changes the number of CPU VPs for the engine the next time the engine is started.

Adding CPU VPs

The ability to dynamically add CPU VPs while the engine is online adds a new dimension of scaling capabilities for the IDS engine. With this feature, the engine can be scaled according to the load on the computer system. If the load placed on the system by other applications increases to a point where the system administrator would like to balance the load and provide additional system resource to users of other applications, the number of CPU VPs used by IDS can be decreased, thus dynamically providing more CPU for applications. This could be done at a time when the load on the IDS engine is low, such as in an OLTP system when the user load is expected to be low (possibly during overnight processing). The syntax for adding VPs using the `onmode` command is as follows:

```
onmode -p +/- <number to add/subtract> <VP Class>
```

The VP class parameter is one of those listed in Table 5-18.

Table 5-18 VP Classes Passed to `onmode`

NET	Network VP
AIO	Asynchronus I/O VP
SHM	Shared memory listener VP
TLI	TLI listener VP
SOC	TCP sockets listener VP
CPU	CPU VP

The number to add/subtract parameter must be an integer number and must be less than 64. The number to subtract must not bring the number of VPs of that type to a number lower than the engine was used when the engine was initialized.

In general, the number of CPU VPs should not exceed the number of actual CPUs available on the platform, though this is not a hard rule. (There are some cases where slightly exceeding the number of CPU VPs will improve the performance of the system.)

To gauge the benefit of adding CPU VPs, a benchmark should be performed. A benchmark application should be developed that closely approximates the queries that are directed at the engine during system processing. This application should send a random set of queries and/or updates to the server and be able to run for at least a 5-minute interval, preferably longer.

The CPU VPs should be added in small increments, preferably one or two, using the onmode command as shown previously in this chapter. After adding the CPU VP, the benchmark program should be rerun to determine whether or not the additional CPU resource has had an impact.When there is no longer any incremental benefit (adding an additional CPU VP has no impact), the optimal number of CPU VPs has been found.

Once the optimal number of CPUs has been found, the IDS system should be brought online and run in production mode using the new configuration settings. The CPU usage should be monitored to determine that it is evenly divided over the CPU VPs on the system.

Tuning a Query

The queries that comprise an application represent the clearest picture of how the application accesses data logically. Once the logical data access is known, the Informix server allows some degree of control over the physical access to the data. The first step in developing this control is to determine the logical data access via the SQL extension set explain.

The set explain command is executed as an SQL statement. Once this command has been executed, it is active for the duration of the database session (the period of time the user is *connected* to the database).

The 'set explain' command writes information about the query plan that will be used to process the query to an ASCII file named 'sqexplain.out' in the user session's current working directory. This file will continue to be appended by *all* user sessions using that current working directory until the 'set explain' option is turned off by the session using the 'set explain off' command. The following is an example of an SQL statement that generates 'set explain' output:

```
set explain on;

select *
from   sales_facts s, time_dim t, region r
where  s.month  = t.month and
       s.region = r.region
order by s.region ;

set explain off;

select *
from   po_facts p, time_dim t, region r
where  p.month  = t.month and
       p.region = r.region
order by p.region ;
```

This series of SQL statements would generate set explain output for the first SQL statement that retrieves data from the sales_facts table. Because the sqexplain output is turned off immediately after this statement is executed, the second SQL statement listed that selects from the po_facts table does not generate set explain output.

The output of the set explain command contains a description of the plan the IDS optimizer has generated for the query. The output of the sqexplain.out file contains the query that has been executed, the number of threads that will be used to process the query, and the filter criteria and indices that will be used to access each table. This output can be used to determine the following:

1. Amount of parallelization
2. Access path for the data tables
3. Join fields
4. Aggregate fields
5. Sort fields

The level of parallelization for a query is determined by the number of threads that are launched. The number of threads launched is determined by a number of factors, including the following:

1. Number of tables in a query
2. Amount of fragmentation in the tables that comprise the query
3. Filters in the query
4. Aggregations in the query
5. PDQ priority currently in effect

The IDS optimizer will only perform parallelization that it believes makes sense. It will not launch two parallel scan threads to read from the same table and/or fragment that is located in the same dbspace under the assumption that this would simply produce disk contention between the two read processes. But if a table is fragmented over multiple dbspaces, then the IDS optimizer assumes that there will be no disk contention in reading from those multiple fragments in parallel.

Fragmenting to the Same Disk

IDS assumes that multiple fragments represent physically separate disks. It does not examine the underlying physical structure of the disk. If an administrator has two separate dbspaces that map to chunks residing on the same disk, then there is a potential for disk contention. For example, the following dbspaces are defined for a system:

dbspace1   chunk1 (/dev/disk1 – offset 0)
dbspace2   chunk2 (/dev/disk1 – offset 50K)

The administrator then creates a table named table1 and fragments the table over dbspace1 and dbspace2 as follows:

```
create table table1
(col1 int,
 col2 char(10),
 col3 char(10))
fragment by round robin in
   dbspace1, dbspace2;
```

The following `select` statement is then executed to retrieve all rows from table1 effectively forcing a full scan of the table:

```
select *
from table1
order by col1
```

With a sufficient PDQPRIORITY setting, the optimizer will launch two threads to read the data from the table named `table1` in this query: one scan thread to read from `dbspace1`, and one scan thread to read from `dbspace2`. This is a read operation that could create disk contention, because even though the `dbspaces` map to separate chunks, the chunks map to the same physical disk. To avoid this problem, the fragmentation plan should use dbspaces on separate disks, if available.

Filters and Fragment Elimination

The Informix server can use filter criteria to make decisions about which fragments to scan; this is known as *fragment elimination*. If a table has been fragmented by expression over several `dbspaces`, then a filter criteria that uses a column in the fragment expression may allow the optimizer to eliminate fragments. The following provides an example.

The table has been created with the following SQL statement:

```
create tablea ( col1 int, col2 char(20) )
fragment by expression
        col1 > 0 and col1 < 200 in dbspacea,
        col1 > 200 and col1 < 300 in dbspaceb,
        col1 > 300 and col1 < 400 in dbspacec,
        remainder in dbspaced;
```

When the following SQL statement is run against the table, there are fragments that can be eliminated:

```
select *
from tablea
where col1 in (10, 20, 210, 230);
```

This query allows fragments in `dbspacec` and `dbspaced` to be eliminated from the search.

In the previous example, because the table was fragmented by an expression that placed records with values 10 or 20 for the column col1 in `dbspacea`, and records with values of 210 or 230 for the columns col1 in `dbspaceb`, and because the query specifically requests rows with *only* those column values, all other fragments can logically be eliminated from the search.

Fragment elimination is possible only when the table is fragmented by expression and then only with an expression that is referenced appropriately in the filter criteria of the query being executed. If the fragment expression includes two columns, then both columns must be referenced in the fragmentation criteria for fragment elimination to be possible.

The PDQPRIORITY Setting

The PDQPRIORITY setting impacts, among other things, the level of parallelization to be applied to the query. This value is used by the optimizer to determine the resources to be applied to a query, with lower settings allocating fewer resources and higher settings allocating more resources. Resources are allocated in the form of scan threads used to perform parallel queries, and in the form of memory as coordinated by the Memory Grant Manager. So a PDQPRIORITY of 0 would yield no parallelization and all portions of the query would be executed serially. A number of query operations can be run in parallel including scans, joins, sorts, aggregates, and groupings. The impact of parallelization can be significant.

For example, if a query contained a scan of a table based on some filter criteria, and then sorted and aggregated the results, there is a potential to execute the scan, the sort, and the aggregation portions of the query in parallel. But if PDQPRIORITY were set to 0, the IDS optimizer would create a query path that had the scan of the data executed first. Then when the scan was complete, the sorting of the results would occur. When the sort was complete, the aggregation of the results would occur. Executing each step serially could yield the following timings:

Process	Time in minutes
Scan	3
Sort	1
Aggregate	1
Total	5

Because each step is being executed in serial, the total time for processing is an accumulation of the time required for each step. But if each step can be executed in parallel, then the time to complete the query is approximately equal to the time required to complete the longest step. So for the preceding query, if executed in parallel with a separate processing thread for each step, the processing time would be three minutes as opposed to five. (This is approximate because there is some overhead for parallelization, to start, synchronize processing, and then shut down processing.)

By way of example, an order entry system would consist of a parent-child table relationship between an orders table and a table used to store constituent items. To get a total price for each order, the price for items for the order would have to be aggregated by order number. The following query would accomplish this aggregation:

```
select orders.order_num, sum(total_price)
from   orders, items
where  orders.order_num = items.item_num
group by 1;
```

Executing this query would provide an aggregate price for each order as shown in the following output:

```
order_num                  (sum)

    1010                  $84.00
    1015                 $450.00
    1006                 $448.00
    1017                 $584.00
    1016                 $654.00
    1002                $1200.00
    1008                 $940.00
    1011                  $99.00
```

The set explain output for this query would describe the query path chosen to process the query: which tables will be read by the query and whether or not an index will be used to read the table, the type of join used to join the tables, and other pertinent query path information. The following is sample output for the sqexplain file for this query:

QUERY:
——

```
select orders.order_num, sum(total_price)
from orders, items
where orders.order_num = items.order_num
group by 1


Estimated Cost: 79
Estimated # of Rows Returned: 1
Temporary Files Required For: Group By

1) informix.orders: SEQUENTIAL SCAN   (Serial, fragments: ALL)


2) informix.items: SEQUENTIAL SCAN



DYNAMIC HASH JOIN (Build Outer)
    Dynamic Hash Filters: informix.orders.order_num = informix.items.order_num

al_price)
from orders, items
where orders.order_num = items.order_num
group by 1

Estimated Cost: 94
```

This set explain output indicates that the join between the orders table and the items table is conducted via a *dynamic hash join*. The orders table index is read to retrieve index (the query does not require any other data of the orders table). The order number retrieved from the index is then joined to rows from the items table via a hash table (thus the name hash join).

The following line in the set explain output indicates that the query will not be processed in parallel:

```
1) informix.orders: SEQUENTIAL SCAN   (Serial, fragments: ALL)
```

On a platform that supports parallel processing, the information in parentheses indicates whether the query will be processed in serial or in parallel. Because this output indicates that serial processing will be used, it's clear that parallel processing is not taking place. Setting the PDQPRIORITY to 0 would have the impact of forcing all scans to be executed serially. Adjusting the PDQPRIORITY setting to value greater than 0 would impact the query path generated for a query and allow portions of a query to be executed in parallel, including scan operations.

Setting and Controlling PDQPRIORITY

The value of PDQPRIORITY can be set in an environment variable allowing it to be set for a user session, or in an SQL statement. The default value of PDQPRIORITY if it is not set in the environment or the SQL session is 0. A number of configuration parameters influence the impact of PDQPRIORITY as explained in Table 5-19. (These configuration parameters are covered in more detail in Chapter 4.)

Table 5-19 PDQ Configuration Parameters

Parameter	Description
DS_MAX_QUERIES	Maximum number of concurrent PDQ queries allowed
DS_MAX_SCANS	Maximum number of concurrent PDQ scan threads allowed
DS_TOTAL_MEMORY	Maximum amount of memory that will be allocated to PDQ queries
MAX_PDQPRIORITY	Maximum PDQPRIORITY setting allowed
OPTCOMPIND	Preferred join type to be used by the optimizer

If the PDQPRIORITY is set in an environment variable and then set in an SQL statement, the SQL statement setting overrides the setting of the environment variable. The MAX_PDQPRIORITY setting limits the PDQPRIORITY setting of an individual session. If MAX_PDQPRIORITY is set to 50 and a session attempts to set PDQPRIORITY to 80, the optimizer will substitute a PDQPRIORITY setting of 50.

As stated previously, setting the PDQPRIORITY to a value of zero means that parallel features will not be used. A setting of 1 indicates to the optimizer that only parallel scans will be used to process a query. A setting of 2 through 100 indicates that some percentage of parallel query resources, as constrained by the environment variables settings indicated in Table 5-19, will be used to process the query.

The use of parallel query processing can have a dramatic effect on some queries, primarily what are deemed decision support queries, queries that process a large number of rows and perform aggregations, sorts, and filters on the rows. For other types of queries, queries that retrieve few rows such as OLTP type queries, parallel processing would be unlikely to have a positive impact and is not recommended. For this reason, a PDQPRIORITY setting of 0 (the default) is recommended for OLTP systems using IDS.

For decision support applications, setting PDQPRIORITY to a value between 2 and 100 is recommended. The impact of various settings on a particular query is dependent on the fragmentation of the tables in the query, the IDS resources available, and the settings of the configuration parameters in Table 5-19.

Experimentation and iterative benchmarking with long-running DSS queries are encouraged. Creating a benchmark application (which could be nothing more than an SQL statement that executes the DSS query and outputs results to /dev/null) and running the benchmark with the PDQPRIORITY environment variables set to various values could reveal the optimal PDQPRIORITY setting for the query.

Note that if allowed, a PDQ query can use a significant portion of IDS resources and could severely limit the processing of other DSS queries. For this reason, the configuration parameters in Table 5-19 should be set to limit the amount of resources used for PDQ. Note that these parameters can be set with the IDS engine online using the onmode command, thus allowing the use of PDQ resources to be limited during certain time periods (such as during production hours) and then raised during off-hours batch processing periods. Table 5-20 lists the onmode commands that can be used to adjust PDQ resources.

Table 5-20 onmode PDQ Settings

Parameter	Setting
-M	Change value of DS_TOTAL_MEMORY
-Q	Change value of DS_MAX_QUERIES
-D	Change the value of MAX_PDQPRIORITY
-S	Change the value of DS_MAX_SCANS

Impacting Optimization with the OPTCOMPIND Parameter

Informix provides an environment variable that provides some hints to the optimizer concerning the joining and merging of data between two or more tables. When a query requires multiple tables to be joined (retrieving related rows from multiple tables), there are several methods of available to perform the join. The environment variable is named OPTCOMPIND and the available settings and their respective impact is shown in Table 5-21.

Table 5-21 Table Joining Methods

Option	Description
0	The optimizer chooses index scans (nested-loop joins) regardless of cost.
1	If the isolation mode is *repeatable read*, then the optimizer operates the same as if the setting were 2. Otherwise the optimizer behaves as if the setting were 0.
2	The optimizer uses costs to determine the optimal query path. This is the default value.

Index Read versus Sequential Read

When a table is read in random order (as it is during a nested loop join with index access to the outer table), disk reads are expensive. The actual disk I/O requires read heads to move around on disk increasing latency times and lengthening the time needed to perform the read. The cost-based optimizer is aware of this expense and adds a corresponding weight to random disk read operations. For this reason, the optimizer will often choose to perform a sequential scan of a table even when an index is available that can be used to satisfy some or all of the filter criteria for the table.

The Read-Ahead Option

The IDS engine provides the ability to read ahead several pages during a full table scan. The read-ahead feature reads a few pages ahead in and places these pages in the shared memory buffer before they are specifically requested by the query process. (The engine is effectively anticipating the next I/O request.) This has the net effect of reducing the amount of time the query process must wait for disk I/O.

The read-ahead feature is configured using two configuration parameters: RA_PAGES and RA_THRESHOLD. The RA_PAGES parameter specifies the number of pages to read from disk when the engine performs a read-ahead operation. The RA_THRESHOLD specifies the number of unprocessed pages that should remain in memory before the IDS engine should do another read-ahead. The `onstat` command can be used to monitor the use of the read-ahead feature using the `onstat -p` option. The following `onstat` listing fragment references read-ahead usage:

```
...
ixda-RA   idx-RA    da-RA     RA-pgsused
87        0         6         71
```

These headings are listed in the bottom row of output of the `onstat -p` command. The meaning of these headings is as shown in Table 5-22.

Table 5-22 `onstat` *read-ahead Information*

idxda-RA	Count of read-aheads from index leaves to data pages
idx-RA	Count of read-aheads traversing index leaves
da-RA	Count of data only scans
RA-pgsused	Number of pages that IDS read ahead has used.

If the `RA-pgsused` value reported is much lower than the value reported for all read-ahead pages (`idx-RA + da-RA`), then the read-ahead parameters may be set too high. It is important that this option be used judiciously. Reading large numbers of pages into the shared memory buffer could stress the LRU management and force a large number of page flushes to free buffer space, which would in fact reduce performance.

> **Note**
>
> Using Optimizer Directives to Improve Performance: With the release of Informix Dynamic Server version 7.3, optimizer directives were made available to provide additional hints to the optimizer concerning the choice of query plans. Chapter 7, "The Relational Database and Informix SQL," provides details on using optimizer hints with the IDS engine.

The Query and the Query Plan

Unlike the hierarchical and network databases that were prolific in the 1970s and 1980s, relational databases do not contain definitions of physical relationships between the data tables on disk. In a relational database, data access paths are not defined as part of the database. Instead, these access paths must be determined when the data is requested from the database. With the IDS database, it is the responsibility of the IDS optimizer to perform this function.

The IDS optimizer uses an internal algorithm to determine the best plan for accessing the data requested by the query. This plan is known as a *query plan*. In order to create the query plan, the optimizer must evaluate the query and make several determinations as follows:

- Access plan
- Join plan
- Evaluation order

While this list is short, the logic involved in performing these evaluations is significant. The following sections provide some of the details behind these evaluations.

The Access Plan

The optimizer must make two basic decisions about how to access a table: whether to use an *index read* to access the table, or to read the table sequentially (i.e., to perform a *table scan*).

The decision whether or not to use an index can be based on a number of factors. If a large portion of the table must be read, then using an index would not necessarily be beneficial, because reading the index plus the data pages simply increases the number of I/O operations to be executed. Reading a large number of rows from a table can be performed more efficiently using a sequential scan than using an index read.

A sequential scan could be performed very efficiently with the IDS engine, through a combination of parallel processing (if the table has been fragmented), disk read-ahead operations, and the general efficiencies of reading consecutive data pages from disk.

The Join Plan

The tables used in a query are joined through equality statements in the `where` clause of the query. Tables can physically be joined in a number of different ways in what is known as the **join plan** of the query. The join plan dictates the method of the join that would be either nested *loop join* or *hash join*. The nested loop join is considered faster when a relatively small number of records is being accessed, and conversely the hash join is considered faster when a large number of records is being accessed.

A **nested-loop** joins two tables by scanning the first table in the evaluation order, also known as the *outer table*. Each of the rows that passes the filter on the outer table are then sought in the inner table. Both the inner and outer table can be scanned using an index, which is the preferred method of access but not required. If the inner table does not have an index, then one may be created using an *autoindex* at the time of query execution. Whether or not an autoindex is created is determined by the optimizer when query plans are evaluated.

Hash Join

A *hash join* involves joining two tables using a hash table, a mechanism for finding a quick match between two values. The significant advantages of this join method is that no index and no sorting are required.

A hash join consists of two activities: a *build phase* where the hash table is built and a *probe phase* where the second (outer) table in the join is read, any appropriate filters applied and the hash table is probed for a join record. Smaller hash tables can be placed in the dynamic portion of shared memory, thus improving the performance of the hash-join.

Evaluation Order

If more than one table is being read in a query, the optimizer must make a determination on the order in which to read the tables in the query. The order is evaluated based on the costs of reading the tables and is determined by the number of rows in the table, the presence of a column index to read the table, the selectivity of the index, the data distribution of the data in the table that is to be filtered, and other factors.

The Cost-Based Optimizer and the 'set optimization' Command

As discussed previously, the IDS optimizer is a *cost-based* optimizer, deriving a statistical cost for each alternative access plan available. This cost is based on factors such as the number of I/O operations required, calculations needed to produce results, the number of rows the optimizer expects to access, any sorting required, the selectivity of indexes available, and other pertinent criteria. By default, the optimizer will evaluate all possible access paths and assign a cost to each. The optimizer will then choose the access path with the lowest possible cost and use that access path.

The default optimization can be overridden using the set optimization command. The syntax for this command is as follows:

```
set optimization high | low | first rows | all rows
```

With the set optimization high option, the optimizer uses the exhaustive review of all possible access paths described previously. This is the default optimization mode.

With the set optimization low option, the optimizer does not use an exhaustive algorithm to evaluate query paths. Instead, it eliminates a number of less likely access candidates early in the optimization process.

The `first rows` and `all rows` options apply to the *query goal*. If the query goal is to retrieve *all rows* then optimization creates a query plan that will ultimately return all rows to the requestor as efficiently as possible.

If the query goal is set to *first rows*, then optimization attempts to formulate a query plan that will optimally bring back the first set of rows as quickly as possible.

Tuning the Query

Tuning a query or set of queries in an application can have a significant impact on both the performance and efficiency of a system. Tuning specific queries also implies a review of the underlying physical and logical database structure—that is, both the design of the tables in the query and the physical layout of the tables as reflected in the fragmentation scheme for the table. In addition to these considerations, the indexing strategy for the table should also be reviewed. Often the addition of an index for a single joined column can increase query performance by several orders of magnitude.

Identifying and Addressing Full Table Scans

A *full table scan* exists when the IDS optimizer decides it must read every row in the table to satisfy the needs of a query. There are some cases where the full table scan is necessary, but in many cases this expensive operation is not required and merely extends the processing time for the query.

A full table scan can be identified in the `sqexplain` output produced by a query run. The following `sqexplain` output provides an example:

```
QUERY:
____

select * from orders where order_date < "05/01/1995"

Estimated Cost: 2
```

```
Estimated # of Rows Returned: 3

1) informix.orders: SEQUENTIAL SCAN  (Serial, fragments: ALL)

    Filters: informix.orders.order_date < 05/01/1995
```

In this example, the section for the scan of the table indicates that there are filter criteria to be applied but no index is listed, therefore the entire table must be read or scanned to satisfy the query. So it is by the process of elimination that we determine that the entire table must be scanned.

When a Full Table Scan Is Acceptable

There are instances where all or almost all of the rows in a table must be read and processed. For instance, a table may contain one year of sales transaction detail. A query may need to produce a summary of four quarters of sales data. Such a query would have to read the entire table in any event, so using an index in this instance would merely add an additional disk read to the query processing overhead. The following provides an example:

```
create index sales_qtr_idx on sales_facts( sales_qtr );
create index cust_id_idx   on sales_facts( cust_id );

select sales_qtr, sum(sales_amount)
from sales_facts
where sales_qtr in (1,2,3,4)
group by sales_qtr;
```

In this example, the table `sales_facts` contains a `sales_qtr` column and an index has been built on this column. The query being run uses filter criteria on the column. At first blush, it would be useful to use the index on the `sales_qtr` column. But knowledge of the table content tells us that only four quarters are stored in the table, so the result of the query will be to read the entire table. If there are 200,000 rows in the `sales_facts` table and the optimizer decides that it will use the `sales_qtr_idx` index to access the table, then the query will read 200,000 index rows plus the 200,000 rows from the table - an extra 200,000 rows.

This query is a typical DSS type query, scanning a large number of rows for summarization and aggregation. It is not uncommon for this type of query to require a full table scan. A typical OLTP type query would need to read fewer rows and would most likely not perform aggregation. The following provides an example of an OLTP query against the sales table:

```
select sales_qtr, sales_id, sales_name, sales_amount
from sales_facts
where sales_qtr in (1,2)   and
      sales_id = 1234       and
      sales_amount > 10000;
```

This query attempts to determine the sales for over $10,000 in the first two quarters of the year for the salesperson with the ID 1234. This is a highly selective query that would select a relatively small number of rows (relative to the DSS query that would need to scan rows for an entire year). But without an adequate index, the engine would have to scan the entire table. Since this query would be retrieving only a small number of rows, scanning the entire table would not be efficient, but without an appropriate index, the optimizer would have no other choice but to choose a query path that scanned the entire table. The following would create an index that could be used to satisfy the query shown previously:

```
create index sales_idx1 on sales( sales_id);
```

This index would provide access to the table using the salesperson ID number (sales_id), an identifier that uniquely identifies a salesperson but would contain duplicates in the sales facts table that lists the sales for all salespersons in the company. But even with the duplicates, there would be a manageable number of records for a given salesperson in a given quarter. With an index on the sales id, the query path could read all sales fact records with the given sales ID and then filter those records for the quarter desired. If it is known that the queries run against the sales_facts table will usually select for **sales_id** and **sales_qtr**, then creating a composite index on sales_id and sales_qtr would provide a more selective index for the query, as follows:

```
create index sales_idx2 on sales( sales_id, sales_qtr );
```

The threshold for choosing a sequential scan over an index is about 20 to 40 percent, meaning that if 20 to 40 percent of the table must be read by the query, then a sequential scan should be chosen over an index. The optimizer should make this decision on its own, but the difficulty is in determining how many rows of a table will be read before the table is actually scanned. The IDS optimizer depends on the statistics generated and stored by the update statistics command. As detailed in Chapter 4, the update statistics command scans each column in the table and stores statistics on the ranges of values in the columns. But the level of detail stored by the update statistics command can vary depending on the level of detail chosen when the update statistics command is run; levels of detail are *low*, *medium* or *high*.

It is possible that with the update statistics command run at the low level that inadequate statistics could be stored for the optimizer to make the correct decision. It is also possible that given the volatile nature of data in some tables (data is updated extensively and continuously), that the distribution of data could have changed since the last set of statistics was generated and the optimizer is working with statistics that are no longer valid and thus making incorrect decisions.

In either case, if it appears that the optimizer is making incorrect decisions in generating query paths, then statistics should be regenerated using the update statistics command at either a medium or high level so that a useful amount of detail is created for the optimizer. If a database contains a set of tables that are updated constantly, then it may be best to run the update statistics command on a regular basis, either weekly or, in some cases, on a nightly basis.

Using Table Fragmentation for Query Tuning

One of the most powerful capabilities of the Informix engine is the ability to provide *static fragmentation* of data and parallelization to support it. When large amounts of data are being scanned, common during a decision support query, performance gains from parallelization can be significant. Likewise, with an OLTP system where data contention can be a problem, static fragmentation can allow data in a single table to be distributed over multiple disks and/or multiple controllers. This distribution can reduce the stress on a particular disk or controller and spread I/O over multiple devices. Without static fragmentation, a less exacting mechanism such as disk striping would have to be used to accomplish the same goals.

Fragmentation Schemes

In order for fragmentation to work ,a proper *fragmentation scheme* must be employed. The fragmentation scheme specifies where data in a table will be located. The scheme may be based on an expression involving a column, or columns, in the table as with expression-based fragmentation (the most common and often the most effective), or it may be based on evenly distributing rows across a specified set of disks as with round-robin fragmentation.

In most cases, fragmentation is used to improve performance, but in some cases it can be used to distribute data for archive and restore purposes. This could be the case where static prior-year data within a table is distributed into a single dbspace and the volatile current data is kept in other dbspaces. The archive and restore of the static prior-year data could be on a monthly basis (during a full archive of the database), and the current data could be archived on a daily and weekly basis.

But the more common use of fragmentation is to improve performance, primarily on long-running queries. In this case, data is usually distributed over multiple disks based on a fragmentation scheme that involves a column or columns that are usually part of filter criteria for retrieval of data. The goal is to evenly distribute the data over multiple disks and reduce I/O contention as much as possible. The following data table forms the basis of an example of fragmentation schemes:

```
create table invoice_facts(
    inv_number int,
    inv_date date,
    inv_flag char(2),
    ship_to_code char(5),
    inv_amount decimal(12,2));
```

This abridged fact table contains information about invoices pulled from an OLTP system for storage in a data warehouse. There are several columns that are candidates for use in an expression-based fragmentation scheme: `inv_date`, `inv_flag`, and `ship_to_code`. These columns contain values that will contain a number of duplicates, so they could be used for expression-based fragmentation schemes. A number of different schemes are possible, and the following sections will provide examples of those schemes.

Fragment by inv_date

There are a number of advantages of fragmenting data by invoice month. The first is that in a data warehouse scenario, most of the `dbspaces` on the system will contain relatively static data. Because current-month data will be going into the current month `dbspace`, prior-month data will reside in relatively static `dbspaces` that can be archived on a weekly or monthly basis. The following demonstrates a fragmentation scheme based on the `invoice_date`:

```
create table invoice_facts(
      inv_number int,
      inv_date date,
      inv_flag char(2),
      ship_to_code char(5),
      inv_amount decimal(12,2))

fragment by expression

  month(inv_date) in (1,2,3) in dbspace1,
  month(inv_date) in (4,5,6) in dbspace2,
  month(inv_date) in (7,8,9) in dbspace3,
  month(inv_date) in (10,11,12) in dbspace4,

  remainder in dbspace6;
```

In this example, the fragmentation scheme is based on the month of the invoice date. The function `month(inv_date)` resolves to a number between 1 and 12 for the month of the year. The fragmentation scheme places data for a given set of months in a specific `dbspace`. An additional benefit of this approach is performance. By distributing the data over several dbspaces, parallelization of queries is possible. Multiple scan threads can be started to read data from each of the dbspaces to return data for a given query. And because an expression-based fragmentation scheme has been used, fragment elimination can be used to eliminate unwanted fragments from the query path.

Fragment by inv_flag

A fragment strategy that involves using a fragment expression on the inv_flag field would allow data to be distributed across the dbspaces in the system. The difficulty in this strategy would be in creating an even distribution of data across the dbspaces. This would require some knowledge of the nature of the data in the system. The following is an example of this fragmentation scheme:

```
create table invoice_facts(
    inv_number int,
    inv_date date,
    inv_flag char(2),
    ship_to_code char(5),
    inv_amount decimal(12,2))

fragment by expression

    inv_flag = "A" in dbspace1,
    inv_flag = "B" in dbspace2,
    inv_flag in ("C", "D", "E" ) in dbspace3,
    inv_flag = ("F", "G", "H") in dbspace4,
    inv_flag = "I" in dbspace5,
    remainder in dbspace6;
```

This fragmentation strategy distributes data across the dbspaces by inv_flag. This strategy attempts to create an even distribution of data by allocating more than one inv_flag setting to a single dbspace. This strategy is built on the belief that an even distribution of data can be obtained via the inv_flag and that most queries request data using the inv_flag as a filter criteria. By running data distributions using the dbschema command (dbschema -d <database name> -hd <table name>), an administrator could determine the distribution of data in a table and develop a fragmentation scheme with a grouping that provided a fairly even distribution of data.

Fragment by ship_to_code

An additional fragmentation strategy involves fragmenting by expression on the `ship_to_code`. This would distribute data in the `invoice_facts` table over a specified set of `dbspaces` based on the contents of the `ship_to_code` column. The following provides an example of this strategy:

```
create table invoice_facts(
    inv_number int,
    inv_date date,
    inv_flag char(2),
    ship_to_code char(5),
    inv_amount decimal(12,2))

fragment by expression

    ship_to_code = "345" in dbspace1,
    ship_to_code = "456" in dbspace2,
    ship_to_code in ("789", "888", "888" ) in dbspace3,
    ship_to_code = ("921", "831", "366") in dbspace4,
    ship_to_code = "987" in dbspace5,
    remainder in dbspace6;
```

Using this strategy, specific `ship_to_codes` are used to distribute records in the `invoice_facts table` across the identified `dbspaces`. The presumption is that this distribution scheme is either based on business knowledge of the nature of the ship_to_code values, or a data distribution has been run using the `dbschema` utility (`dbschema -d <database name> -hd <table name>`) and this distribution indicated that this scheme could create a relatively even distribution of the data records in the table.

Fragmentation and RAID

RAID is a hardware facility that allows a series of disk drives to appear as one disk drive to a computer system. It provides a number of implementations, named RAID 1 through 5, that provide differing implementations of the same strategy. Failure recovery is a big draw for these systems because the failure of a single disk is transparent to the system; disk reads and writes would continue uninterrupted.

But RAID suffers from the same implementation problem that *disk striping* (a method for randomly distributing data across multiple physically separate portions of disk) does—IDS is not aware of the physical distribution of the data and does not provide parallelization on data distributed in this fashion. For this reason, the use of RAID provides no special benefit for IDS.

This does not preclude using RAID with IDS. If RAID is used transparently, so that disk chunks are mapped to RAID disk as it would be to normal disk, then there can be parallelization with RAID using data should be distributed over this logical *disk* (dbspaces) as though it were normal disk, thus allowing IDS to provide parallel data scans against the data.

Chapter Summary

This chapter has provided details on the process of monitoring and tuning the IDS database. The onstat utility, the staple of Informix database administrators the world over, provides much of the basic information on engine operation. A number of basic informational screens are available including a series of onstat -g commands is available to provide more specific information on multithreading and internal memory allocation operations.

There are two basic approaches to engine tuning: tuning the actual operation of the engine and tuning specific queries. Though there is obvious overlap between the two approaches, there are also significant differences.

The LRU queue manages the process of writing dirty pages to disk to provide space for new data pages that must be placed in the shared memory buffer. The process of tuning the LRU queue, as covered in this chapter, can provide significant performance improvement for an update-bound system.

The onmode command can be used to make changes to specific engine tunable parameters while the engine is in operation. This provides a convenient means of evaluating changes to tunables without having to incur the overhead of restarting the engine. This also provides a means of altering system resource usage to match system load.

The IDS engine provides for parallel processing of queries based on the fragmentation of the query, the dispersion of the query across multiple logical disks (dbspaces). The proper fragmentation of a table can yield significant performance benefits.

Next Chapter

The next chapter examines the process of administering the IDS database. The tasks of starting and stopping the engine, adding and dropping logical logs, archiving and restoring data, and administering security are covered. The IDS engine provides the powerful capability of altering a number of configuration parameters while the engine is online; the process for making these changes is also covered in the next chapter.

Database Administration in the Informix Dynamic Server

With virtually any commercial database product, a certain amount of database administration is required, and the IDS engine is no exception. With IDS, this administration effort includes the basic operations of starting and stopping the engine, performing archives of the database and logs, and administering security. In addition, IDS includes facilities for dynamically altering database configuration parameters and controlling engine resources while the database is online. Understanding and using these administration facilities is a key component of maximizing the utility of the IDS engine. The following sections discuss these and other administration topics in more detail.

Starting and Stopping the Database

An IDS database instance is started using the `oninit` command. This program and the numerous internal threads it instantiates performs the bulk of the work done by the IDS engine. Only the user `informix` or `root` (the Unix superuser) can run the `oninit` command. Table 6-1 lists the options that can be passed to the this command.

Table 6-1 `oninit` *Command Options*

Parameter	Description
-p	Delete temporary tables
-s	Bring to quiescent mode only
-i	Initialize disk
-y	Answer yes to all questions

Engine Operating Modes

The `oninit` command starts the database and brings it into an operating mode. The IDS database has three operating modes: *offline*, *quiescent* (single user), and *online* (multi-user). There are a limited number of database tasks that can be performed with the database offline. And there are some tasks that require the database to be in quiescent mode (for instance, dropping a logical-log file). For multiple users to access the database and perform useful work, the database must be online.

The `oninit` command can initialize shared memory and start an existing database instance, or it can initialize shared memory and disk and create a new database instance.

When `oninit` starts an existing database, it reads environment variables and the configuration file, initializes the shared memory buffer for the engine, and places the system reserved pages and control tables used by the engine into shared memory. It then executes a fast recovery and performs any other additional housekeeping and startup tasks required by the engine. When all startup tasks are complete, the engine is brought into the operating mode specified by the parameters passed to `oninit`. The command used to start an existing database involves calling `oninit` with no parameters as follows:

```
oninit
```

Optionally, oninit could be instructed to delete all temporary tables and bring the engine to quiescent mode using the following command:

```
oninit -ps
```

To initialize a new database instance, the oninit command would be passed the -i parameter instructing it to initialize the disk (essentially just the root dbspace) and create a new, empty database instance. Unless the -y parameter is passed to oninit, this command will prompt the user before continuing with the creation of the new instance. The reason for this prompt is the destructive nature of oninit disk initialization; any existing database instance, including system reserved pages, system catalog tables, and all constituent databases, would be deleted by this command. The following is an example of database instance initialization with oninit.

```
oninit -i
```

> **Note**
> When oninit is used to initialize disk and create a new database instance, the oninit -i command is used. If used in conjunction with the -y parameter, oninit will quietly delete any existing database instance and create a new database instance. Needless to say, this is a command that has the potential to inflict great harm on an unsuspecting database instance and should be used with caution.

Startup Problems

Problems can occur during engine startup. If during startup the engine cannot understand the contents of the configuration file, cannot find the configuration file, or cannot understand the contents of the sqlhosts file, it will not start.

Problems can also occur with the dbspaces that comprise the database. During startup, the engine does not necessarily read from all of the dbspaces in the database instance; only the dbspaces containing information and storage needed for startup are read (physical logs, logical logs, system reserved pages). It is primarily the root `dbspace` that contains the information needed to start the engine. If the root `dbspace` cannot be read, the engine is not able to start and the database must be recovered from a backup.

Online Engine Modifications

A number of aspects of engine operation can be modified while the engine is in online mode. The `onmode` command provides command line access to these options. The parameters that can be passed to the `onmode` command are shown in Table 6-2. These commands are described in the following sections.

Bringing the Engine to Offline Mode

The `onmode` command with the -k parameter can be used to take the database engine to offline mode. When executed, this command (after prompting the user who executed the command) aborts all running database transactions and brings the engine offline. Only the user `informix` or `root` can execute this command, which is usually executed as follows:

```
onmode -ky
```

When executed with this syntax, the `onmode` command immediately kills any running threads and takes the engine to offline mode. Using the -y option bypasses the question requiring the user to validate the action and immediately takes the engine to offline mode. If the -y parameter is omitted, then the user is prompted as follows to abort all user sessions and continue:

```
onmode -k

This will take INFORMIX-OnLine OFF-LINE -
Do you wish to continue (y/n)?
```

Table 6-2 IDS onmode Options

Option	Description
-a <kbytes>	Increase shared memory segment size
-b <version>	Revert IDS disk structures to a previous version
-c	Perform checkpoint
-D <max PDQ priority allowed>	Set the MAX_PDQPRIORITY configuration parameter to a specified value
-d {standard|{primary|secondary <servername>}}	Set the data replication server type for this server
-m	Bring the engine to an online mode
-F	Release unused memory segments
-k	Bring the engine offline
-l	Begin using next logical log
-M <decision support memory in kbytes>	Set the memory to use for decision support in kilobytes
-n	Set shared memory buffer to nonresident (allow shared memory to be swapped)
-O	Allow a checkpoint to complete even if the DBSPACEDOWN parameter specifies it should not complete
-p <+-#> <class>	Add or remove virtual processors of specified class
-Q <max # decision support queries>	Set the DS_MAX_QUERIES configuration parameter
-z <sid>	Kill specified session ID
-Z <address>	Heuristically complete specified transaction
-y	Do not require confirmation for the specified command
-u	Kill all sessions and shutdown
-s	Bring the engine to single user mode
-S <max # decision support scans>	Set the DS_MAX_SCANS configuration parameter
-r	Set shared memory buffer cache to resident (shared memory cannot be swapped to disk)
-R	Rebuild the /INFORMIXDIR/etc/.infos.DBSERVERNAME file

If the user responds "y" (yes) to the prompt requesting the user to continue, then the engine begins the process of moving to offline mode. If there are user threads running, then the user is prompted to abort those threads as follows:

```
onmode -k
This will take INFORMIX-OnLine OFF-LINE -
Do you wish to continue (y/n)? y
There are 1 user threads that will be killed.
Do you wish to continue (y/n)?
```

Responding "y" (yes) to the prompt will kill the user thread and bring the engine to offline mode.

Bringing the Engine to Single-User Mode

The engine can be brought from online mode to single-user mode using the onmode command with the '-s' parameter. Once in single-user mode, only the user informix or root can access the engine in this mode. Other users can view engine activity using utilities such as the onstat command but cannot connect to the database. This database mode is usually used to add and drop logical logs or perform other administrative functions and is entered as follows:

```
onmode -s
```

This command first prompts the user executing the command as follows:

```
onnmode -s
This will perform a GRACEFUL SHUTDOWN -
Do you wish to continue (y/n)?
```

If the user enters "y" (yes), then the engine is brought to quiescent mode. Alternatively, the onmode command could have been entered with the –y option (onmode -sy), and the engine would have begun the process of moving into quiescent mode without prompting.

The –u option kills all currently running user sessions. This is a useful parameter to use with the "–s" option to assure that all running sessions are killed and would be used as follows:

```
onmode -suy
```

Executing this command would kill all running sessions and bring the engine to quiescent mode.

Bringing the Engine to Online (Multi-User) Mode

The `onmode` command with the `-m` parameter can be used to bring the engine from quiescent mode to online mode. Note that this command assumes that shared memory has already been initialized with the `oninit` command. If shared memory has not been initialized, then the `onmode` command returns an error. To bring the engine from quiescent mode to online, the `onmode` command can be used as follows:

```
onmode -m
```

This command brings the engine from quiescent mode to online mode.

Tip

The engine must be in quiescent mode to add or drop logs. It is not uncommon to bring the engine to quiescent mode from online mode, add or drop logical logs, and then bring the engine back to multi-user or online mode. The following would be the sequence of commands used to execute these actions:

```
onmode -suy
onparams -a -d dbspace
onmode -m
```

First in this example, the engine is brought to single-user mode using the `onmode -s` command. Next, logical logs are added using the `onparams` command. Once the logs have been successfully added, the `onmode -m` command is used to return the engine to multi-user mode.

Adding and Removing CPU Resources

The `onmode` command with the -p option can be used to apply or remove additional CPU resources to the engine. As discussed previously, the IDS engine allows CPU resource to be allocated to various tasks indirectly through allocation of virtual processors (VPs). These VPs can be allocated or deallocated using the `onmode` syntax shown as follows:

```
onmode -p +/- <number of VPs to add> <VP type>
```

The VP type can be one of those shown in Table 6-3.

Table 6-3 VP Types

Type	Description
NET	Network VP
AIO	Asynchronus I/O VP
SHM	Shared memory listener VP
TLI	TLI listener VP
SOC	TCP sockets listener VP
CPU	CPU VP

Using this syntax, a single CPU VP can be added as follows:

```
onmode -p +1 CPU
```

Alternatively, the following command would remove two CPU VPs as long as executing this command did not reduce the number of CPU VPs to a number lower than the number in place when the engine was started:

```
onmode -p -2 CPU
```

DSS Parameter Changes

A number of engine parameters are available to impact the execution of long-running, DSS-type queries. Parameters are available to adjust the maximum number of DSS queries and DSS

> **Tip**
> If additional CPU resource is available, allowing the IDS engine to access this resource could potentially have a significant impact on performance. On a symmetrical multiprocessor machine where multiple CPUs are available, some portion of these CPUs may be allocated to the IDS engine. If an SMP machine has six CPUs and three are initially allocated to the engine, there is still the potential to allocate an additional two or three CPUs to the engine. (On most platforms, a single CPU is left available to the operating system and the remaining CPUs are allocated to the applications running on that platform.)

scans that can be run concurrently and the amount of memory to apply to DSS queries. The maximum PDQPRIORITY value allowed can also be set using the `onmode` command. These DSS parameters are as shown in **Table 6-4**.

Table 6-4 DSS Parameters

Parameter	Description
-D <max PDQ priority allowed>	Set the MAX_PDQPRIORITY configuration parameter to a specified value
-M <decision support memory in kbytes>	Set the memory to use for decision support in kilobytes
-Q <max # decision support queries>	Set the DS_MAX_QUERY parameter
-S <max # decision support scans>	Set the DS_MAX_SCANS parameter

The `onmode` command can be used to raise MAX_PDQPRIORITY as in the following command:

```
onmode -D 40
```

Executing this command would set the MAX_PDQPRIORITY to a value of 40. To adjust the amount of memory to be allocated to decision support queries, the following command could be executed:

```
onmode -M 20000
```

This command would set the maximum amount of memory to be used for decision support queries to 20,000 kilobytes.

> **Tip**
>
> Altering the MAX_PDQPRIORITY setting using onmode has the same impact as changing the DS_TOTAL_MEMORY configuration parameter. Setting this parameter can be used to help balance a system that is used for both online transaction processing and decision support. During periods of busy OLTP activity, the MAX_PDQPRIORITY can be set to a lower value to reduce the heavy toll that decision support can place on an engine and leave additional resource available for OLTP processing. When OLTP processing is lowered or nonexistent, the MAX_PDQPRIORITY can be increased to allow more resource to be allocated to decision support queries.

Using onmode to Alter Shared Memory Parameters

A number of onmode options are available to alter shared memory parameters. These options are as shown in Table 6-5.

Table 6-5 onmode Options to Alter Shared Memory Parameters

Parameter	Description
-a <kbytes>	Add a shared memory virtual segment of a specified size
-r	Set shared memory buffer cache to resident (shared memory cannot be swapped to disk)
-F	Release unused memory segments
-n	Set shared memory buffer to nonresident (allow shared memory to be swapped)

Adding Virtual Shared Memory with the 'onmode –a' Command

The onmode command with the -a option can be used to add a virtual shared memory segment to the IDS instance for processing decision support queries. This value must be a positive integer and must not exceed memory available to the engine.

Generally, the IDS engine allocates virtual shared memory segments as needed up to the defined limit specified by the DS_TOTAL_MEMORY to avoid reaching the operating system limit on the number of share memory segments available. This parameter should be used to allocate a segment large enough to avoid forcing the engine to allocate a number of smaller segments (as defined in the SHMADD configuration parameter) for decision support queries. This parameter is passed a value in kilobytes for the memory to be added to the instance. The following is an example of this option:

```
onmode -a 10000
```

This command would add 10 megabytes of shared memory (10,000 kilobytes) to the database instance.

Setting the Shared Memory Buffer to Resident Status with 'onmode –r'

The onmode command executed with -r option would set the shared memory buffer cache to resident. By default, shared memory (as with all Unix memory) can be swapped to disk. Executing this command would not allow the shared memory segment to be swapped to disk. The following is an example of this command:

```
onmode -r
```

This command would set the shared memory buffer to resident and not allow the shared memory buffer to be swapped to disk.

The onmode command with the -F option can be used to release unused memory segments from the IDS instance. The following is an example of executing this option:

```
onmode -F
```

This command would release memory segments acquired for the virtual memory portion of the IDS instance and should be run on a regular basis. Note that there will be some performance degradation while this command is being run, generally for about one or two seconds.

The onmode command executed with the -n option would set the IDS instance shared memory buffer to nonresident, thus allowing this segment to be swapped to disk. On a server where

> **Note** If shared memory is being swapped to disk, then the performance of the system, including the database engine and other running applications, would be noticeably impacted. Setting the Informix shared memory to resident would avoid swapping shared memory and should improve performance for the engine.
>
> But the fact that shared memory is being swapped is indicative of memory constraints on the system as a whole. Locking the IDS shared memory buffer would leave less memory available for the other applications on the system and could force them to be swapped to disk and degrade performance for other applications. It may be that the only resolution to the problem of memory swapping would be the addition of more physical memory for the system.

memory is constrained, this would allow memory being used for the IDS engine to be removed to disk and free the shared memory to be used by other applications. The following is an example of this command:

```
onmode -n
```

Executing this command would immediately set the shared memory buffer cache to non-resident.

Miscellaneous onmode Commands

The onmode command can also be used to perform a number of additional administrative tasks. These tasks are as follows:

Option	Description
-l	Move to the next logical log
-Z	Heuristically complete the specified transaction
-z	Kill the specified process
-R	Set the replication type for this server
-d	Rebuild the /INFORMIXDIR/etc /infos.DBSERVERNAME file

These command options are explained in the following sections.

The 'onmode -l' Command

The onmode command with the -l option is used to force the IDS engine to move to the next logical log. Certain SQL DDL (data definition language) statements are not recognized until the next logical log is used. Executing this onmode command moves IDS to the next log and allows the results of the DDL statement to be recognized by the engine.

The 'onmode -Z' <transaction id> Command

The onmode command with the -Z option and an additional parameter that contains the transaction ID logically kill the distributed transaction specified by the shared memory address passed as a parameter. (The shared memory address is available in the onstat -x output for transactions.) This command can be used only when the time specified in the TXTIMEOUT parameter has expired for the transaction. Only the user informix or root can execute this command.

The 'onmode -z' <pid> Command

The onmode command with the -z option can be used to kill a specific process. This command requires an additional argument indicating the process ID of the process to kill (available from onstat -u output).

The 'onmode -R' Command

The onmode command with the -R option can be used to re-create the Informix information file used by certain database utilities. Some utilities require this file to determine the configuration of the IDS instance while the instance is offline. Should the file become corrupt or be inadvertently deleted, it can be re-created using this command.

The 'onmode -d' Command

The `onmode` command with the -d option can be used to set the replication type for the current database instance or a specified database instance when the *secondary* option is used. The syntax for this command is as follows:

```
onmode - d {standard|{primary|secondary <servername>}}
```

This command asserts that the database instance referenced is running IDS replication. The following is an example of this command:

```
onmode -d standard
```

Executing this command would set the current database instance to *standard* replication. To change a currently running primary instance to secondary, the following command would be used:

```
onmode -d secondary remote_ids_instance
```

IDS Database Security

The security model originally used with the Informix engine was on the user level. Table access was assigned to users using the user login name. Users were given permission to perform specific actions on tables and/or table columns. This security model did not involve user *groups* or *roles*.

Later revisions of IDS have added a type of permission known as *user roles*. Roles are assigned permissions related to specific tables, and users are then assigned roles. Using roles, the process of administering security for a database can be greatly simplified.

Security or privileges with IDS exist for the database and for the table. Users can be assigned permissions relating to a database and the tables within the database. Database-level privileges can be either *resource, dba,* or *connect*. Table-level privileges can be either *select, update, delete, alter index,* or *references*. These permissions are explained in more detail in the sections that follow.

Database-Level Permissions

There are a number of permissions that relate directly to the database. These permissions allow a user to connect to the database—a requirement to be able to do anything of use—to add tables to the database, or to be a superuser and have database administrator privileges to the database. They are as follows:

* Connect
* Resource
* dba

These permissions are assigned to either a user or role and are explained in the following sections.

Database connect Privileges

With database `connect` privileges, a user has permission to connect to the database. The user can then access tables in the database and add, update, delete, alter, or grant permissions on a table based on the permissions the user has been granted for the table. The user with these privileges cannot add tables, indexes or stored procedures to the database.

Database resource Privileges

A user with `resource` privileges can perform all of the functions of a user with connect privileges plus create new tables, indexes, and procedures. This level of privilege would be appropriate for a developer or database administrator.

Database dba Privileges

The user with `dba` privileges can perform all of the functions of a user with resource privileges plus a number of additional functions. A user with `dba` privileges can grant any privilege to another user, perform any action on a system catalog table, create tables or views and specify another user as the owner, and execute `drop database`, `drop distributions`, `start database`, and `roll forward` database statements.

Database-level permissions are assigned using the `grant` statement syntax shown as follows:

```
grant <database privilege> to <user name | PUBLIC >
```

A common approach is to grant connect to public and then restrict table-level permissions to a specified set of users or roles. Each user is therefore assigned a role or roles, or is assigned specific permissions for each table in the database. The following statements provide an example:

```
grant connect to public;
grant insert, delete, select on customers to jamesj, henryj;
```

This example first grants `connect` privileges on the database to `public` (to all users). The next statement then grants `insert`, `delete`, and `select` privileges on the customers table to users `jamesj` and `henryj`.

Creating and Using User Roles

With the current versions of IDS, the most common approach to user security is through the creation of user *roles*. Roles are created using the `create role` statement with the following syntax:

```
create role payroll;
```

This statement would create a roll named payroll for payroll department users. The users in the payroll department would then be granted the use of this role using the `grant` statement as follows:

```
grant payroll to hannaht;
grant payroll to erict;
grant payroll to carolynt;
```

Users can have more than one role granted. A payroll user may have the need to access accounting and personnel roles. These user roles can also be assigned as follows:

```
grant acctg to hannaht;
grant personnel to hannaht;
```

Executing the grant statements would allow the user to use any one of their roles. But users would not be able to use the role without specifying which role they intend to use. The user role must be specified at the start of each database session using the `set role` statement. To set the user role to payroll and later in the same session switch the user role to accounting, the following statement would be executed:

```
set role to payroll;
... <SQL statements to execute>
set role to accounting;
... <SQL statements to execute>
```

Table Permissions

Each table created in a database has a set of permissions associated with it. Permissions can be one of `insert`, `update`, `delete`, `select`, `index`, or `alter`. These permissions are explained in Table 6-6.

Table 6-6 *Table Permissions*

Permission	Descrption
insert	Ability to insert (add) rows in the table
delete	Ability to delete rows from the table
udpate (column list)	Ability to update all or some columns in the table; if no columns are listed, all columns in the table are implied
select (column list)	Ability to select some or all columns in the table; if no columns are listed, all columns in the table are implied
index	Ability to create an index on the table; the user must also have resource privilege to use index privilege
alter	Ability to alter the table; the user must also have the resource privilege to use the alter privilege
references(column list)	Ability to create referential constraints on some or all columns in the table; if no columns are listed, all columns in the table are implied
all	Grant all privileges to the user

The `insert` and `delete` statements do not act on specific columns—they act on full rows inserting or deleting full rows so they do not specify columns for permissions. The `update`, `select`, and `references` statements act on either full rows or specific columns so a column can be specified. If no column list is provided, then all columns are assumed.

Table permissions are assigned using the `grant` statement. The syntax for the grant statement is as follows:

```
grant <permission> on <table name> to <user list | role>
```

If table privileges are granted to user `public`, then all users are allowed to use those privileges on the table. For example, the following statement grants select privileges on all columns:

```
grant select on sales_facts to public;
```

This statement allows all users, whether or not they have been granted specific privileges on the `sales_facts` table, the privilege to select rows from the table.

A number of users can be granted permissions in a single statement as follows:

```
grant insert on sales_facts to erict, hannaht;
```

This statement grants `insert` permission on the `sales_facts` table to users `erict` and `hannaht`.

The 'with grant option' Statement

If permissions are granted using the `with grant option` statement, the specified privileges are granted to the user along with the permission to grant those privileges to another user. The following statement grants update permission to the user `johni`:

```
grant update on customers to johni with grant option;
```

The user `johni` can then grant update privileges to additional privileges, as follows:

```
grant update on customers to janetr, paulaj;
```

This statement, executed by user `johni`, grants `update` permissions on the `customer` table to users `janetr` and `paulaj`.

Removing Permissions with the 'revoke' Command

The `revoke` option can be used to remove table- or database-level permissions that have been granted to a user. Users can revoke only privileges they have granted unless they have dba privileges, in which case users can grant or revoke permissions to other users. The `revoke` statement specifies a specific privilege and identifies a user using the following syntax:

```
revoke insert on sales_facts from erict;
```

This statement revokes insert privileges on the `sales_facts` table from user `erict`. The `revoke` statement can also be used to revoke database privileges, as follows:

```
revoke connect from erict;
```

This statement revokes connect privileges from the user `erict`. If the user `erict` does not have permission to connect to the database, the fact that he has permission to access specific tables in the database would be moot; the user would not be able to access the database and would not be able to use the tables in the database.

Managing IDS Logs

The Informix database uses logical logs for data recovery purposes. Logical logs are buffered in memory, then written to disk files. Leaving the logical logs on disk would not provide recovery in the event of a disk failure, one of the more serious hardware failures for a database system. Additionally, logical log files on disk cannot be freed until they have been backed up to tape. For these reasons, logical logs on disk should be archived to tape as soon as possible, preferably on a continuous basis .

The IDS database provides two means of logical log backup: *periodic* backups where the administrator chooses to backup logical logs at specific times, or *continuous* backup where as each log file fills it is backed up to disk.

If the logical logs on disk fill the engine will not be able to start new transactions and database activity could come to a standstill. It is therefore imperative for database administrators to monitor logical log activity in the database. Specifically, administrators should be aware of how many logical log files are available and how quickly the log files are filling. The following sections discuss the process of monitoring and archiving logical log files.

Monitoring Logical Logs

The number of logical log files can vary depending on system activity. Because it is primarily heavy update activity that uses logical logs, periods of intensive read activity would not require many logical logs. But periods of extensive updates, such as the periodic load of a large database table, could require a large number of log files. Administrators should review the transaction profile of their database and try to foresee the number of logical log files required to manage peak activity. Because the process of adding logical logs is not trivial, requiring the addition of the log file and a level 0 archive, logs should be added ahead of time and left in place for peak system activity.

The onstat -1 option can be used to monitor logical logs. As shown below, the output of this command lists the logical logs on the system and the current status of the individual log files:

```
Physical Logging
Buffer  bufused   bufsize   numpages  numwrits  pages/io
  P-1   0         16        0         0         0.00
        phybegin  physize   phypos    phyused   %used
        10003f    500       214       0         0.00


Logical Logging
Buffer  bufused   bufsize   numrecs   numpages  numwrits  recs/pages  pages/io
  L-2   0         16        1         1         1         1.0         1.0

address    number   flags    uniqid    begin      size    used    %used
832bb110   1        U——      1         100233     250     250     100.00
832bb12c   2        U——      2         10032d     250     250     100.00
```

```
832bb148  3        U——       3      100427      250       250    100.00
832bb164  4        U——       4      100521      250       250    100.00
832bb180  5        U——       5      10061b      250       250    100.00
832bb19c  6        U——       6      100715      250       250    100.00
832bb1b8  7        U——       7      10080f      250       250    100.00
832bb1d4  8        U--C-L    8      100909      250       120     48.00
832bb1f0  9        F——       0      100a03      250         0      0.00
832bb20c  10       F——       0      100afd      250         0      0.00
```

The logical logging section of the output lists the address of each logical log file, the log file number and the status flags for the log file. The status flags for the log files are as shown in Table 6-7.

Table 6-7 *Logical Log Status Flags*

Log Status	Description
A	Newly added
B	Backed up
C	Current logical log file
F	Free, available for use
L	Contains the most-recent checkpoint record
U	Used

When the logical log is listed with the flag of either B for backed up or F for free, the log file is available for use. Logs with other flags are either waiting to be backed up or are unavailable for use.

If available log files are needed, then it may be necessary to back up used log files to tape; this will make those log files available for use. The `ontape` command can be used to back up log files as detailed in the following sections.

Backing Up Log Files

With *continuous* backup of logical log files, logical logs are backed up to tape as they become full. This approach provides a high degree of failure recovery; the most that would be lost in the event of a catastrophic disk failure would be the transactions that were in process within the partial log file.

Using continuous logging requires a tape drive devoted to storing the logical log tape. On a system that uses tapes for database archives, there would be a total of two tape drives required to support the IDS database: one for archives and one for continuous logical log backups.

The `ontape` command for initiating continuous logical log backups is as follows:

```
ontape -c
```

The tape device used by `ontape` is defined by the LTAPEDEV configuration parameter. As with other commands that impact logical logging, the user must be logged in as user `informix` or `root`.

If continuous logical log file backup is not a possibility, then completed logical log files can be accumulated on disk and then backed up all at once using the following command:

```
ontape -a
```

This command initiates a backup of all completed logical logs in what is referred to as an `automatic` logical log backup. As with continuous logical logging, the log files are archived to the device specified in the LTAPEDEV parameter.

Changing the Size and Location of the Physical Log

The physical log is used constantly by the IDS database. Each time a page in the shared memory buffer is changed for the first time in a session, the *before image* of the page (before the update) is written to the physical log. The constant writes to the physical log could create a large amount of disk I/O on a busy system. For this reason, it may be beneficial to move the physical log to a location where the disk I/O will not interfere with other database disk activity.

When a database instance is created, the physical log is placed in the `root dbspace` by default. Because when a database instance is created there are no other `dbspaces`, there is no

If LTAPEDEV is set to /dev/null, logical log files are freed when they become full—there is no attempt to backup the log. This effectively precludes any logical log roll-forward during recovery; recovery is effective only up to the point of the last complete backup.

Occasionally, it may be useful to set LTAPEDEV to /dev/null;. for instance, when a large portion of the database is being loaded using the insert or update statement (e.g., using a load program that filters or transforms the data as it's being loaded) or when the Informix-SQL load statement is being used. In this case, it may not be necessary to use a log roll-forward to recover the database. Instead, the loads that failed could simply be restarted. Using an LTAPEDEV setting of /dev/null would simply avoid the overhead of maintaining a large number of logical logs that would not be needed. On completion of the load, the engine could be taken offline, the LTAPEDEV parameter changed to the tape device for the logical log, and the engine restarted.

other choice but to allow the physical log to be placed in this location during the initialization of the database instance. But once additional dbspaces have been added to the database instance, the location and size of the physical log can be changed in using one of the following methods:

* onmonitor utility
* Change the PHYDBS or PHYSFILE configuration parameters
* onparams command

Using either approach, the shared memory for the database instance must be reinitialized. Additionally, it is a good idea to create a level 0 backup of the database. This level 0 backup would allow recovery of the database (including the newly altered physical log) in the event the database was destroyed. The following sections detail the processes for sizing and moving the physical log.

Changing the onconfig File

Two parameters in the onconfig file are used for directly controlling the physical log: PHYDBS and PHYSFILE. The PHYDBS configuration parameter is used to identify the dbspace where the physical log will be located. The default location for the physical log is the root dbspace. As discussed previously, it is best to put the physical log in a location where what could be significant disk I/O for the log will not impact the performance of the system. This generally involves placing the physical log either alone in a dbspace or in a dbspace with tables that are fairly static and require limited disk I/O. The value supplied for this parameter must be a valid dbspace and must have adequate contiguous space for the physical log. (Chapter 5 provides tips for setting the size of the IDS physical log.)

The PHYSFILE configuration parameter is used to set the size of the physical log in kilobytes. By default, the size of the physical log file is 200 kilobytes. The entry for this parameter must be equal to or greater than 200 kilobytes.

Using the onparams Command

The onparams command allows the size and location of the physical log to be moved using the following syntax:

```
onparams -P -s <size> -d <dbspace>
```

The -P parameter indicates that the physical log is being altered. The -s parameter indicates the size of the physical log and is followed by an unsigned integer value that indicates the size of the physical log. This size must be greater than or equal to 200. The -d parameter is followed by the name of the dbspace where the physical log file is to be stored. The value supplied this parameter must be a character string name of a valid dbspace. Within this dbspace there must be adequate contiguous space for the physical log.

Adding Logical Logs

If logical log files are needed, they can be added using the onparams command. When the logical log file is added, the administrator must specify the `dbspace` and size for the logical log file. Because the logical log will perform a great deal of disk I/O when used, the logical log files should be located in a `dbspace` or set of `dbspaces` where the additional I/O will not create a problem. The `dbspace` specified must have the contiguous space specified for the logical log or the command will fail. The `onparams` command used to add a logical log is shown as follows:

```
onparams -a -d dbspace [-s <size>]
```

If the size of the logical log is not specified, then the log size specified by the LOGSIZE configuration parameter is used. This command adds a *single* log file in the `dbspace` specified; to add several logical log files, the command must be executed repeatedly. The log file added does not become available until a level 0 archive has been created. The user running the `onparams` command must be user `informix` or user `root`, and the database must be in quiescent (single-user) mode.

Dropping Logical Logs

There may be cases when the space used by logical logs must be freed and allocated to other purposes. Logical logs can be dropped from the database instance using one of two methods: using the `onmonitor` utility or using the `onparams` command.

All the usual administrative caveats for the `onparams` command apply. The database must be in quiescent mode, and the user executing the command must be user `informix` or user `root`. Additionally, the logical log being freed must have a status of "F" for free, or "A" for newly added. The syntax for this command is as follows:

```
onparams -d -l <logid>
```

The `logid` must be valid log ID for a free or newly added logical log as indicated by the `onstat -l` command. Logical logs must be dropped one at a time; to drop 10 logical logs, the `onparams` command must be executed 10 times—once for each logical log.

Archiving and Recovery

Informix provides three utilities to archive data in the database: ontape, onarchive, and onbar. This book covers the ontape utility, a simple, straightforward means of archiving and restoring data. The onbar utility is used in conjunction with a storage management device (a tape silo or other backup device that automates a great deal of the media management effort) and is documented in the Informix technical documentation. The onarchive utility provides some additional functionality over the ontape utility but has been largely superseded by the capabilities of the onbar utility.

Archiving can be performed online. This means that as users are accessing database data, reading and writing records, a database backup can be in progress. By reviewing the time stamp on a buffer page, the IDS backup thread can determine whether or not a page belongs in the archive.

Recovery can be done as either a *cold restore* or a *warm restore*. A **cold restore** is performed when the database is completely offline; this type of restore is required for the restoration of critical dbspaces. A **warm restore** is performed when the database is online (though some functions are restricted).

Archive Levels

The IDS backup utilities provide three levels of incremental archives: level 0, level 1, and level 2 archives. Using multiple archive levels reduces the amount of data that must be written to tape by incrementally archiving data.

A **level 0 archive** is used to archive all data in the database. All data pages regardless of the time stamp on the page are archived.

A **level 1 archive** is used to archive all data pages that have been modified since the last level 0 archive. The ontape archive threads would examine the datetime stamp of each page in the database instance and only select pages that have been modified since the last level 0 archive (as recorded in the system reserved pages).

A **level 2 archive** is used to archive all data pages that have been modified since the last level 1 archive. The `ontape` archive threads would examine the `datetime` stamps on all data pages in the database instance and select pages for backup that have been modified since the last level 1 archive as recorded in the system reserved pages.

Performing an Archive

The `ontape` utility is the tried-and-true workhorse of the Informix engine, providing the basic features required of an IDS archive. Using `ontape`, administrators can create level 0, level 1, and level 2 archives for the database as a whole. (Archiving a single `dbspace` or set of `dbspaces` is not supported by `ontape`, though a set of dbspaces can be identified for restore purposes.)

The syntax of `ontape` for archiving is as follows:

```
ontape -s -L <archive level>
```

The -s parameter is passed to `ontape` to indicate that an archive is being performed. The -L parameter is followed by a value that indicates the archive level that is being performed. Valid values are, of course, 0, 1, and 2.

The `ontape` program was designed with certain expectations. One expectation is that because it is possible for the archive to span multiple tapes, an operator is required to change tapes. Though given the tape storage capacity of current backup media, this may not always be the case; the result of this expectation is that the `ontape` utility is not designed to run in a batch process. The `ontape` program reads and writes prompts and messages to the Unix `stdin` and `stdout` devices. This means that `ontape` reads input from the terminal keyboard that started the program (`stdin`) and outputs to the terminal display (`stdout`).

What many administrators would like to do is create an unattended archive—an archive that is run off hours and requires no user intervention. Unfortunately, `ontape` was never written with this purpose in mind. It is possible to redirect `stdin` and `stdout` and run `ontape` from within a Unix batch file, but operation can be unwieldy and difficult. Given the importance of archives and their significance, it is best not to attempt this.

> **Note** The onarchive and onbar utilities provide the capability to create unattended archives. The onbar utility allows interaction with a storage management device that provides additional archive functionality. Users requiring unattended archives should review the documentation for these utilities.

Restoring Data

Unfortunately there may come a time due to hardware or software failure that the database must be recovered from archives. A full recovery requires at the very least, a level 0 archive. If a level 1 or level 2 archive has been done since the level 0 archive, then it should also be used for recovery. And finally, the logical logs that have been written to tape since the last archive (level 0, 1, or 2) must be available. When all of these tapes are ready, the recovery process can begin.

Ideally, the combination of the level 0, level 1, and level 2 archive will bring the database up to the point of the previous night's archive; the logical logs will then be used to roll forward the database up to the point of the last checkpoint. With this recovery process complete, only the data written to the database since the last checkpoint will be lost—all other data will be restored. The ontape options to perform a restore are as follows:

```
ontape -r [-D <dbspace list for restore>]
```

To perform a full database restore, after placing the first tape (the start of the level 0 archive) in the tape drive designated as the archive tape device (TAPEDEV configuration parameter), the following ontape command would be executed with the IDS engine offline:

```
ontape -r
```

To restore a single dbspace, the following command would be executed:

```
ontape -r -D dbspace1
```

Executing this command would require that a level 0 archive be available in the tape drive.

The `ontape` utility will prompt the administrator for additional tapes for each archive level if it detects that additional tapes are needed. Once the level 0 archive has been restored, it will request any additional archive levels and prompt for those tapes if they are available. Once archive tapes have been restored, the `ontape` utility will prompt for any logical tapes available for the log roll-forward operation. Note that a logical log roll-forward is to perform a `dbspace` level restore, but it is not required for other restores, though it would obviously provide for a more complete recovery of the database

Cold Restores and Warm Restores

In the event the entire database must be restored, or some critical portion of the database such as the `root dbspace` must be restored, a **cold restore** must be conducted. A cold restore means that the database is offline during the restore operation. (Of course, in the event the root `dbspace` were corrupted, it is probable the database would not start in any event.)

A cold restore consists of both a physical restore (restoring the level 0 and other archives) and a logical restore (performing a logical log roll-forward with the log tapes).

The IDS engine will be offline when the restore begins but will enter recovery mode when the system reserved pages are restored. It will then remain in recovery mode until the logical restore is complete or `onmode` is used to force it into another mode.

A **warm restore** can be used to restore a noncritical `dbspace`. With a warm restore, the database can be in online or quiescent mode. If the database is in online mode, database queries will succeed as only as they do not need to access data that is in the `dbspace` being recovered.

Changing the Database Logging Status

The Informix IDS engine, unlike other relational databases, does not require database logging to be in place; it is possible to operate an IDS database without logging, though this does preclude using transactions within the database.

Database logging is specified in the create database statement, with the "with log" clause used to specify that the database is to be created with logical logging. Once a database is running, the ontape command can be used to change the logging status of the database. To add logging to a database, a level 0 archive must be performed; this is required in the event it is necessary to perform a restore on the database. The ontape commands shown in Table 6-8 are used to change the logging status of a database.

Table 6-8 Changing logging status with ontape

Parameter	Description
-B	Add buffered logging to the database
-N	End logging for the specified database
-U	Change logging status to unbuffered logging
-A	Change logging status to ANSI compliant logging

These commands are executed as follows:

```
ontape -s [ -A | -B | -N | -U | -A <database name> ]
```

To change the status of the sales_db from buffered to unbuffered logging, the following command could be executed:

```
ontape -s -U sales_db
```

To change the status of the sales_db to buffered logging, the following command could be executed:

```
ontape -s -B sales_db
```

Chapter Summary

This chapter covered the basic administrative features of the IDS engine, from the basic administrative options such as starting and stopping the engine, to the process of archiving and restoring the IDS database. The aspects of database security were also covered, detailing the IDS implementation of user roles and table-level permissions.

The IDS `onmode` command allows certain configuration parameters to be set while the engine is online, a powerful capability that allows the engine to dynamically change to suit the needs of its environment. These `onmode` commands and their impact were covered in this chapter.

Logical and physical logging are critical components of the data integrity features of the IDS engine. Logical logging provides an important failure recovery mechanism for the database after physical restore of the database has been performed. It is therefore important that logical logs be written to tape, preferably using continuous logical logging. The process of establishing a logical log backup and other logging administration was covered in this chapter.

Next Chapter

The next chapter covers the Informix version of the Structured Query Language. Informix-SQL is the means by which administrators and developers interact with the IDS database. The proper use of SQL is an important part of the process of maintaining the database, providing the administrator with the facility to perform the management operations required. An application developer also needs to have a thorough understanding of the Informix version of SQL to adequately program efficient and productive applications against the IDS engine. The following chapter will provide useful information for both the developer and administrator, covering important Informix-SQL statements in detail and providing practical tips and suggestions on their usage.

The Relational Database and Informix-SQL

Relational databases are considered the database of choice, dominating the database server market, from the low-end Unix and NT platforms, to the high-end Unix servers. Understanding the history of this popular data storage medium helps provide a clear perspective on the nature of relational database theory.

Contributing to the success of the relational database has been the pervasive usage of the Structured Query Language as an access language for relational database data. Because SQL has been a prominent standard endorsed by virtually all database vendors, relational databases have been able to provide a data storage platform with an interface that is familiar to a large number of users. A programmer who has been using SQL to access a Sybase database can take those same basic skills and apply them to writing a program to access an Informix database.

This chapter covers the basics of the relational databases and introduces basic terms and concepts. Each database vendor has implemented minor extensions to its version of SQL, and Informix is no exception. Since SQL is a nonprocedural language, there are limitations in the logic that can be expressed through

SQL alone. For that reason database vendors have created a stored procedure language (SPL) to express procedural logic when performing database I/O; this language is also covered in this chapter.

History of the Relational Database

The relational database model had its theoretical start in the late 1960s. In 1968, while at an IBM research institution, Dr. E. F. Codd began researching the concept of applying mathematical rigor to the world of database management systems. Codd's ideas were later published in a landmark paper, "A Relational Model of Data for Large Shared Data Banks" (Communications of the ACM, Volume 13, No. 6, June 1970). The ideas laid out in this paper had a sweeping influence on the nature of database systems for years to come. Today, they are the theoretical standard of all relational database systems.

The relational database was favored in academic institutions because it was based on provable mathematical foundations. This differentiated the relational database from other database formats and made the process of developing a query language somewhat easier.

Relational Database Concepts

The relational database is conceptually a collection of tables. Each table in the database represents a data *entity*, and each entity is a collection of data *attributes*. An entity is a distinguishable object about which information is to be recorded. An example of such an object is a car. An attribute is a characteristic or property associated with the distinguishable object. An example of attributes for a car entity would be the color of the car, the make of the car, the size of the engine, and the age of the car.

Entities, Attributes, and Relationships

The process of designing a relational database involves first identifying the entities (the objects) to be modeled. In the design of a system to take catalog orders, for example, the entities would be objects such as a catalog item, an order for an item or items, the manufacturer of an item, and the customer who purchased an item.

The next step would be to identify attributes. The attributes for an entity are the characteristics—or the features of the entity or object. In the case of a catalog item, characteristics would be a description of the item, the cost of the item, the weight of the item, the size of the item, and the manufacturer of the item. The characteristics of another entity, such as the customer, would be the name of the customer and the address of the customer with the zip code. And the order would contain characteristics or attributes for the customer making the order, the item or items being ordered, and the cost of the order.

Entities can have relationships. Relationships are the connections between the objects being modeled. An order does not exist alone. There are customers who have made the order, and there are items on the order that represent items the customer has purchased. The customer and item entities are therefore related to the order entity.

Relationships have several forms: *one-to-one, one-to-many*, and *many-to-many*. A one-to-one relationship indicates that for a particular entity there is one and only one related entity. An example of a one-to-one relationship would be the relationship between a manufacturer and an item. For any particular item record, there is one and only one manufacturer record. (An alternative design could allow multiple manufacturers for an item, but for our purposes, a different manufacturer would entail a different item.)

A one-to-many relationship indicates that for a given entity record there are one or more than one related entity records. This would be the case for the orders entity and the line items on the order. For every order record, there could be multiple items purchased, and each of these items would be represented by line item records.

A many-to-many relationship indicates that for the multiple records in a given entity, there are one or more than one records in a related entity. An example of a many-to-many relationship is the relationship between cars and family members. A single family member can drive more than one car, and a single car can be driven by more than one family member.

A relational database is often diagrammed using an entity-relationship diagram (ERD); these diagrams provide a series of specialized lines, boxes, and symbols to represent the relationships between entities.

Normalization

Once the attributes and entities of the database have been identified, there is usually a process of normalization that the database developer must complete. Normalization generally involves the elimination of repeating attributes in an entity, and the identification of attributes that belong in a particular entity and attributes that belong elsewhere. The data analyst must usually go through several iterations of review and modification before the proper level of normalization has been achieved.

Several levels of normalization have been defined by Codd and other academics. Each level provides for examination and review of the entity and its attributes and a determination of what belongs and does not belong to that entity. The most common level of normalization is known as *third-normal form*, though a fifth-normal form has been defined.

The normalization of a relational database is an important part of the database design process. Normalization reduces data redundancy and thus reduces the amount of data storage required for the data. A normalized design also simplifies the process of making the inevitable modifications required of most databases.

The Structured Query Language in IDS

Informix provides a version of SQL that supports both an ANSI standard SQL and a slightly expanded version to support the unique features of the IDS engine such as fragmentation. This language provides all the functionality needed to interact with the IDS database.

> **Note** This SQL portion of this book does not cover the entire set of Informix-SQL statements. Many statements are relatively obscure and rarely used. The focus of this book is on the statements that provide the most utility to database administrators and developers.

SQL Statement Types

Informix-SQL statements are divided into two types: Data Definition Language (DDL) and Data Manipulation Language (DML) statements. As the names imply, DML statements concern manipulating and maintaining the data in the database and DDL statements concern the definition of storage for the data. These statements are as outlined in Tables 7-1 and 7-2.

Table 7-1 *SQL DDL Statements*

DDL Statement	Description
create database	Create an empty IDS database
create table	Create an empty table; specifies columns, data types, and optionally constraints and default values .
create view	Create a view based on existing tables
drop table	Drop or delete an existing table
drop view	Drop or delete an existing view
drop database	Drop or delete an existing empty database
alter table	Alter an existing table; can be used to change columns, add columns, drop columns, and perform other functions

Table 7-2 *SQL DML Statements*

Statement	Description
select	Retrieve rows from a specified database table or tables. Used to join two or more related tables
update	Update existing rows in the database
insert	Insert new rows into the database
delete	Delete existing rows from the database

Extended SQL Statements

Informix provides a number of extended SQL statements. These statements perform special functions for the database and are as outlined in Table 7-3.

Table 7-3 Extended SQL Statements

Statement	Description
load	Load rows from an ASCII file and insert the contents into a database table. ASCII file must be delimited
unload	Unload rows from a database table to a delimited ASCII file
update statistics	Update the optimizer statistics in the database

Creating Data Storage—The DDL Statements

The IDS engine supports DDL statements to define the data storage requirements for a database and its constituent tables. These statements are explained in the sections that follow.

Create Database

The `create database` statement assigns data storage for a database. The syntax for this statement is as follows:

```
create database [in <dbspace>] [with log];
```

By specifying the `dbspace` for the database, the administrator can specify the location for the system catalogs for the database. Additionally, this `dbspace` becomes the default location for tables created in the database. This feature allows the administrator to apply a degree of organization and control over the location of databases and tables.

The "with log" clause allows database logging to be specified. Informix enables you to create a database without logging. Such a database does not provide the recovery mechanisms that logging provides, so SQL statements that provide transaction control (begin work, commit work) could not be executed in a database created without logging.

A "no log" database is not completely without logging. A logical and physical log are still created with the database. Logical logging continues to be used for DDL statements, and each SQL statement is treated as a "singleton transaction," meaning that a set of two or more statements cannot be rolled back, but the failure of a single statement can and will be rolled back by the engine to preserve data integrity. This means that for certain statements executed in a "no log" database, a significant number of logical logs can be used. For example, the load statement discussed next can be used to load a large number of records from an ASCII file into the database. This entire statement would be logged and could potentially require a large number of logical log records to complete.

While not generally recommended, a "no log" database can be useful in some instances. For example, a database that contains data that represents a daily or weekly snapshot of information and is updated only on a periodic basis could be run effectively without logging. With this type of database, periodic loads run on a daily or weekly basis could be designed to be rerun in the event they failed, thus eliminating the need for the ability to run transactions within the database. And because there are no complex online updates occurring, there is no need for online transactions to provide a logical rollback of a series of updates. A data warehouse is an obvious example of this type of database.

The create table Statement

The create table statement is used to define data storage for a database table. This statement provides for the basic definition of a table name and columns and the data type and length of columns. In addition, it allows the definition of referential and integrity constraints and fragmentation schemes for the table. The following is the syntax for this statement:

```
create table <table name> ( <column name> <column data
type>| <data length> [ constraint definition ] [default
values], ... )
    [in <dbspace name> ] |
[fragmentation definition]
```

Table Name, Column Names, and Data Types

A failure in syntax for any portion of the `create table` statement causes the entire table build operation to fail. A table create statement is used to specify the table name for the table. With IDS, the table name is limited to 18 characters. The table name must be unique in the database in which the table is created; it need not be unique in the database instance.

The **column name** for a table is subject to the same naming limitations of the table name. It must be 18 characters or fewer in length. A column name must be a unique column name for the table but need not be a unique column name for the database (i.e., there can be another table with the same column name, but not another column with the same name in the same table.)

The **data type** for the column must be one of those listed in Table 7-4 and is subject to the size limitations identified.

Table 7-4 *Valid Data Types*

Data Type	Length	Minimum Value	Maximum Value
smallint	2	-32,767	+32,767
integer, int	4	-2,147,483,647	+2,147,483,647
smallfloat, real	4	platform-dependent	platform-dependent
float, double precision	8	platform-dependent	platform-dependent
decimal, dec, numeric	precision/2 + 1	-32 significant digits	+32 significant digits
money	precision/2 + 1	-32 significant digits	+32 significant digits
date	4	1/1/0001	12/31/9999
char, character	programmer defined	1 byte	32,767 bytes

Note that Informix `insert` and `update` statements usually do data type conversion when it makes sense. So creating a column as a character column and then inserting integer numbers into the column would be allowed. Likewise, an integer column would accept the input of a character string of integer numbers if the converted value of the integers did not exceed the limit of the Informix integer. If tight control over the contents of a column is desired, then constraints should be placed on the column as detailed in the section that follows.

The **dbspace name** clause of the `create table` statement allows the table to be created in a specific `dbspace`. By default, if no `dbspace` is specified in `dbspace` clause or a fragmentation clause, the table is placed in the `dbspace` where the containing database was created.

IDS Fragmentation Definition

The fragmentation definition for a table defines a fragmentation scheme for the data in that table. Fragmentation can be either *by expression* or using a *round robin* scheme.

A round-robin fragmentation scheme specifies that the data will be distributed across the `dbspaces` specified in the `dbspace` list. Data will be distributed in a serial fashion to the `dbspaces` in the list, being written first to the first `dbspace` in the list, then to the second `dbspace` in the list, and so on. The following is the syntax for the "fragment by" clause in the `create table` statement:

```
... fragment by  round robin in <dbspace list> |
            expression <expression1> in <dbspace name>,
            <expression2> in <dbspace name> ...;
```

The round-robin fragmentation scheme is useful in cases where even distribution of data across multiple disks is desirable or an expression-based fragmentation scheme can simply not be developed. The following provides an example of round-robin fragmentation:

```
create table sales (
            sales_id integer,
            region char(10),
            product char(10),
            sales_amt decimal(12,2))
        fragment by round robin in dbspace1, dbspace2,
dbspace3;
```

In this example, the data in the `sales` table will be fragmented over three `dbspaces`: `dbspace1`, `dbspace2`, and `dbspace3`. These three `dbspaces` are known as *fragments*. This fragmentation scheme will evenly distribute data over the three dbspaces, first writing records to dbspace1, then to dbspace2 and dbspace3. After writing to dbspace3, it will then start over on the dbspace list and write the next record to dbspace1.

If the access to this table is through a detached index (not in the same dbspace as the table), then the even distribution of the data over three fragments should have little impact on data access because the data access operation will read the index to get the address of the page where the data record is located. This data record information in the index will indicate the fragment, page and page offset where the data record is located, so there will not be a need to read through the data in the other fragments to find the record.

But if queries are run against the table that must scan the table in its entirety, then it may be useful to somehow eliminate scanning some of the table fragments. This can be accomplished using **expression-based fragmentation**. Expression-based fragmentation uses expressions to determine where data rows will be written. The syntax for this fragmentation scheme is shown as follows:

```
... fragment by expression
        <expression1> in <dbspace name>,
        <expression2> in <dbspace name> ...;
```

Using this syntax, a series of expressions are used to write data to specific dbspaces. Once this has been done and the update statistics command has been run to update optimizer information for the table, the IDS optimizer is then aware of the nature of the data in the fragments. Given this information, the optimizer can then make intelligent decisions about which fragments to scan to retrieve data rows from a table. The following provides an example of fragmentation by expression:

```
create table sales (
        sales_id integer,
        region char(10),
        product char(10),
        sales_amt decimal(12,2))
    fragment by expression
        region in ("NW","NE") in dbspace1,
        region in ("SW","SE") in dbspace2,
        region in ("MW","HW") in dbspace3;
```

This `create table` statement fragments sales data records across several `dbspaces` based on the `region` column of the sales record. Queries that must scan this entire table can take advantage of fragment elimination by the optimizer by using filter criteria that filter the data by region, thus allowing the optimizer to intelligently eliminate fragments from the search path.

As the previous sections indicated, the Informix `create table` statement allows a great deal of the specifics of data storage to be defined. The basic information about the data table, the table name, column name, and data types are defined as well as information about constraints on the data and how to distribute the data through fragmentation. Taken as a whole, the `create table` statement lays the groundwork for the efficient access of data in the database.

Fragmentation of data can be a crucial part of providing efficient data access. It is one of the key features that distinguishes the IDS database from the offerings of other relational database vendors. A more thorough discussion of this important features relative to performance tuning is provided in Chapter 5.

Creating Database Views

Database views can be used for a number of purposes. They can be used to express logical views of relationships between tables and filter criteria for those tables. A view can reference a single database table or multiple tables in a complex join. Once created, a view is accessed as a database table would be accessed with a few minor restrictions. A view can be used in an SQL `update` statement unless it contains one of the following:

- View restrictions for updatable views
- Select list with aggregate values
- Use of the `unique` or `distinct` keyword
- `Group by` clause
- Derived value for a column created using arithmetic expressions

Database views are an excellent tool for hiding and encapsulating the complexity of a relational database. Complex joins and filters can be expressed in a view and then accessed in a more simplified manner as a database table. The real names of table columns can be renamed using the `as` clause, hiding or simplifying the column name to a more familiar name for a developer or user. The syntax for the `create view` statement is as follows:

```
create view <view name> [ ( <column name list> ]
    as < select statement >
```

The optional `with check option` clause can be used to enforce a set of rules when updates are performed with a view. For example, the following view would restrict updates to sales within region "NW":

```
create view sales_nw as
    select *
    from sales
    where region = "NW"
    with check option;
```

An SQL `update` statement could use the view name as a table name but would be restricted to updating only rows where the region column had the value "NW." Likewise, an insert statement could insert rows into the table but would only be able to insert rows with the value of "NW" for the region column.

A view can be used to store a common but complex query in the database. This query could then be accessed by programmers and database administrators as "shared code." This approach allows queries to be standardized and shared among developers, a means of storing the business rules for an organization in a centralized location.

Enforcing Security with views

Often database security must be expressed at the row level, restricting certain users to a view of a set of rows in a table. For instance, users from a certain sales region should be allowed only to view rows of data from their region. Informix database security provides table and column security, but not row-level security. But views combined with Informix keywords can provide this capability. The following `create view` statement provides an example:

```
create table user_perms (
    login_name char(10),
```

```
        region char(10) );

create table sales_recs (
        sales_id integer,
        sales_date date,
        sales_amt decimal(12,2),
        prod_id char(5),
        region char(10));

create view sales_view as
   select sales_recs.*
   from sales_recs, user_perms
   where sales_recs.region = user_perms.region and
          user_perms.login_name = user;
```

In this example, records are selected from the `sales_recs`
table based on the login ID of the user accessing the table as
resolved from the `user` keyword in the query. This query
enforces security via a join between the `user_perms` table that
stores the valid region for the user and the `sales_recs` table.
The details of this query can be hidden by simply selecting sales
records using the view as follows:

```
select  *
from    sales_view
where   sales_date between "1/1/1998" and "3/30/1998"
```

Running this query would retrieve `sales` records between
January 1, 1998, and March 30 1998. But because the
`sales_view` is being used, only the sales records the user is
allowed to view (as defined in the `user_perms` table) will be
retrieved by the query.

Using Keywords in Views

The `today` keyword could also be used in conjunction with this
query to return only today's sales. This query could also be stored
as a view as follows:

```
create view todays_sales as
      select * from sales_view
      where  sales_date = today;
```

Using this view, the `select` statement shown as follows would retrieve only the sales entered for today's date in the region in which the user is allowed to view records as returned by the `sales_view` view referenced in the "from" clause:

```
select * from todays_sales;
```

Referencing Complete Queries

A fully normalized or even partially normalized database can sometimes require complex queries to retrieve data. Database views can be used to hide this complexity. The next query shown is used to hide a complex three-table join used to retrieve sales data.

```
create view sales_startup as

    select sales_rec.*
        from sales_rec, region, product, sales_code, periods
        where
                sales_rec.region = regions.region and
region.region_type = "S" and
product.prod_code = sales_rec.prod_code and
product.prod_scale = "X" and
product.sales_period = period.period_code and
period.flag = "CURRENT";
```

Using this view, sales records that met that criteria could be retrieved for a specific sales person using the following query:

```
select * from sales_startup
where sales_startup.sales_id = 123;
```

This query would retrieve the records that matched the join and filter criteria of the view and were for the salesperson with the `sales_id` of 123.

Dropping Database Tables

The `drop table` statement can be used to drop an existing database table. Only the table creator, user `informix`, or the database administrator can drop a database table. The table need not be empty to be dropped. When a table is dropped, all database objects directly related to and dependent on the table (views, triggers, constraints on table columns) are also deleted from the database.

Using tools such as `dbaccess` and SQL Editor, the user executing the `drop table` statement will be prompted. But note that with some of the language tools such as ESQL/C, the user will *not* be prompted to drop the table. The syntax for the `drop table` statement is as follows:

```
drop table <table name>;
```

To drop the `sales_recs` table, the following statement would be executed:

```
drop table sales_recs;
```

Dropping Database Views

A database view can be dropped using the `drop view` statement. When a view is created, a series of entries are made to a system catalog tables to define the view. This statement effectively removes the view from the database by deleting the rows pertaining to the view from the system catalog tables. The syntax for the `drop view` statement is as follows:

```
drop view <view name>
```

To drop a view named `sales_view`, the following statement would be executed:

```
drop view sales_view;
drop database
```

Dropping a Database

The `drop database` statement can be used to drop a specific database. Only an empty database, a database with no tables other than system catalog tables, and a database with no active user sessions can be dropped. This effectively eliminates the possibility that an administrator can inadvertently drop a database that is currently in use. Only the user `informix` or `root` or the database administrator can drop a database.

Removing a database removes the system catalog tables for that database from the `dbspace` where the database was located. The syntax for the `drop database` statement is as follows:

```
drop database <database name>
```

To drop a database named `salse_dw`, the following statement would be executed:

```
drop database sales_dw;
```

The 'alter table' Statement

The `alter table` statement can be used to alter an existing table. The work performed by the `alter table` statement could be performed by executing a number of SQL DDL and DML statements and so provides a convenient means of performing this operation with less work for the administrator. The syntax for the alter table statement is as follows:

```
alter table <table name> <action>
```

The action performed is one of those shown in Table 7-5.

Table 7-5 alter table Statement Actions

Function	Description
add	Add a column to the table
modify	Modify a column in the table
drop	Drop a column
add constraint	Add a constraint to the table
drop constraint	Drop a constraint from the table
modify next size	Modify the next extent size
lock mode	Alter the lock mode for the table

The most common use of the `alter table` statement is the addition or modification of a column in the table. The syntax for this operation is as follows:

```
alter table <table name> add ( <column name> [<default clause>]
[not null] [<constraint definition>] [before <column name>] )
```

Or the `alter table` statement can be used to drop an existing column as follows:

```
alter table <table name> drop ( <column name> )
```

Another use of the `alter table` statement is to modify an existing column using the following syntax:

```
alter table <table name> modify ( <column name> [<default clause>]
[not null] [<constraint definition] [before <column name] )
```

The following SQL statement uses the `alter table` statement to drop an existing column from the `sales` table.

```
alter table sales drop ( region );
```

If more than one column is to be dropped, a comma-separated list of the columns can be included in the statement as follows:

```
alter table sales drop ( region, sales_code );
```

To add a column to the `sales` table, the following statement could be executed:

```
alter table sales add ( region char(5), sales_code char(2) );
```

To modify the `region` column and change it to a character field with a length of 10 instead of its original designation as a character field with a length of 5, the following `alter table` statement could be used:

```
alter table sales modify ( region char(10) )
```

Alternatively, the `alter table` statement can be used to add a constraint to an existing table using the following syntax:

```
alter table sales add constraint  check ( region in ( "NW", "SW", "SE",
"MW", "W" ) );
```

Note that the `alter table` statement *cannot* be used to change the name of a column. The `rename column` statement is used to accomplish that task.

> **Note**
> The `alter table` statement performs its work by creating a new table with the original and altered added columns and then copying the work from the old table to the new table and deleting the old table. What this means is that the size of the original table is doubled until the old table is deleted. Administrators should take this into account when executing the `alter table` statement. (Note that in versions 7.3 and higher, an *in-place* `alter table` exists that eliminates this space problem.)

The rename column Statement

The `rename column` statement can be used to change the name of an existing column. A column name must be unique within that table, but it need not be a unique name for the entire database. The syntax for this statement is as follows:

```
rename column <table name>.< column name >
                to < new column name >
```

The change the name of the `sales` table column named `region` to `sales_region` the following statement could be executed.

```
rename column sales.region to sales_region
```

The rename table Statement

The `rename table` statement can be used to change the name of an existing table. The syntax for this statement is as follows:

```
rename table < table name > to < new table name >
```

This statement can be useful in SQL script to make database changes. The following script creates a new `sales` table and copies data from the old `sales` table to the new `sales` table:

```
create table tmp_table ( sales_id integer,
                         region char(5),
                         sales_amt decimal(12,2) );

insert into tmp_table select * from sales where region in
( "NW", "NE" );
rename table sales to sales_bak;
rename table tmp_table to sales;
```

This script creates a new table initially named `tmp_table`. Selected rows from the `sales` table are then copied into this table. When the copy operation is complete, the name of the `sales` table is changed to `sales_bak` and the table to which data has been copied is renamed to `sales`.

Column Integrity and Referential Constraints

The IDS engine supports both *referential* and *integrity* constraints. Referential constraints allow relationships with other tables in the database to be enforced automatically at the database level. Integrity constraints allow an attribute domain (a set of valid values) to be established and enforced at the database level. Together these facilities can greatly enhance the integrity and quality of the data stored in the database. Using these facilities, the database administrator need not depend on the applications using the database to ensure data quality; enforcement can become part of the database.

Constraints can be established when the database table is created using a simple syntax. The syntax for `constraint` creation with the `create table` statement is as follows:

```
create table <table name > (
       <column name> <data type> check <check constraint> |
          references <table reference>
...
```

Constraints that are created as part of a column definition can reference only a single column (the column on which they are created). The following statement places several constraints on columns in a table containing sales data:

```
create table sales (
sales_id serial primary key,
region char(5) check ( region in ("NW","SW", "NE", "SE" ) ),
sales_code char(2) references sales_codes( sales_code ),
. . . .
```

The `create table` statement here places three constraints on `sales` table columns. The first constraint identifies the `sales_id` column as a *primary key*, a column that contains a value that uniquely identifies a row. Because by definition a primary key uniquely identifies a row in the table, the key must be a unique identifier. To implement the primary key constraint, the IDS engine will therefore place a unique index on this column.

The next constraint placed on the table limits the `region` column to the values specified in the "in" clause expression. Any attempt to insert a record with a `region` value that does not satisfy this check constraint causes the insert to fail with an error indicating that a constraint has been violated.

The third constraint placed on the `sales` table is a referential constraint placed on the `sales_code` column. This referential constraint indicates that the `sales_code` column references the `sales_code` table and that any column value inserted into the `sales_code` column must be contained in the `sales_codes` table as a value of the `sales_code` column.

To identify more than one table column in a constraint definition, a table-level constraint must be defined. This capability is demonstrated in the following section.

Primary Key/Foreign Key Definition at the Table Level

Primary key and foreign key definitions can be placed at the table level. In fact, if a multicolumn primary or foreign key constraint is being placed, it must be entered at the table level not at the column level. The following example creates table-level primary and foreign key definitions:

> **Note**
>
> Note that primary key and referential keys are implemented creating indexes on the primary and referenced tables. When a primary key is created, a unique index is created on the primary key column in the table where the primary key was defined. When a referential constraint is placed on a column, an index is created on the referenced table for that column (thus avoiding the need to scan the entire table for a value).
>
> Indexes can improve performance on read operations using that key, but incur a penalty on write (update and insert) operations. Thus, creating a large number of referential constraints on a table would create a large number of indices and could impact performance during update operations. But any impact on performance should be balanced with the significant data integrity gains that can be derived from using referential and integrity constraints.

```
create table region_link (
        sales_id integer,
        region char(5),
        reg_flags char(3),
    primary key ( sales_id, region ),
    foreign key (sales_id) references salesmen (sales_id) )
```

This `create table` statement defines a multi-column primary key definition. A foreign key definition is also created, which references the `salesmen` table. (Note a foreign key referential constraint must reference a column in the referenced table that has been identified as a primary key.)

Any constraint that references more than one column must be defined at the table level. For instance, a check constraint that involves more than one column must be defined as shown as follows:

```
create table sales_stats (
        sales_id integer,
        trans_id integer, gross_sales decimal( 12,2),
        cost_of_sales decimal(12,2),
        gross_profit   decimal(12,2),
            check ( cost_of_sales <= gross_sales ) );
```

In this table, a constraint is created that limits the `cost_of_sales` to a value less than or equal to the value of `gross_sales`. This check constraint therefore enforces a business rule that states that the cost of making a sale cannot be greater than the gross revenue for the sale.

Creating a Unique Column

A unique column can be created using the `unique` constraint. The `unique` constraint has the same impact as creating a unique index on a column (which is, in fact, how it is implemented). The following SQL `create table` statement demonstrates the use of this constraint:

```
create table region (
        region char(5) primary key,
        region_type char(3),
        region_id integer unique );
```

This `create table` statement creates a table named `region` and identifies the `region_id` column as a unique identifier.

Naming a Constraint

By default, the IDS engine assigns a name to a constraint. A constraint can, however, be explicitly named. This could be useful should the constraint need to be dropped (through the `alter table` statement). The following provides an example for naming a constraint:

```
create   table region (
        region char(5) primary key constraint pk_region,
        region_type char(3) check ( region_type in ("SK","ZE"))
            constraint region_type_check );
```

In the following example, a primary key constraint is created on the `region` column and is named `pk_region`. In the event this constraint needed to be dropped using the `alter table` statement, the constraint name could be referenced as follows:

```
alter table sales drop constraint ( pk_region);
```

Note that all constraints contain a name that can be referenced in the `alter table` statement. If a constraint name is not
explicitly assigned, the IDS engine assigns it a default name. This
default name can be identified using the following SQL statement:

```
select  sc.constrname, sc.constrtype
from    systables st, sysconstraints sc
where   sc.tabid=st.tabid and
        st.tabname = "sales";
```

In this SQL statement, a pair of system catalog tables are
read—the `systables` and `sysconstraints` table. The tables are
joined on the `tabid` column, the unique identifier for tables in
the IDS database. The query uses filter criteria to select just the
`sales` table (`tabname = "sales"`), but any valid table name
could be substituted to retrieve constraints for that table.

By default, constraints are tested immediately when a table is
updated. This behavior can be changed to defer checking until a
set of `insert` statements is committed to the database. The `set`
`constraints` statement is used to alter this behavior using the
following syntax:

```
set constraints [all]| <constraint name> immediate|deferred
```

Using this statement, constraint checking can be deferred until
a transaction is committed. This statement must be executed
within a transaction.

Accessing Data—DML Statements

A number of statements are available to manipulate and update
data within the database. These statements are known as Data
Manipulation Language and are the `select`, `update`, and
`delete` statements. Together they constitute the bulk of the
database interaction performed using SQL. These statements are
covered in the following sections.

The select Statement

The `select` statement is the workhorse of SQL statements. This statement is used to query the database and retrieve a desired set of rows. Using the `select` statement "where" clause, rows can be filtered and joins between two or more tables can be expressed. The format for the `select` statement is as follows:

```
select    [ first  n ] <column list>
from      <table list>
[where    <filter criteria> ]
[group by <column list> ]
[having   <filter criteria>]
[order by <column list>]
```

The Select List

The *select clause* contains a column list of the columns that will be retrieved as part of the query. These column lists can contain expressions to perform mathematical calculations or string manipulation. An asterisk indicates that all columns in an identified table will be retrieved. The optional `first  n` clause allows a specified number of rows to be returned by the query; any records that satisfy the query beyond this number will be ignored (this feature is available only in IDS version 7.3 and beyond). The `select` clause is a required part of the `select` statement. The following query selects two columns from the sales table to be returned for each row of the query results:

```
    select region, sales_amount
  from sales
```

An expression can be part of a select list as shown in the following query:

```
    select region, sales_amount * 1.1
  from sales
```

The from Clause

The *from clause* of the select statement lists the tables that will be queried to satisfy the query. This clause can be used to specify the type of join between the tables listed—either a natural join (the default) or an outer join as specified with the `outer` keyword. This clause is a required part of the `select` statement. The following example selects records from the `sales` table as specified in the from clause:

```
select *
from sales
```

The where Clause

The optional *where clause* is used to express the filter and join criteria for the SQL statement being executed. The *join criteria* indicate the columns that will be used to join one or more tables listed in the from clause. And the *filter criteria* indicate what rows will be included or eliminated from the entire set of rows in the tables that have been identified.

A `select` statement to retrieve all of the rows in the `sales` table would be written as follows:

```
select *
from sales
```

Because no `where` clause has been included, all rows in the table are retrieved. To filter the result set for this query, a `where` clause would be included as follows:

```
select *
from sales
where region = "NW"
```

This `select` statement would retrieve rows from the `sales` table but limit the result set to rows that contain the value "NW" in the `region` column. To further filter the result set, the following query would be written using parentheses to group query results:

```
select *
from sales
where region = "NW" and
      sales_code = 23   and
      (sales_date = "1/1/1998" or
       sales_date = "2/1/1998)
```

This `select` statement adds additional filter criteria in the `where` clause to limit the result set to rows that contain a `sales_code` of 23 and a `sales_date` equal to January 1, 1998 or a sales_date = February 1, 1998. To express a join condition between two tables in query, the following select statement would be written:

```
select sales.*, region.region_name
from   sales, region
where  sales.region = region.region
```

This `select` statement joins the `sales` table with the `region` table. The join condition joins the `sales` table to the `region` table using the `region` column. Had the `where` clause been eliminated (which is allowed), the join between the two tables would have retrieved the *outer Cartesian product* between the two tables, effectively joining every row in the first table to every row in the second table.

Assigning Display Labels

A column in the select list can be assigned a display label. This can be useful for expression columns or for columns where the column name does not clearly identify the contents of the column. These column labels are meaningful only within the query in which they are created. The following query provides an example of defining display labels for a select list column:

```
select     region, sales_amount base_sale,
           (sales_amount * sales_discount) discounted_amt
from sales
```

This query contains column labels for the `sales_amount` that is named `base_sale` because it does not contain a discount, and `discount_amt` for an expression that applies a sale discount to the `sales_amount` column.

Identifying a Sort Order

The `order` by clause allows sort criteria to be specified for a query. Any columns identified in the `order` by column list must be listed in select list. If an expression is being identified in the sort column list, it can be identified by the ordinal position in the select list or by the display label created for the column as shown in the following query:

```
select region, sales_amount base_sale,
       (sales_amount * (1-discount_amount)) discounted_sale
from sales
order by base_sale, discounted_sales, 1
```

This query uses the display label for base_sale and discounted sale as the first two sort criteria for the select statement. The final column identified in the sort list is referenced by the ordinal position in the select list, in this case position one, the region column, the first column to appear in the select list. By default, the sort order for a column is in ascending order. Optionally, a descending sort order can be specified using the desc keyword as shown in the following query:

```
select region, sales_amount base_sale,
       (sales_amount * (1-discount_amount)) discounted_sale
from sales
order by base_sale desc, discounted_sale desc, 1
```

This query will return the same results as the previous query but with the results sorted in descending order of the base_sale amount, the discounted_sale amount, and the region. Thus, the result set would be sorted in the order of the largest base_sale to the smallest base sale, then the largest discounted_sale to the smallest discounted sale, and finally by the region column.

Specifying a Maximum Number of Rows Returned

The first n clause allows a maximum number of records to be returned to be specified for the query. This number is specified by a single numeric parameter for the first n clause. Any records beyond the specified number will be ignored. The following query retrieves a maximum of 50 records that satisfy the query. Because the query results are filtered by region and sorted by sales_amount, this will return the top 50 sales for the specified region.

```
select first 50 *
from sales
where region = "NW"
order by sales_amount
```

Grouping Records

The `select` statement allows record groups to be specified.
These record groups can be used with aggregate functions to provide a series of aggregate expressions such as subtotals for data
groups in the return set. The column list elements to be used as
aggregate groups are specified by the `group by` clause which
must appear after the `where` clause and before the `order by`
clause. Only columns appearing in the select list can appear in
the `group by` clause. If an expression is being used in the grouping, it must be specified by its ordinal position in the `select`
list. Aggregated columns cannot be specified in a `group by` list.
The following query groups the results of a query against the
`sales` table by `region`:

```
select region, sum( sales_amount ) base_sale,
       sum( (sales_amount * (1-discount_amount)) )
discounted_sale
from sales
group by region
order by base_sale desc, discounted_sale desc, region
```

This query retrieves records from the `sales` table and applies
aggregate functions to the `sales_amount` column and an aggregate function that applies a discount to the `sales_amount`. The
region column is specified in the `select` list as the column that
will be used to group the data returned. This query will return
rows that are aggregated by `region`, returning a total of the
`sales_amount` for each region and a discounted `sales_amount`
for each region. The sort order is applied after the aggregations
and groupings have taken place and sorts the results by the sum
of the base sale in descending order (specified by the `desc` keyword in the `order by` clause) for the region and the discounted
sale for the region in descending order and the region. The following is a sample result set returned by this query:

region	base_sale	discounted_sale
NW	115466.65	77362.65550000
SE	105559.98	70725.18660000
SW	92373.32	61890.12440000
MW	4773.32	3341.32400000

The `having` clause of the `select` statement specifies filter criteria for the grouped results (and thus can be used only in conjunction with a 'group by' clause. To filter the query shown previously for aggregated base sales of greater than 10,000 for the region, the following query could be used:

```
select region, sum( sales_amount ) base_sale,
       sum( (sales_amount * (1-discount_amount)) )
discounted_sale
from sales
group by region
having sum( sales_amount) > 10000
order by base_sale desc, discounted_sale desc, region
```

Note that the `having` clause appears after the `group by` clause and before the `order by` clause. This query would return the following results:

region	base_sale	discounted_sale
NW	115466.65	77362.65550000
SE	105559.98	70725.18660000
SW	92373.32	61890.12440000

Table Aliasing

Informix enables you to use a *short name* for a table, otherwise known as a table name *alias*. This facility allows a short name of a table to be specified in the `from` clause list for the table as follows:

```
select
from    parts p
where   p.initial_date < today and
        p.parts_code in ("E","F","C");
```

In this example, the filter criteria for the table is specified using a table alias. The table alias is specified in the from list using the following syntax:

```
. . .
    from parts p
```

Once the letter "p" has been specified as the alias for the table, the alias must be used throughout the select statement in place of the table name.

Using Subqueries

Subqueries provide a means to insert a query within a query. Subqueries can be placed throughout the where clause as a right-hand portion of expressions used in the filter criteria of the query. The following provides an example of a subquery:

```
select *
from sales
where sales.region in
    (select unique region
     from    sales_tmp
     where   region_type = "E");
```

This subquery provides a set of regions that will be used as filter criteria for the query. (Note that the unique keyword is used in the subquery to eliminate duplicate values.) Once the set of regions is known, this statement effectively evaluates to a statement similar to the following:

```
select *
from sales
where sales.region in ( "NE", "SE", "NW" );
```

Subqueries can form the basis for constructing complex queries. They provide a means of clearly stating the logic of a query. The following provides an example of a query with several subqueries:

```
select *
from    sales
where   region in (
    select unique region
    from sales_tmp
    where sales_amt > 10000) and
sales_disct <= (
    select max(sales_disct)
```

```
           from sales_tmp ) and
    sales_code not in (
           select unique sales_code
           from sales_reject )
```

This query provides an example of a more complex set of sub-queries and of the different expressions subqueries can be used where. The first subquery returns a set of regions that is examined by the expression for equality. This is identical to the previous example. But the next subquery performs a "<=" expression evaluation as follows:

```
... sales_disct <= ( select max(sales_disct) from sales_tmp )
```

The aggregate expression max(sales_disct) is used to select the maximum value of the sales_disct column from the sales_tmp table. Assuming this query were being used to produce a comparative report that compared the values in the sales_tmp table with the values in the sales table, then this query would filter on the sales_disct column (which we can assume would contain the discount on the sale) and retrieve rows that used the same or lower discount.

The final subquery (as follows) uses the "not" operator to filter the records being retrieved from the sales table based on the sales_code contained in the sales_reject table:

```
... sales_code not in (
           select unique sales_code
           from sales_reject )
```

The "not" operator forces the SQL processing to reject any records that contain a sales code found in the sales_reject table. In this case, the subquery produces a set of sales codes (sales_code) that is to be eliminated from the final result set. Likewise, the subquery could have returned an inclusive list as follows:

```
... sales_code in (
           select unique sales_code
           from sales_reject )
```

This subquery directs the SQL statement to retrieve a list of sales codes that will be used as an inclusive list for the query. The query will retrieve records where the sales codes are in the set of sales codes returned by the subquery.

If a subquery references the table of the main query, it is known as a *correlated subquery* as follows:

```
select *
from    sales s
where   s.region in (
    select unique region
    from sales_tmp st
    where st.sales_amt > 10000 and
          st.scode  = s.scode );
```

In this query, the sales table is scanned looking for a set of regions found by scanning the `sales_tmp` table. The `sales_tmp` table is scanned for sales where the amount of the sales (`sales_amt`) is greater than 10,000 and the `scode` in the `sales_tmp` and `sales` table match. This is a query that can be rewritten as a join instead of a subquery as follows:

```
select s.*
from    sales s, sales_tmp st
where   s.region = st.region and
        st.sales_amt > 10000 and
        st.scode  = s.scode;
```

In this query, the `sales` table is scanned and rows are returned based on a join between the `sales` table and the `sales_tmp` table. The `sales_tmp` table is scanned for only those rows where `sales_amt` is greater than 10,000 and the `scode` in the `sales_tmp` table matches the `scode` in the `sales` table.

Recursive Queries

There are times when the relationship of the data stored in a table requires a recursive data retrieval operation. This is the case with a parts table that contains rows with parts that are in turn created with other parts. Retrieving rows from this table would involve retrieving a row and then, for that row, determining if there are any related rows in the same table. The following is an example of this type of data relationship:

```
create table parts
    ( part_id integer,
      subpart_id integer,
      part_name char(20)
```

This simple table contains a part number and some information about the part, including a `subpart id`. The subpart ID references parts that reside in the *same* parts table. Each of these constituent parts can in turn have other related parts with their own constituent parts. Table 7-6 provides an example.

Table 7-6 Sample Parts Table Output

part_id	subpart_id	part_name
10	0	Door
11	15	Door handle
15	18	Lock
18	0	Lock tumbler

This table provides a partial list of the parts for a car door. The door contained a door handle and a lock in the door handle. These parts are listed as four separate parts but they are all still components of a single part, the car door. A recursive query to retrieve both the car door and its constituent parts is known as a *parts explosion* and could be partially expressed as follows:

```
select pa.*, pb.*
from    parts pa, parts pb
where   pa.part_id = pb.subpart_id
```

This query will retrieve records from the parts table *recursively*. As a record is retrieved, the `subpart_id` column will be examined and the table will be searched for a record that has the value of the `subpart_id` as a `part_id`, effectively retrieving all of the subparts for a given part. This will achieve a partial parts explosion of all of the parts in the table, but only two levels deep. To get a more complete parts explosion, a language that more completely supports recursion would be required.

Using Outer Joins

Most joins represent a *natural join* between the tables. With a natural join, only matches between the two tables for the join criteria specified are returned. If a row exists for one join table but no match exists in the other table, no row is returned.

An *outer join* allows rows to be retrieved even though the join condition specified in the query has not been satisfied. The following provides an example of an outer join:

```
select  sales.*, items.*
from    sales, outer items
where   sales.items_id = items.items_id and
        sales.sale_date <= today;
```

This query joins the `sales` table to the `items` table using the `sales_id` column, a primary key in the sales table and a foreign key in the `items` table. The query filters the results on the `sales_date` column and indicates the join to the `items` table is an outer join; this allows rows to be retrieved from the `sales` table regardless of whether a corresponding (joined) row exists in the `items` table. The results for this query could be as follows:

sales_id	sale_date	items_id	item_name
10	1/28/58	222	coffee mugs
11	2/1/56	NULL	NULL
13	6/6/91	123	dino poster
15	8/17/88	NULL	NULL

Note that result rows that satisfy the filter criteria for the `sales` table but do not satisfy the criteria for the `items` table substitute NULL values for the `items` table columns. Applications that are programmed using outer joins should be aware of this behavior and be prepared to manage NULL values for these columns.

SQL Unions

The `union` clause in SQL represents the union of two sets as specified by the SQL `select` statement. By default, the `union` clause will eliminate duplicate rows. This default behavior can be overridden by using the `all` keyword as part of the `union` clause. Multiple `union` operations can be specified in a single `select` statement as follows:

```
select *
from sales
where sales_id = 10
union
select *
from sales_tmp
where sales_id = 20
union
select *
from db1@svr1:sales
where sales_id = 30;
```

This SQL statement represents the union of three `select` statements. Use of the `union` clause requires that the number of columns in the `select` statement match and the data types relative to the ordinal position of the columns match. By default, duplicate rows are eliminated from the result set, though this behavior can be overridden.

Often a `union` clause can be expressed differently as a join condition; such is the case with the previous statement as follows:

```
select s1.*, s2.*, s3.*
from sales s1, sales s2, db1@svr1:sales s3
where s1.sales_id = s2.sales_id and
      s3.sales_id = s1.sales_id and
      s1.sales_id = 10 and

      s2.sales_id = 20 and

      s3.sales_id = 30;
```

This statement retrieves the same rows as the previous query, albeit with duplicate rows.

Segmenting Values with the union Clause

The `union` clause can be a useful means of segmenting return values by inserting a constant value into each of the `select` column lists returned by the query. This value is then used in the order by clause that follows the final query as shown in the following `select` statement:

```
select "C",* from sales
where region = "NW"

union

select "B",* from sales
where region = "SW"

union

select "A",* from sales

where region = "MW"

order by 1
```

This query retrieves rows from the `sales` table and sorts the results based on the first column of the `select` list. This column is a character constant that is used to force an artificial sort order on the result. This results in the values returned by the first `select` statement sorting first in the return results (sorted on the string constant "B" in the column list), followed by the second `select` and then the third (based on the "B" and "C" values in their column list) as shown in the following results:

(constant)	sales_id	sales_amount	sales_discount	region
A	1	1193.33	0.300000	MW
B	1	23093.33	0.330000	SW
C	1	23093.33	0.330000	NW

By default, the union clause eliminates duplicates. Since the incidence of duplicates in a query that returns sales results should not necessarily be eliminated (sales are often for the same amount by the same salesperson in the same region), the `all` keyword should be used with the `union` clause as shown in the following query:

```
select "C",* from sales
where region = "NW"

union all
```

```
select "B",* from sales
where region = "SW"

union all

select "A",* from sales

where region = "MW"

order by 1
```

This query retains duplicates and produces a return set that contains all sales that satisfy the filter criteria specified as shown in the following results:

(constant)	sales_id	sales_amount	sales_discount	region
A	1	1193.33	0.300000	MW
A	1	1291.33	0.300000	MW
A	1	2193.33	0.300000	MW
A	1	1193.33	0.300000	MW
B	1	23093.33	0.330000	SW
B	1	22011.23	0.330000	SW
B	1	13093.33	0.330000	SW
B	1	23093.33	0.330000	SW
C	1	11192.22	0.330000	NW
C	1	23093.33	0.330000	NW
C	1	183.32	0.330000	NW
C	1	1309.11	0.330000	NW
C	1	23093.33	0.330000	NW

The insert Statement

The insert statement adds rows to the specified database table. Rows are inserted using the following syntax:

```
insert into <table name> [(column list)] values (<value
list>)
```

The column list is optional. If the column list is not specified, then all columns in the table are used (an implied column list). The number of columns in the column list must match the number of columns in the value list or an error is returned. The columns are matched to the value list based on ordinal position. Data types must be compatible; the engine must be able to convert the value in the value list to the data type of the column or else an error is returned. If a column list is used and does not reference all columns in the table, the NULL value is substituted for columns omitted from the list.

The following provides an example of the `insert` statement:

```
insert into sales values ( 10, "1/28/58", 233.33, 10);
```

This statement would insert the specified values into the `sales` table. Alternatively, a column list could have been used as follows:

```
insert into sales (sales_id, sales_date, sales_amt)
     values (10, "1/28/58", 233.33);
```

This statement specifies a column list with three columns, and a value list is used to specify three values that directly relate to the columns in the column list.

The `insert` statement can use the `select` statement to retrieve values for an `insert` statement. This allows data from other tables to be copied to this table. The tables can reside in the same database instance, or in another database instance on another machine. The following provides an example of this use of the `insert` statement:

```
insert into sales select * from db1@new_jersey:sales;
```

This statement retrieves data from a sales table in a remote database instance. This effectively copies the data from that instance into the local instance. (Note that because another database instance is being accessed, it is required that both database instances be operating in the same logging mode.)

The update Statement

The `update` statement is used to update rows in a table. The statement specifies a table name and columns within the table to be updated. An optional `where` clause is used to specify the rows to be updated; if the `where` clause is omitted, all rows in the table are updated (without error). The syntax for this statement is as follows:

```
update <table name> set <column list = column value list>
   [where clause]
```

To update the `items` table, the following statement could be used:

```
update items
set     price = price * 1.1
where   item_code in ("XX","Z1", "BA" );
```

This statement would update all rows in the `items` table and raise the value of the price column by 10 percent (price * 1.1). This statement would update only rows where the `item_code` was one of the three codes referenced in the `where` clause of the `update` statement. If the `where` clause were eliminated from the `update` statement, it would read as follows:

```
update items
set    cost = cost * 1.1;
```

This statement updates *all* rows in the items table effectively executing a 10 percent price increase for all items. If a 10 percent increase in cost were desired, then this would be a logical statement to execute. If, however, a more restrictive update were desired, then this statement would represent a logical error but not a database error. This would be a logical statement to execute if a 10 percent cost increase needed to be executed for all items in stock.

Note Updating all rows in a table with a single statement does not constitute a database error. Executing an update that touches all rows in a table would not return an error message if executed in an Informix language tool (Informix-4GL, Informix-ESQL/C), but it does generate a warning (`sqlca.sqlwarn4`).

If the update is being performed in a transaction, it can be rolled back; but if not, the data would have to be restored from an archive. Application programmers should be aware of this behavior and program accordingly.

The delete Statement

The `delete` statement is used to delete rows from an existing table. The statement uses the following syntax to specify a table and filter criteria for the delete operation:

```
delete from <table name>
[ where   <filter criteria> ]
```

By default, in the absence of the `where` clause, this statement deletes *all* rows in the table. This delete operation would take place without an error.

> **Note**
>
> The `delete` statement is one of the more dangerous of the SQL statements. In the absence of a `where` clause, the `delete` statement deletes all rows in table. Executing a `delete` statement that touches all rows in a table would not return an error message if executed in an Informix language tool (Informix-4GL, Informix-ESQL/C), but it does generate a warning (`sqlca.sqlwarn4`).
>
> If the delete operation is being performed in a transaction, it can be rolled back; but if not, the data would have to be restored from an archive. Application programmers should be aware of this behavior and program accordingly.

Miscellaneous SQL

The following section covers a number of topics that do not fit neatly into SQL DDL or DML statements that preceded this section. The process of copying records from one table to another and using temporary tables is covered. Additionally, the Informix-SQL extension statements `load` and `unload` are covered in this section.

SQL Copy Operations

Informix (and SQL in general) does not provide an explicit *copy* statement. Data is copied from one table to another using a combination of `insert` and `select` statements. The following is the syntax of this operation:

```
insert into <target table name>
    select from <source table name>
```

A limitation on a `select` statement used in this manner is that the number and data type of the columns in the `select` statement are compatible with the number and data type of columns in the insert statement for the target table. The number of columns must match exactly, and the data types of the source columns must be the same or convertible into the data type of the target columns. The following provides an example of this operation:

```
insert into sales_holding( sales_id, region, sales_amt)
    select (sales_id, region, sales_amt)
    from    sales
    where region in ("NW", "SW", "NE" );
```

This statement selects specific columns from the `sales` table and *copies* them into the `sales_holding` table. The filter criteria on the `select` statement selects only rows where the `region` is one of "NW," "SW," or "NE."

The load and unload Statements

The `load` statement is an Informix SQL extension that allows data to be loaded from ASCII delimited files into the database. Files must be delimited using a pipe character (|) delimiter or a delimiter that has been referenced in the `load` statement using the optional `delimiter` clause. The syntax of the `load` statement is as follows:

```
load from <file name> [ delimiter 'c'] insert into <table
name> | values (<column list> )
```

Note that the `insert` statement component of the `load` statement supports a column list as the Informix-SQL `insert` statement does. The following statement illustrates the use of the load statement:

```
load from sales_data.dat
        insert into sales values (sales_id, region, sales_amt);
```

In this statement, data is loaded from the sales.dat file and inserted into specific columns in the sales table. All other columns in the sales record would be set to a NULL value for each row inserted. The contents of the sales.dat file would be in ASCII format and would contain the following:

```
101|NE|1222.22|
```

Note that no delimiter is required to start the first column. Note also that character strings do not need to be enclosed in quotes. The load statement reads the data and then performs conversion as long as the conversion makes sense. To include a special character in a load file, the "\" character must precede the character. For instance, to include the delimiter character as input into a table, the following line could appear in the load file:

```
101|\|N\|E|1222.22|
```

To unload data from a table to an ASCII file, the unload statement would be used. The syntax for the unload statement is as follows.

```
unload to <table name> [ delimiter 'c' ] <select statement>
```

The unload statement uses a select statement to identify the records to be converted to ASCII and written to the unload file. The unload file will contain rows of ASCII data with columns delimited by the delimiter character for the unload process. The delimiter character defaults to the pipe symbol (|) but can optionally be specified by the delimiter clause in the unload statement. The following statement unloads data rows specified by the select statement from the sales table to an ASCII file. Only the records from the "NW" region will be unloaded to the file.

```
unload to sales.dat select * from sales where region = "NW"
```

Using Temporary Tables

It is sometimes advantageous to use temporary tables. Though this can increase the amount of disk I/O that must be performed, it may nevertheless be a necessary part of the processing cycle, allowing data to be stored and then manipulated using SQL statements.

Temporary tables can be created explicitly using the `create temp table` statement (a variation of the `create table` statement), or temporary tables can be created by using the `into temp` clause of the `select` statement.

Temporary tables exist for the life of the session that created the table. Any processing that must be accomplished with a temporary table must therefore be accomplished during that session. This is generally considered a useful mechanism because a developer of a batch process need not be concerned with the housekeeping operation of removing temporary tables created during processing; it will happen automatically when the engine session ends. The following statement provides an example of a temporary table creation using the `create temp table` statement:

```
create temp table sales_tmp
   ( sales_id integer,
     region char(5),
     sales_amt decimal(12,2));
```

This statement creates a temporary table with three columns. This table would be created in one of the `dbspaces` specified as a temporary `dbspace` in the DBSPACETEMP configuration parameter, or if no temporary `dbspaces` were identified, in the root `dbspace`.

The explicit temporary table creation requires that the data type and size of each column of data to be stored in the table be specified explicitly in the statement. An alternative to this syntax is to use the `into temp` clause with the `select` statement. This clause allows a temporary table to be created implicitly using the data type and length of the columns specified in the `select` statement. An example of this statement is as follows:

```
select sales_id, region, sales_amt
from   sales
where  region in ("NW", "NE", "SW" )
into temp sales_tmp;
```

This statement would create a temporary table with the name `sales_tmp`. This temporary table would contain three columns: `sales_id`, `region`, and `sales_amt` as specified in the column list of the `select` statement. Data rows from the sales table that satisfy the filter criteria would be copied into the temporary table, and the temporary table could then be accessed by the process that created the table.

Informix Stored Procedure Language

The SQL language was never intended to be a programming language. It is a nonprocedural language that does not provide variables, has no flow-of-control statements, provides no specific error-reporting facilities, and does not provide the ability to create and save functions. The Informix stored procedure language provides these capabilities.

Stored procedures provide a limited programming language that can be used in conjunction with SQL. Informix-SPL expands the capabilities of SQL and allows some degree of business logic to be stored and accessed in the database.

Informix SPL allows variables to be created and manipulated in any valid SQL data type with limited exceptions for Byte, Serial, and Text. Variables can be declared using the convenient "like" syntax, which provides a type of database binding for variables and instructs SPL to retrieve the data type and length information using the database table declaration.

Stored procedures can receive values as parameters and can return one or more values. Parameters can be any valid data type.

Informix-SPL provides a number of programming flow-of-control statements as shown in Table 7-7.

The IDS stored procedure language allows *recursion* when a stored procedure function calls itself. This is a useful feature for solving a number of logical problems, often providing a more elegant solution to a problem than the corresponding iterative solution.

Comments can be inserted using the same syntax as Informix-SQL statements, with the following notations:

Table 7-7 *SPL Flow-of-Control Statements*

Statement	Purpose
foreach	Iterate thorough select results
for	Looping for a specified number of iterations
while	Looping while Boolean condition is satisfied
if	Conditional statement
let	Variable assignment

```
— this is a comment
{this is a comment}
```

A stored procedure is created using the following syntax:

```
create procedure <procedure name> ( [<parameter list>] )
 [returning <return value list>;]
<SPL statements>
end procedure;
```

To create a procedure named `sales_update`, the following statement would be executed.

```
create procedure sales_update( sales_id integer )
...
end procedure;
```

The body of the stored procedure would contain any number of valid SPL or SQL statements. When combined with SQL, the SPL flow-of-control statements provide a great deal of utility in manipulating database objects. The following sections detail the various language statements that comprise Informix-SPL and provide examples of usage.

The if Statement

The SPL `if` statement is used for conditional branching. A conditional expression is evaluated and if the expression evaluates to TRUE, then the block of statements following the `then` clause are executed. If the conditional expression evaluates to FALSE, the statements in the `then` clause are ignored and if the optional `else` clause has been coded, the statements there are executed; otherwise, statement execution begins after the end of the `end if` clause which terminates the `if` statement. Unlike the C programming language, which allows a conditional expression to evaluate to a mathematical value for TRUE or FALSE, SPL conditional expressions must involve two values and a relational (see Table 7-8) or an SQL Boolean expression and evaluate to a TRUE or FALSE value.

Table 7-8 Informix Relational Operators

Operator	Description
<	Less than
>	Greater than
<=	Less than or equal to
>=	Greater than or equal to
=	Equal to
!=	Not equal to

The Informix SQL operators IN, NOT IN, and EXISTS can also be used in SPL conditional expressions in conjunction with SQL subqueries. The following is the syntax for the `if` statement:

```
if [ NOT ] <conditional expression(s)> then
    <SPL statements>
[else <SPL statements> ]

end if;
```

Using a subquery within a conditional expression provides for a concise means of expression, as shown in the following examples:

```
...
if ( "NW" in (select unique region from sales) )
    then
        return 1;
else
```

```
        return 0;
end if;

if ( var1 in ( 1,2,3 ) )   then
    return 1;
else
    return 0;
end if;
...
```

SPL does not support a `case` or `switch` statement, so procedures that require multiple evaluations must use an `if/then/else` style of conditional evaluation as follows:

```
...
    if ( psales_code = "A" ) and
       ( s1.region = "NW" )    then

          select region_code
          into   pregion_code
          from   region
          where  region_type = 5;

          let region_count = region_count + 1;

       elif ( psales_code = "B" ) and
            ( s1.region = "NE" )   then
              select region_code
              into   pregion_code
              from   region
              where  region_type = 6;

              let region_count = region_count + 1;

       elif ( psales_code = "E" ) and
            ( s1.region = "SW" )   then
              select region_code
              into   pregion_code
              from   region
              where  region_type = 4;

              let region_count = region_count + 1;

    end if;
...
```

In this example, the region of the current record is evaluated against the sales code that has been assigned to this record. This `if/then/elif` statement clause allows the combination of region and sales code to be mapped to a region type code (in the `select` statement that is executed in the `if/then` block). This is complex logic that would be difficult if not impossible to code in SQL alone. (The SQL `case` clause introduced in version 7.3 does provide the ability to perform conditional mapping in SQL `select` statements; this clause is discussed later in this chapter.)

The return Statement and the returning Clause

Informix-SPL procedures can return one or more values. Return values must be declared in the optional `returning` clause of the stored procedure declaration. The syntax for the `returning` clause is as follows:

```
create procedure <procedure name> ( <procedure parameters> )
        [ returning <data type declaration>... ]
```

The `returning` clause can identify multiple return values of any valid SPL data type. When values are returned using the `return` clause, data types must match in number and position the data types that were declared in the `returning` clause. The following provides an example of a `returning` clause in an SPL declaration:

```
        create procedure proc1()
                                returning integer, integer, char(20);
                        ....
        end procedure;
```

To return one or more values from a procedure, the `return` statement would be used. The `return` statement uses the following syntax:

```
...
        return <variable list> [ with resume ]
...
```

The object of the `return` statement is a variable list containing one or more variables that are within scope (declared in the procedure or having global scope) for the `return` statement. By default, the `return` statement will return values and exit the stored procedure. If a stored procedure must iterate through a result set and return multiple rows of data, then this behavior must be overridden. The `with resume` clause allows values to be returned from a stored procedure and then allows procedure execution to resume with the statement following the `return` statement, as follows:

```
...
    return var1, var2, var3 with resume;
...
```

The foreach Statement

The `foreach` statement is used to effectively create a cursor in SPL. It executes an SQL statement and then iterates through the results, executing a set of SPL statements for each tuple of the result set. The following is the syntax for the `foreach` statement:

```
foreach <controlling SQL statement>

  <SPL statements to execute>

end foreach;
```

The `foreach` statement continues to loop or execute for each row returned by the execution of the SQL statement. When the SQL statement indicates that it has no more rows to return, the `foreach` loop terminates and SPL begins execution with the statement after the `end foreach` statement. The following SPL sample executes a `foreach` loop and returns results using the `return` statement with the `resume` clause:

```
...
    foreach select sales_rec_code
            into    psales_rec_code
            from    sales

        if psales_rec_code = 8 and
           psales_rec_code
             then
                 return ( psales_rec_code ) with resume;
        end if;
```

```
        end foreach;
...
```

This SPL fragment iterates through the select statement and, for each value returned, it evaluates the value and if certain conditions are met, the value is returned from the procedure.

The call statement

The SPL call statement executes a stored procedure from within an SPL statement. The syntax of the call statement is as follows:

```
    call <procedure name>( <parameter1>, <parameter2> )
[returning <value1>, <value2> ]
```

Using the call statement, a stored procedure can call another stored procedure to retrieve additional information. This allows a modular approach to stored procedure development to be used. The following provides an example of the call statement:

```
    ...
    foreach select sales_id into psales_id from sales

        call getAddLData( psales_id ) returning pdata1, pdata2;
    end foreach;
```

This call statement is executed from within a foreach statement. For each iteration of the foreach loop, the stored procedure getAddLData is called with the sales_id and returns two values into variables: pdata1 and pdata2.

The while Loop

The while loop is used to execute a set of statements while a certain loop condition is satisfied. The condition being tested in the loop is a valid SPL condition. The following is the syntax for the while loop:

```
while <condition>
  <statement block>
```

```
end while;
```

To execute a loop until a variable is set to a certain value, the
following statement would be executed:

```
...
let cflag = 1;
while ( cflag = 1 )

    select sales_id, sales_amt, region
    into    psales_id, psales_amt, pregion
    where scode = pscode;

    if psales_amt/10000 < 10000 then
        let cflag = 0;           — force exit from loop
        continue while;
    end if;

    if ( cflag ) then

            insert into sales_tmp (sales_id, sales_amt, region)
                        values ( psales_id, psales_amt,
                                        pregion );
    end if;

    insert into tracking_table values ( sales_id, sales_amt );

end while;
...
```

This code performs a loop as long as the cflag is set to 1. The
value of the cflag variable is dependent on the sales_amt. The
conditional statement that checks the value of the psales_amt
variable and, if it meets a certain condition, the value of cflag is
set to 0, which forces the loop to exit on the next pass.

The for Statement

The for statement is a looping statement used to perform one or
more actions for a set number of iterations. The syntax for this
statement is as follows:

```
for <control variable> ( <starting value> to <ending value> [STEP] <step value>)
```

```
<statements to execute>

end for;
```

An alternative format for execution of the for loop is as follows:

```
for <control variable> = <starting value> to <ending value> [
STEP <step value>]
```

The `for` loop expressions are computed before the start of the loop. The loop ends when the control variable reaches the value specified as the end value. The increment value is 1 by default, unless the `step` clause is used, in which case the increment value is the value specified in the `step` clause.

The control variable must be a previously assigned variable but need not be initialized before the loop, because it must be initialized at the start of the loop. The statements within the loop are executed on each iteration of the loop.

Iteration for a range of control variable values can be specified in two ways. One method would be to assign a starting value to the control variable using the "=" sign and assign an ending value with the "to" clause. The following statement demonstrates this approach:

```
. . .

for n = 2 to 20 step 2

    insert into table test_table values (n, 1, 2, 3, 4);

end for;

. . .
```

This statement performs 10 iterations, executing the `insert` statement on each iteration. The control variable is the variable n. The variable starts with the value of 2 and then increases in increments of two until the control variable reaches the value of 20.

The begin/end Statement Block

The `begin/end` statement block is used to group a set of statements together. Variable declarations can be made within a `begin/end` block, and these declarations can mask declarations

Tip

A `for` loop can be a useful means of generating test data. The following stored procedure inserts test sales records into a sales table by creating a `for` loop and iterating for the number of iterations specified as a function parameter, and executing an insert into the `sales` table for each iteration:

```
create procedure sales_test_data( iteration_count integer )

define loop_counter, n integer;
define region_code like sales.region;
define sales_code  like sales.sales_code;
define sales_amt   like sales.sales_amt;

for n = 1 to iteration_count

let sales_amt = n * 239.22;

- make some attempt to disperse these values among the data
set
if ( mod(n,2) = 1 ) then
   let region_code = "NW";
else
   let region_code = "NE";
end if;

if ( mod(n,3) = 1) then
   let sales_code = 6;
else
   let sales_code = 10;
end if;


   insert into sales values (n, region_code, sales_code,
sales_amt );

end for;
end procedure;
```

This procedure receives a number indicating the number of test records to create. This number is used to set the number of iterations for the loop to execute. The increment value is left at the default value of 1. Within the loop, there is some attempt to create a realistic set of values. The dollar amount of the sale is a function of the loop counter, and the values of the sales code and region code are dependent on whether or not the loop counter is an even or odd number.

elsewhere in the stored procedure, thus providing a certain level of encapsulation for the code within this block. Variables can also be declared close to where they are used in the code, making the code more readable. The following provides an example of the use of this statement:

```
create procedure sales_proc()

define n integer;

for n = 1 to 20

    begin
        define n integer;

        for n = 1 to 30

            insert into sales(n,"NW",3, 3334.33);

        end for;
    end; - ends the block

end for;
end procedure;
```

This statement demonstrates the use of the begin/end block by executing two for loops. The outer for loop uses a control variable named n. The inner for loop is enclosed within a begin/end block, thus masking any variable declarations made within this block. The variable n that is declared in this block is therefore separate and distinct from the variable declared at the start of the procedure. The inner declaration of the variable n is *out of scope* outside of the begin/end block, so the outer for loop can continue to execute correctly while the inner for loop executes.

The use of begin/end blocks can provide more concise code, allowing variables to be declared close to where they are used and masking any previous declarations.

The continue Statement

The continue statement is used to branch program execution to the start of an enclosing for/while/foreach loop. When this statement is encountered, the remaining statements within the loop are ignored. The syntax for this statement is as follows:

```
continue while | for | foreach;
```

The following SPL fragment demonstrates the use of the
`continue` statement:

...

```
foreach select sales_id, sales_name
        into   psales_id, psales_name
        from   salesman

        if psales_name = "FRED" then
            continue foreach;
        end if;

        insert into sales_bonus values ( psales_id, psales_name
);

end foreach;
```

...

In this procedure, a `foreach` loop is executed to retrieve
records from the salesman table. For each iteration of the loop,
the `psales_name` variable is checked to determine whether or
not the `sales_name` is "FRED." If the `sales_name` is "FRED,"
then the `continue foreach` statement is executed, branching
execution to the start of the loop and bypassing the `insert`
statement that follows the `if/then` statement. This code has the
effect of eliminating the insert operation (or any other statements that could follow) based on a set of conditions that are
part of the `if/then` statement.

The raise exception Statement

The `raise exception` statement is used to generate or raise a
specific SQL error. This allows the procedure to generate an error
based on a set of conditions that may not necessarily generate an
SQL error. The following is the syntax for the `raise exception`
statement:

```
raise exception  < SQL error>, <ISAM error>, <error text>
```

The "SQL error" is an integer that identifies one of the designated Informix-SQL error numbers, and the "ISAM error" is an integer that identifies one of the designated Informix ISAM error numbers (generally a lower-level data access error). The error text is a string that provides information on the error encountered.

The exception raised can be an existing SQL error (useful in the case where a procedure is used in an SQL statement and the developer would like the SQL statement to fail with an error code being trapped for other SQL statements). Alternatively, an error message that is unique to the stored procedure could be used to generate an error using a special error number -746 as follows:

```
...
  if psales_amt < 0 then raise exception -746, 0, "Bad data in
procedure sales_update"
  end if
...
```

In this SPL fragment, if the conditional statement is true, an exception -746 is raised with an error text that indicates the nature of the error. Code that is executing this stored procedure would trap the error and receive both the error number and error text and act accordingly.

The let Statement

The let statement is used to perform variable assignments. Unlike some languages, SPL will *not* perform assignments based on the use of the equality operator (i.e., n = 1). The let statement, like SQL, makes some attempt at type conversion, converting an integer to a decimal and converting a string to a numeric if the string contains a numeric value.

The let statement is flexible; it can be used to perform multiple-value assignments in a single statement and can use an SQL statement as a right-hand expression. The syntax for variable assignment is as follows:

```
let <variable1>, <variable2> ... = <value1>, <value2> ...;
```

The values on the right side must match the number of variables on the left side or an error will be returned. To perform value assignment for three variables in a single statement, the following syntax could be used:

```
let var1,var2,var3 = val1, val2, val3;
```

Data types of the values and target variables must either match or involve a conversion that makes sense. The values on the right side of the expression can be an expression that resolves to one or more values that match the data types of the variables on the left side of the expression, as follows:

```
let var1,var2 = spl_func1(), spl_func2();
```

Alternatively, an SQL statement can be used to return values on the right-hand side of the expression as follows:

```
let var1 = (select col1, col2 from qtab where scode=10);
```

Note that the SQL statement must be enclosed in parentheses for the value assignment. This form of variable assignment is equivalent to the `select into` statement but is in some ways clearer and more concise. The following statements demonstrate variable assignment using SPL:

```
let x,y,z = 2 * 3, 3 + 3, 2 + 2;
let avg_sales = (select avg( sale_amt) from sales where region = "NW" );
let full_name = first_name || middle_initial || last_name;
```

The first assignment statement assigns the value of the expressions 2*3, 3 + 3, and 2 + 2 to the variables x, y, and z respectively. The next assignment statement assigns the value returned by the right-hand expression, in this case an SQL statement, to the variable avg_sales. And the final SPL statement performs string concatenation to create a string variable with a full name, a concatenation of first name, middle initial, and last name.

The system Statement

The system statement allows an external program to be executed. This effectively provides SPL limited access to the operating system and applications that can be run there. The external application is run under the permissions of the user who has called the stored procedure. The following is the syntax of the system statement:

```
system  <external program and parameters>;
```

The program and parameters can be in a string constant enclosed in double quotes, in a string (`character/varchar`) variable, or in an expression that evaluates to a character string. The following `system` statement is used to send an error message to a log file:

```
system "echo Error in SPL processing >> spl_errors.log";
```

This statement writes an error message to an external log file using the redirected output of the Unix `echo` statement. Alternatively, the Unix `mail` program could have been invoked to send e-mail to a specific user.

SPL `system` Statement Return Values

Unfortunately, the only value returned from a program executed with the `system` statement is a nonzero exit status that is raised as an ISAM error along with an appropriate SQL error, so this is not a good mechanism for calling and returning values from external programs. In order to return a value from an externally executed program to a stored procedure, the external program would have to write data to a database table, and the stored procedure would then read the data from that table. The SPL `system` statement is probably best used to invoke external programs to send e-mail notification to users or to write to external log files.

The 'on exception' Statement

The `on exception` statement is used to trap runtime errors encountered during SPL processing. This statement allows programs to branch to specific procedures in the event an error is encountered. The following is the syntax for the `on exception` statement:

```
on exception
    | in (<error number list>)
    | < statement block >
    | set <sql error variable>, <isam error variable>, <error string>
    end exception | with resume;
```

The on exception statement can either execute a statement block based on the error being trapped or set other variables with the value of the SQL and ISAM error and a string that describes the error that has been encountered.

The on exception statement must be used after the variable declaration statements but before language statements in a stored procedure. The on exception statement is not explicitly executed; it merely defines a course of action to be taken if specific errors occur.

The in clause is used to specify a list of specific errors to trap. In the event the "in" clause is omitted, the on exeception statement would specify a course of action to be taken for all errors encountered.

Using the with resume clause specifies that after executing the statements in the on exception block, program execution would continue after the line of SPL that raised the error. The following procedure demonstrates the use of the on exception statement:

```
create procedure sales_update()
define psales_id like sales_id;
define psales_amt like sales_amt;
define error_flag integer;

let error_flag = 0;

on exception in ( -323 )

   let error_flag = error_flag +1;

end exception with resume;

foreach select sales_id, sales_amt
        into    psales_id, psales_amt

        insert into sales_upd ( sales_id, sales_amt)
           values ( psales_id, psales_amt );
end foreach;
insert into control_file( "sales_upd", "errors", error_count );

end procedure;
```

In this SPL fragment, an exception trap is created for the error -323. If that error is raised by SQL or by the procedure (with the raise exception statement), then the error_count variable will be incremented and execution will resume at the statement following the error. Before the procedure ends, the error count is written to a control file to record the number of errors encountered.

The define Statement

The define statement is used to declare variables within stored procedures. Variables can be virtually any valid SQL data type. Variables can also be declared to be *like* a table column, thus allowing variables to be bound directly to a table column. The syntax for the define statement is as follows:

```
define [ global ] <variable name> <data type> | like
<table_name.column_name> [ default <default value> ]
```

Variables are defined with local scope by default. Using the optional global keyword, variables can be declared to have global scope. Default values can be declared only for variables with global scope. To define a series of variables to be used in a stored procedure, the following statements would be executed:

```
....
define counter_variable integer;
define psales_id like sales.sales_id;
define pregion like sales.region;

define x,y,z smallint;
...
```

In this SPL fragment, a variable is first declared as integer to be used as a counter variable. The next two declarations declare variables to be bound in data type to a table column; these variables are declared using the like clause. The variable is declared to be the data type of the column when the procedure was created (at the time the procedure was compiled to pcode).

Note that variables by default have *local* scope—they are visible only in the procedure or begin/end block in which they are declared. For a variable to have global scope, it must be declared as a global variable as described in the following section.

Using Global Scope Variables in SPL

The `define` statement can be used to declare *global* variables—
variables that are visible to all procedures running during the
current session. Global variables are visible only within the current database instance during the current database session. The
following stored procedure demonstrates the use of a global SPL
variable:

```
create procedure demo_global1()
define global gvar1 char(20) default "this is global";
system "sleep 200";

end procedure;

create procedure demo_global2()
    returning char(20);

let gvar1 = "this is a new value";

return gvar1;

end procedure;
```

Executing the stored procedure `demo_global1` would first set
the value of `gvar1` to "this is global" and then execute a system
statement to sleep for 200 seconds, allowing the procedure to
pause long enough for the second procedure to execute Next, executing the stored procedure `demo_global2` would access the
global variable and set the value of `gvar1` to "this is a new value"
and return the value to the process that called the procedure.

The exit Statement

The `exit` statement can be used to unconditionally branch to a
statement following a control loop. The `exit` statement uses the
following syntax:

```
exit while | for | foreach;
```

The following stored procedure demonstrates the use of a
branching statement to exit a `foreach` loop:

```
create procedure get_vals()

define psales_id   like sales.sales_id;
define psales_code like sales.sales_code;

foreach select sales_id, sales_code
        into    psales_id, psales_code
        from    sales

        if psales_code not in ( "NW", "NE", "SW", "SE" )
            then
                    exit foreach; — bad value

            else
                    insert into sales_holding values (
psales_id, psales_code );
        end if;

end foreach;


end procedure;
```

Producing Debug Output with trace Statements

Informix-SPL provides a facility for producing debug output that is written to a file designated by an SPL statement. Debug output is known as *trace* and can be turned on and off using SPL statements. The syntax for these statements is as follows:

```
set debug file to <debug file name> | with append;
trace on  | off | procedure | <trace output string> ;
```

The set debug file statement is used to open the debug file or to create the file if the file does not exist. This statement must be executed before executing the trace statements that are to produce the debug output. By default, the debug file will be deleted and new output will be written. The with append clause overrides this default behavior and appends to the debug file.

Using the dbinfo Function in Procedures

The Informix tool set uses an internal structure to track errors and warnings, and to store information on the last statement executed. This internal structure is known as the `sqlca` structure and carries critical information such as the last serial value inserted by the current session and the number of rows that have been updated by the last `update` or `delete` statement executed. The original version of SPL did not provide the ability to interrogate the `sqlca` structure. Fortunately, the `dbinfo` function has since been added to the list of functions available in Informix-SQL. This function provides information on the `sqlca` structure as well as other important information that is of use to stored procedures.

Specifically, the `dbinfo` function can return several pieces of useful information, as follows:

* Last value generated by an `insert` into a `serial` column,
* Number of rows processed by certain SQL statements
* Session ID of the current engine session
* Name of a `dbspace` or `tblspace` for a `tblspace` or `dbspace` number or expression

The syntax for the `dbinfo` function is as follows:

```
dbinfo ( <parameter 1> [, <parameter 2>] )
```

The `dbinfo` function returns a single value. It accepts either one or two parameters depending on the first parameter passed to the function. The parameters passed are shown in Table 7-9.

Table 7-9 dbinfo Function Parameters

Parameter1	Parameter2	Information Supplied
dbspace	tblspace number	Table space number
sqlca.sqlerrd1		Last serial value inserted
sqlca.sqlerrd2		Number of rows updated
sessionid		Current session ID

The `dbspace` option reveals the name of the `dbspace` where a `tblspace` is located. The `tblspace` number is an integer or an integer expression that corresponds to an existing `tblspace`.

The sqlca options reference components of the sqlca informational structure, the structure used in Informix development tools to provide information and track errors concerning SQL operations. Executing the dbinfo function with the sqlca.sqlerrd1 option returns an integer corresponding to the last serial value generated by an insert operation into a serial column. Executing the dbinfo function with the sqlca.sqlerrd2 option returns an integer representing the number of rows touched by a select, insert, update, delete, or execute procedure statement. The following SPL fragment demonstrates the use of the dbinfo function:

```
. . .
    insert into sales_man( 0, psale_name, psales_address );
    let psales_id = dbinfo( 'sqlca.sqlerrd1' );
    insert into sales_region_assgnmt values( psales_id,
psales_region1);
    insert into sales_region_assgnmt values ( psales_id,
psales_region2);
. . .
```

This code fragment creates a sales_man record that contains a serial field, an automatically maintained unique identifier for a table stored as an integer value. This serial ID is used to uniquely identify the salesman—it is the salesman ID (sales_id). This sales_id is used as a foreign key in the sales_region_assgnmt table that defines the region assignments for the salesperson. Using the dbinfo function, the serial ID (sales_id) for the newly inserted salesman record is retrieved and stored in a program variable and then written to the sales region_assgnmt table where it will function as a foreign key to the sales_man table.

IDS Database Triggers

The IDS engine supports triggers, events, and corresponding actions that are initiated by database updates. Database updates are SQL insert, update, and delete statements.

Database triggers are an excellent means of enhancing database integrity. They can be used to enforce business rules, perform data validation, replicate data, and log system activity. IDS triggers can be cascading triggers, where an executed trigger carries out an action event that in turn initiates another trigger, and can use a snapshot of the data before the triggering action takes place.

The Create Trigger Statement

Database triggers are created using the `create trigger` statement. The syntax for IDS triggers is as follows:

```
create trigger <trigger name> insert on <table name> |
                              delete on <table name> |
                              update on <table name>
                [referencing <referencing clause> ]
                <action statements>
```

The `referencing` clause allows the data record from the triggering table to be referenced before the triggering action. This clause is needed because the nature of the table varies depending on the type of trigger (there is no *old* record before an `insert` operation).

The `action` statements provide a list of actions to be performed within the body of the trigger. Other than a conditional clause (using the `when` keyword), only specific SQL statements can be used in this statement block. Fortunately, the full SPL syntax is available to the trigger by allowing the trigger to execute a stored procedure statement in `action` statement blocks.

Only one trigger is allowed for an `insert` or `delete` statement. If certain conditions are met, then multiple triggers can be defined for an `update` statement.

Triggers can impact performance because no longer is a single SQL statement being executed for a triggered event—instead, multiple statements are being executed. Performance of triggering SQL statements should not be evaluated relative to single SQL statements but relative to the full set of SQL statements executed by the trigger.

Syntax and restrictions for triggers vary depending on the type of trigger being executed. The following sections detail the specific types of triggers and their syntax.

Insert Triggers

An insert trigger traps an insert event (an SQL `insert` statement) and allows actions to be specified for that event. The syntax for an insert trigger is as follows:

```
create trigger insert on <trigger name>
[referencing <referencing clause> ]
[before] | [for each row] | [after]
                        <action statements>
```

The trigger name must be a unique name for the database for which the trigger is created. The optional `referencing` clause is used to assign a name to correlate with the newly inserted row (as distinguished from the table name). The syntax for this clause is as follows:

```
...
        referencing  new as <correlation name>
...
```

The correlation name specified can be used within the `for each row` clause of the action statements (it logically can't be used in the `before` clause because no such row existed before the trigger event). This clause could be used as follows:

```
...

    referencing new as new_one
        for each row ( insert into sales_log values
(new_one.sales_id, new_one.region, new_one.sales_date) );
```

The action statements for the trigger are used to specify the actions to be executed for the triggering event. Actions can be an `insert`, `update`, or `delete` statement. An insert trigger cannot have an action clause that contains an insert or delete statement that references the triggering table. The syntax for trigger action statements is as follows:

```
...
before (<action statements>)
  for each row ( <action statements> )
    after ( <action statements> );
```

The `before` statement action statements are executed once before the row or rows are inserted. The `for each row` action statements are executed once for each row inserted. The `after` action statements are executed once after the row or rows are inserted. The following provides an example of action with an `insert` trigger:

```
create trigger ins_sales
      insert on sales
      referencing new as post
      for each row ( insert into sales_log values (
post.sales_id, post.sales_date, post.region, post.sales_code ) );
```

The trigger shown traps inserts into the `sales` table and, using a `for each row` statement, inserts `sales` records into the `sales_log` table. When a row is inserted into the `sales` table, the insert trigger trips and inserts the `sales_id`, `sales_date`, `region`, and `sales_code` columns together as a row into the `sales_log` table. This creates a running log of entries made into the `sales` table at any particular time.

Delete Triggers

A `delete` trigger allows record deletion events in a table to be trapped. This provides a useful means of storing rows before they are deleted from the target table should they be needed for some purpose, or for recording deletion activity: who deleted the record and when. The syntax for the delete trigger statement is as follows:

```
create trigger delete on <trigger name>
[referencing <referencing clause> ]
[before] | [for each row] | [after]
                <action statements>
```

Logically, a delete trigger will not be able to reference a new row, because it is the purpose of the `delete` statement to eliminate a row or rows from the table. The `referencing` clause can therefore reference only the old row as follows:

```
create trigger
   ...
      referencing old as <correlation name>
   ...
```

Note that if a delete trigger contains a `referencing` clause, it must include a `for each row` clause in the body of the trigger. The valid action clauses for a delete trigger are as follows:

```
create trigger
    ...
        before <action statements> |
        for each row <action statements> |
        after <action statements>
```

These action statement blocks are the same as for the other triggers, allowing actions to be executed before the delete, for each row being deleted and after the delete. If the delete trigger contains a referencing clause, it must contain a `for each row` action block. The following provides an example of a delete trigger:

```
create trigger del_sales
        delete on sales
        referencing old as pre
        for each row ( insert into sales_delete_log
                    values ( pre.sales_id, pre.sales_date,
                            pre.region,
                            pre.sales_code ) );
    ...
```

The delete trigger shown contains a `referencing` statement that assigns the correlation name for the old row (the row to be deleted) as `pre`. The `for each row` statement for the trigger will execute for each row that is deleted. As rows are deleted, part of the previous record will be written to the `sales_delete_log`.

In addition to writing what could be a recovery record to a recovery table, it may be useful to write a log record to a table to create a record of who is deleting sales records and when the records are being deleted. Because this log record should be written only once per delete operation and not for every row deleted, it should be placed in the `before` statement block that is only executed once for a trigger event as shown in the following trigger:

```
create trigger del_sales
        delete on sales
        referencing old as pre
        before ( insert into sales_log  values
                    ( sales_id, "DELETE", user, today ) )
        for each row ( insert into sales_delete_log
```

```
              values ( pre.sales_id, pre.sales_date,
                      pre.region,
                      pre.sales_code ) );
```

Within the `before` statement block, an `insert` statement is
executed to insert a record into a sales log table. The record contains information on who executed the delete operation: the
sales ID, a string indicating a delete operation has taken place,
the user name, and the current date provided by the keywords
"user" and "today" respectively.

Update Triggers

An `update trigger` is tripped when an `update` statement is
executed against a table. Like the `delete` statement, an `update`
statement can affect multiple rows; the `for each row` action
statement can be executed for each row affected by the `update`
statement. An `update` statement also has a valid `before` record
(before the update took place) and an after record (after the
update took place). The `referencing` clause can be used to
establish correlation names for both of these records using the
following syntax:

```
referencing old as <correlation name> | new as <correlation name>
```

This referencing clause allows both the old (pre-update) record
and the new (after-update) record to be referenced in the action
statement of the trigger.

As with the insert and update triggers, the action statements
can be executed for `before`, `for each row`, and `after` trigger
events using the following syntax:

```
create trigger
    ...
    before <action statements> |
    for each row <action statements> |
    after <action statements>
```

The `before` and `after` statement blocks are executed only
once during the trigger event—before the update has taken place
and after the update has updated the row or rows designated in
the statement. The `for each row` statement is executed for every

row updated by the trigger. If an update trigger contains a `refer-encing` clause, it must also contain a `for each row` clause.

As with the insert and delete triggers, the update trigger is a useful way of tracking changes to a table. When a user changes a record, the event could be logged and a before image of the record could be written to a recovery table as shown in the trigger that follows:

```
create trigger upd_sales
     update on sales
     referencing old as pre new as post before ( insert into
sales_log   values
                    ( sales_id, "UPDATE", user, today ) )
     for each row ( insert into sales_upd_log
             values ( pre.sales_id, pre.sales_date,
                     pre.region,
                     pre.sales_amt),
             insert into sales_upd_recs
               values ( post.sales_id,
                       pre.sales_date,
                       pre.sales_amt) )
```

The trigger shown here trips when an `update` to the `sales` table occurs. The `referencing` statement references both the previous record, the record before the sales update, and the postrecord, or the record that exists after the update. A `before` clause is used to store a log record indicating that the `sales` record is being updated, the user who made the update, and the date of the update.

In the `for each row` statement block, two `insert` statements are executed. The first `insert` statement inserts records into the `sales_upd_log` table to create a more complete log record for the update operation by inserting the previous (before update) version of the sales record. The next `insert` statement inserts a portion of the `post` (after the update) record into the `sales_upd_recs` table. The combination of the pre- and post-images of the record could be used to provide a useful view of the nature of the updates being made to the `sales` table.

The Utility of Triggers

In addition to the features outlined previously, triggers also provide the ability to call stored procedures and return values and to use a conditional clause to evaluate an expression and perform an action based on the evaluation of the expression. These features allow triggers to be used for logging, replication, user notification, and other functions. The following sections provide some examples of using triggers to perform these functions.

Executing Stored Procedures within Triggers

Triggers provide only a limited syntax for programming purposes. The IDS stored procedure language provides a much more extensive set of programming statements and facilities. Fortunately, the two features are combined by providing the ability to call stored procedures within triggers as is demonstrated in the following statement:

```
create trigger del_sales
      delete on sales
      referencing old as pre
      for each row ( execute procedure log_sales( pre.sales_id ) );
```

This statement creates a trigger that executes a stored procedure when sales records are deleted. For each row that is deleted, the stored procedure log_sales is called and is passed the sales_id of the record being deleted. The log_sales procedure could contain code to write a record to a sales log table adding additional information about the deletion, such as the name of the user executing the deletion and the date of the deletion. This procedure could even add additional integrity checking, which could abort the deletion if a set of business rules was not met. By using a stored procedure, more complex logic can be executed before the deletion occurs.

Update triggers can call stored procedures that return values using the into clause. These values can be returned *into* columns for the triggering table only. And a stored procedure with an into clause can be executed only within a for each row block of a trigger. The following is an example of such a trigger:

```
create trigger upd_sales
      update of sales_amount on sales
      referencing old as pre new as post for each row (
excecute procedure count_item( pre.item_id ) into
curr_in_stock);
```

This procedure executes during the update of the `sales` table. When a sales record is updated, this trigger executes a stored procedure to get a count of in-stock items for the item being updated. This count is stored in the `curr_in_stock` column of the record being updated. This effectively calculates the value of a calculated field as the data is being inserted into the database.

Using the when Clause in Triggers

The when clause is available to perform conditional tests in triggers. The when clause can perform conditional tests as with any other SQL conditional expression using tables, columns, and stored procedures that were in existence when the trigger was created. If the conditional expression resolves to TRUE, then the action statements are executed. If the conditional statements resolve to FALSE or unknown, the action statements are not executed. The following provides an example of the trigger statement when clause:

```
create trigger upd_sales
     update on sales
     referencing old as pre new as post
    for each row   when ( pre.sales_amt > 10000 )
              ( insert into sales_log values ( pre.sales_id,
pre.sales_amt, today ) );
```

This trigger performs a conditional test on the `sales_amt` column and if the `sales_amt` is greater than $10,000, a record is written to the `sales_log` table. If necessary, more than one when clause can be used to evaluate data in a trigger.

Using Triggers and Stored Procedures for Custom Replication

A useful feature of triggers is to perform finely grained and customized replication. Using insert triggers, entire records, specific columns, or expression values executed on columns can be replicated to tables in the current database or to tables in a remote database. Conditional statements in the trigger statement can be used to make decisions on where to replicate data. The following trigger provides an example of data replication using triggers:

```
create trigger ins_sales
        insert on sales
        referencing new as new
        for each row (
            insert into region11@corporate_hq:sales_replicate
                        values ( new.sales_date,
                                    new.region,
                                    new.sales_code,
                                    new.sales_amt );
```

This insert trigger takes rows being inserted into a table in the local database and for each row inserted, data from that row is moved to remote machine (region11) into a table named sales_replicate. This trigger has the effect of copying the row currently being inserted and replicating that row to another machine.

The replication scheme shown requires both the local and remote machine to be online for the trigger to complete successfully. Should the remote machine be offline for any reason, then the write to the remote table would fail and the entire insert operation would fail. This would mean that both the local and the remote machine would have to be online for inserts into the local sales table to succeed. An alternative to this form of custom replication would be to store rows or keys to rows to be replicated in a local table and then periodically flush the local table to the remote table. This method of replication is shown in the following example.

First, a table is created to record the records being inserted. To reduce the amount of system effort needed to accomplish the replication, only the primary key for the record is written to this table. The table contains a record with several columns to store the key field and then the name of the source table and the target table as follows:

```
create table replicate (
        key1 char(10),
        key2 char(10),
        key3 char(10),
        key4 char(10),
        stable_name char(18)
        rflag char(1)
);
```

An insert trigger is created for the table to be replicated. The trigger writes a record to the `replicate` table for the record being inserted as follows:

```
create trigger ins_sales
        insert on sales
        referencing new as new
        for each row (
            insert into replicate (key1, rflag, stable )
                          values (  new.sales_id, "N", "sales" ) );
```

This trigger inserts the primary key for the `sales` table into the replicate table and a flag with the value "N" that indicates the record is "new" and has not been replicated. A stored procedure would then read the records from the `replicate` table and replicate `sales` records to the remote table as follows:

```
create procedure replicate_sales()
define pkey char(10);

foreach select key1
        into    pkey
        from    replicate
        where   stable = "sales" and
                rflag  = "N"

        insert into region11@corporate_hq:sales_replicate
            select * from sales
            where   sales_id = pkey;

        update replicate
          set rflag = "U"
          where key1 = pkey;

end foreach;

end procedure;
```

This stored procedure reads records from the `replicate` table that have been written by the insert trigger for the sales table. The specific records can be retrieved by filtering on the `stable` (source table) field and the `rflag` field is set to "N" (for not replicated). A single primary key column is retrieved for this example, but a multipart primary key could also be stored in the `replicate` table and retrieved to replicate records.

The primary key is stored in an SPL variable that is then used to retrieve the record from the source table (the sales table) and insert the single replicated record into the `region11@corpo-rate_hq:sales_replicate` table. Once the record has been written to the remote table, the `replicate` record for the current record is updated and the `rflag` column is set to "R" for replicated.

Because the `replicate` table record being updated is being used in the controlling loop for the stored procedure, there may be restrictions on updating the `replicate` table in this case, depending largely on the isolation mode being used. An efficient alternative would be to use a *hold cursor* for the `foreach` loop and then update the replicate table using the `where current of` clause for update statement.

A more complex and robust implementation of this replication scheme would perform the process of replicating the records within a transaction, thus providing a higher level of data integrity and control. Note that because this replication scheme uses a *store-and-forward* approach to replication, there is some flexibility in when the actual replication of the records takes place. The `replicate` table could be read and records replicated once a minute or once a day; it is entirely dependent on the needs of the application for which the replication is being performed.

IDS String Manipulation Functions

IDS version 7.3 contains a set of long-awaited string manipulation functions that were added to the IDS engine. These functions allow substring operations to be performed with variable parameters (unlike SQL syntax, which require integer constant parameters). String functions are also available to trim strings, replace characters in strings, and pad strings with characters. Table 7-10 shows the string functions available in the 7.3 version of IDS.

The following sections detail each of these functions and provides examples of their usage.

Table 7-10 *New IDS String Functions*

Function	Description
trim	Trims trailing or leading blanks from a string
substring	Creates a substring from a string based on input parameters
substr	Creates a substring from a string based on input parameters
replace	Replaces specified characters in a string
lpad	Pads a string with characters starting from the left side of the string
rpad	Pads a string with characters starting from the right side of the string
upper	Converts a string to upper case
lower	Converts a string to lower case
initcap	Converts a string to initial capital letters

The trim Function

The trim function trims leading characters, trailing characters, or both from string expressions depending on the first parameter passed into the function. A single character is specified as the character to trim with the default being the space character. If the first parameter is specified, then both leading and trailing trim operations are performed. The following is the syntax for the trim function:

```
trim ( leading/trailing/both <single character to trim) from
<string to trim>) )
```

To trim question marks from the end of a string, the following SQL statement could be used:

```
select sales_id, trim( trailing "?" from sales_code ),
sales_amt
from    sales;
```

This SQL statement would retrieve a number of columns from the sales table including the sales_code, which could contain trailing "?" characters. These characters are trimmed from the end of the column string value using the syntax shown.

The substring Function

The substring function resolves to a substring of the string passed into the function based on the parameters passed to the function. A starting position and ending position are both passed into the function. If the ending position is eliminated, the function returns a string to the end of the string passed into the function. A negative parameter can be used to count back from the end of the string. The following is the syntax for the substring function:

```
substring( <string expression> from <starting postion> to <ending position> )
```

To take a substring of the character string stored in a column, the following syntax could be used:

```
select sales_id, substring( region from 1 to 3 ), sales_amt
from sales;
```

This query will retrieve the sales_id, the first three characters of the region, and the sales amount from the sales table. In some cases, specific character positions in a column string can have a specific meaning; the substring function is a useful means of extracting this information.

The substr Function

The substr function performs the same functions as the substring function but with different syntax. A source string is specified along with parameters for the starting position and ending position for the substring. The following is the syntax for the substr function:

```
substr( source, start, length)
```

The following query performs the same function as the previous substring function query but uses the substr function instead:

```
select sales_id, substr( region, 1, 3 ), sales_amt
from sales;
```

The replace Function

The `replace` function is used to replace characters in a string. The following is the syntax for the `replace` function:

```
replace( string_to_process, string_to_replace [,
replacement_string] )
```

If the replace function is called with all three parameters, then the occurrence of the `string_to_replace` is replaced with the string value of the `replacement_string` parameter. If the optional `replacement_string` parameter is not included in the function arguments, then the `string_to_replace` string within the source string is deleted. The following is an example of the replace function:

```
select sales_id, replace( region, "SW", "NW" )
from sales;
```

This SQL statement uses the `replace` function to change every occurrence of the string "SW" within the `region` column to "NW" and then returns that value.

The lpad Function

The `lpad` function is used to left pad strings—to add spaces or blanks to the left of strings, a common requirement of many key fields. The syntax for this function is as follows:

```
lpad ( source_string, length [,pad_string] )
```

If the `pad_string` parameter is eliminated, then spaces will be used to pad the string. To left pad a column value four spaces before inserting it into a table, the following syntax would be used:

```
insert into sales ( sales_id, sales_code ) select sales_id,
lpad( sales_code, 4) from sales_db@remote_machine:sales;
```

The rpad Function

The `rpad` function performs the same function as the `lpad` function but performs right padding instead. It adds a specified number of spaces to the right-hand side of a string expression. The syntax for this function is as follows:

```
rpad( source, length [, pad string ] )
```

The Case Conversion Functions

A number of case conversion functions are available to work on strings. These functions effectively allow case-insensitive queries to be performed by shifting character strings up or down on both data insert and retrieval. These functions are listed in Table 7-11.

Table 7-11 *Case Conversion Functions*

upper	Shift each character in the string to uppercase
initcap	Every word in the string gets an initial capital letter
lower	Shift each character in the string to lowercase
Initcap	Shift each initial letter of each word to upper case

To shift a string to upper case before inserting it into a table, the following syntax would be used:

```
insert into sales_tmp (sales_id, sales_code)
        select sales_id, upper(sales_code) from sales;
```

To set a column to initial capitals before retrieval, the following syntax could be used:

```
select sales_id, initcap( salesman_name ) from sales;
```

New Version 7.3 Features

The 7.3 release of IDS added several important new features to the engine. These features enable you to quickly return the first page of rows from a query, to force a table to become memory resident, to execute decision logic in queries using a "case" statement, and to provide directives to the optimizer for use in developing its query plan. Though small in number, these features add a tremendous amount of flexibility to the engine. The following sections detail the use of several of these new features.

The case Statement

The case statement is used as an SQL expression that allows a series of conditions to be tested and values returned based on those conditional tests. The case statement can be used wherever a column expression is valid, such as in a select list or the where clause of the select statement. The following is the syntax of the case statement:

```
case [value]
    when <condition>
        then
            <expression>
            ...
    else
        <value>
end
```

A case expression allows conditional value substitution to be performed in the select statement, a useful feature that greatly expands the power of SQL queries. The following provides an example of the case statement:

```
select sales_id, case region
                    when "SW"
                        then "South West"
                    when "NW"
                        then "North West"
                    when "SE"
                        then "South East"
                    else
                        "Unknown Region"
                end,
        sales_amt,
        sales_date
    from sales
```

This SQL statement retrieves values from the sales table and evaluates the region column. As is common in relational databases, the `region` column does not contain the full text of the region name but is instead a three-character code that relates to the region name. The `case` statement is used to evaluate the `region` code and return the region name without requiring a join to the `region` table. The `else` condition is used if none of the other conditional expressions evaluates to TRUE. If the `else` condition had been eliminated and all the conditional expressions returned FALSE, then the `case` expression would return a NULL value.

A common problem in relational databases is that of NULL values. A NULL represents the absence of data and thus has no mathematical value. What is often required in situations where a column is to be used in a mathematical expression is to convert any NULL values to a valid number, as follows:

```
select region, avg( case sales_amt
                         when NULL
                              then 0
                    end )
from sales
group by region
```

This `select` statement retrieves data from the `sales` table and converts any NULL values that may exist in the `sales_amt` column to a value of 0. The `avg` function is used to compute the average sales amount for a region, but the `avg` function does not count NULL values in its average. It is important, therefore, to convert the NULL values to a 0 in order to get an accurate average count for the column.

The decode Function

The `decode` function has a utility similar to that of the `case` statement—it evaluates a condition and returns a result based on that condition. The following is the syntax for the `decode` function:

```
decode ( <expression>, <when expression>, <result expression> ...)
```

The functionality of this statement is similar to that of the `case` statement as shown in the following example:

```
select sales_id, decode( region,
```

```
                                        "SW",  "South West",
                                        "NW",  "North West",
                                        "NE",  "North East",
                                        "SE",  "South East",
                                        "Unknown Region" ),
                    sales_amt
        from sales
```

In this `select` statement, the `region` code is evaluated to the region name and based on the value of the region column, a region name is returned for the column value. The `when` `expression`/`result` `expression` pairs are passed to the function for a series of expressions to evaluate. The last value to appear in the function argument list is an `else` expression value to be used if all previous conditional statements fail. If the final `else` expression is not passed to the function, a NULL value is returned.

The nvl Function

The `nvl` function is an alternative means of managing NULL values. The `nvl` function evaluates a pair of expressions—`expression1` and `expression2`. If `expression1` is NULL, then `expression2` is returned. The following is the syntax for the `nvl` function:

```
nvl( expression1, expression2 )
```

To manage NULL values in the `sales_amt` column of the `sales` table, the following expression could be used:

```
select region, avg ( nvl( sales_amt, 0 ) )
from    sales
group by region
```

This `select` statement retrieves data from the `sales` table and generates an average sales amount for each region. To eliminate the undesired effect of NULL values on the `avg` function, the `nvl` function is called to convert any NULL values to 0 before being evaluated by the `avg` function. (Note that this expression serves the same purpose as the `case` statement in the previous example.)

Creating Memory Resident Tables and Indexes

All IDS data pages are read into the shared memory buffer before they are processed. But there is a limited amount of memory available to handle these buffers. Once pages have been read into memory, the LRU queue management then makes decisions about when these buffer pages should be flushed to disk to make room for new pages. A least recently used mechanism attempts to find pages that have not been used (recently) and should thus minimize the instances where a page that is needed has been flushed to disk.

To avoid situations where pages that are needed have been flushed to disk, the capability to define a table as memory resident has been added to IDS 7.3. This does not guarantee that a table that has been specified as memory resident will always be present in memory when a process requests data from that table, but the database engine will make an effort to flush those pages from tables designated as memory resident to disk last. The syntax for designating a table or index as memory resident is as follows:

```
set table <table name> | index <index name>  [ ( <dbspace list>
) ] memory_resident | non_resident [<fragmentation options>]
```

The dbspace list allows portions of the table or index in specific dbspaces to be designated as memory resident. To set the entire sales table (including all fragments in various dbspaces) to memory resident, the following syntax would be used:

```
set table sales memory_resident;
```

To set specific fragments from the sales table to memory residency, the following statement would be executed.

```
set table sales ( dbspace1, dbspace2)  memory_resident;
```

This statement would place the fragments of the sales table in dbspace1 and dbspace2 to memory residency status. To set the sales_idx1 index to resident, the following statement could be used:

```
set index sales_idx1 to memory_resident;
```

To remove the `sales` table from residency, the following statement would be used:

```
set table sales to non_resident;
```

Note that table residency is in effect only during the session in which the `set to resident` statement is executed. Once an instance has been shut down and restarted, no tables are kept resident until the set residency statement is executed again.

Using Optimizer Directives

Though the Informix optimizer generally makes very good decisions about query paths, there are occasions where the optimizer does not have sufficient information in the form of statistics to make the correct decision. When this occurs, there are optimizer directives available (as of IDS version 7.3) to provide hints to the optimizer so that the best query path is chosen. Optimizer directives are available in several forms, as follows:

- Access method
- Join order
- Join method
- Optimization goals

In order to provide compatibility with previous versions of the engine that did not support optimizer directives, the optimizer directives appear in an SQL comment block. This allows the same query with optimizer hints to be directed at IDS 7.3 engines and pre-IDS 7.3 engines where the optimizer directives, because they appear in a comment block, will be ignored. A comment block can be one of the following:

```
- this is a comment
{ this is a comment }
```

The optimizer directive appears in a comment block with a "+" sign as the first character. The syntax for optimizer directives is as follows:

```
{+ <optimizer directive>}
```

Note that the optimizer directives can be used in the `select`, `update`, and `delete` statements. A number of factors are considered by the optimizer when a query path is chosen. Optimizer directives enable the developer to provide hints for a number of these directives. Multiple directives can be included in a query as long as they appear in the same comment block. The IDS 7.3 optimizer directives are listed in Table 7-12.

Table 7-12 *Optimizer Directives*

Directive	Type	Description
INDEX	Access method	Consider only the identified index for accessing the table
AVOID_INDEX	Access method	Do not consider the identified index for accessing the table
FULL	Access method	Forces the optimizer to choose a full table scan on the specified table
AVOID_FULL	Access method	The optimizer is directed to avoid a full table scan on the specified table
ORDERED	Join order directives	Forces the optimizer to join tables in the order in which they appear in the from clause
USE_NL	Join method	Forces the optimizer to choose the nested loop
USE_HASH	Join method	Forces the optimizer to choose a hash join method
AVOID_NL	Join method	Directs the optimzer to avoid the nested loop join method
AVOID_HASH	Join method	Directs the optimizer to avoid the hash join method
FIRST_ROWS	Optimization goal	Directs the optimizer to process the query to retrieve the specified number of rows first
ALL_ROWS	Optimization goal	Directs the optimizer to process the query to retrieve all rows for the query (this is the default behavior)

To direct the optimizer to efficiently retrieve the first 100 rows of a query, the following statement could be executed:

```
select —+ FIRST_ROWS(100)
         sales_id, sales_code,sales_amt
from   sales
where region = "NW"
```

To direct the optimizer to use a nested loop join to join rows from two tables, the following statement could be executed:

```
select {+ USE_NL( region )}
        sales_id, r.region_name, sales_amt
from  sales s, region r
where s.region = r.region;
```

To have the optimizer choose a specific index to access a table in the query, the following syntax could be used

```
select -+ INDEX( sales sales_idx1 )
        s.sales_id, s.region, r.region_name
from  sales s, region r;
```

This query joins the `sales` table to the region table and directs the optimizer to use a specific sales index to access the table.

Chapter Summary

This chapter has covered a subset of the Informix-SQL query language, specifying the most important SQL statements for administrators and developers, from the basic SQL select statements to the Informix Stored Procedure Language (SPL). Table constraints and triggers have also been covered, and practical applications of these statements have been demonstrated.

A number of long-awaited features have been added in the Informix 7.3 release, including string manipulation functions, the SQL `case` expression, and optimizer hints. These new features have been explained and demonstrated in this chapter.

Next Chapter

The next chapter begins coverage of the Informix-4GL programming tool. Informix-4GL is a robust fourth-generation programming language capable of performing data retrieval, formatting, manipulation, and updating with speed and functionality not available in Informix-SQL or SPL. The learning curve for Informix-4GL is faster and the ease of use for Informix-4GL is greater than that of third-generation languages such as C or C++. And Informix-4GL provides a level of language safety not available in many third-generation languages.

With these significant capabilities, Informix-4GL is an invaluable tool for the database administrator or application developer working with the IDS engine. The following chapters will provide solid coverage of all important aspects of this language.

Introduction to INFORMIX-4GL

Informix-4GL is a proprietary application language and tool developed early in the history of Informix. Despite its age, it has survived as a classic product, a well-designed and focused product that at one time had captured a significant portion of the Unix application development market.

Informix-4GL is an excellent adjunct to the IDS database, providing extensive data manipulation and reporting capabilities. It is an extremely easy-to-learn language with English-like syntax and seamless Structured Query Language (SQL) integration. It provides capabilities and performance that surpass that of Stored Procedure Language (SPL), filling a niche for a tool that can easily be used to program those one-up reports database administrators and application developers are so often tasked with creating. And in the current IT world of the ubiquitous data warehouse and data store, this is a tool that can handily be used to perform the task of data filtering, transformation, and aggregation efficiently and with minimal programming effort relative to using a language such as C.

The INFORMIX-4GL Language

Fourth-generation languages (4GLs) were designed to reduce programming effort through the use of nonprocedural language statements. Whereas *procedural* statements (e.g., if, while, for statements) require a programmer to tell the computer specifically how to do something, *nonprocedural* statements can be used to simply tell the computer what to do; it is up to the language to handle the details. Fourth-generation languages represent the current culmination in the progression of programming languages, as shown in Figure 8-1.

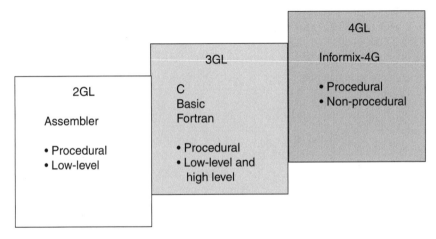

Figure 8-1 *The History of Language Generations*

What distinguishes INFORMIX-4GL from other fourth-generation languages is a very flexible mix of procedural and nonprocedural statements. As the designers of INFORMIX-4GL knew, a 4GL cannot depend on nonprocedural statements alone. In order to be flexible and provide sufficient functionality to develop a complex application, a language must contain an adequate number of procedural statements. Without an adequate set of procedural statements, a 4GL programmer would be forced to resort to 3GL statements in order to complete the application; this is a tedious process that quickly eliminates any advantage of using a 4GL in the first place.

The INFORMIX-4GL language is composed of *statements, operators, blocks,* and *functions.* An INFORMIX-4GL program can be defined as any arbitrary combination of any of these with a valid entry point and a valid exit. The valid entry point is through the main program block, and the valid exit is either implicit (as with the `end main` statement that indicates the end of the main program block) or the `exit program` statement.

Statements and Operators

INFORMIX-4GL statements control program operation. They can be *flow-of-control, conditional branching* operations, or *nonprocedural* statements. A block can be a *program* block, a *function* block, or a *report* block.

Program Blocks

Of the program blocks, only the **main** block is required; all other INFORMIX-4GL blocks are optional. There are no requirements for other program blocks, though adhering to the principles of modular programming would certainly encourage the use of the function block.

At runtime, blocks are executed in a serial fashion with the main program block being executed first. Additional blocks, such as a function block or a report block, are executed when the program flow of control passes control to one of these blocks. Program execution finishes when an `exit program` statement is encountered, or when the `end main` block-terminating statement is encountered.

A *function* is composed of all the language statements and operators between the function declaration (`function function_name`) and the `end function` statement. More than one function can be contained in a source code module. A function declaration cannot be made within a function declaration.

Language Operators

INFORMIX-4GL operators can be mathematical operators such as addition, subtraction, multiplication, division, module, or string-oriented operators such as the string concatenation operator.

Operators can optionally be grouped explicitly using parentheses. Order of precedence and a description of operators are provided in Chapter 9, "Screen Forms."

Memory Control

INFORMIX-4GL performs all memory allocation, providing a level of safety not generally available in other languages such as C. The programmer does not have direct access to program memory. While this may seem a hindrance to some who are used to the freewheeling access to memory provided by the C language, it does eliminate the need to spend several days tracking down an infamous C language *memory leak,* which usually doesn't reveal itself until the program is already in full production.

Data Typing

INFORMIX-4GL provides fairly strict data typing. Variables must be declared to be a specific data type before they are used; variables do not simply spring into existence with data type implied by assignment statements. With this level of control, the programmer can be reasonably confident of the value and characteristics of a variable at a particular point in time.

Strict data typing can be constraining when data conversion is needed. With Informix-4GL, a range of data conversion is implied during assignment statements. In order to convert the data type of a value contained in a variable, the programmer need only make an assignment of the variable to a variable of the desired data type; if the conversion is appropriate and can be performed, then Informix-4GL makes the conversion.

Database Interaction

The INFORMIX-4GL language is tightly bound to Informix through the industry-standard Structured Query Language (SQL). Informix data types are the equivalent of Informix-SQL data types and SQL is seamlessly integrated into the language.

Parts of a 4GL Application

Informix-4GL applications make use of a *two-tier* architecture, composed of a *front-end* application (which comprises the compiled program), and the *back-end* (which is essentially the IDS database). Communication from the front-end to the back-end program is accomplished using the IDS database connectivity layer, the same communication layer used in the ESQL/C tool.

An INFORMIX-4GL application is composed of a set of source code *modules*. A source code module contains a set of statements, data variables, and operations performed on the data variables. Only the main block statement is required in at least one of the source code modules; all other statements are optional. The modules are compiled and linked together to form the executable INFORMIX-4GL application (see Figure 8-2). This process can be streamlined using the Unix `make` utility or the INFORMIX-4GL programmer's environment.

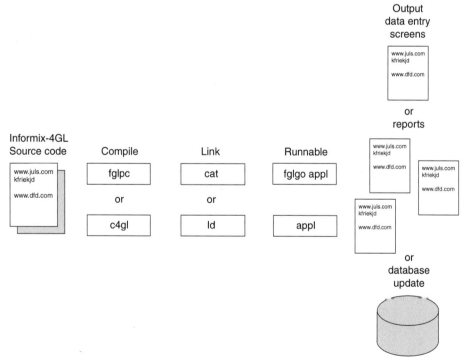

Figure 8-2 INFORMIX-4GL Development

There is no specific rule for the composition of INFORMIX-4GL program modules. A particular module is usually composed of a set of function blocks. Each module then contains a group of INFORMIX-4GL functions, which would all logically perform some portion of the overall task of the application.

Adhering to the rules of modular programming would produce a program that is composed of a set of source code modules, each module containing a set of statement blocks. There would, by definition, be only one main statement block. There should be multiple function blocks spread across several different program modules. Each function block would have a limited number of program statements and operations. The size of each function would be kept small to improve readability and maintainability of the application.

User Interaction with Informix-4GL

INFORMIX-4GL performs the majority of its screen interaction using the *screen form*. The screen form is a character-based facility for performing user interaction, either through data entry or output of data to the screen. The Informix-4GL screen form allows data screens to be developed in text files, compiled, and then used by the application at runtime. Informix-4GL programs interact with screen forms using a series of statements to input, validate, and display data to the screen.

Reporting and Data Filtering

Informix-4GL provides a rich nonprocedural reporting syntax. This syntax allows a programmer to create one or more SQL statements to scan data in the database, sort the data, pass the data to a report function, and execute a series of nonprocedural statements to create control breaks and format the data being processed. Informix-4GL control breaks are useful points to process the data being scanned using procedural language statements. This facility can also prove very useful when filtering and transforming data for inserting into a data warehouse or data mart.

Modular Programming with INFORMIX-4GL

INFORMIX-4GL provides a balance of procedural and nonprocedural statements; it does so with block-oriented statements that are designed to promote a modular method of application development. Though meant as a COBOL replacement, it does not contain any of the modular programming failings of COBOL. In fact, its design borrows more from such block-oriented modular languages as PASCAL, ALGOL, and C than COBOL or FORTRAN.

The benefits of modular programming have been known and documented for some time. INFORMIX-4GL was written with modular programming in mind. The language is block-oriented and contains a variety of both structured procedural and structured nonprocedural statements that make modular application development easier.

Modular programming requires that an application be developed from a set of small to medium-sized source code modules. Complexity is managed by keeping the size of modules small and encapsulating functionality in small, reusable functions. Many of these functions could be *black-box* functions; they could contain code with which the programmer need not be concerned. The programmer need only be concerned with how to use the functions, not with the specifics of their operation. The programmer only needs to know what parameters will be passed into the function and what parameters will be returned.

INFORMIX-4GL was designed to be used in this manner. Its full-featured implementation of functions provides the capability to receive multiple function parameters of virtually any valid data type and return any number of values. This implementation of functions makes the development of modular function libraries easier.

Informix Data Types and Operators

As a language that must interact with the IDS database, the Informix-4GL language supports all IDS data types and operators required to manipulate these data types. The following sections detail the Informix-4GL data types and valid data type operators.

Informix-4GL Data Types

INFORMIX-4GL supports the full range of data types supported in most 3GL languages. INFORMIX-4GL simple data types have a one-to-one correspondence with the data types supported by the Informix database, including the Binary Large Object (Blob) data type. (More complex data types, such as arrays and records, obviously do not have this correspondence.) Table 8-1 lists all INFORMIX-4GL data types along with their storage size and their minimum and maximum values.

Table 8-1 *Valid INFORMIX-4GL Data Types*

Data Type	Length	Minimum Value	Maximum Value
smallint	2	-32,767	+32,767
integer, int	4	-2,147,483,647	+2,147,483,647
smallfloat, real	4	platform-dependent	platform-dependent
float, double precision	8	platform-dependent	platform-dependent
decimal,dec, numeric	precision/2 + 1	-32 significant digits	+32 significant digits
money	precision/2 + 1	-32 significant digits	+32 significant digits
date	4	1/1/0001	12/31/9999
char, character	programmer-defined	1 byte	32,767 bytes

Smallint

The INFORMIX-4GL smallint is a two-byte integer and corresponds to the C short integer. It is signed and supports a minimum/maximum value of +/- 32,767. An integer overflow is an error in INFORMIX-4GL. In the p-code/RDS version of INFORMIX-4GL, this error is trapped by default. In C-code-compiled INFORMIX-4GL, this error is only trapped if the whenever any error statement is in effect.

Integer

The INFORMIX-4GL integer is a four-byte integer that corresponds to the C long integer. It is also signed and supports a minimum/maximum value of +/- 2,147,483,647. Integer overflow errors are trapped as they are with the `smallint` data type.

Unfortunately, there are no macro constants provided to test for maximum integer values; the programmer must store these values in variables and check them accordingly. If an Informix-4GL screen form is being used to allow the user to input these values, the screen form automatically validates the numeric data being entered and returns an error code if the number entered greater than the maximum allowed value for an Informix `integer`.

Smallfloat

The INFORMIX-4GL `smallfloat` is roughly equivalent to the C language `float` or `real` data type. It has a minimum and maximum value that is officially machine-dependent but is generally on the order of +/- 10^{16}.

Decimal

Because of the difficulties and variations associated with using floating-point numbers on early Unix machines, Informix developed their own form of floating-point number representation: the `decimal` data type. This design move had the added advantage of making it easier to move data over the network, because the numeric data was stored in a consistent format from machine to machine.

Internally in the INFORMIX-4GL program, the decimal data type is stored as shown in Table 8-2.

The decimal data type can be either fixed-point in representation if a precision is specified during the declaration process, or floating-point if no precision is specified. Its precision is very

Table 8-2 *Decimal Data Type Storage*

Component	Storage
Exponent	2-byte Integer
Decimal position	2-byte integer
Number of digits	2-byte integer
Digits	Character with a length of declared precision/2

large, on the order of +/- 10^{32} or 32 significant digits. The INFORMIX-4GL declaration for this data type is:

```
define dec_var    decimal
```

Because this declaration does not specify precision, this variable will have the default of 16 digits of precision and the decimal point will float. If, however, the variable had been declared as:

```
define dec_var decimal(10)
```

it would create a `decimal` variable with a maximum number of 10 significant digits; or the variable could have been defined as:

```
define dec_var decimal( 10, 2 )
```

This would create a `decimal` variable of 10 digits with a precision of 2 (2 digits to the right of the decimal place).

If m is the precision and n the scale, the largest value that can be placed in a decimal data variable declared:

```
define dec_var decimal(m,n)
```

would be 10^{m-n} - $10^{-n.}$ This means that a decimal could be declared:

```
define dec_var decimal(2,0)
```

This variable could then store a maximum of 10^{2-0} - 10^{-0}, or 99(100-1). Any attempt to store a number larger than this would generate an expression error, which should be trapped whenever any error mode of error checking is in effect (current versions of INFORMIX-4GL may not trap this error by default).

Money

The `money` data type is a special case of the decimal data type. It is, by default, a fixed decimal number with a scale of two. When the money data type is displayed, the default currency symbol is displayed to the left of the digits being displayed. The default output currency symbol may be changed by using the DBMONEY environment variable, which has the following format:

```
DBMONEY=scb
```

In this format, s is the symbol that will precede the money value, c is the symbol that will separate the whole currency portion from the fractional portion, and b is the symbol that will follow the money value. The valid values for c are "." or ",". The valid values for s or b are any series of characters that do not include a comma or a period.

Float

The float data type in INFORMIX-4GL usually has the same precision as a C double on the machine platform. Once again, the precision is machine-dependent but is usually limited to 10^{32}. The language-definition double precision is a synonym for float.

Date

The INFORMIX-4GL date is represented internally as a four-byte integer that represents the number of days since January 1, 1900, inclusive. INFORMIX-4GL automatically formats this value according to either its default format or the format specified by the DBDATE environment variable. The DBDATE environment variable is set as:

```
DBDATE=dmync
```

where d is the day being set, m the month being set, y the year, n the number following the year position (valid digits can be a two or a four); and c is the character used to separate the components of the date.

Datetime

The datetime data type is a means of representing an instant in time; it contains both date and time components. The datetime data type has a variable degree of precision. The user can define a datetime variable to be of a particular precision, but then dynamically change the precision as needed. The datetime data type is composed of the fields year, month, day, hour, minute, second, and fraction of a second. This data type is very handy for applications that require a timestamp to be stored with a record. The datetime data type is declared as follows:

```
define variable_name datetime first to last
```

In this example, the identifier *first* or *last* is one of the fields from Table 8-3, where the level for a *last* entry cannot precede a *first* entry from the list in the same datetime definition.

Table 8-3 *Datetime Identifiers*

Field	Valid Entries	Level
Year	Number from 1 to 9999	1
Month	Number from 1 to 12	2
Day	Number from 1 to 31, depending on month	3
Hour	Number from 0 to 23	4
Minute	Number from 0 to 59	5
Second	Number from 0 to 59	6
Fraction	5 decimal digits	7

Interval

The interval data type is used to represent a span of time. It represents the difference between two datetimes. It also supports a varying degree of resolution, which can be defined when the variable is defined or changed at runtime.

Because the interval data type is specifically designed to represent a span of time independent of dates, it must be represented by specific components that cannot mix dates and times. There are two interval types: those that represent a year/month span of time, and those that represent day/hours/minutes/seconds. An interval would be declared with the following format:

```
define interval_var interval first to last
```

In this example, the identifier *first* or *last* is one of the fields from Tables 8-4 and 8-5, where the level for a *last* entry cannot precede a *first* entry from the list in the same datetime definition.

Table 8-4 *Year/Month Intervals*

Field	Valid Entries	Level
Year	Number 1 to 9999 (default)	
	Number 1 to 999,999,999 (max)	1
Month	Number 1 to 99 (default)	
	Number 1 to 999,9999,9999 (max)	2

Table 8-5 *Day/Hour Intervals*

Field	Valid Entries	Level
Day	Number 1 to 99 (default)	
	Number 1 to 999,999,999 (max)	1
Hour	Number 1 to 99 (default)	
	Number 1 to 999,999,999 (max)	2
Minute	Number 1 to 99 (default)	
	Number 1 to 999,999,999 (max)	3
Second	Number 1 to 99 (default)	
	Number 1 to 999,999,999 (max)	4
Fraction	Number 1 to 999 (default)	
	Number 1 to 99,999 (maximum)	5

The default entries are system defaults that can be overridden during the declaration of the interval variable. The following declaration statement demonstrates this:

```
define interval_var interval year(5) to month
```

In this example, the interval variable has been defined to allow five digits in the year, instead of the default value of four digits.

Character

The character data type in the INFORMIX-4GL language is a string of characters of up to 32,767 characters in length. It is always blank-padded to its defined length. Though it is usually null-terminated, it does not depend on a null terminator to determine its length. Its length is fixed when the character variable is defined.

Complex Data Types

Unlike many 4GL languages, INFORMIX-4GL supports complex data types. Records, arrays, and database binding to variables are available. These complex data types are a big part of the power of the INFORMIX-4GL language.

Arrays

INFORMIX-4GL arrays are homogeneous collections of data elements. Arrays can be declared up to three dimensions. Arrays are fixed in size at compile time and are currently not allowed to grow dynamically.

By default, array bounds are **not** checked at runtime in compiled C INFORMIX-4GL. However, a special compiler flag can be passed to the compiler, which will force the compiler to check array bounds at runtime. Because the checking of array bounds on every array reference operation can become expensive, it is recommended that this flag only be used during the debugging stage and not with the production version of the program.

Whereas arrays of records are allowed, arrays of arrays are not allowed. Arrays cannot be passed as function parameters.

Records

INFORMIX-4GL supports records of non-homogeneous data types of virtually unlimited length. Elements within the record can be any valid simple or complex data type, such as records. Arrays may also be record components.

Records may be passed as function parameters. Note that when this occurs, the function will process this using *call by value*; that is, the entire record variable will be pushed and pulled off the function stack. (This differs from the C language, where a record or structure would be *called-by-reference* using a pointer, thus allowing the function to act on the actual variable, not just the value of the variable.)

Database Binding

INFORMIX-4GL allows variables to be bound to database tables at compile time. These variables then have a direct correspondence with the database tables. This increases the safety of the language and virtually eliminates the data type errors that are so common when retrieving data from a database. Database binding takes place when the like keyword is used during variable declaration, as follows:

```
define lcustomer like customer.first_name
```

The asterisk character in the following declaration is then resolved to all of the columns in the database table, as the following example shows.

```
define lcustomer_rec record like customer.*
```

This statement would produce a record where all of the columns match, in ordinal position and data type, the columns within the database table that has been referenced.

The `through` clause can be used with the `define` statement to identify only a subset of a data tables columns to be used in the record declaration. An example of this clause is:

```
define lcustomer record like
        customer.first_name through customer.last_name
```

The benefits of this capability cannot be underemphasized. The ability to declare records in this manner eliminates the need for the programmer to constantly refer to the database schema for clues on how to declare variables. Whenever possible, this feature should be capitalized.

Note that the database binding that occurs when using this statement occurs during the compile phase. For this reason, if a record is bound to the `customer` table using the `like` keyword, the program is compiled, and then the `customer` table is modified before the program is run, there is a potential for a type mismatch error at runtime. In a structured development environment, database schemas should come under the same, or stricter, controls as source code, thus minimizing the potential for this error.

Null Data Values

The NULL data type is a special case of data values that represents the *absence* of data and has a different internal value that depends on the data type being evaluated. The NULL data type can be used to distinguish between values such as the number zero, blanks, or date zero, and an unknown value for these data types.

For instance, a column that stores the balance of an account could have the value zero. This could be an indication that the account had carried a non-zero balance, but was set to zero by a transaction. This zero value could be distinguished from a NULL value, which would indicate that the account had not been used.

Using NULLs in INFORMIX-4GL expressions can be problematic. A NULL data value, in any Boolean expression, returns FALSE for the entire expression. Consider the following example:

```
define val1, val2 integer
let val2 = 100000
initialize val1 to NULL

if ( val2 > val1 ) then
        display "val2 is the larger number"
else
        display "val1 is the larger number"
end if
```

This Boolean expression would evaluate to FALSE, and the display statement would not display the message "val2 is the larger number," even though the value of val2 appears to be larger than the value of val1. This is intentional behavior based on the theoretical assertion that a NULL value is the absence of data and cannot have a value greater or less than any other value.

This implies that in order for expressions to behave as a programmer may expect, if it is possible for a data variable to contain a NULL value, then the data variable must be tested *explicitly* for a NULL value within an expression, as follows:

```
define val1, val2 integer
let val2 = 100000
initialize val1 to NULL


if val1 IS NULL and val2 IS NOT NULL
```

```
          then display "val2 is a number and val1 is nothing."
end if
if val2 IS NOT NULL and val1 IS NOT NULL and  val2 > val1 then
          display "val2 is the larger number"
else
          display "val1 is the larger number"
end if
```

A technique sometimes practiced when using numeric values in INFORMIX-4GL programming is to eliminate NULLs in expressions by scanning data values before they are used and mapping NULLs to zero values. This technique is shown as follows:

```
define val1, val2 integer
let val2 = 100000
initialize val1 to NULL

     ....

if val1 IS NULL then
        let val1 = 0
end if
if val2 IS NULL then
        let val2 = 0
end if


if val2 > val1 then
        display "val2 is the larger number"
else
        display "val1 is the larger number"
end if
```

Data Conversion in Assignments

INFORMIX-4GL performs automatic data conversion in expressions as long as the conversion follows some simple rules. This implicit data conversion allows an integer to be converted into a string with a simple assignment operation. The following statement performs such a conversion:

```
define x        integer
define str   char(10)

let x = 1 / 2 * 3
let str =   x
```

This statement creates a string with the integer value 1.

In some cases, integer values may be right-shifted and prepended with blanks. In many cases, this may not be desirable. This is especially true when the integer string is being stored in the database as a database key and will be sorted when returned. With that being the case, the sorted data will not appear in sensible order. A simple solution to this problem is to format the data so that it is no longer right-shifted when assigned into the string. This can be done with the using clause, a clause generally referred to only in reference to display or printing options. The syntax is:

```
let sir = x using "<<<<"
```

The left arrows indicate that the integer being formatted should be right-shifted when placed into the string. The complete set of format operators for the using clause are listed in Table 8-6.

Using these formatting characters, in order to place an optional column at a specific position, the following format string:

```
let x     =   133444555
let str = x using"<<<,<<<,<<<<"
```

would produce the following result:

```
133,444,555
```

INFORMIX-4GL performs a variety of conversions when it deems necessary. Table 8-7 details a number of these conversions.

Assignment and Conversion in Expressions

INFORMIX-4GL uses a set of internal rules to perform type conversion during expressions. Each expression is parsed, and individual arguments are placed on the INFORMIX-4GL stack along

Table 8-6 *Formatting Characters with the Using Clause*

Format Character	Action
#	Insert blank for zero.
&	Insert 0 for 0.
<	Left-shift results.
$	Place $ at end of the number.
*	Insert * for 0.
.	Place period at this position in the stream of numbers.
,	Place comma at this position in the stream of numbers.
( )	Surround negative number in parentheses.
-	Place negative sign in number if the number is negative.
+	Place positive sign in number if the number is positive.
mm	Insert the month number.
dd	Insert the day number.
mmm	Insert the month name.
ddd	Insert the day name.
yy	Insert 2-digit year.
yyyy	Insert 4-digit year.

Table 8-7 *Assignment Conversion Rules in INFORMIX-4GL*

Expression	Default Rule
let string = numeric	Left-shifted, blank-padded.
let integer = string	Acceptable if string is a stream of ASCII characters that represent integers, or else a fatal error may occur.
let integer = decimal	Truncated to integer.
let string1 = string2	No errors or warnings if the length of string1 is long enough to hold string2. If the length of string1 is less than the length of string2, truncation occurs but signals a warning, not an error.
let decimal1 = decimal2	Will alter the scale of the left-hand argument as needed as long as precision is not exceeded. If precision is exceeded, a fatal error may occur.
let date = datetime	Datetime must be in the format year to day.

with the data type and length of the argument. As arguments are pulled off the stack, type conversion takes place as long as the conversion is sensible.

Character Conversions

INFORMIX-4GL converts any valid data type into a character string without generating errors. If truncation occurs, a warning is generated. If these warnings are not trapped, program execution continues. If both sides of the expression are characters, but the left-hand side of the expression is shorter than the right-hand side, then truncation occurs, a warning is generated, and program execution continues. The following code fragment demonstrates this concept:

```
define str1    char(5)
define str2    char(10)

let str2 = "0123456789"
let str1 = str2
display "str1 is ", str1
```

This would produce the following output:

```
01234
```

If the right-hand side of the expression is numeric, it is placed into the character variable left-shifted. If the string is not long enough to hold the number, then it is truncated and a warning is generated. Program execution continues. This behavior is true for all numeric data types used on the right-hand side of a character conversion expression.

Arithmetic Operators and Numeric Conversion Rules

INFORMIX-4GL supports a full range of mathematical operators. These operators have a specific order of evaluation, which may not be exactly what the user expects. Table 8-8 lists the valid INFORMIX-4GL operators and their level of evaluation or grouping.

In numeric operations, all operands are converted to the INFORMIX-4GL data type decimal, and the resulting number is

Table 8-8 *Grouping of Operators*

Operation	Symbol	Evaluation Level
Associative	()	1
Exponentiation	**	1
Multiplication	*	2
Division	/	2
Modulus	mod	2
Addition	+	3
Subtraction	-	3

decimal. Rules concerning the precision and scale of the result are detailed in Table 8-9. If the result can be placed in the left-hand value, no errors are returned. If significant digits are lost, a fatal error is sometimes returned. Using the whenever any error mode of error checking provides error checking for all expression errors.

Table 8-9 *Precision and Scale of Result of Mathematical Operations*

Operation	Precision	Scale
Addition or Subtraction	$MIN(32, MAX (p_1 - s_1, p^2 - s_2) + MAX(s_1, s_2) + 1)$	$MAX(s_1, s_2)$
Multiplication	$MIN(32, p_1 + p_2)$	$s_1 + s_2$
Division	32	$32 - p_1 + s_1 - s_2$

The table details the precision and scale of the result of a mathematical operation. Here, p_1 and s_1 are the precision and scale of the first operand, and p_2 and s_2 are the precision and scale of the second operand.

Initialization

Note that INFORMIX-4GL variables are, by definition, not initialized when defined. The p-code version of the compiler initializes data space to binary zero. This can cause significant surprise when moving a p-code application to a compiled version of INFORMIX-4GL. The C language is a language that, by definition, does not initialize variables, leaving their value indeterminate until assigned; and as most programmers know, indeterminate data values can wreak havoc on an application.

Language Constants

One limitation of INFORMIX-4GL is its lack of constants, a program value that can be referenced by name but cannot be altered once it has been set in the program. An obvious workaround is to use a variable in place of a constant. Because the INFORMIX-4GL language does not restrict a variable from modification during compilation, it is up to the programmer to enforce the behavior of a constant. By using a style convention that easily identifies *constant variables*, this task is made somewhat easier. The simplest choice is to use only uppercase letters when naming constants (a common C language convention). The following example demonstrates this convention:

```
— Create global 'constants'
—
globals
        define   MAXRECS integer
        define   MAXARR  integer
end globals

main

        — Initialize CONSTANTS
let MAXRECS = 100
let MAXARR  = 200
...
```

In this example, the integer variables MAXRECS and MAXARR are defined as global variables. At the start of the main program block, they are initialized to a specific value. From this point on, they can be used much as any other constant would be in the program. Obviously, constants of other data types could be declared, initialized, and used in the same manner.

Flow of Control Statements in INFORMIX-4GL

INFORMIX-4GL provides a set of standard iterative flow of control statements. Statements are available to provide iterative loops: the `for` statement and the `while` statement. A `foreach` statement is also available to provide an iterative loop through the result set returned by a SQL `select` statement. Table 8-10 lists the iterative flow of control statements found in Informix-4GL.

Table 8-10 INFORMIX-4GL Iterative Flow of Control Statements

Statement	Parameters	Function
for	Initialization expression, limit expression, optional step expression	Perform loop with index variable beginning at initialization expression, looping until value of index variable exceeds limit expression.
while	Boolean evaluation expression	Performs loop until Boolean expression evaluates to false.
foreach	Cursor name	Performs loop until cursor fetch operation returns not found condition.

The `for` Statement

The `for` statement is used to perform a loop for a specified set of iterations. The statement can evaluate complex expressions for initialization and terminating values. The index variable being used may be altered within the loop (though strict adherence to the rules of structured programming would not allow this). The `for` loop can be initialized with the return value of a function call, as in the following example:

```
for n = get_val(a,b,c) to limit_val(a,b,c)
        do_this(a,b,c)
        do_that(a,b,c)
end for
```

In this example, the functions get_val and limit_val are called on this first iteration of the loop in order to get the initialization and terminating values for the loop. However, because loop index values can change within the loop, these expressions must be reevaluated on each iteration of the loop. If loop index variables are not being changed within the loop, this is not efficient. Storing the initialization and terminating values in variables optimizes the looping operation. This approach is shown as follows:

```
let x = get_val(a,b,c)
let z = limit_val(a,b,c)

for n = x to z
        do_this(a,b,c)
        do_that(a,b,c)
end for
```

Conditional Expressions in INFORMIX-4GL

Conditional expressions in Informix-4GL provide conditional flow of control branching based on the evaluation of Boolean expressions. Boolean expressions in INFORMIX-4GL are evaluated as they are with the C programming language. A non-zero value is evaluated as TRUE; a zero value is evaluated as FALSE. For programmers familiar with the C language, this concept should not be difficult to follow. The statement:

```
if (1) then
        display "It's true"
end if
```

would display "It's true". But, the statement:

```
if (0) then
        display "It's false"
end if
```

would produce no output. Because INFORMIX-4GL allows programmers to negate Boolean expressions, this statement could be written as:

```
if NOT (0) then
      display "It's false"
end if
```

   Likewise, negating a non-zero value would produce a value of false, as in the expression:

```
if NOT (1) then
      display "It's true"
end if
```

   This statement would produce no output.

   What is interesting about INFORMIX-4GL is its treatment of expressions in Boolean statements. It is a rule that regardless of the Boolean operators in a Boolean statement, all expressions are evaluated. So, in the Boolean statement:

```
if ( funct1(x,y,z) and funct2(x,y,z) and funct3(x,y,z) ) then
      do_this_funct(x,y,z)
end if
```

all expressions are grouped using the and operator. This requires that *all* conditions must test TRUE in order for the statement to be true. With this knowledge, we could then evaluate the statement from left to right and, as soon as a FALSE is evaluated, quit evaluating the statement. We could do this because we know that a single false value will force this statement to fail.

   INFORMIX-4GL does not make this assumption. Boolean statements are evaluated from left to right with no conclusions about statement groupings. Unless there are parenthetical groupings, expressions are evaluated two at a time, with the result being applied to the next expression. In order to optimize the preceding statement, it could be rewritten as follows:

```
if ( funct1(x,y,z) )   then
   if ( funct2(x,y,z) ) then
      if ( funct3(x,y,z) ) then
             do_this_funct(x,y,z)
      end if
   end if
end if
```

In this code fragment, if the expression `funct1` fails, none of the other statements are executed. The same holds true for the expression `funct2`. This provides a certain level of optimization, because the odds are favorable that unneeded statements will not be executed.

The Concatenation Operator

In INFORMIX-4GL, the string concatenation operator is the comma (,). The operator allows two strings to be concatenated using the following syntax:

```
let str1 = str2, str3
```

In INFORMIX-4GL, strings are always padded to their defined length. In order to eliminate this padding, the `clipped` operator must be used. For example:

```
define str1 char(40), str2 char(40), str3 char(40)

let str2 = "012345"
let str3 = "012345"

let str1 = str2, str3
```

In this example, the final statement would be rejected at run-time, because the padded length of `str2` and `str3` combined is greater than the defined length of the target `str1` (40). Using the `clipped` operator, this problem could be eliminated, as follows:

```
define str1 char(40), str2 char(40), str3 char(40)

let str2 = "012345"
let str3 = "012345"

let str1 = str2 clipped, str3 clipped
```

This statement would execute, because the clipped length is 12, which will easily fit in the 40-byte character string `str1`.

Using SQL in INFORMIX-4GL Applications

An important element of the nonprocedural component of INFORMIX-4GL is SQL and its seamless integration into the language. If used correctly, SQL can greatly reduce the amount of procedural code required to program an application. Long, tedious procedural steps can be compressed into a single SQL statement.

Virtually all valid SQL statements are supported in INFORMIX-4GL, with only minor restrictions. These are significant capabilities, but in order to capitalize on these capabilities, it is important that the underlying database be well designed and normalized. If not, the advantages of SQL will be lost, and SQL will be no more useful to the programmer than ISAM-type function calls.

A small number of Informix-SQL statements are not supported by INFORMIX-4GL. Most of these are administrative in nature, and are recognized and processed by the `dbaccess` program, but are not interpreted by the engine. For instance, the following `info` statements are not recognized by INFORMIX-4GL:

```
info tables
info status for <table_name>
info indexes for <table_name>
info columns for <table_name>
```

These are administrative statements, but it is not uncommon for INFORMIX-4GL applications to handle some database administrative functions. For these instances, the following `select` statement can be used to retrieve information about a table:

```
select tabname
from   systables
where  tabid > 99
```

Because all Informix system catalog tables have a `tabid <= 99`, this returns a list of the tables in the current database exclusive of the system catalog tables. The informational statement `info columns for table_name` can be emulated with the following statement:

```
select colname, coltype
from    syscolumns, systables
where   syscolumns.tabid  = systables.tabid and
        systables.tabname = <table_name>
```

If the column allows NULL values, the integer value for the column `coltype` is masked with a specific bit pattern. To eliminate this mask using 4GL, the following statement could be executed:

```
let pcoltype = pcoltype mod 256
```

Otherwise, the statement could make use of the built-in SQL modulo operator, which could be incorporated into the `select` statement as follows:

```
select colname, mod( coltype, 256 )
from    syscolumns, systables
where   syscolumns.tabid  = systables.tabid and
        systables.tabname = table_name
```

Likewise, the informational statement `info indexes for table_name` can be emulated with the following SQL statement:

```
select idxname
from    systables, sysindexes
where   systables.tabid = sysindexes.tabid   and
        systables.tabname = table_name
```

This statement would return the index name for all indexes for the table name used in the `where` clause.

Type Conversion with SQL Statements

As with other statements that assign values in INFORMIX-4GL, SQL statements support type conversion when it makes sense. In all cases, any Informix data type can be converted into a character string as long as the character string is long enough to hold the entire value.

The `select` statement retrieves data from the database and assigns values to host variables using the `into` clause. It is not an error to retrieve fewer data elements than there are host variables; INFORMIX-4GL considers this a warning and not an error.

This behavior will be capitalized upon later in this text in using dynamic SQL statements to retrieve data.

During retrieval of data, data conversion occurs freely much as it does during variable assignment. This is demonstrated in the following example:

```
define str1 char(20), str2 char(20), str3 char(20)

- column int_col contains an integer value
- column dec_col contains a decimal value
- column date_col contains a date value

select int_col, dec_col, date_col
into   str1, str2, str3
from   sample_table
```

In this example, all data types are converted according to the defaults. The resulting values are placed into the strings as long as the strings are the appropriate length. If the strings are not long enough, asterisks are placed into the string up to the size of the string.

Database Binding in INFORMIX-4GL

One of the most useful features of INFORMIX-4GL is the ability for program variable definitions to be *bound* to database table columns using the `like` keyword. This allows a simple set of statements to ensure data integrity of data being retrieved from the database, as follows:

```
database mycust

define customer_rec record like customer.*

select customer.*
into   customer_rec.*
where  cust_numb = 1
```

This code allows the customer record for customer number 1 to be retrieved into a program variable without concern of data type incompatibilities. Note that it is a requirement for the database statement to appear before the data binding `define` statement.

The data binding feature is implemented by having the INFORMIX-4GL compiler read the schema for the database table at compile time, determine the data type and length of the variables, and then produce definitions for the variables to match the database table column definitions in ordinal position and type. The compiler **expands** the record definition into its appropriate components. Note that the database statement must precede a `define like` statement in the source code module. The resulting C code generated by the preceding definition would appear as follows.

Using the schema:

```
create table customer (
        first_name char(15),
                    middle_i char(1)
                    last_name char(15),
                    phone_number char(10),
                    address1 char(20),
                    address2 char(20)  )
```

with the INFORMIX-4GL declaration of:

```
define customer_rec record like customer.*
```

the generated C code would be:

```
struct {
        char first_name[16];
        char middle_i[2];
        char last_name[16];
        char phone_number[11];
        char address1[21];
        char address2[21];
}       customer_rec;
```

However, this feature can cause problems when the structure of the data table has changed in data type or order. Because INFORMIX-4GL quietly converts data types whenever possible, invalid data may be read into the record, and the error may not be readily apparent. Assume that in the following example, the `customer` table was initially defined to have the following schema.

Schema 1

```
create table customer (
            first_name char(15),
            middle_i char(1)
            last_name char(15),
            phone_number char(10),
            address1 char(20),
            address2 char(20) )
```

However, the schema is changed to the following structure.

Schema 2

```
create table customer (
            first_name char(15),
            last_name char(15),
            phone_number char(10),
            address1 char(20),
            address2 char(20) )
```

If the program example were **compiled** while schema 1 was in place and then **run** when schema 2 was in place, the data record defined like the schema 1 definition would receive incorrect values. This would not necessarily cause the program to fail. It is likely the program would quietly continue operation, placing the first letter of the user's last name into the middle_i component of the record and putting the customer's last_name field into the phone number fields. The first address1 record component would receive the address2 part of the database record, and the address2 field in the program record would be untouched; its value would be indeterminate. Because INFORMIX-4GL assumes all data variables are NULL-terminated, attempts to manipulate this component of this record could fail randomly at runtime.

prepare **Statement**

The prepare statement serves two purposes in the INFORMIX-4GL language. First, it is used to perform dynamic SQL in INFORMIX-4GL. Using the prepare statement, a query can be built dynamically at runtime.

However, the prepare statement is also considered an optimization tool because it can be used to reduce the inter-process communication (IPC) traffic between the engine and the front end. Because a prepared statement is optimized before it is executed, it reduces the need to continually re-optimize the statement every time it is executed.

To create dynamic SQL, the `prepare` statement can take a string variable as a parameter; within this string variable, virtually any valid SQL statement is supported; the exceptions are the `close`, `declare`, `execute`, `load`, `open`, `prepare`, and `unload` statements.

The `prepare` statement merely packages the string it is passed and sends it to the engine for evaluation; it does not examine the SQL statement. All parsing and optimization are performed by the database engine, not in the front end.

There are occasions when the database engine supports syntax not yet supported by INFORMIX-4GL.

The solution to this problem is to place the SQL statement in a string and pass it to the engine using the `prepare` statement, as follows:

```
let qstr = "execute procedure myproc()"

prepare ex_stmt from qstr

execute ex_stmt
```

In this example, we want to call the stored procedure `myproc`, but the version of INFORMIX-4GL being used does not currently support the `execute procedure` statement. We must therefore place the statement in a string and use the prepare statement to pass the string to the engine. Because the engine recognizes the statement, it will have no problem processing the statement and returning a statement id to the INFORMIX-4GL program. The INFORMIX-4GL program then issues an `execute` statement for this statement id. Note that if the stored procedure retrieves data, a cursor must be declared for the statement id; otherwise, a runtime error would occur when the statement was executed.

Optimization with the `prepare` Statement

When a query is executed in INFORMIX-4GL, the database engine must parse the query, examine the query for validity and syntactical correctness, optimize the query, create temporary tables if needed, access the data files, and then begin retrieving data. Not all of these steps may be necessary each time the query is executed.

When the database engine first encounters a query, it must parse the query. Because SQL database objects are not examined until runtime, complete parsing and optimization of the query cannot be done until runtime.

When the database engine checks the query, it will examine the SQL statement for correct syntax (it must do this to determine where the database objects are within the statement). Database objects are examined, and then the database is searched to determine that these objects exist.

In the next step, the engine optimizes the query. Informix version 4.0 engines and later use a cost-based optimizer. This optimizer optimizes queries by examining every possible access path in conjunction with costs for various components of that access path. It chooses the access path with the least cost, and therefore the most efficient access. Because it is quite possible that the elements of the query examined in this step do not change between each execution of the query, it is not necessary to repeat this step. The `prepare` statement can be used to bypass this step.

In transaction-processing environments, optimization with the `prepare` statement is also important because CPU cycles spent preparing a query are CPU cycles that could have been spent processing other applications.

SQL Processing: Front-End *vs.* Back-End Activity

Informix products were originally designed to make use of a two-process architecture. Though this is changed slightly in version 6.0 of their products, the concept of **front-end** and **back-end** processing is still valid. The **front end** of the application controls the application; the back end performs the database interaction. Certain portions of the SQL statement are processed in the application, and other portions are processed in the engine.

Every SQL statement that is encountered by INFORMIX-4GL is processed in several steps. First, it is parsed to determine the validity of the SQL syntax. Some cursory syntax-checking may be performed by the INFORMIX-4GL compiler in order to ensure that a valid statement is being used, but the bulk of the SQL statement-parsing is performed by the database engine.

The parser in the database engine reviews the various sub-clauses of the SQL statement for correctness. The objects that these statements invariably reference are evaluated based on several criteria. First, it must be determined that they exist in the current database. Then it must be determined that they are valid database objects for the current clause. Next, expressions must be resolved, data type consistencies evaluated, and any necessary conversion performed. Finally, optimization must be performed. The database engine optimizer evaluates various access paths and an optimal access path is selected.

Optimization with the prepare and declare Statements

If an SQL statement is going to be executed repeatedly, performance can be improved by using the prepare statement to parse and optimize the statement before it is used. Alternatively, in the case of select statements, the declare statement can be used to accomplish the similar optimization.

If the SQL statement is only going to be executed once, then using the prepare or declare statement does not provide *any* optimization. The following example demonstrates this point. Assume that, in this example, the code shown is executed only once during the application startup procedure:

```
            — build the query
    prepare qstmt from  "select application_name ",
                            "from control_file ",
                            "where control_code = 1 "

    declare curs1 for qstmt

            — fetch the data
    fetch curs1 into appl_name
```

In this example, assume the contents of the entire query are known at compile time. There is no benefit to performing a prepare, declare, and fetch for a singleton query of this type. It would have been just as efficient to execute the following:

```
— execute the query
select  application_name
into    appl_name
from    control_file
where   control_code = 1
```

This statement requires fewer lines of code and is clearer; it is easier to read the `select` statement here and understand what is being selected, than to read a lone `fetch` statement, far removed from the code that declared the cursor, and understand what is being retrieved.

Where an SQL statement is being used to validate data being input on a screen, a hard-coded SQL statement versus a prepared SQL statement will probably not produce notable changes. However, in the case of a report that must scan one million rows and execute miscellaneous SQL statements for each row, preparing a statement before repeated execution may make very good sense. The following code samples demonstrate this point. This example demonstrates the use of the `prepare` statement within the body of a report:

```
on every row

        select fld_stats
        into fld_stats
        from field_stats
        where empl_numb = pempl_numb
```

This query is executed for each tuple passed to the report. If the report is reading and processing a large number of rows, the execution and parsing of this query will slow the execution time of the report. In order to speed up this process, the statement could be prepared as follows:

```
        first page header

        declare fld_stats_curs cursor for
           select fld_stats
           into fld_stats
           from field_stats
           where empl_numb = pempl_numb


        . . . .
```

```
on every row
```

```
        open stmt1
        fetch stmt1 into fld_stats
```

In this example, the statement is prepared in the first-page
header block, which will only be executed once. Once this block
of code has been executed, the optimized statement in the `on`
`every  row` block is executed for every row passed to the report.
The steps of unnecessarily evaluating database objects and optimization and the related IPC traffic are avoided in this solution.

In the case of the SQL `update` or `delete` statements, which
are usually executed to act on a single row at a time, the `pre-`
`pare` statement can be used to optimize these operations. For a
batch update program that must update numerous rows based on
varying criteria, using the `prepare` statement can produce significant performance improvements. This is demonstrated in the
following example:

```
on every row
```

```
        if ( do_update )   then
        update customer
        set     customer.addr1 = customer_rec.addr1,
        customer.addr2 = customer_rec.addr2


               . . . .
```

In this example, a report program is being used to perform
batch updates based on a flag set elsewhere in the application.
Assuming that a large number of rows are being processed, optimizing this update could have a significant impact on this program's execution speed. The following code demonstrates this
optimization:

```
        first page header
```

```
            prepare upd_stmt
        from "update customer set customer.addr1 = ?,  ",
            " customer.addr2 = ?   ",
               " where customer_num = ? "
        . . .
```

```
        on every row
```

```
if ( do_update )  then
       execute upd_stmt using customer_rec.addr1,
                              customer_rec.addr2,
                              customer_rec.cust_numb

  . . .
```

In this example, the page header block is used to prepare the update statement. When the `on every row` statement is executed, the `do_update` flag is evaluated, and if it is set to TRUE, the update statement is executed via the `upd_stmt` statement id. In a large batch program processing a large number of rows, this could provide a significant performance improvement.

Optimization should not be limited to using the `prepare` statement alone. Numerous other factors can affect the performance of a query: the existence of appropriate indexes, sort criteria, and the duplicity of indexes. If database access is viewed as a bottleneck, these factor should be reviewed.

Cursors in INFORMIX-4GL

Cursors are a means of reconciling a row-at-a-time, serial language such as the procedural statements in INFORMIX-4GL, with the set-at-a-time, set-oriented statements of SQL. Cursors provide the means of managing this impedance mismatch of language statements. In the case of a `select` statement, cursors provide a pointer into the active set that is referenced by the select statement.

The `foreach` Statement

The `foreach` statement combines some of the properties of a procedural statement with those of a nonprocedural SQL statement. A `foreach` statement relates to a cursor and all of the tuples within that cursor; in that respect, it is an extension of a cursor. However, it is also used to create a loop structure similar to that of a `while` loop. It is a `while` loop that loops until a not-found condition is satisfied. At this point, program execution begins at the first statement following the `end` of the `foreach` statement.

A substitute for the `foreach` is a cursor open followed by a `while` loop, which continues to loop until a not-found condition is detected. However, the `foreach` statement is a more attractive alternative to programming this logic. The `foreach` statement provides a useful structure for loading arrays scanning large numbers of rows and producing reports.

Data Variables Used in SQL Statements

INFORMIX-4GL variables used in SQL expressions are evaluated for data type and length at compile time. They are checked for content at runtime. Values to be used in SQL statements can be supplied at runtime using one of several alternatives. The statement can be declared as a cursor using the variables that have been defined as parameters in the `where` clause of the SQL statement, or the statement can be prepared using the '?' as placeholders for values that will be substituted at runtime.

There is no real performance advantage to using one versus the other. The internal implementation is virtually the same. The only issue to consider is that of programming convenience and style.

One method of supplying runtime values is to simply include the programming variable references in the cursor declaration. This method is shown in the following example.

```
declare cursor c1 cursor for

    select *
    from customer
    where cust_numb = customer_rec.cust_numb

open c1
fetch c1 into customer_rec.*
```

In this example, the cursor is declared with the filter criteria of the SQL `where` clause referencing the INFORMIX-4GL variable record element. This record element will be bound to the cursor. When the cursor is opened, the contents of the host variable are examined and substituted for filter criteria. This method is the *only* supported method of passing parameters into a `foreach` statement, because this statement does not support a `using` clause.

In the next example, the cursor is created with placeholders for the filter criteria.

```
prepare s1 cursor for " select *   ",
```

```
                                " from mycust ",
                                " where cust_numb = ? "

        declare c1 cursor for stmt1

        open c1 using customer_rec.cust_numb
```

In this example, a statement id is first established for the select statement and then a cursor is declared for that statement id. Finally, the cursor is opened with the using clause. This clause is necessary in this example because the cursor must access the filter criteria to open the cursor. (Note that in the current version of INFORMIX-4GL, the cursor declaration must precede its use in the source code module.)

There is no single correct way to bind data variables in INFORMIX-4GL; both methods shown are valid and could be considered modular in form. The first example requires slightly less coding, but the second example makes it clear in the open statement where the criteria for the cursor filter is to be found. It is up to the programmer to choose which method to use.

Cursors in INFORMIX-4GL

A cursor is a data structure in the **front end** that references a data control structure in the database engine. Use of this data control structure in the engine requires that inter-process communication (IPC) facilities be used. Reduction of this IPC traffic is one means of optimizing cursor use.

Cursors cause activity to occur on both the front and back ends of the application. When the cursor is created via the declare statement, data space is allocated in the application programs data area. This data space is a structure containing information about the cursor: the database object or objects it references, the table columns it retrieves, and any data binding that is to occur for parameters within the statements and data values to be retrieved by the statement.

When the cursor is opened, the SQL statement is parsed, and any fatal errors are reported to the program. The database objects are examined for availability and, with the Informix cost-based optimizer, a number of access paths for the query are evaluated. An access path to the data is determined. If any temporary tables are needed, they are opened.

When data is retrieved from the database using the `foreach` or `fetch` statement, a certain amount of buffering will occur. Buffering occurs in the database engine and, to a limited extent, in the application. This buffer is usually around 1K in size and currently cannot be changed by the programmer.

Types of Cursors

There are four types of cursors in INFORMIX-4GL: the serial (or normal) cursor, the *scroll* cursor, the *update* cursor and the *insert* cursor. These cursors are explained as follows.

The **serial** cursor is the most common type of cursor. This cursor reads the selection set in a serial fashion, beginning at the start of the set and proceeding to the end of the set. This cursor cannot maneuver backward and forward through the set.

Whereas a serial cursor may directly access a table or set of tables through an index, a **scroll** cursor requires that a temporary table be created. A scroll cursor can move forward and backward through a set of data, and thus requires a *snapshot* of the data at a particular point in time. The movement can be forward and backward relative to the start of the set or to the current position in the set. Because a temporary table is required, some performance degradation can be expected when using this type of cursor.

Scroll Cursor

The following code demonstrates the use of a scroll cursor. This application displays a screen form for the customer table and then allows the user to *browse* the table. The user will be able to move forward a record or back a record, jump to the start of the select set with the *first* option, or jump to the end of the select set with the *end* option. These movements within the current set will be made using a scroll cursor.

```
define customer_rec record like customer.*
define recno integer

open form f1 from "customer"
display form f1

— select the key fields
declare c1 scroll cursor for
```

```
                    select  *
                    from customer

          open c1
          fetch c1 into customer_rec.*
          display customer_rec.* to customer.*

               menu "Customer "
                    command "Next" "Display next record"
                         fetch relative 1 c1 into customer_rec.*
                         display customer_rec.* to customer.*
                    command "Previous" "Display previous record"
                         fetch relative -1 c1 into customer_rec.*
                         display customer_rec.* to customer.*

                    command "First" "Display first record"
                         fetch first c1 into customer_rec.*
                         display customer_rec.* to customer.*

                    command "Last" "Display last record"
                         fetch last c1 into customer_rec.*
                         display customer_rec.* to customer.*

                    command "Goto" "Go to a specific record"
                         prompt "Enter record number: " for recno
                         fetch absolute recno c1 into customer_rec.*
                         display customer_rec.* to customer.*

                    command "Quit" "Quit this menu "
                         exit menu

               end menu
```

In this example, a `scroll cursor` is created for the customer record. The scroll cursor is then opened, and the first record is retrieved by the `fetch` statement. (By default, a `fetch` statement with no record number qualifier on a scroll cursor is considered a `fetch next` statement, a request to fetch the next record.) This record is then displayed to the screen.

Next, a menu is displayed, allowing the user to choose an option for *next, previous, first, last,* to go to a specific record, or *quit* the menu. For the *next* and *previous* options, the fetch relative statement is executed with either a +1 for the *next* option or a -1 for the *previous* option. This moves the cursor to either the next record for the +1 or the previous record for the -1. This move is **relative** to the current cursor position. Alternatively, the `fetch previous` statement could have been used to fetch the previous record, or the `fetch next` statement could have been used to fetch the next record. The *first* and *last* options simply execute either the `fetch first` statement to retrieve the first record or the `fetch last` statement to retrieve the last record.

The *goto* option allows the user to specify a record number in the current set and move to that record number. In this case, the move is relative to the start of the set, so the `fetch absolute` statement is used. If it were desirable to move relative to the current position in the active set, then the fetch relative statement would have been used. Both of these statements take either an integer constant or an integer expression as an argument.

Problems with Scroll Cursors

There are two problems associated with some implementations of scroll cursors. Both problems are exhibited by the example shown previously, and both are easily solved.

The first problem is that of stale data. When the scroll cursor is first executed, a temporary table is created; a snapshot is taken of the current state of the select set. This snapshot is then used for the duration of the cursor's existence. This means that as the user browses the rows in the set, it is possible that the data has been changed by another user.

The second problem is associated with the use of the temporary table. If the size of the selected tuple is large and the number of rows large, the temporary table could grow to a significant size. This could use a large amount of system resources and time to create.

The solution is to use two cursors: one to retrieve the primary key from the target table or tables, and the second to retrieve the rest of the data. The following example demonstrates this approach:

```
define customer_rec record like customer.*
    define recno integer

open form f1 from "customer"
    display form f1

— select the key fields
```

```
declare c1 scroll cursor for
        select   customer_num
        from     customer

declare c2 scroll cursor for
    select *
    from customer
    where customer_num = customer_rec.cnum

open c1
open c2

fetch c1 into customer_rec.customer_num
fetch c2 into customer_rec.*

display customer_rec.* to customer.*


menu "Customer "

        command "Next" "Display next record"
           fetch relative 1 c1 into customer_rec.customer_num
           open c2
           fetch c2 into customer_rec.*
           display customer_rec.* to customer.*

        command "Previous" "Display previous record"
           fetch relative -1 c1 into customer_rec.customer_num
           open c2
           fetch c2 into customer_rec.*
           display customer_rec.* to customer.*

        command "First" "Display first record"
           fetch first c1 into customer_rec.customer_num
           open c2
           fetch c2 into customer_rec.*
           display customer_rec.* to customer.*

        command "Last" "Display last record"
           fetch last c1 into customer_rec.customer_num
           open c2
           fetch relative c2 into customer_rec.*
           display customer_rec.* to customer.*

        command "Goto" "Go to a specific record"
           prompt "Enter record number: " for recno
           fetch absolute recno c1 into customer_rec.customer_num
```

```
open c2
fetch c2 into customer_rec.*
display customer_rec.* to customer.*

command "Quit" "Quit this menu "
  let cont = "N"
  exit menu
```

end menu

In this example, two cursors are declared: one a scroll cursor and the other a simple cursor. As the scroll cursor is traversed for each row retrieving just the primary key, the remainder of the data record is retrieved from the database using the simple cursor. The data is then displayed to the screen.

Update Cursors

An *update* cursor performs row retrieval similar to that of the serial cursor: it moves serially through the data set, retrieving rows. This cursor cannot move back rows and can only move forward one row at a time.

It is different from the serial cursor in two respects. First, it obtains a shared lock on each row as it is retrieved, and it releases the lock when it moves to the next row. Second, it has a number of restrictions associated with its use. These restrictions generally apply to the fact that, because it is intended to be used to update a single database table row, the underlying select statement can only reference one table and must reference the table directly. There cannot be an order by clause in the select statement, because this may require a sort table to be created and read instead of the target table.

One very significant advantage to using update cursors is the performance advantage gained when performing database updates. Because the current cursor position can be used to update a record, the expense of finding the record to update is averted.

The update cursor is sometimes referred to as a *locking cursor*. As the update cursor accesses a row, it places a shared lock on the row. A shared lock means that other users can read the row, but they cannot update the row until the user who acquired the shared lock has released the lock. As the cursor moves to the next row, the lock is released.

Insert Cursor

Unlike the other cursors mentioned, the *insert* cursor does not retrieve rows from the database. As the name implies, it is used to insert rows into the database. And unlike the simple `insert` statement, which inserts a single row into a database table, the insert cursor buffers the rows before inserting them into the table, inserting multiple rows in a single insert request sent to the database engine.

With the simple insert statement, a single row is sent through the IPC facility to the database engine where it is written to the database. When the row is sent to the engine by the front-end application, in this case an INFORMIX-4GL program, it waits for an acknowledgment from the engine that the row has been received. It is this acknowledgment and the time spent accessing the IPC facility that slows down the process of inserting multiple rows into the database and it is this step that is largely eliminated using an insert cursor.

With an insert cursor, rows are buffered in the front-end process before they are sent to the engine. The front-end buffer is usually about 1K in size, which for a 30-byte row would allow around 330 rows to be buffered before sending them to the engine. Instead of waiting for 330 separate acknowledgments for the rows, only a single acknowledgment is issued for the entire set of buffered rows. For a process inserting 20,000 rows, only 60 buffers would be passed and 60 acknowledgments returned, versus 20,000 buffers and 20,000 acknowledgments using a simple insert statement. This yields a 98-percent reduction in pipe traffic and usually produces about a 40-percent performance improvement.

The insert cursor is useful when a large number of rows are being input to the database during a single execution of the program, such as a batch load of data. An insert cursor being used in conjunction in a data entry program would probably not yield a notable performance improvement. In a data entry program, the time required for the user to perform data entry offsets any possible performance improvement of buffering the rows. The rows will not make it to the database any faster, because the application must still wait for the user to enter the rows. An example of an implementation of the insert cursor is as follows:

```
define journal_rec record like journals.*

declare ins_curs cursor for insert into journal_hist⇐
      values ( journal_rec.* )
declare j_curs cursor for select * from journals where⇐
      journal_date < "1/1/1993"

open ins_curs

foreach  j_curs into journal_rec.*

    put ins_curs

end foreach

delete from journals where journal_date < "1/1/1993"

close ins_curs
```

In this example, two cursors are declared. One cursor reads rows from a journals table less than a specific date. These rows are then input to a history table (journal_hist) using an insert cursor. After the end of the foreach loop, the insert cursor is closed; this flushes the remaining rows in the buffer. Note that it is important to close an insert cursor; otherwise, the rows remaining in the last buffer will not be output to the database.

Using an insert cursor also raises data integrity issues. Rows buffered in the **front end** do not come under the control of the database engine's data integrity facilities. Should the machine fail, these rows are lost. As noted in the previous example, a significant number of rows could be lost this way. It is the programmer's responsibility to provide contingencies for this type of failure.

Closing the Cursor

The process of closing a cursor requires communication with the database engine with IPC facilities. The database engine must be informed of the **front end's** desire to close the cursor. If the cursor is successfully closed, the database engine returns an acknowledgment or response that the cursor has been closed or the process has failed. In an application where a cursor may be reopened several times as filter criteria change, performance can be improved by simply eliminating the cursor close operation.

This is allowed in INFORMIX-4GL because a cursor open implies a close and then an open of the same cursor. Using this technique eliminates unnecessary IPC traffic and, depending on the specifics of the application, may improve performance significantly.

Views

One of the most overlooked features of SQL is the `view`. A view is a name associated with an SQL statement; referencing the name is virtually identical to referencing the SQL statement. The following SQL statements provide an example.

```
create view   cust_profile
                    ( cust_name,
                      cust_num,
                      cust_city,
                      cust_balance ) as
                  select cust_name,
                          customer_num,
                          city,
                          balance
                  from    customer, cust_balance
                  where   customer.customer_num =
cust_balance.cust_num
```

This SQL statement creates a view that relates to an SQL statement that joins the `customer` table with the `cust_balance` table. Once this view has been created, any references to `cust_profile` will execute the select statement shown as follows:

```
select *
from cust_profile
where   cust_num = 101
```

This statement accesses the `cust_profile` view and executes the underlying query, appending the `where` clause criteria in the preceding `select` statement shown to the `where` clause criteria contained in the view. The preceding SQL statement is the equivalent of the SQL statement that follows:

```
select cust_name,
        customer_num,
```

```
                          city,
                          balance
                 from     customer, cust_balance
                 where    customer.customer_num =
cust_balance.cust_num   and

                          customer.customer_num = 101
```

Obviously, using an SQL view, a great deal of the complexity of a query can be stored in the database, thus simplifying data access for the programmer. Reducing the difficulty and complexity of data access helps reduce the code required to develop an application, the overriding goal of any 4GL.

The SQL view can also be used to provide limited access to a table. Making use of the SQL keyword users and a control table, a restricted view of any number of tables can be provided. The following example demonstrates this:

```
— define a permissions table
create table user_perms ( logname char(20),
                          perm_level );

— table to access
create table menu_header ( menu_id integer,
                           menu_name char(20),
                           perm_level );

— create view to access menu_top table based on user login name

    create view menus   as
       select   menu_name,
                menu_id
       from     menu_header, user_perms
       where    logname = user       and
                user_perms.perm_level = menu_header.perm_level
```

In this example, a table is first created that relates each user login name to a permission level. This table is then populated with user login names and permission levels (not shown). Next, a view is established that joins the user_perms table to the menu_header table using the perm_level column; this relationship is a 1-to-many relationship-for each perm_level, there are multiple menu_header entries in the menu_header table. (These menu_header table entries represent menus that this user is allowed to view.) Note that the view menus makes use of the SQL built-in keyword user, which resolves to the login name of the user executing the SQL statement. The result of the join being issued will be a restricted view of the entries in the `menu_header` table. All that must be done to extract this selected view is to execute the following query:

```
select *
from    menus
```

The view essentially represents the natural join of two sets: the `user_perms` and `menu_headers` tables. The view is a shorthand for this relationship. This set-oriented approach to data management is central to SQL. Because SQL is so tightly integrated into INFORMIX-4GL, the judicious use of this language helps ensure meaningful results when using INFORMIX-4GL.

Modularity and SQL

In keeping with the overall goal of maintaining modularity in INFORMIX-4GL applications, SQL statements should be centralized and kept together in one or more source code modules. These modules should be devoted to similar operations, such as retrieving data or updating data. Additionally, for readability and maintainability, cursor or statement id declarations should be placed on a source code line close to where the cursor is to be used. The same holds true for statement ids.

An additional incentive for placing cursor declarations close to where they will be used in the code is in the INFORMIX-4GL requirement that cursor declarations precede their usage in the source code; that is, a cursor must be declared on a previous line in the source code, as follows:

```
— define a module scope variable as a flag
define first_pass smallint

function f()

let first_pass = TRUE

while ( continue = TRUE )
        call get_data( key1, key2 ) returning data_rec.*

...
```

```
function get_data( k1, k2 )
...

if ( first_pass )    then
        declare data_curs cursor for ...
              let first_pass = FALSE
end if
```

In this example, the variable first_pass is declared to have module scope. Module scope variables are visible within the entire source code module in which they were declared and are static, retaining their value between function calls. These variables are not visible beyond the source code module in which they were declared. This technique overcomes the disadvantage of no static local variables. This type of variable is needed for the first_pass flag, because it must retain its value between calls to the function get_data, something that simple local (automatic) variables will not do.

Within the function get_data, the first_pass flag is evaluated. If the flag is set TRUE, the initialization code within the if/then statement is executed; this includes the cursor declaration. If the flag is set FALSE, the initialization code is not executed. This allows the overhead of excessive cursor declaration to be avoided and enhances modularity by placing all code relevant to the cursor together in the same location.

Chapter Summary

This chapter has introduced the Informix-4GL language. As this chapter detailed, this language provides for seamless interaction with the IDS database. Informix-4GL data types mirror those of the IDS database and the language provides a full set of SQL statements that can be used virtually without restriction in an Informix-4GL program.

Data retrieved from an IDS database can be placed in native program variables and data in program variables can be inserted into an IDS database. The 4GL language provides cursors to match the set-at-a-time logic of nonprocedural SQL with the record-at-a-time logic of Informix-4GL. Cursors have a variety of capabilities associated with them to allow for random access to a set defined by a `select` statement, or to allow efficient updates or inserts using either *update* cursors or *insert* cursors.

Next Chapter

The next chapter covers the process of performing input and output with an Informix-4GL program. Screen forms, the method for interacting with a data terminal, are covered along with the process of producing reports using the Informix-4GL report writing syntax.

Chapter 9

Screen Forms and Reports

The INFORMIX-4GL screen form is a template for screen interaction. It describes the data to be output to the screen, the characteristics of the data, and the attributes to be used on display of the data. A great deal of data binding can take place if desired. Screen fields can be bound to table columns; the data type and length of those columns will then match the data type and length of those columns when the form was created.

INFORMIX-4GL uses a form compiler, named `form4gl`, which reads the screen form image and outputs a compiled image of the screen form. The data in this file maps to internal structures that are used by the INFORMIX-4GL program at runtime. The INFORMIX-4GL screen form interface is designed to be dynamic.

The characteristics of the terminal are read at runtime from the `termcap` or `terminfo` definition file. This means that, by definition, specific terminal characteristics are not known until runtime. Therefore, the compiler cannot determine the validity of certain screen form interaction statements. This can make the screen form development process frustrating. Some tips to make this process easier and more predictable are presented in this chapter.

Managing Screen Size

The size of the screen form defaults to 24 lines at 80 characters per line, but this can be changed by using the `screen size` statement in the screen form. Because different terminals can have different screen sizes, the validity of these parameters is not checked until runtime. As long as the terminal capabilities match those needed to run the application, the application will run.

Screen Form Programming

The INFORMIX-4GL screen form is composed of a `database` section, a `screen` section, a `tables` section, an `attributes` section, and an optional `instructions` section. The `screen` section contains an image of the screen. The image is composed of plain text and screen *fields*. Screen fields are labels that indicate where input or display is to take place. These fields are identified by screen labels, which are composed of an open brace, an initial alpha character, and/or additional alpha characters and numbers. After the label, the field is padded by spaces up to the defined length of the field. The end of the field is identified by a closing brace. Alpha characters used in the screen field labels can be upper or lower case; the screen form compiler is not case-sensitive. A single character can be used to create a field label for a single character field and the maximum number of single character fields that can be placed in a screen form is therefore 26.

Database Binding in Screen Forms

Because INFORMIX-4GL screen forms were designed to interact with a database table or tables, a form of database binding is available within the screen form interface. Once the database has been identified in the `database` section of the screen form, database table fields can be bound to fields on the screen form in the `attributes` section. The data type of these fields is then presumed to be the data type of the field in the database table. The length of the field, however, is the length of the field on the screen form. At runtime, when data is input into these fields, its data type is checked against the data type of the database table field. If the data that has been input cannot be converted to the data type of the table field, an error is signaled and user input remains in the same field. If the data length differs and truncation does not cause a loss of significant digits, truncation will occur. In this case, no error is signaled.

The `attributes` section further provides the means of specifying additional attributes for the screen form field. Most of these attributes can be specified within the INFORMIX-4GL application as well as in the screen forms. If they are specified in both places, some contention can occur.

The `instructions` section of the screen form is optional. It can be used to redefine the field delimiter characters used in INFORMIX-4GL or create screen records. Screen records are a useful means of grouping screen form fields together in a single record, which can be referenced in INFORMIX-4GL screen interaction statements.

`formonly` Screens

If the screen form will not be interacting with a specific database, the database statement can specify `formonly` as the database. In this case, the `tables` section cannot be used.

The `formonly` screen form provides an excellent mechanism for designing generic screens—screens not bound to a particular database. These screens can be used to develop library routines usable for manipulating data from a variety of tables. Such routines are the building blocks of a modular application.

A `formonly` screen is designated by indicating in the database section of the form that no database will be used. The syntax for this is as follows:

```
database formonly
screen {

...

```

Of course, designating a form as `formonly` precludes using any database binding within the form. Using database binding does not limit the screen to `formonly` fields. As the following form shows, it is possible to mix fields bound to table columns with `formonly` fields.

```
database inventory
screen
```

```
{

Product Name        [f001                      ]
Wholesale Price      [f002          ]
Markup               [f003          ]
Total                [f004          ]


}

tables
inventory
stock

attributes
f001 = stock.product_name;
f002 = stock.curr_price;
f003 = inventory.markup_amt;
f004 = formonly.total;
...
```

In this example, the inventory database is selected because the majority of the fields in the form are from tables in that database. However, one of the fields, the total field, is a computed field; the data in this field does not come from any database tables. For this reason, the field is designated as a formonly field.

Because there is no data type declared for the formonly field, it is treated as a character field with a length equal to the length of the screen form field in the screen form, including blanks. Even though a numeric is displayed to this field, there should be no problem because data conversion occurs freely as it does in most INFORMIX-4GL statements. A data type could have optionally been declared for this field using the following syntax:

```
....

attributes
f004 = formonly.total, type decimal(5,2);
```

Manipulating the Screen Form in INFORMIX-4GL

INFORMIX-4GL manipulates data on the screen via the screen form. Screen forms can be displayed in a window, and multiple windows and screens can be opened and displayed at the same time. The only real restriction on the number of screen forms opened is the number of file descriptors available on the application platform, because each open screen form represents an open file.

The open form statement is used to open a screen form. This statement is used to associate a screen form identifier with a screen form. It also identifies where the runtime application can find the compiled screen form file necessary to open the screen form. The validity of this information is not checked until runtime.

Screen Form Identifiers

The screen form is identified by an identifier that has global scope in the application. The identifier is static and is created at *compile* time; it cannot be created at *runtime*. This implies that a form opened in one INFORMIX-4GL source code module will be recognized in another source code module.

As with all global identifiers, this can create problems. A screen form that is opened, used, and closed within the same function could have a name collision with a screen form opened and used in an unrelated function. One workaround for this problem is to name generic screen forms using a leading underscore character, as shown in the following example:

```
open form _custf1 from "cust_form"
display form _custf1
```

Modularity and Screen Form Interaction

When developing an application, there are several decisions that must be made relative to screen forms. One programming style would elect to open all screen forms in the same function. These forms are opened during application initialization and are then ready for use. This eliminates the need to open the screen form when the application finds it necessary to use it; the form will already be opened—all that will be necessary is to display the screen form.

There is some minimal overhead associated with opening a screen form. The screen form file must be opened, which requires operating system overhead. The contents of the file must be read into INFORMIX-4GL's internal screen form structures; data space must be allocated for these structures. While this may have been an issue on some older, less-efficient platforms, most current hardware performs these functions in a virtually imperceptible period of time.

A coding style that enhances modularity and improves maintainability is to place all INFORMIX-4GL screen form operations together in one or more screen form modules. In this module, screen forms are opened, displayed, and, when necessary, closed.

An alternative to opening screen forms together in a single function designated solely for opening screen forms is to open the screen form in the function in which it will be displayed and used. The advantage to this approach is maintainability. The programmer need look no further than the current function to determine which screen form is being used to display the screen.

Managing Multiple Windows

It has become something of an art to determine the correct window size for an INFORMIX-4GL screen form. A window can be opened with a screen form, but the default window size is not always that needed for the application. The following formula can be used to size a window for an INFORMIX-4GL form:

number of lines needed = (form line - 1) + (form length + 1 for the comment line)
+ 2 (if the window has a border)
number of columns needed = position of right-most column + 2
(if the window has a border)

By default, the form line starts at line 1 of the screen. This can be changed with the options statement. As the formula shown indicates, changing the form line can impact the sizing of the screen.

The Current Window

INFORMIX-4GL allows multiple screens to be opened and displayed. Control can be passed from one window to another, with each window displaying separate screen forms and performing separate input operations.

The current window statement is used to shift control
between windows. When the statement is executed as current
window is screen, the effect is to have the bottom-layer window, the blank screen, brought to the top and all other windows
layered below it. Once this statement has been executed, any displayed windows or forms will be displayed on this blank screen.
The following program demonstrates this functionality:

```
main

open window w1 at 5,5
    with 10 rows, 10 columns
    attribute (border )
display "1" at 1,1

current window is screen
open window w2 at 10,10
    with 10 rows, 10 columns
    attribute(border)
display "2" at 1,1

current window is screen
open window w3 at 15,15
    with 7 rows, 10 columns
    attribute( border )
display "3" at 1,1

sleep 10

end main
```

This program displays three-bordered windows to the screen,
each with a separate number displayed to the window. But as
each window is displayed, the current window is screen
statement is executed and eclipses the previous window with a
blank screen. The result is, after the last window has been displayed, that it is the only window visible, as shown in Figure 9-1.

To obtain a set of layered windows, the current window is
screen statement must be eliminated, as shown in the following code. The result is a set of three layered windows.

```
main

open window w1 at 5,5
    with 10 rows, 10 columns
```

Figure 9-1 *Managing INFORMIX-4GL Windows.*

```
    attribute (border )
display "1" at 1,1

open window w2 at 10,10
   with 10 rows, 10 columns
   attribute(border)
display "2" at 1,1

open window w3 at 15,15
   with 7 rows, 10 columns
   attribute( border )
display "3" at 1,1

sleep 10

end main
```

In this code, each window is displayed sequentially. The result is that the first window displayed is the bottom layer, the next window displayed is the second layer, and the third and last window displayed is the top layer. The result is shown in Figure 9-2.

Unfortunately, there is no easy way to determine the current window. This makes it advantageous to keep window-manipulation statements close to the code in which the windows are used, preferably within the same function block. If this maxim is followed, it is relatively easy to determine which window is the current window merely by looking to the start of the current function. The following code sample illustrates this concept:

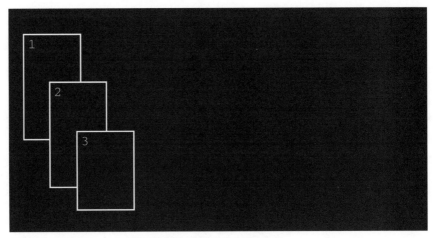

Figure 9-2 Managing INFORMIX-4GL Windows

```
define wflags array[3] of smallint

main

initialize wflags to NULL

call f1()
call f2()
call f3()

end main

function f1()

if wflags[1]  IS NULL then
    open window w1
    open form f1
    let wflags[1] = TRUE
end if
current window w1

. . .

end function

function f2()
```

```
if wflags[2] IS NULL then
    open window w2
    open form f2
    let wflags[2] = TRUE
end if
current window w2

...

end function

function f3()

if wflags[3] IS NULL then
    open window w3
    open form f3
    let wflags[3] = TRUE
end if
current window w3

....

end function

function close_windows()
define n smallint

for n = 1 to 3

    if wflags[n] is NOT NULL  then
        case n
          when 1 close window w1
                  close form f1
          when 2 close window w2
                  close form f2
          when 3 close window w3
                  close form f3
        end case
    end if

end for

end function
```

This sample application demonstrates a modular approach to window and form management. First, an array of three `small-int` variables (`wflags`) is declared with module scope. These variables are used as flags in the functions that make use of the screen forms. In the main program block, the array of flags is initialized to NULL.

Next, the functions are called in sequence. In the body of each function, the flag variable is tested; if it is NULL, the window and screen form for that function is opened and the screen form displayed. If the flag is not set, the current window is set to the appropriate window and function execution continues. The `close_windows` function is used to close only those windows that have been opened; it can determine this information by evaluating the `wflags` array element for the window in question.

This approach to screen window operations modularity places the majority of window operations in the functions that use the window, thus keeping the control for these operations close together. The advantages to this approach are improved modularity and efficiency; windows and forms are only opened if they are used.

`display` Statement

The `display` statement is used to display output either to the current screen or to specific fields on the current screen form. Because there is no supported method of determining the current screen form, it is the programmer's responsibility to have knowledge of the current open screen form.

The most simple form of the `display` statement can be used to perform simple output of data to the current position on the terminal screen. When this form of the statement is used, there is no effort to clear or initialize the current terminal screen. The statement acts like the C language `puts` function call; it simply takes the data variables passed to it, converts them to a string data type, and outputs the data at the current terminal cursor position. This means that, in its simplest form, the `display` statement can be used to produce simple reports, as the following code demonstrates:

```
main
define salesm record like salesman.*

declare sales_curs cursor for
              select *
              from   salesman
```

```
             where region   = "NE"

foreach sales_curs into salesm.*
        display "Salesman:   First Name: ",
                salesm.first_name,
                " Last ",  salesm.last_name,
                " Phone: ",  salesm.phone

        end foreach

end main
```

In this example, a report of all the salespersons in the northeast region is printed to the terminal screen. Because no screen interaction statements that would reset the terminal screen have been executed, the display statement will simply take its output and send it to the terminal screen, displaying a newline character at the end of the output. The output of the program could be output to the system printer using the Unix `lp` command, as follows:

```
rpt_prog | lp
```

The simple form of the display statement can take any INFORMIX-4GL simple data variable and output it to the screen. Unfortunately, in its current form, it cannot take expressions as arguments, even if those expressions evaluate to a simple data type. The following example illustrates this problem:

```
function funct_s()

        return   "hello world"

end function

display funct_s()
```

This code example would fail to compile, because `funct_s` is considered too complex a data type for the `display` statement, even though the expression `funct_s()` resolves to a simple character string. The following statement would also fail to pass a compile:

```
define x,y smallint
```

```
let x = 1
let y = 2

       display ( x + y / 2 )
```

Once again, the compiler would consider the simple mathematical expression too complex for the `display` statement. The only solution to this limitation is to use temporary variables to store the results of these expressions, as follows:

```
let str = s()
let x = x + y / 2

display x,str
```

This `display` statement would not only compile, but would also execute without incident.

The `display` Statement and Screen Form Interaction

The `display` statement can make explicit use of database binding with the `by name` clause. When this clause is used, the INFORMIX-4GL runtime screen form component searches for column names that match the record component names of the record being used. These record component names must provide an exact match for the screen form field names; otherwise, the statement will fail. An example of this statement is as follows:

```
database sales
screen
{
                                        Customer Record

        First Name          [f001                                      ]
        Last Name           [f002                                      ]
        Address             [f003                                      ]

                     }
tables
customer

attributes
f001 = customer.first_name;
```

```
f002 = customer.last_name;
f003 = customer.address;
```

```
....
```

```
— INFORMIX-4GL program

        define cust_rec record like customer.*
```

```
...
        display by name cust_rec.* to customer.*
```

In this example, because the fields in the screen form are
named identically and in the same order as the columns in the
customer table, they can be referenced in the display statement.

It is not necessary for an entire table to be referenced for the
by name clause to be used; a portion of one table or portions of
a number of tables could be referenced. As long as the *names* of
the columns are identical to the record element name and sensible data type conversion can take place, the by name clause can
be used. The following example demonstrates this capability
using a screen record:

```
database sales
screen
{
                           Customer    Record

        First Name        [f001                              ]
        Last Name         [f002                              ]
        Salesman Number   [f003                              ]


                }
tables
customer
salesman

attributes
f001 = customer.first_name;
f002 = customer.last_name;
f004 = salesman.number;

instructions
```

```
screen record scr1 ( customer.first_name,
       customer.last_name,
       salesman.number)

...

-- INFORMIX-4GL program to display data to the screen form

       define scr_rec record like customer.first_name,
       customer.last_name,
       salesman.first_name,
       salesman.last_name

....
       display by name scr_rec.* to scr1.*
```

In this example, the screen form is created to interact with two tables: the salesman table and the customer table. The columns used in these two tables are identified and referenced in the attributes section of the screen form. These columns are then placed in a screen record. In the INFORMIX-4GL program, this screen record is then used as the target of the display statement. The entire contents of the scr_rec record will be displayed to the scr1 screen record, matching the names of the record elements to the names of the columns.

input Statement

The input statement uses the INFORMIX-4GL screen form to retrieve data from the terminal. While the majority of the data entry control rests with the INFORMIX-4GL program, the screen form definitions also affect data entry. The INFORMIX-4GL program interacts with the screen form to retrieve data from the terminal. This interaction is performed using the input statement.

The input statement retrieves data from each field in its target form. It moves through the fields in a serial fashion, beginning at the top of its internal input list and finishing with the last field in its input list. The order of input is controlled by the order of fields listed in the attributes section of the screen form if a screen record is *not* being used, or the order of fields listed in the screen record if a screen record is used.

```
define cust_rec record like customer.*

- the order in which the fields appear in the screen
- form will control the order of input

input cust_rec.* from customer.*
```

A number of events can be trapped during the execution of the `input` statement. These event traps are one of the more unique and interesting aspects of the INFORMIX-4GL language. The events are *before field, after field,* and *on key.* The `before field` statement is used to take control of the input operation before entering the named field. The `after field` statement takes control after the cursor leaves the field. The `on key` statement is used to take control of the application when a defined function key is pressed by the user. Examples of these statements are shown in the next section.

Moving Past an Input Field

There are times when it is desirable to keep the cursor from entering a field on the screen form. The field may be used to display lookup information or a field derived from other fields on the screen form. There are two methods for skipping this field. In the following code sample, the screen field is skipped using a `next field` statement in the `before field` block.

```
database sales
screen
{

     Salesman Information

First Name          [f001                                    ]
Last Name           [f002                                    ]
Territory Code      [f003    ]
Name                [f004                                    ]
}

tables
salesman
territory
```

```
attributes
f001 = salesman.first_name;
f002 = salesman.last_name;
f003 = salesman.territory;
f004 = territory.territory_name, reverse;

instructions

screen record sc1 (salesman.first_name, salesman.last_name,
salesman.territory, territory.territory_name)

...

define scr_rec record like salesman.first_name,
salesman.lastname, salesman.territory, territory.territory_name;

input scr_rec.* from  sc1.*

   before field territory_name
        display scr_rec.territory_name to
        territory_name_
        next field salesman.first_name
...
```

In this example, the input statement skips the
territory_name field because the before field statement for
this field directs input to the salesman.first_name field before
the cursor can enter the territory_name field. This same functionality could have been provided by declaring the screen field
attribute in the screen form to be a noentry field, as follows:

```
...
f004 = territory.territory_name, reverse, noentry;
```

Either approach is correct. Placing attribute entries in the
screen form has the advantage of reducing the code required in
the INFORMIX-4GL application. However, a maintenance programmer reviewing the input loop of a given application would
not immediately know what attributes are being used on the
screen form fields. By placing attribute information within the
input statement block, the programmer uses a structured syntax
to achieve the same functionality.

Highlighting the Current Field

Often, it is desirable to have the current input field highlighted, as shown in Figure 9-3. This makes it easier for the user to detect which field is currently being input. Unfortunately, INFORMIX-4GL does not currently have a clause that triggers this behavior. However, as the following example shows, it is not difficult to achieve this functionality.

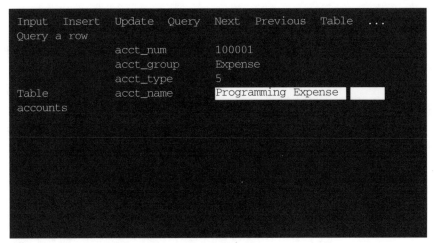

Figure 9-3 Highlighting the Current Field

```
— highlight the current field in the input loop

input scr_rec.* from scr1.*

before field first_name
        display scr_rec.first_name to first_name
              attribute ( reverse )

after field first_name
        display scr_rec.first_name to first_name
              attribute ( normal )

before field last_name
        display scr_rec.last_name to last_name
              attribute( reverse )
```

```
after field last_name
        display scr_rec.last_name to last_name
                attribute( normal )
```

In this example, the current field is highlighted in the `before field` statement by displaying the data in that field to the screen using the `attribute (reverse)` clause. This leaves the entire field (length defined in the screen form) in the reverse attribute while the user is entering data and the cursor remains in this field. In order to eliminate the reverse video when the cursor leaves the field, the code in the `after field` statement is required. This code displays the current contents of the data record, which may have changed during input, back to the screen field using the *normal* video attribute. The `attribute` statement in this `display` statement is redundant because normal attribute is the default attribute for the `display` statement, but it is included here to make the code more readable. A maintenance programmer would be more likely to understand the purpose of the `display` statement because the normal attribute is being emphasized by use of this clause.

Termcap Issues

A number of the capabilities of INFORMIX-4GL are dependent on the definitions of the terminal being used. With Unix systems, these definitions are contained in a file known by the name `termcap` in the `/etc` directory. If a terminal attribute is not available (it is not defined in the `termcap` file) and INFORMIX-4GL attempts to invoke this attribute, the statement will generally be ignored by the screen form runtime component.

For instance, if the terminal does not support reverse video, reverse video will simply not be displayed. Additionally, if the function keys are not assigned in the `termcap` for the terminal, INFORMIX-4GL will fail on attempts to access these function keys.

Redefining Function Keys

INFORMIX-4GL allows specific keys to be remapped through the `options` statement. If a programmer wishes to turn off certain keys during input, the `options` statement may be used to redefine these keys to a function key that is undefined for the terminal being used.

Turning Off the Insert Key and Delete Key
in `input array`

If an application uses an `input array` statement that should not allow the user to insert or delete rows, the `options` statement can be used to map the insert or delete keys to function keys undefined for the terminals being used, as follows:

```
options
        insert key f39,
        delete key f40
```

This code redefines the `insert key` to function key 39 and the `delete key` to function key 40, keys that cannot be generated on most terminals. If the terminal doesn't allow these function keys, the `insert key` and `delete key` have been turned off during the `input array`.

Adding Additional Function Keys
in the `termcap` File

Adding additional function keys to the INFORMIX-4GL `termcap` is relatively simple. The programmer must first determine the escape sequence transmitted by the terminal. This can usually be accomplished by pressing the function key and redirecting its output to a file. This file can then be read using either a text editor that will display control keys or a Unix utility, such as `od`, that displays the ASCII or hexadecimal value of the contents of the file.

Once the function key escape sequence has been determined, it is simply a matter of making the appropriate entry in the `termcap` file. For example, if the terminal being used was found to be sending the escape sequence \E (escape) OP for function key 1 (f1), the correct entry to make in the termcap for that terminal would be as follows:

```
v1|vt100|vt-100|DEC vt100:\
...
        :k0=\EOP:k1=\EOQ:k2=\EOR:k3=\EOS:\
...
```

If a *page-up* or *page-down* key is needed, then the process is similar to that of the function keys. The programmer must first determine the escape sequence transmitted. Once this is known, the termcap entry must be made to relate this escape key sequence to a function key number that will be used to trap the page-up and page-down keys. This process is shown as follows:

```
v1|vt100|vt-100|DEC vt100:\
...
        :k31=\EOP:k32=\EOQ:k2=\EOR:k3=\EOS:\
...
```

Next, in the options statement for the application, the function keys for next key and previous key should be set to the function keys that have been mapped for the page-up and page-down keys, as follows:

```
options
        next key f31,
        previous key f32
```

Once these steps have been taken, whenever an input array or display array statement is executed, the page-up and page-down keys for the terminal will cause the screen array to scroll forward or backward appropriately.

Trapping the Interrupt Key

INFORMIX-4GL provides a means of trapping the interrupt key when the application is waiting for user input. This interrupt trap is achieved using the defer interrupt statement. By default, if the interrupt signal is received by the program, the application will abort. Because this is not always desirable behavior, it is useful to trap the interrupt key in the application. If the interrupt key is trapped, the interrupt flag (int_flag) must be checked at the end of `input` statements to determine whether or not the user has pressed the interrupt key. The following code demonstrates this method:

```
database accounting

main
define ar record like accounts.*

defer interrupt

options  message line last - 1

open form accts from "accts"
display form accts

let int_flag = FALSE
input by name ar.*

    before field acct_num
        message "Enter Account Number"
        display ar.acct_num to acct_num attribute( normal )

end input
if int_flag  then
    error "Input Aborted.
    initialize ar.* to NULL
    return ar.*
else
    return ar.*
end if
```

In this example, the `defer interrupt` option is set before the screen form is opened and displayed. Before the start of the input loop, the `int_flag` is set to FALSE. This is necessary to allow for the contingency when the `int_flag` has not been reset by the application after the last interrupt.

After the input block, the `int_flag` is tested. If it has been set, an error message is displayed, the `int_flag` is reset, the `ar` record is set to NULL and the function returns a NULL record. If the `int_flag` has not been set, the function simply returns the record.

INFORMIX-4GL Reports

In creating the INFORMIX-4GL report writer, the developers sought to provide a productive report generation environment that would overcome the limitations of Ace, the precursor to the INFORMIX-4GL report writer. The syntax of Ace was placed in the INFORMIX-4GL report writer virtually intact, and was combined with virtually all of the 4GL procedural and nonprocedural statements. The result was the INFORMIX-4GL report facility.

The INFORMIX-4GL report facility is a set of program statements that provides a block-oriented, structured set of statements for report production. Control blocks are provided to define format, initialize control variables, and produce report output. With report blocks, any procedural and most nonprocedural statements (including SQL) can be executed. This allows calculations to be performed, database tables to be updated, and report output to be formatted within report statement blocks. Tables 9-1 and 9-2 list the statements that make up the INFORMIX-4GL report facility.

Table 9-1 *Report Statements*

Statement	Function
`report report_name( parameter1, parameter2, )`	Indicates the start of the report block.
`define`	Defines static variables local to the report.
`format`	Indicates the start of the block that defines how to format the data being passed to the report.
`on every row`	Within format section—indicates how data is to be formatted for every row passed.
`after group of / before group of field_name`	Within format section—indicates control breaks for the data stream being passed to the report.
`on last row`	Within format section—indicates actions taken at the end of the report.

Virtually all other INFORMIX-4GL statements can be executed in the `format` block of a report function with few restrictions, but some restrictions do apply. Screen interaction statements such as `close form`, `input`, `display`, and `construct` cannot be executed within the body of a report. (The simple workaround for this limitation is to call a function, which then executes the screen interaction statement.)

Report Statements

A report has a specific start triggered by a `start report` statement, and a specific end triggered by a `finish report` statement. The `start report` statement opens the file or device for output. The `output to report` statement is used to output data to the file or device; it is called for each tuple to be output to the report. The `finish report` statement flushes the remainder of the buffer being used to the output device and closes the device. Failure to issue a `finish report` statement could result in an incomplete report (a common error). The effect of these statements is shown in Table 9-2.

Table 9-2 Report Interaction Statements

Statement	Function
`start report <report name>`	Starts the report; can optionally identify an output device.
`output to report <report name>`	Sends output to the report device/file.
`finish report <report name>`	Completes the report; closes the output device.

Variables are declared within the `define` section and, unlike other INFORMIX-4GL function variables, these variables retain their value between successive calls. This is currently the only instance of static local scope variables within INFORMIX-4GL.

The report block is declared with the `report` statement. It uses a function-like syntax that identifies the parameters to be passed to the report using the `output to report` statement on each iteration of the report. These parameters must be passed to the report, and must match in number and ordinal position and have compatible data types. If the number of parameters in the `output to report` statement does not match that declared in the report declaration statement, the **compiler** signals a fatal error. If the data types passed in the `output to report` statement cannot be converted, a fatal **runtime** error is signaled. Figure 9-4 illustrates the effects of report statements.

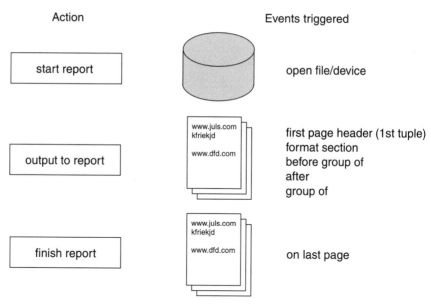

Action		Events triggered

start report — open file/device

output to report — first page header (1st tuple) / format section / before group of / after / group of

finish report — on last page

Figure 9-4 *Effect of Report Statements*

Declaring a Report

The body of a report is declared using a syntax similar to that of an INFORMIX-4GL function, as follows:

```
report sales( sales_rec )
define sales_rec record like sales_person.*
```

This code declares the report `sales_report` and indicates that it will be receiving the `sales_rec` record. In the `define` section of the report, `sales_rec` is identified as a record with a structure identical to that of the `sales_person` table.
The report declaration need not appear in the same module in which the report is started and executed. Internally, the report declaration creates a function that will be called when the `output to report` statement is executed, as follows:

```
start report sales_report

foreach report_curs into srec.*

    output to report  sales_report ( srec.* )

end foreach
```

```
finish report sales_report
```

In this example, the `output to report` statement is executed within a `foreach` loop. The `foreach` loop provides an excellent mechanism for report generation. It creates a loop within
which report parameters can be created and then output to the
report, all within the same control block. Before the start of the
`foreach` loop, the `start report` statement can be executed;
upon termination of the `foreach` loop, the `finish report`
statement is usually executed.

Generating a Default Report

INFORMIX-4GL has the capability to create a simple default
report using very little code. The report produced is very simple
and lacks formatting, but it does represent a quick and easy
method to produce a report. The following code demonstrates
this capability:

```
database sales

main
define sr record like sales_person.*

declare c1 cursor for
    select *
    from sales_person

start report sales

foreach c1 into sr.*
    output to report sales( sr.* )
end foreach

finish report sales

end main

report sales( sales_rec )
define sales_rec like sales_person.*

format
    every row
```

```
end report
```

In this example, on the first line of the program module, the compiler is informed of the database to use for record declarations, the `sales` database. Next, a record is declared to have the same structure as the `sales_person` table. A cursor is declared to select every row, and every data element in the rows, from that table. A `foreach` loop is then started, and the data retrieved is output to the default report. The output from this report is as follows:

```
first_name    Frank
last_name     Salesguy
territory     Buffalo
quota         1,000,000

first_name    Greg
last_name     Techguy
territory     SW
quota         1,000,000
```

The `output` Section

The `output` section of the report, as the name denotes, defines where data will be output and provides some basic formatting instructions for that output. This section of the report is optional and, if omitted, various defaults will take effect. The defaults for the report output section are listed in Table 9-3.

Table 9-3 Output Section Defaults

Parameter	Default
report to <character>	Terminal screen (stdout)
left margin <integer>	5
right margin <integer>	132
top margin <integer>	3
bottom margin <integer>	3
page length <integer>	66
top of page <character>	Not used

The parameters for these options must be constants; variables may not be substituted. While this may appear to force the report format options to be defined at program compile time, the fact is that these parameters are easy to adjust dynamically at runtime, as shown in the sections that follow.

The `report to` statement is used to direct the output of a report to a particular location. Note that by default, the report data will be sent to the terminal screen in a continuous stream. Unless `pause` statements are inserted into the body of the report, the report will scroll continuously off the screen until the report is complete.

If the `report to` statement has been used in the body of the report, and the `start report` statement has a `to` clause, then the `start report` statement takes precedence, and the `report to` statement in the body of the report is ignored.

The `report to` statement can specify `printer` as the output device. In this case, the contents of the environment variable DBPRINT are examined, and output is sent to the program specified in the environment variable. If this environment variable is not set, then, under the Unix operating system, the program "lp" is opened as a receiving pipe, and data is output to this program.

The `right margin` parameter in the output section is only effective within a default report or if the `wordwrap` clause is used; if this is not the case, the `right margin` statement is **ignored** by the INFORMIX-4GL report writer. This means that, in most cases, INFORMIX-4GL does not enforce the right margin; it is up to the programmer to do that, using logic similar to that shown throughout the following sections.

The `order by` Section

The `order by` statement is used to specify the order in which the report grouping statements (`before group of`/`after group of`) should be executed. If the sort order of the report is specified here, the report *front end* will sort the data. Informix has made a great deal of effort to improve the speed of engine or *back-end* sorts. The back end has the intelligence to make use of indices if available, use parallel sorting schemes, or sort merge techniques, methods that are not necessarily available to the front-end sort facility. If the data will be output to the report in the order expected, the order need not be specified.

Because it would obviously be more efficient to have the data sorted by the engine than by the front end, it is recommended that sorts be performed there. This can be done by specifying the correct sort order using the `order by` clause in the SQL statement.

The `format` Section

The `format` section represents the body of the report. Subclauses within this section identify the actions to be taken during the preparation of the report. It is the capability of using virtually any INFORMIX-4GL procedural or nonprocedural statement within this block that allows the INFORMIX-4GL report writer to be used for more than just simple reports.

First Page Header

The `first page header` section is executed once per report. It is triggered by the transfer of the first tuple to the report function. The `first page header` does *not* trigger the `page header` block, so if it is necessary to print a page header for the first page, the page header print statements must also appear in the `first page header` section of the report. This section is usually used to print the first page header, but is also useful for performing initialization of variables to be used in the report, as the following code demonstrates.

```
define

    col1 integer,
    col2 integer,
    col3 integer,
    page_header1 char(50),
    page_header2 char(50)


first page header

— initialize variables
let col1 = 10
let col2 = 20
let col3 = 30
```

```
— create the page header strings to be printed on every page
let page_header1 = "Regional Sales Report"
let page_header2 = "Date: ",today, " Time: ",time

— print the page header
print  col1, page_header1
print  col1, page_header2
...
```

In this example, the `first page header` section is used to initialize integer variables that will be used to hold the multiple column position for the data to be printed on the report. Next, two character strings are initialized to hold the page headers for the report. Finally, the page headers are printed.

This demonstrates initialization of variables within the `first page header` section of the report. These variables are local to the report function and are not visible outside of the report function. However, unlike other local variables in INFORMIX-4GL, they will retain their value on each iteration of the report. This allows subtotals and totals to be maintained and allows local report variables to be used to hold column positions, which is demonstrated in the next section.

Creating Dynamic Column Positions in Reports

It is not uncommon during the development of a report to have to constantly change the format of the report. By using the integer variables to hold column positions, report modification is made easier.

If all column one data is being printed at a column position stored in an integer variable, it is merely a matter of changing the value of that integer variable once in the `first page header` section to effectively move the data throughout the report. Storing the column position in this manner also allows the data to be moved around on the report at runtime if needed.

A variation on this method is shown as follows. With this method, all column positions are relative to the starting column (column one) position. In this way, adjusting the column position for one column will automatically adjust the column position of the remaining columns to the right of that column. This technique is shown as follows:

```
first page header
```

```
let col1 = 3
let col2 = col1 + 10     - sales man first name
let col3 = col2 + 5      - sales man last name
let col4 = col3 + 5      - region name
let col5 = col4 + 10     - sales amount in that region

on every row
        print column col1, sr.first_name,
              column col2, sr.last_name,
              column col3, sr.region_name,
              column col4, sr.sales_amount
```

In this example, the column positions are all set relative to the column position of the previous column, with the exception of the first column, which is assigned an integer constant value. This simplifies modification of the report. In order to adjust the report to allow the length of the salesperson first name to be fifteen characters instead of the current 10 characters, the only modification necessary would be to the col2 assignment statement, as follows:

```
let col2 = col1 + 15
```

This assignment adds five column positions to the starting column position for column two. Because all columns greater than column two are assigned their column position relative to column two, this will have the effect of pushing those columns over five column positions.

The format Section—before group of/ after group of Clauses

The INFORMIX-4GL report facility uses the before group of/after group of statements to provide report control breaks. The grouping logic assumes that the data is being sent to the report in a sorted fashion, and the default sequence for the grouping is the order in which they appear in the format section. As stated previously, this can be overridden and made specific using the order by clause in the output section of the report. If this clause is used *without* the external keyword, the report will ensure the report data is sorted by performing its own

Table 9-4 *Aggregate Functions*

Function Name	Purpose
sum	Compute sum of field.
avg	Compute average of field.
count	Compute count of all rows passed.
percent	Compute percentage of total (count(*)/total).
min	Minimum value of field.
max	Maximum value of field.

sort of the incoming parameters. Because the report has no knowledge of how the data is being sent to it, it will perform a complete sort.

A variety of aggregate functions can be used within the body of the report. These functions provide powerful nonprocedural capabilities which can reduce the code necessary to generate the report. They are listed in Table 9-4.

Aggregates also support the use of a where clause. This clause can be used to filter the data that will be used to compute the aggregate function; only the data that fulfills the where clause criteria will be used in the computation of the aggregate—all other rows are ignored. The syntax of the where clause used with aggregates is similar to that of the where clause used in SQL statements: a number of Boolean operators can be used to create a list of conditions that rows must meet before they are accepted. The following example demonstrates the use of the where clause with aggregate group functions:

```
    . . .

on last row

        print  "New Jersey Sales Person Count: ", count(*) where
                             sales_man.region = "NJ"
```

In this example, a count of rows where the salesperson's region is "NJ" is obtained on the final row of the report. The count is obtained by using the where clause in conjunction with the INFORMIX-4GL aggregate function count(*).

Batch Processing in Reports

A variety of processing can be performed within the `before group of`/`after group of` clauses. A common practice in production systems is to perform batch processing during the report run. This is representative of a typical batch-processing report run where database tables are updated as a report is generated. The following example demonstrates such a report.

```
{schema for acct_master and acct_balances table}

create table acct_master (   acct_code char(10),
                                    sub_code char(3)
                                    acct_group char(3),
                                    acct_name char(15) );
create table acct_balances ( acct_code char(10),
                                    acct_group char(3),
                                    acct_period smallint,
                                    acct_balance decimal(12,2) );
```

```
{function and report for acct_group report }

function acct_rpt_drv()

define accts record like acct_master.sub_code,*

declare c1 cursor for
     select acct_master.acct_code,
              acct_master.acct_name,
              acct_master.acct_group,
              acct_balances.balance
     from acct_master,
              acct_balances
     where acct_master.acct_code = acct_balances.acct_code and
     acct_balances.period = 1
       order by acct_master.acct_code,
                acct_master.acct_group

start report accts

foreach c1 into accts.*
    output to report accts( accts.* )
end foreach
finish report accts
```

```
end function
```
_____

```
report accts( act_rec )
define act_rec record like acct_master.*
define sum_amt array[2] like acct_master.balance

output
    left margin 5
    top of page "^L"

format
after group of acct_code
        let sum_amt[1] = group sum(balance)

      print "Acct Code Balance: ", sum_amt[1]

      update acct_subs
      set   sub_bal = sum_amt[1]
      where sub_code = act_rec.sub_code


after group of acct_group

        let sum_amt[2] = group sum(balance)
          print "Acct Group Balance: ", sum_amt[2]

      update acct_groups
      set     group_bal = sum_amt[2]
      where group_code = act_rec.acct_group

on last row

              print file "report.trailer"


end report
```

The goal of this report is to determine the account balances and totals for the account codes and account groups. First, the `acct_master` table is read in sorted order. On control breaks for account codes and account groups, the balance subtotals are stored in their respective tables. (The practical reason for such a *roll-up* table will be faster retrieval of rows from the sub-account table than would be possible if the accounts table had to be scanned for this information.)

The report begins by declaring a cursor for an SQL statement that will simply retrieve data from the `acct_master` table in order of account code and account group. Because the data is being retrieved in the order expected by the report, there is no need to sort the data using the report sort facility. Also, because the order in which the `after group of` statements appear in the `format` section is the order in which the groupings should be executed, there is no need to specify the order using the `order by` clause in the `format` section. If this were not the case, an explicit `order by` clause would be included in the `output` section of the report.

In the `after group of` blocks, subtotals for the balance are taken and stored in an INFORMIX-4GL variable, which is then used to update the `acct_subs` and `acct_groups` tables with the subtotals. The subtotals are taken using the built-in aggregate statements of the INFORMIX-4GL report facility: the `group sum` statements.

The statements in the `on last row` clause are triggered by the `finish report` statement. In the preceding example, the `on last row` clause contains a statement that uses the `print file` statement to print a report trailer. The `print file` statement will print the text document specified at the current location in the report.

`print` Statement

The `print` statement makes use of the `using` clause. It is only recognized in the format section of the report block. The syntax for this clause within the `print` statement is as follows:

```
print column 10, acct_name, col 15,
      acct_balance using "Balance:   $<<<<<.<<"
```

One of the more difficult aspects of printing a report is that of keeping important information together and not allowing it to be printed across pages. With INFORMIX-4GL, this can be accomplished with the `need` statement, as follows:

```
after group of acct_sub

      need 3 lines
      print "Account Name: ",   accts.acct_name
```

```
print "Account Group Total: ",  sum_amt[2]
print "Sub Account Total: ",  sum_amt[1]
```

In this example, it is desirable to keep the three lines of information printed together in the same location on the report; split-
ting this information across pages would make it difficult to read.
The need statement is used to keep these lines together and force
a page break if necessary.

Managing Text Fields in Reports

INFORMIX-4GL provides several useful statements for managing Blob data types within a report. In general, if the Blob data
type is a Text column, the report writer has facilities for managing the data type. If the Blob data type is Binary, there are no
facilities provided for managing this data type; functions, most
likely C functions, would have to be called to process Binary
blobs.

The Text data type is a subset of the Blob data type that provides a variable-length field limited to 2 GB in size. The contents
of this field are limited to the printable ASCII character set plus
the control characters ^L (line-feed) and ^J (form-feed).
Extensions added to the print statement in INFORMIX-4GL version 4.1 are used to format this data type. These extensions are
demonstrated as follows:

```
format
      on every row
      print "Description : ", description_field
                       wordwrap compress right margin 80
```

In this example, the description_field is a Blob Text data
type. It is printed using the wordwrap clause to wrap words at
the right margin. The compress option is used to compress
extra spaces out of the field, leaving just a single space between
words. The right margin defaults to 132 bytes, but is overridden
for this Blob field by using the right margin clause to force it
to print with 80 columns. (Note that currently, the column position in the print section is ignored when the wordwrap option
is used.)

Page Breaks

The default method for forcing page breaks with INFORMIX-4GL is to print blank lines up to the length of the page. Besides being slow, this method is prone to error, and if the page length is not exact, can cause the page header to drift down the page as successive pages are printed. A preferable method of moving the printer to the next page is to use the page feed character, Control-L. This can be specified in the `output` section of the report using the following syntax.

```
output
    top of page "^L"
```

This statement will direct the INFORMIX-4GL report writer to use the Control-L character to move to the next page. Virtually all printers support using this control character to move to the next page.

A page break will trigger the `page header` section of the report block, where the code to produce the page header will be placed. In an effort to control the format of the report and ensure consistency, an `if` statement with a `print` statement used in this block must print the same number of lines in both portions of the `if/then/else` statement. The following example illustrates this behavior:

```
page header

        if rpt_rec.acct_group = 3   then
                print "Report Group Three being printed"
else
        let counter = count+1
end if
```

This statement would not be allowed. The INFORMIX-4GL report writer expects the page header to *always* be a consistent size. The belief is that if this statement were allowed, the report would produce unbalanced formatting results. The following code would be required:

```
    . . .

page header
        if rpt_rec.acct_group = 3   then
```

```
                          print "Report Group Three being printed"
     else
                     skip 1 line
                     let counter=count+1
          end if
```

In this example, the report output is kept balanced by printing (skipping) one line in the `else` clause of the `if/then` statement. This will effectively compensate for the one line printed in the `then` clause above that clause.

If it is necessary to keep report information together on a page, or if an entire page is needed to print the information, the `skip to top of page` statement can be used. This forces the printer to move to the next page. The following example demonstrates the use of this statement:

```
after group of acct_group

          - print accounts rolled into account group
          if num_accounts > 40 then - print on a separate page
                    skip to top of page
          end if
          for n = 1 to num_accts
          - print one line for each account


               . . . .
```

In this example, after the control break for subaccounts, a loop is executed to print a list of accounts that are contained in the account group. An `if/then` statement is used to evaluate the number of accounts to be printed. If the number of accounts is greater than 40, the report forces a page break using the `skip to top of page` statement.

If the goal in printing the account detail information is to keep *all* of the account information together on one page, the above approach is flawed. The current position on the page is not taken into consideration. A better approach that would evaluate that information is shown as follows:

```
report sub_acct_rpt( page_length, rec )

          define page_length integer,
                    rec record like ...


     . . .
```

```
                   after group of sub_accounts                  .
                   — determine whether or not there is room
                   — print the list of accounts
                       if ( page_length - lineno -  num_accounts ) <= 0
                       then
                        skip to top of page
                   end if

                   — print the information
                   for n = 1 to num_accts
                        . . .
```

In this example, the `page_length` of the report is supplied as a parameter. In addition to this parameter, the current line number on the page (`lineno`) is evaluated, along with the number of accounts to be printed. If there is not enough room to print all of the accounts together, determined by the equation `page_length - lineno - num_accounts`), then the `skip to top of page` statement is executed to move to the next page.

Modular Dynamic Reports

A more modular approach to controlling the format of a report based on parameters supplied at runtime can be accomplished by placing all relevant parameters in a record and then passing this record to the report. An example that demonstrates this approach is shown as follows:

```
database sales

main

define rpt_control record
           out_file char(10),
           page_length  integer,
           right_margin  integer,
           left margin    integer
      end record

define sales_rec record like sales_person.*

let rpt_control.out_file     = "SCREEN"
```

```
let rpt_control.page_length  = 22
let rpt_control.right_margin = 80
let rpt_control.left_margin  = 3

start report sales_rpt

declare c1 cursor for
        select *
        from    sales_person
foreach c1 into sales_rec.*

    output to report sales_rpt( rpt_control.*, sales_rec.* )

end foreach

finish report sales_rpt

end main
_____

report sales_rpt( rc, sr )

define rc record
                out_file char(10),
                page_length   integer,
                right_margin  integer,
                left_margin   integer
    end record
define sr record like sales_person.*

output
        page length   55
        right margin  0
        left margin   0
        top margin    0
        bottom margin 0

format


    on every row
        print "Sales Person: ", sr.first_name, " ",sr.mi," ",
                        sr.last_name

        if lineno = rpt_control.page_length  then

            — automatically handle output to the screen
```

```
if rpt_control.out_file = "SCREEN"   then
    pause "Press Return to Continue"
end if

skip to top of page

end if

        . . .
```

In this example, report parameters are stored in a record before calling the report. This record contains entries for page length, output file name, right margin, and left margin. In the `output` section of the report, the page length is set to a number higher than the actual page length that will be enforced.

The page length parameter is evaluated as data is being printed; if the current line number on the page, contained in the built-in variable `lineno`, is greater than the specified page length, the report jumps to the start of the next page using the `skip to top of page` statement. Assuming that the `page_length` parameter entered in the control record is greater than the page length setting in the report `output` section, this effectively removes page breaks from the control of the INFORMIX-4GL report writer.

The report control record is also examined for the output device setting. If the output device is set to "SCREEN," then a `pause` statement is executed to allow the user to press return when they are ready to see the next screen displayed. This allows the report to dynamically support screen output as well as a printer device. (Because `pause` does nothing if this output is not to the screen, this conditional clause is not needed. But other code specific to screen output could be inserted here.)

Report Issues

It is not uncommon for the format of a report to be in a constant state of flux. Users often request different report formats from week to week. With some foresight and planning, report modification can be made easier, as the following examples demonstrate.

The right margin and page length of a report can vary depending on the output data and output device. When the right margin changes, it is up to the report code to make adjustments for

this change. The examples that follow demonstrate how to manage changes in these format parameters.

```
...
first page header

        let header1 = "Accounts Report "
        let pos = right_margin - length( header1 clipped)   / 2
        let header1 = spaces pos, header1 clipped
        let header1[1,16] = "Date: ", today
        let header1[right_margin - 12, 12 ] = "Time: ", time

        let header2= "Group Breakdown"
        let pos = right_margin - length( header2 clipped ) / 2
        let header2 = spaces pos, header2 clipped
        let header2[ right_margin - 9, 9] =  pageno using
                                              "Page: <<<"
page header
        let header2[right_margin - 9, 9] = pageno using "Page:
<<<"
        print column col1, header1 clipped
        print column col1, header2 clipped
```

In this example, because the right margin can vary, it is treated
as a parameter in preparing the page headers for the report. The
report title is centered in a string using an equation that makes
use of the current right margin to place the title in the center of
the string. This equation is as follows:

```
        pos = ( right_margin - length_of_string ) / 2
```

This equation identifies a starting column position that is half-
way to the right margin, taking into account the length of the
string to be placed at that position by padding spaces to the
desired position. The next INFORMIX-4GL statement in the
example places the string to be centered at that position.

```
        let header1 = spaces pos, header1 clipped
```

This statement uses the built-in spaces function to blank-fill
the string out to the starting position for the centered string. The
string to be centered, in this case the contents of the string variable header1, are then concatenated onto this string. The page

header and time are also inserted into the string using the built-in string manipulation operators of INFORMIX-4GL.

Once the two header strings have been formatted, taking into account the variable right margin, they are then printed in the `page header` section of the report. Because they have been formatted in the `first page header` section executed at the start of the report, it is not necessary to format them again each time the page header is printed. However, because the page number varies, it is necessary to insert this into the string on each `page header` block iteration.

In addition to the headers, the row-by-row output of the report must take into account the varying right margin. The following code demonstrates this:

```
on every row

    let row1_data = "Account Name: ", Acct_name ...

    if right_margin > 80   then
      let row1_data = row1_data clipped, "Additional info: ",
          acct_info.group, column col3,
          acct_info.acct_status
          let row2_data = NULL
    else
        let row2_data = "Additional Information: ",
                        acct_info.group, column col3,
          acct_info.acct_status
    end if

      print column col1, row1_data
      if row2_data IS NOT NULL then
          print column col1, row2_data
      end if
```

In this example, the data that will be printed regardless of the length of the right margin is placed in a string. The `right_margin` variable is then evaluated to determine its length. If the length is large enough to support printing the additional data, the data is added to the `row1_data` string and the `row2_data` string is set to NULL. If the length is not long enough, the additional data is placed in the `row2_data` string. Finally, the `row1_data` string is printed and, if it is not NULL, the `row2_data` string is also printed.

Modularity in Reports

Some general rules can be applied to enhance the modularity of reports. Whenever possible, local variables should be used within the body of the report. Because local report variables are static local scope variables, one of the most common needs for global variables in INFORMIX-4GL is eliminated. While there is often the temptation to use globals to reduce the number of values that must be passed to the report function, minimizing this practice enhances the modularity and readability of the report.

As mentioned previously, the `first page header` section of the report is useful for initializing variables that will be used in the report. Because most INFORMIX-4GL programmers are aware that initialization can be performed in this section, it is recommended that initialization be performed in this block rather than elsewhere in the report. Local variables as well as module scope or global variables may be initialized in this block. It is also recommended that strings or variables that will be used throughout the report be initialized or formatted in this section. For instance, if a complex page header is to be printed consistently throughout the report, a series of strings could be assigned the values of the page header in the `first page header` section and then simply printed on each page of the report.

As the complexity of a report grows, it becomes more and more difficult to maintain a modular structure within the report. Because the `print` statement is only recognized within the body of a report, a function cannot be called to print the information required in a particular control block (trying to execute a `print` statement in a function would result in a compiler syntax error). Therefore, it is not uncommon for the body of a complex report to swell to a thousand lines or more, much larger than a modular format would recommend. To reduce the number of lines of code within the report body and enhance modularity, functions can be called to load strings, which are then printed on the report. This technique is aided by the fact that the INFORMIX-4GL `let` statement allows formatting with the same using clause employed by the `print` statement. The following code sample demonstrates this method:

```
report accts( jrec, acctrec )
...
define line1_string char(132)
```

```
after group of acctrec.sub_accts

        let gsum = group sum(acctrec.balance)
        call sub_accts( gsum, jrec, acctrec )
                    returning line1_string

        print column 1, line1_string

....



function sub_accts( gsum, jrec, acctrec )
define ret_str1
define jrec like journals.*
define acctrec like accts_master.*
define gsum, totals decimal

select jour_name, jour_type, acct_type
into    jrec.jour_name, jrec.jour_type, acctrec.acct_type_name
from journals, accts_crx_ref, accts_master
where journals.journal_number =
        accts_crx_ref.journal_number   and
        accts_crx_ref.acct_number =
        accts_master.acct_number

let ret_str1 = gsum using "Sub-Accts total: <<<<",
                " Journal Activitity ",
                jrec.jour_name," ", jrec.total, jrec.jour_type

return ret_str1

end function
```

In this example, several records are passed into a report. Two strings are defined to the default width for INFORMIX-4GL reports. The contents of these strings is loaded with calls to the functions `sub_accts`. This function executes a series of `select` statements to retrieve data, load the data into strings, and then return those strings to the calling function.

By calling functions rather than coding the `select` statements directly in the body of the report, the report is kept more modular, and the details of the `sub_accts` function are isolated from the report program block.

Synchronous Reports

Having the capability to take the same data stream and produce two distinct reports is a practical capability. INFORMIX-4GL supports such synchronous reports: sending output to two separate reports at the same time, as the following code demonstrates.

```
main

define sr record like sales_person.*

declare c1 cursor for   select *
                            from sales_person

start report sales1
start report sales2
foreach c1 into sr.*

    output to sales1( sr.* )
    output to sales2( sr.* )

end foreach

finish report sales1
finish report sales2

end main
```

In this example, two separate reports are started: `sales1` and `sales2`. Within the `foreach` loop, data is retrieved from the `sales_person` table and is then output to the two reports. At the end of the `foreach` loop, both reports are completed with the `finish report` statement.

Dynamic Reports Driven by the Construct Statement

A number of reports are considered dynamic in nature—their requirements change constantly. Many MIS organizations devote a great deal of programming resources to report writing and modification for these dynamic reports. However, what is often considered a *dynamic* report is really only a report with dynamic selection criteria; the format for the report remains virtually the same, only the selection criteria changes. A very useful facility for processing the varying selection criteria needed to drive these reports is query-by-example capabilities supplied by the `con-struct` statement (see Figure 9-5). The following example demonstrates this type of report.

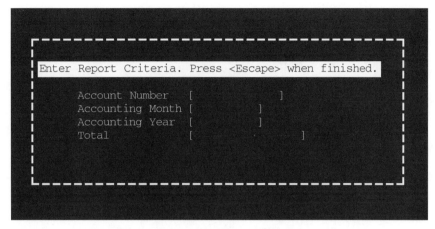

Figure 9-5 *Construct Statement for Report Criteria*

Many organizations use a large number of bookkeeping accounts. When it is necessary to produce reports for these accounts, it is most likely that only a small subset of the accounts will be examined. For instance, if management wanted to determine expenses, they would run an accounting report for just expense accounts. Or management may want to further narrow their review to examining expenses just for January for a small set of expense accounts. Rather than write separate reports for each possible set of selection criteria, it would make more sense to simply write a single report and use different selection criteria to drive the report. Using the `construct` statement to drive this report would make this an easy task, as the following example demonstrates.

The main program block in this example merely calls two functions: the `qry_acct_totals` function, which displays the screen form and executes the `construct` statement, and the `rpt_drv` function, which receives the results of the construct statement, opens a cursor and then outputs data to the report.

```
database accounting
```

```
main
define where_clause char(500)

call qry_acct_totals() returning where_clause
call rpt_drv( where_clause, "acct_totals.out" )

end main
```

The `qry_acct` Function

The `qry_acct` function is used to retrieve the selection criteria for the report. It first opens a window, and then displays the screen form and a message explaining to the user how to enter the criteria. The `construct` statement is then executed. When the `construct` statement is completed, the criteria for the `where` clause of the `select` statement that will be used to drive the report will be in the `where_clause` string variable. The window is then closed, and the contents of the `where_clause` variable is returned to the calling function.

```
function qry_acct_totals()
define where_clause char(500)

open window w1 at 5,5
  with 12 rows, 60 columns
  attribute( border )

open form f1 from "acct_tot"
display form f1
message "Enter report criteria.  Press <Escape> when finished."
    attribute ( reverse )

construct by name where_clause on acct_totals.*

close window w1
return where_clause clipped

end function
```

The `rpt_drv` Function

The `rpt_drv` function receives the `where` clause criteria prepared by the previous function and the name of the output file to be produced by the report. It defines local string variables to hold the query to be used to drive the report, the record that will receive the data from the database, and the name of the account being processed.

The first step taken in this function is to build the query string that will be prepared. The `where` clause criteria that was passed into the function as a string are appended to a string constant of the `select` clause of the query statement. The `select` clause must be a constant because the report that is to be called contains static report format statements that expect a fixed record structure.

Once the query statement has been created, default error checking is turned off and the query statement prepared. After the `prepare` statement, the `sqlca.sqlcode` is checked; if an error has occurred, an error message is displayed and the function returns. If the `prepare` statement has been executed successfully, a cursor is declared for the prepared statement.

If the cursor is declared successfully, the report is started. The report will be output to the file name passed into the function. A `foreach` statement is then started, which will receive the data from the database and output the data to the report. If an error is encountered, an error message will be displayed and the function will return.

```
function rpt_drv( where_clause, file_name )
define where_clause char(500),
       file_name      char(50),
       qstr           char(1000)
define at_rec record like acct_totals.*
define acct_name like accounts.acct_name

— build the query
let qstr = "select acct_totals.*, accounts.acct_name from ",
           " acct_totals, accounts where ",
            where_clause clipped,
           " and accounts.acct_num = acct_totals.acct_num ",
           " order by acct_totals.acct_num, ⇐
                   acct_totals.acct_year, ",
           " acct_totals.acct_month"

whenever error continue
prepare s1 from qstr
if sqlca.sqlcode < 0 then
   call err_print( sqlca.sqlcode )
   call err_msg( "Error on prepare." )
```

```
        return
    end if

declare rpt_curs cursor for s1
if sqlca.sqlcode < 0 then
    call err_print( sqlca.sqlcode )
    call err_msg( "Error on declare." )
    return
end if

start report acct_totals_rpt to file_name

— main output loop
foreach rpt_curs into at_rec.*, acct_name

    if sqlca.sqlcode < 0 then
        call err_print( sqlca.sqlcode )
        call err_msg( "Error on fetch." )
        return
    end if

    output to report acct_totals_rpt( at_rec.*, acct_name )

end foreach

finish report acct_totals_rpt

end function
```

The `acct_totals` Report

The `acct_totals` report receives the account totals record and
the name of the current account being processed. Variables are
declared to hold the column position of the columns where the
report record is to be output. Variables are also declared to hold
the report header strings.

In the `output` section of the report, the left margin is set to
zero. This effectively removes margin control from the
INFORMIX-4GL report-writing facility. Margin control will be
maintained by the local variables holding the column positions
for the report data.

In the `first page header` block, the variables used to print
the page headers are initialized. The `all` function is used to create a string composed of a series of identical characters. In this
case, a series of "=" characters is stored in the strings that will be

used to print lines on the page header. These strings are loaded in the `first page header` block to avoid the overhead of formatting these header strings each time a page header is printed.

Column positions are also loaded in the first page header block. Loading the column positions in this way will allow them to be modified easily during the application development and maintenance process. Note that all the columns are declared to be relative to the previous column (to the left of the current column). This allows a change to the second column to impact all columns that follow it sequentially on the report line.

Once the page header strings have been loaded, they are printed. INFORMIX-4GL does not execute the page header section of the report if the first page header section appears in the report, so the page header strings must be printed here. They will be printed at the column position defined in the col1 variable using a series of print statements. These same print statements will be executed again in the page header section.

A string containing the column headers is then printed. The use of the column position strings make printing these headers at the correct position an easier task. The total line is shifted to the right eight spaces to align this header with the formatting of the decimal number to be printed in this column.

```
report acct_totals_rpt ( acct_rec, acct_name )
define acct_rec record like acct_totals.*
define acct_name like accounts.acct_name
define col1, col2, col3, col4   smallint
define header1, header2, header3 char(80)

output
 left margin 0

format

first page header
    let header1 = all("=", 80)
    let header2 = center( "Account Totals Report", 80 )
    let header3 = all("=", 80)


    — set column positions
    let col1 = 4
    let col2 = col1 + 15
    let col3 = col2 + 15
    let col4 = col3 + 10
```

```
        — print page headers
        print column col1, header1
        print column col1, header2
        print column col1, header3

        — print column headers
        print column col1, "Acct Number",
              column col2, "Month",
              column col3, "Year",
              column (col4 + 8 ), "Total"

    page header
        print header1
        print header2
        print header3
        print column col1, "Acct Number",
              column col2, "Month",
                  column col3, "Year",
                  column (col4 + 8), "Total"
```

In the on every row section of the report, the acct_rec
record elements are printed at the column position specified in
the integer variables set in the first page header section of
the report.

In the before group of block for the acct_rec.acct_num,
the name of the account to be printed is output. In the after
group of block for the acc_rec.acct_num record element,
the total for the account just processed is printed.

```
on every row
    print column col1, acct_rec.acct_num using "<<<<<",
          column col2, acct_rec.acct_month using "<<",
          column col3, acct_rec.acct_year  using "<<<<",
          column col4, acct_rec.acct_total using ⇐
      "###,###,###.##"


before group of acct_rec.acct_num
    skip 1 line
    print column 1, "Account Name: ", acct_name
    skip 1 line

after group of acct_rec.acct_num

    print column col4, "================="
```

```
        print column 1, "Account Total ",
                column col4, group sum( acct_rec.acct_total )
                                        using  "###,###,###.##"
        skip 1 line

end report
```

Example 9-1 *Report Output for Account Totals Report*

```
============================================================
                    Account Totals Report
============================================================
Acct Number      Month            Year               Total

Account Name: Electricity Exp

    1                1              1993              100.00
    1                2              1993              100.00
    1                4              1993              100.00
    1                5              1993            1,100.00
    1                6              1993            1,011.00
    1                7              1993              553.00
    1                8              1993              133.00
    1                9              1993            1,133.00
    1               10              1993              133.30
    1               11              1993              556.00
    1               12              1993               44.30
                                                ================
Account Total                                       4,963.60


Account Name: Miscellaneous E

   11                1              1993            1,333.30
   11                2              1993              334.00
   11                3              1993            1,334.00
   11                4              1993              133.30
   11                5              1993               33.40
   11                6              1993              333.40
   11                7              1993               33.44
   11                8              1993              300.00
   11                8              1993              300.00
   11                9              1993              500.00
   11               10              1993              600.00
   11               11              1993              234.00
   11               12              1993              560.00
                                                ================
Account Total                                       6,028.84
```

Example 9-1 *Report Output for Account Totals Report (continued)*

```
============================================================
                   Account Totals Report
============================================================
Acct Number      Month              Year              Total
Account Name: Water

        2            1              1993             400.00
        2            3              1993             500.00
        2            4              1993             600.00
        2            5              1993             550.60
        2            6              1993           1,133.00
        2            7              1993             554.00
        2            8              1993             443.00
        2            9              1993             334.00
        2           10              1993           1,100.10
        2           11              1993           1,193.00
        2           12              1993           1,110.00
                                              =================
Account Total                                     7,917.70
```

Table-Driven Dynamic Report

The possibilities for report formats are virtually limitless, but there are trends that tend to repeat. One such report format is a report in which a series of numbers are printed across the report page. Also, each number printed on the report is the result of a separate `select` statement, most likely one that retrieves aggregate totals. An accounting expense report that prints monthly totals across the report and account groupings on each row is an example of such a report and is shown in Example 9-2. Another example would be an accounting balance sheet where each line of the report represents a total of a series of accounts.

To write distinctive custom reports for each of these reporting needs could become a tedious task. A more modular approach, which would allow a significant amount of code to be reused, would be preferable. The example in Figure 9-6 presents such an approach.

Such a dynamic report requires a table to store the information, which specifies the report format and the data to be retrieved for each column and row of the report. This is the information that will ultimately drive the report. At runtime, this table will be read. All the rows that match this report will be

report_ctrl table

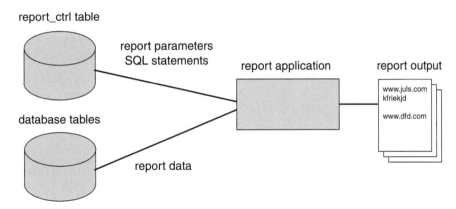

Figure 9-6 *Table Driven Dynamic Report*

selected. For each row, the query statement will be prepared and executed. The result of executing the query statement will be output to the report, along with other formatting information contained in the control record. Figure 9-6 shows this process.

Example 9-2 *Report Ouput for Dynamically Generated Expense Report*

```
=============================================================
3/19/1994               Expense Report              15:05:01
=======================================================Page: 1
                  Jan              Feb              Mar


Water             100.00           100.00
Phone             400.00                            500.00
Labor             600.00           100.00           123.00
Subtotals         1100.00          200.00           623.00

Cleanup           2274.40          1133.00          123.33
Misc.             1333.30          334.00           1334.00
Subtotals         3607.70          1467.00          1457.33

Grand Total       4707.70          1667.00          2080.33
```

Each row of this table specifies the report name, information about where the data will be printed on the report, and the SQL statement used to retrieve the data. Table 9-5 shows the contents of the table used to drive this report.

Table 9-5 *Report Control Table*

Column	Purpose
rept_name	The name of the report.
line_no	The line number of the report. This relates to the rows of the report.
header	If line_no = 0, this is the header or report title for the report. If line_no is not zero, this is the header or title for the row.
col_pos	The column position where the data to be retrieved will be printed.
col_no	The column number or row number for this row. This number is used to identify the data in this column. It is used to store subtotals and grand totals and to sort the data retrieved from the report_ctrl table.
sign	Stores the sign (+/-) of the data in this row-column. If the data in this column to be printed is negative, a negative 1 is stored here. If the data to be printed is positive, a positive 1 is stored here.
action	A single-byte flag for this row. Indicates the action to be performed. Possible settings are listed below.
q_stmt	Stores the query statement that will be used to retrieve the data for this row, column.

```
create table report_ctrl
    (
        rept_name char(10),
        line_no smallint,
        header char(20),
        col_pos smallint,
        col_no smallint,
        sign smallint,
        action char(1),
        q_stmt char(500)
    );
```

The main Program Block and the rpt_drv Function

The main program block simply calls the rpt_drv function with the name of the report, the column width of the report, and the file where the report will be output, as follows.

The rpt_drv function reads rows from the report_ctrl table that describes the report and then passes the contents of each row to a function that will process the row. First, a cursor is declared to read all rows from the `report_ctrl` table that match the report name being run. Once the cursor is declared, the report is started and output to the file name that has been passed into the function.

The `foreach` loop is then executed, and all elements of the `report_ctrl` table are retrieved into the `report_ctrl` record. The `action` element of the `report_ctrl` record is a flag that indicates the type of row being processed. The possible settings for the action flag are shown in Table 9-6.

Table 9-6 Action Flag Settings

Flag Setting	Purpose
N	This indicates that the data in the row-column is numeric data. This means that the `proc_line` function must be called to process the data.
S	This indicates that the row-column will be used to trigger a subtotal.
G	This indicates that the row-column will be used to trigger a grand total.
H	This is a header row. The contents of the header column will be printed as the report header.

If the action flag is set to "N," the `report_ctrl` record is passed to the `proc_line` function, which will process the query contained in the record and return an amount into a decimal variable. The amount variable, the report control record, and the column width for the report are then output to the report. When the `foreach` loop is finished, the report is closed with the `finish report` statement.

```
database testit
main

call rpt_drv( "Accounting", 80, "acctg.out" )

end main
```

```
function rpt_drv( rept_name, col_width, file_name )
define rept_name like report_ctrl.rept_name
define col_width smallint,
       file_name char(50)
```

```
define rc record like report_ctrl.*
define amt decimal


declare c1 cursor for
   select *
   from    report_ctrl ct
   where   ct.rept_name = rept_name
   order by line_no

start report sql_rpt to file_name

foreach c1 into rc.*

    if rc.action = "N" then
        call proc_line( rc.* ) returning amt
    end if
    output to report sql_rpt( rc.*, amt, col_width )

end foreach
finish report sql_rpt

end function
```

The proc_line Function

The proc_line function takes the report control record as a
parameter. A decimal is defined to be used as a return value. The
default error checking mode is turned off, and the statement contained in the q_stmt element of the report control record is prepared. If an error has been encountered, an error message is
displayed along with the query statement that failed. A cursor is
then declared for the prepared query statement. The cursor is
opened, and the data is fetched and returned to the calling function.

Note that there is no attempt to read additional rows from the
cursor; it is asserted that the query will only retrieve a *single* row
of numeric data, presumably an aggregate sum of a series of
numeric values.

```
function proc_line( rc )
define rc record like report_ctrl.*
define retval decimal

whenever error continue
```

```
prepare rpt_stmt from rc.q_stmt
if sqlca.sqlcode < 0 then
   error "Error on prepare.", sqlca.sqlcode
   initialize retval.* to NULL
   return retval.*
end if

declare rpt_curs cursor for rpt_stmt

open rpt_curs

fetch rpt_curs into retval

return retval * rc.sign

end function
```

The sql_rpt Report

The sql_rpt report receives as parameters the report control record, a decimal value of the amount for the row, and the column width of the report. Variables are declared to hold the header of the report and the current line of the report. Because of the manner in which data is processed in this report, subtotals and grand totals cannot be processed by report aggregates (group sum, group subtotals, and so forth). (This would not make any sense, because report aggregates only act on parameters passed into the report; they would not recognize the multiple columns output on the report.) Therefore, 2 arrays of 50 dimensions each are declared to hold the totals and grand totals for the report. Variables are also declared to be used as counter variables and flags within the report.

In the output section of the report, the left margin is set to zero to allow the report complete control of the placement of the report columns. In the first page header section, initializations are performed. The subtotal and grand total flags are set to false, and the subtotal and grand total arrays initialized to zero; the logic of the report demands that this be done.

Because the report header must be built before other rows are output from the report, the report control data must be input in such a way that the report header row from the control table will be the first row passed into the report. That has been accomplished in this example by setting the column number (the `col_no` column from report_ctrl table) for the header record to zero. Because the report control records are sorted in ascending column number and all other nonheader rows have column numbers greater than zero, this causes the report control header record to be passed into the report first. The code in the `first page header` section takes the additional precaution of verifying that the `action` element of the `rc` record is set to "H." In fact, if the first row passed to the report is the header record, there is no need to check this value.

Within the `first page header` control block, the report header is created and stored in a series of three strings. The `all` function is used to initialize strings that will be used to store the column totals. Because these strings will be inserted into substrings of the current line string variable, it is necessary to set the entire string to blanks so that indeterminate values are not left in portions of the string that have not been explicitly assigned.

The title of the report is contained in the `header` element of the report control record. Also, the column headers are contained in the `q_stmt` element of the report control record; these are merely assigned to the `colheader` string. The date, time, and page number are also placed in the report header strings. All header information is placed relative to the column width parameter passed into the function.

Once they have been created, the header strings and the column header string are output. The only information in the third page header string that changes is the page number. This is reinserted into the `header3` string on each page.

```
report sql_rpt( rc, amt, col_width )
define rc record like report_ctrl.*
define amt decimal,
       col_width   smallint
define header1, header2, header3, colheader char(132)
define tstr char(50)
define curr_line char(132)
define n,x,colno smallint
define sub_totals array[50] of decimal
define grand_totals array[50] of decimal
define sub_total_flag, grand_total_flag smallint

output
   left margin 0
```

```
format

first page header

- initialize
let sub_total_flag   = FALSE
let grand_total_flag = FALSE

for n = 1 to 50
    let sub_totals[n]    = 0
    let grand_totals[n] = 0
end for

- these need to be passed in 1st to force initializations
if rc.action = "H"   then - build the header

    let curr_line = all(" ", col_width )
    let colheader = all(" ", col_width )
    let header1   = all("=", col_width )
    let header2   = all(" ", col_width )
    let header2 = center( rc.header, col_width)

    let colheader = rc.q_stmt     this field contains column⇐
        headers
    let tstr       = today
    let n          = length(tstr clipped)
    let header2[1,n+1] = tstr clipped
    let tstr = time
    let n = length( tstr clipped)
    let header2[ col_width - n, col_width ] = tstr clipped
    let header3 = all("=", col_width )

end if

    let tstr = pageno using "Page: <<<"
    let n = length( tstr clipped )
    let header3[ col_width - n , col_width ] = tstr

    print header1    clipped
    print header2    clipped
    print header3    clipped
    print colheader clipped
    skip 1 line


Page header
```

```
let tstr = pageno using "Page: <<<"
let n = length( tstr clipped )
let header3[ col_width - n , col_width ] = tstr

print header1 clipped
print header2 clipped
print header3 clipped
print colheader clipped
skip 1 line
```

The on every row Report Block

The on every row section of the report performs a great deal of
the processing. The report flags used in this report are "N" for
numeric output, "S" for subtotals, and "G" for grand totals. If a row
has any of these flags set, then the amount supplied must be stored
at the correct offset in the current line (the curr_line variable)
string. The code currently implemented allows 10 characters for the
amount column. The offsets for loading the amount into the current line string are calculated and stored in local variables. This is
largely necessary due to peculiarities in the INFORMIX-4GL parser,
which occasionally complains about expressions in a substring reference. The amount will therefore be inserted into the current line
strings into the substring of the starting column position passed in
the report control record plus 10 bytes.

First, based on the setting of the action flag in the report control record element, an amount will be stored in the current line
substring. If the action flag is "S," a subtotal should be inserted
into the current line for the column number being processed.
Columns are numbered on the report in a left-to-right fashion,
with the first column being one and the maximum column
being 50. The column number is used as an array index into the
subtotal and grand total arrays, and because the arrays are
defined as 50 element arrays, they should only accept element
values between one and 50.

If the action record element is set to "S," "G," or "N", then
the amount value from the appropriate array is placed in the current line string at the column position (the report control
col_pos record element) offset. A series of if/then statements is
used to determine which variable to use. If the action flag is "S"
or "G," then the subtotal flag or grand total flag is set to TRUE.
This flag will be used to trigger other actions later in the program.

The row header is also loaded into the current line at the sub-string, starting at the first column position and extending for the length of the header string element of the report control record.

Next, the amount value is tested. If the amount is NULL, it is set to zero to allow sane mathematical processing later in the program. The subtotal flag is then evaluated to determine whether or not the subtotal flags should be cleared. If the subto-tal flag is set and the current row being processed is not a subto-tal row (rc.action != S), the subtotals can be cleared. (Because grand totals are only printed once, there is no reason to clear them.) The subtotal flag is then set to false so that subsequent iterations do not execute this code unnecessarily.

If the action flag for the current row is set to "N," this is a numeric line and needs to be added to both the subtotal accumu-lator and the grand total accumulator for that column.

Because the current line is made up of a series of rows from the report control table, each of the rows have the same report line number. Each row of the report control table should not be output as it is passed to the report. It is only when all of the report control rows for the current report line number have been passed to the report that the current line (contained in the cur-rent line string) should be output to the report output file. After the line is output, the current line string is reinitialized. On the final row of the report, if the grand total flag is set, then grand totals are output to the report file.

```
on every row

if rc.action = "N" or rc.action = "S"  or rc.action = "G" then
    let n = rc.col_pos
    let x = n + 10
    let colno = rc.col_no

    — load the amount
    if rc.action = "S" then    — subtotal
        let curr_line[n,x] = sub_totals[colno]
        let sub_total_flag = TRUE
    end if

    if rc.action = "G" then — grand total
        let curr_line[n,x] = grand_totals[colno]
        let grand_total_flag = TRUE
    end if
```

```
        if rc.action = "N" then
            let curr_line[n, x] = amt
        end if

        — load the row header
        let n = 1
        let x = n + length( rc.header clipped )
        let curr_line[n,x] = rc.header clipped

        — process the amount or subtotal
        if rc.action = "N" then
            if amt IS NULL then
                let amt = 0
            end if
        end if

end if

    — clear subtotals if necessary
if sub_total_flag and rc.action != "S"  then — clear the ⇐
        subtotals

        for n = 1 to 50
            let sub_totals[n] = 0
        end for

        skip 1 line

        let sub_total_flag = FALSE

end if

    if rc.action = "N"  then
        let sub_totals[colno]   = sub_totals[colno] + amt   — ⇐
        accumulate the total
        let grand_totals[colno] = grand_totals[colno] + amt   — ⇐
        accumulate the grand total
    end if


after group of rc.line_no
    print curr_line clipped
    let   curr_line = all( " ", col_width)


on last row
```

```
if grand_total_flag then
    skip 1 line
end if
print curr_line clipped

end report
```

Chapter Summary

This chapter demonstrated the process of performing input and output using the Informix-4GL language. The process of using screen forms to design and present a user interface was shown in conjunction with the use of the `input` and `display` statements that interact with the screen form to retrieve and display data respectively.

The capabilities of the Informix-4GL report syntax were also presented. Using the Informix-4GL report blocks, reports can be developed quickly and easily. Because procedural statements can readily be intermixed with the nonprocedural statements for SQL and the Informix-4GL report blocks, complex reports can be created using this language.

Next Chapter

The next chapter provides more detail on the use of three components of Informix-4GL: functions, error handling, and the use of help facilities. The proper use of functions is an important part of modular programming with a language like Informix-4GL. Informix-4GL provides a flexible facility for calling functions allowing multiple input parameters, multiple return parameters, and recursion, all of which are demonstrated in the next chapter.

Informix-4GL provides the ability to trap IDS errors and display meaningful error messages (rather than just the error number). In the next chapter, the process of using the error facilities is presented in conjunction with a discussion on the use of the Informix-4GL help screen syntax.

Functions and Error Handling in INFORMIX-4GL

One of the most significant features of INFORMIX-4GL is the ability to create functions. Informix-4GL allows the creation of functions in a manner that is modular and block-oriented in the tradition of such third-generation languages as Pascal, Algol, and C.

4GL functions have a block beginning designated by the `function function_name` statement, and a block ending designated by the `end function` statement. Within this block, any variables declared in the variable declaration section of the function have a *local scope* – they are only recognized within the block scope of that function. (Note that a local variable name declaration masks the declaration of any variables declared with the same name with *module* or *global* scope.)

This treatment of variable name scope in Informix-4GL mirrors that of C or Pascal and is a very useful language design feature. Programmers are free to name all array index variables without fear of altering other array index variables in use elsewhere in the program. Additionally, the use of local variables makes more efficient use of memory because space for local variables is allocated on function entry and deallocated on return from the function.

Unfortunately, the use of local variables does not come easily to programmers more familiar with such languages COBOL, in which variables are declared in a single statement block and then used throughout the program; a style of programming antithetical to that of modular programming.

INFORMIX-4GL does not force applications to be written in a modular manner. However, the benefits of limiting variable scope, especially with local variables in functions, are significant. The benefits of modular programming in INFORMIX-4GL should not be underestimated.

Function Parameters

In INFORMIX-4GL, functions can receive parameters of any data type except arrays, and can return parameters of any data type except arrays. Also, unlike many languages, INFORMIX-4GL can return multiple parameters.

Functions in INFORMIX-4GL are *call-by-value*. A parameter passed to a function is passed as a *value*; it cannot be modified by that function.

The data type of incoming parameters must be defined within the variable declaration section of the function body. These data types should correspond to the data types, in ordinal position, of the parameters used to call the function, but this is not required. The reason for this is INFORMIX-4GL will, when possible, convert the data type passed to the function to the appropriate data type for that parameter. Failure to define the data types of incoming function parameters will result in a compiler error.

Implementation

The implementation of functions in INFORMIX-4GL is similar to that of other modular languages. Function parameters are pushed onto the INFORMIX-4GL stack in a left-to-right order. As they are pushed onto the stack, the data type of the variable is recorded on the stack. When INFORMIX-4GL calls the function, the function is sent the number of parameters pushed onto the stack. This stack is shown in Figure 10-1.

Before the function retrieves its parameters from the stack, it will first retrieve the number of parameters it has been passed. If

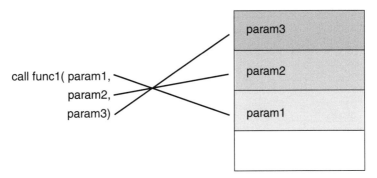

param3

call func1(param1,
param2,
param3)

param2

param1

Figure 10-1 *The INFORMIX-4GL Stack*

this number is not the correct number of parameters, the function will signal a fatal error and the program will abort.

If the correct number of parameters has been passed, they are retrieved from the stack in reverse order of the order in which they were placed on the stack, (i.e., right to left). As the parameters are retrieved from the stack, the data type required for the parameter is compared to the data type of the parameter being retrieved. If the parameter can be converted, it will be; if not, a fatal error is returned and program execution is terminated. INFORMIX-4GL does not explicitly support passing a variable number of parameters to a function—The number of parameters is effectively fixed.

Once all parameters are retrieved, the body of the function is executed. Any valid INFORMIX-4GL statement may be placed within the body of a function except a function declaration. On finishing execution of the function block, INFORMIX-4GL will place return parameters on the stack, and then return, or send, the number of parameters placed on the stack. Return parameters are treated as are the function parameters: They are retrieved in reverse order and data type conversion takes place if it is sensible. On return from the function, all space used for storage of local variables is deallocated—The variables cease to exist.

All parameter type conversions and testing of the number of parameters are not performed until runtime; the INFORMIX-4GL compiler does not check the validity of function calls.

Functions as Expressions

Function calls can also be treated as expressions in INFORMIX-4GL. The following statements are valid:

```
—the function isvalid_state() returns integer 0 for
—false and 1 for true

let x = isvalid_state("CA")


define x integer
if x then
      call do_something()
end if
```

In this code, the assignment statement

```
        let x = isvalid_state("CA")
```

automatically assigns the return value of isvalid_state to the variable x. This assumes that the function isvalid_state returns only one parameter (if it did not, a runtime error would occur).

INFORMIX-4GL Boolean expressions also allow functions as expressions. The following code is valid:

```
        if  isvalid_state("CA")   then
                call do_something()
        end if
```

Note how making use of this capability reduces the number of lines of code required to make the validation and creates more modular, readable code. More complex, nested function expressions are also allowed, as follows:

```
let state = "ca"
let country = "us"

if isvalid_state( upshift(state) )         and
            isvalid_country( upshift(country))  and
            isvalid_zip("08833")                    then
            call do_something()
end if
```

Use of Variables Within a Function

As mentioned previously, INFORMIX-4GL variables declared within a function have local scope—they are only visible within that function. The space for these variables is allocated on entry to the function and deallocated on exit from the function. This means that between successive function calls, the variable does *not* retain its value. In most cases, this may not be a problem. However, in cases where the function must retain information from a previous call, a variable that can retain its value is needed. Because the use of global variables is discouraged in modular coding, something short of a global variable is desired.

The solution is to use a variable declaration with module scope. This is a variable that is only visible to the INFORMIX-4GL source code module (source code file) in which it is declared. These variables are simply declared outside of a function block and outside of a global statement block, as follows:

```
—
— declare module scope variables
—
define first_pass_flag smallint
define pass_counter     integer


—
— function declarations start here
—

function get_data(rec_key)
#
# Purpose: to retrieve data from the tab1 table
#
define rec_key   like tab1.key_col
define rec_var   record like tab1.*
— assert first_pass variable is initialized to TRUE in main
— We only want to execute the following code once, on the
— first pass through the function
—
if first_pass then

            declare c1 cursor for
              select *
              from tab1
              where key_col = rec_key
```

```
            open c1

            let first_pass = false

end if

fetch c1 into rec_var.*

—
— assert pass_counter was initialized to 0 in main
let pass_counter = pass_counter + 1

call display_counter( pass_counter )

return rec_var.*

end function
```

In this example, the declaration of the two module scope variables, `first_pass` and `pass_counter`, allow the function `get_data` to *remember* whether or not it has been called before. If it has been called before, it will avoid the overhead of having to declare and then open the cursor (an expensive database operation). Also, a count of the number of passes can be kept in the variable `pass_counter`, which is passed to a function that presumably would display a count of the number of records returned so far. Note that `first_pass` and `pass_counter` would be visible to other functions in the source code module and could be modified by them, but they would not be visible or modifiable in other source code modules.

Passing a Variable Number of Parameters to Functions

INFORMIX-4GL does not explicitly allow a variable number of parameters to be passed to a function. However, by making use of some simple string manipulation capabilities of INFORMIX-4GL, a variable number of parameters can be passed to, and returned from, an INFORMIX-4GL function.

The key to this capability is to place delimited function parameters into a string and then pass that string as a function parameter. This method is shown as follows:

```
let table_list = "table1, table2, table3 "
```

```
let column_list = "col1, col2, col3 "
call get_data( table_list, column_list )
```

The function would then take the delimited string and parse
the parameters, placing each parameter into a variable. These
variables would then be used by the function as function parameters. The string manipulation required to do this is as follows:

```
function get_data( tables, cols )
define tables char(100)
define cols    char(100)
define x,y     smallint
define len     smallint
define table_parms array[10] of char(20)
define col_parms   array[10] of char(20)

—
— initialize the parameter strings.
—
for n = 1 to 10
    for y = 1 to 20
        let table_parms[n][y] = " " — a blank character
    end for
end for


—
— move through tables string, getting parameters
—
let len = length( tables )
let n = 1
let y = 1

for x = 1 to len

  —
  — 'copy' to parameter array
  —

  let table_parms[y][n] = tables[x]
  let n = n + 1


  —
  — test to see if we are on a delimiter.  If so,
  — jump to the next parameter
  —

  if tables[x] = "," then — terminate the parameter
```

```
        let x = x + 1        — move past the delimiter
        let y = y + 1        — next parameter
        let n = 1            — start at the beginning
    end if

end for


—
— do the same for the columns list passed
— into the function
—
...
```

In this example, the input parameters are parsed in a `for` loop that manages to get all the parameters passed up to a safe limit (supplied by the built-in `length` function) and store them in an array of character variables. However, before the character array can be used, it must be initialized to a set of safe values. This is necessary for two reasons. First, as mentioned previously, declared variables in INFORMIX-4GL always have an indeterminate value (the p-code version runner makes this appear otherwise, but a programmer should always code as though the value were indeterminate). Second, character strings in INFORMIX-4GL are always assumed to be padded to their defined length. INFORMIX-4GL assignment statements that reference an entire string will pad the string with blanks if the whole string is being referenced. However, in cases where individual elements of the string are being assigned, the string is not (and cannot be) padded with blanks.

The `initialize` statement is usually used to initialize these variables, but in the case of character variables, initialize will simply set the first character to a NULL character. (This behavior improves performance—Instead of having to modify 20 bytes of a 20-byte string, only one byte need be modified.)

For our purposes in the code example, this won't work because we are directly addressing elements of the string with assignment statements. If we did not initialize all elements of the string to spaces, odd characters would creep into the end of the string following the last byte we explicitly assigned.

Once the array of strings has been initialized in the example, a `for` loop is used to parse the parameters from the string passed to the function. Various integers used to serve as indexes are initialized to appropriate values.

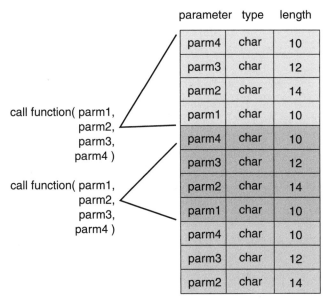

parameter   type   length

parm4	char	10
parm3	char	12
parm2	char	14
parm1	char	10
parm4	char	10
parm3	char	12
parm2	char	14
parm1	char	10
parm4	char	10
parm3	char	12
parm2	char	14

call function(parm1,
        parm2,
        parm3,
        parm4)

call function(parm1,
        parm2,
        parm3,
        parm4)

Figure 10-2 The INFORMIX-4GL Stack

A `for` loop is then started for the entire length of the string containing the parameters. For each iteration of the `for` loop, the contents of the string containing the parameters is copied, byte by byte, to the array of string parameters. When a delimiter character is detected, in this case a comma, the index variables that keep track of the current parameter array element are incremented and reset. The result is that at the end of the `for` loop, the `tables_parms` array contains all of the tables' parameters passed into the function.

Note that this example does not provide coding to handle instances where more than 10 parameters are passed into the function. A more complete example of using this method of passing function parameters to create a generic validation function is shown later in this chapter.

Recursion in INFORMIX-4GL

One of the more powerful function-related language capabilities is available in INFORMIX-4GL: recursion. Recursion is generally considered one of the necessities of a modular third-generation language. INFORMIX-4GL supports recursion in both its procedural code and nonprocedural code with only minor limitations. INFORMIX-4GL places no restriction on the levels of recursion allowed: recursion can continue as long as there is memory available to support the associated stack operations.

Recursion essentially allows a function to call itself. Because INFORMIX-4GL is using a stack and placing arguments on the stack in a push-down fashion, function parameters will not become confused by recursion. However, recursion comes with a cost: Function calls require stack operations, and stack operations can be expensive in terms of resource usage. Often, even though a recursive solution is available, an iterative programming solution is chosen to avoid the overhead of recursion.

Recursion offers a relatively simple, elegant solution to problems that would be difficult to express with an iterative algorithm. The following code provides an example of recursion in INFORMIX-4GL:

```
—
—define module scope variable to hold counter value
—
define levels smallint — indicates the depth of recursion

main

let levels = 0
call recurse()

end main

function recurse()
define col smallint


—
— increment level counter
—
let levels = levels + 1


—
— stop at a depth of 20
—
if levels = 21   then
    display "Finished run." at 8,10
    sleep 2
    return
```

```
end if


—
— display message
—
display levels using "Recurse level << "
                at 10,10
let col = 9 + levels
display "*" at 12, col



—
— go even deeper
—
call recurse()

end function
```

In this example, a module scope variable is declared to provide a counter variable that will hold its value between calls. On each call, the counter is incremented and the recursion levels count displayed along with a text graph that indicates the same information. When 20 levels of recursion have been reached (on the 21st iteration), the program will exit.

An Example of Recursion—
The Parts Explosion Problem

The use of recursion is not limited to such esoteric problems as the Towers of Hanoi; recursion provides solutions to some common relational database problems. The most notable of these problems is that of the self-referencing table. A very good *real-world* example of this is shown in the parts explosion problem.

The table definition that follows is for an auto parts database. Parts stored in the table are made up of component parts that are themselves parts. By definition, the level of self-referencing is unlimited. A good implementation of recursion will support recursion to a depth limited only by available memory, which is the case with INFORMIX-4GL.

The Informix-SQL script shown below creates the parts database, creates the parts table and indices, and then loads data into the parts database.

```
{ create the parts database }
create database partsdb;

{ create the parts table and indexes }
create table parts ( pname                 char(20),
                     pnum                  integer,
                     component_of_pnum integer );
create index pidx1 on parts ( pnum );
create index pidx2 on parts ( component_of_pnum );

{ load the data for the parts table }
insert into parts values ( "alternator-p1", 1, 0 );
insert into parts values ( "gear-ax1z", 2, 1 );
insert into parts values ( "bearing", 3, 1 );
insert into parts values ( "stabilizer-rod", 4, 2 );
insert into parts values ( "coil-assembly", 5, 1 );
insert into parts values ( "wire-assembly", 6, 5 );
insert into parts values ( "wire-frame", 7, 5 );
insert into parts values ( "coil-assembly-gasket", 8, 5 );
insert into parts values ( "clips-a2", 9, 6 );
insert into parts values ( "washer-w2", 10, 5 );
insert into parts values ( "clip-w2", 11, 7 );
```

The following is the INFORMIX-4GL programmatic solution to the parts explosion problem. This code uses the previous data and recurses to a depth of three levels to provide a listing of all auto parts, their component parts, and the component parts of those component parts.

```
database partsdb

—
— define module scope variables to use as program
— counters and program constants
—
define levels      smallint
define MAX_LEVELS  smallint

main
define pr record like parts.*

declare c1 cursor for
select  *
from    parts

—
```

```
— Initialization
—
let MAX_LEVELS = 5
let levels    = 0

foreach c1 into pr.*

    display pr.pnum using " Part number <<<<   Name: ",
                               pr.pname

    call get_parts( pr.pnum )

end foreach

end main


_____

function create_cursor( plevel, lpnum )
—
— DECLARE and OPEN the cursor needed for
— this level number
— hardcoded limit of five levels.
—
define plevel smallint
define lpnum  like parts.pnum
define qstr char(100)

let qstr = " select * from parts where ",
           " parts.component_of_pnum = ? "

case plevel
    when 1  prepare stmt1 from qstr
            declare cl1 cursor for stmt1
            open cl1 using lpnum

    when 2  prepare stmt2 from qstr
            declare cl2 cursor for stmt2
            open cl2 using lpnum

    when 3  prepare stmt3 from qstr
            declare cl3 cursor for stmt3
            open cl3 using lpnum

    when 4  prepare stmt4 from qstr
            declare cl4 cursor for stmt4
            open cl4 using lpnum
```

```
            when 5    prepare stmt5 from qstr
                      declare cl5 cursor for stmt5
                      open cl5 using lpnum


      end case

      end function


      _____

      function fetch_cursor( plevel )
      define plevel smallint
      define pr record like parts.*

                  case plevel
                      when 1
                              fetch cl1 into pr.*
                      when 2
                              fetch cl2 into pr.*
                      when 3
                              fetch cl3 into pr.*
                      when 4
                              fetch cl4 into pr.*
                      when 5
                              fetch cl5 into pr.*
            end case

      return pr.*

      end function


      _____

      function get_parts( lpnum )
      —
      — recursively retrieve component parts
      —
      define lpnum  like parts.pnum    — part master
      define cpr record like parts.*   — components of master

      let levels = levels + 1

      if levels > MAX_LEVELS then
                      display  "Too many levels"
                      exit program
      end if

      call create_cursor( levels, lpnum )
```

```
call fetch_cursor( levels ) returning cpr.*


    --
    -- Continue to loop as long as data is found
    -- at this level
    --
    while cpr.pnum IS NOT NULL  and sqlca.sqlcode = 0
        display cpr.pnum using
            "       Component part number: <<<<    Name: ",
                cpr.pname clipped, lpnum using
                    " Component of <<<<",
                        levels using " Recurse level: <<"

            --
            -- Now get its component parts, if any
            --

            call get_parts( cpr.pnum )

            call fetch_cursor( levels ) returning cpr.*
    end while
    let levels = levels - 1  -- going back one level

end function
```

This program begins by declaring a cursor to read all rows from the `parts` table. The cursor is then opened implicitly by the `foreach` statement, which continues to read data from this cursor until no more rows are found.

For every row read, the function `get_parts` is called. The `get_parts` function determines whether or not component parts exist for this part and displays information on those component parts if they exist.

INFORMIX-4GL supports recursion completely, but unfortunately, the cursors it creates do not. Cursors created in INFORMIX-4GL have module scope, not local scope. Their data space is allocated from the heap, and they retain their value between successive function calls. (This was an intentional design—cursors are expected to retain their values as long as they are open.)

This behavior causes problems in a recursive function. If a single cursor were opened in the `get_parts` function, and `get_parts` was called recursively in a `foreach` loop, the `get_parts` function would terminate the `foreach` loop before returning to the `get_parts` function one level up. On return to the `get_parts` function, the program would begin executing within the `foreach` loop, but the cursor controlling the `foreach` loop will have been closed by the previous recursive call to `get_parts`—it will no longer be opened.

The solution to this problem is to write code that will create a series of cursors to potentially be used. This is done in the `create_cursor` function that is passed the parts number parameter and the level parameter. Based on the recursion level, a cursor is created that selects all component parts for that part number. The cursor is also opened in this function.

Instead of a `foreach` loop, a `while` loop is used as a control structure for retrieving the rows for the component parts. The `fetch_rows` function is called with the recursion level as a parameter. Because the recursion level was used as an *index* value when we created the cursor, we can also use it to fetch rows from the same cursor.

As each row is retrieved, the part number, part name, master part number (the part number of which this part is a component), and recursion level are displayed. Before the end of the `while` loop, the fetch_cursor function is called again to retrieve any additional rows. If no rows are found, the `while` loop is terminated. On exit from the `while` loop, the `levels` variable is decremented because program execution is returning to the previous level.

This implementation of the parts explosion problem is limited to five levels of recursion, but because of the modular nature of this code, it would be fairly simple to add additional levels to the `create_cursor` and `fetch_cursor` functions and adjust the MAX_LEVELS value accordingly.

Error Handling and Help Messages in INFORMIX-4GL

INFORMIX-4GL provides several different methods for displaying error messages and help screens. Some facilities are intended to help the programmer during the debugging phase of application development, and others are intended to provide useful, informational error messages for the user at runtime.

INFORMIX-4GL provides three types of error messages: **SQL errors**, INFORMIX-4GL **language syntax errors**, and **screen form errors**. INFORMIX-4GL language syntax errors are trapped by the compiler. Errors that refer to SQL syntax are also checked at compile time, with the exception of SQL statements *prepared* using the SQL `prepare` statement; these statements are effectively *invisible* to the compiler. The syntax for these statements is not checked until runtime, and then they are checked by the engine, not by the INFORMIX-4GL front end.

Forms errors include both errors that occur during screen form interaction as well as runtime errors that occur with a variety of expressions. This includes errors such as division by zero, decimal overflow, and date/date-time operations. Forms errors are *not* trapped by the simple `whenever error` statement; the `whenever any error` statement must be used.

`whenever error` Statement

INFORMIX-4GL provides very good default error reporting. This error report includes the SQL error number that occurred, if any, the source code module and line number where the error occurred, and a brief description of the error. By default, the INFORMIX-4GL runtime component will display this error message and then terminate the program (see Figure 10-3). This method of error trapping, which may not be the preferred method to use in a production environment, is very useful during the debugging process.

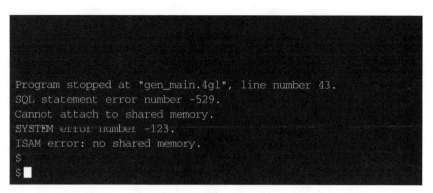

```
Program stopped at "gen_main.4gl", line number 43.
SQL statement error number -529.
Cannot attach to shared memory.
SYSTEM error number -123.
ISAM error: no shared memory.
$
$
```

Figure 10-3 Default INFORMIX-4GL Error Reporting

In order to override the default error checking, the INFORMIX-4GL language provides the `whenever error` statement to trap errors and trigger various events based on these errors.

The syntax for this message is:

```
whenever | any | error | stop | continue | goto label | call⇐
    function
```

The `whenever error` statement has module scope. It can be thought of as a *compiler directive* because its impact is controlled by the compiler. Upon encountering this statement, the compiler will begin to generate the appropriate code to execute the method of error handling chosen, serially, from the point where the `whenever error` statement was encountered in the source code module. The impact of the `whenever error` statement is therefore from the point at which it is encountered to the next occurrence of a `whenever error` statement or the end of the source code file (see Figure 10-4).

The `whenever error continue` method of error trapping will, as the statement implies, continue on receipt of an error. If this method of error handling is used, then following the line on which an error occurred, the global status variable will be set to the error number of the error that occurred. It is the programmer's responsibility to examine this variable and respond accordingly. Generally, because of the need to continually check the status variable after statements, it is advisable to limit the scope

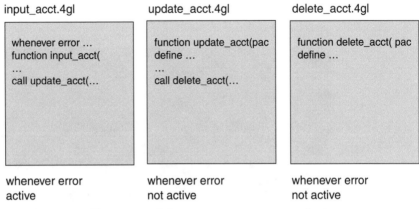

Figure 10-4 The Scope of the `whenever error` *Statement*

of `whenever error continue` statements and provide some other consistent method of error trapping in production applications. The sample code that follows demonstrates a common use of the `whenever error continue` statement:

```
function get_data( rec1 )
define rec1 like table1.*

whenever error continue
select *
into rec1.*
from table1
where table1.col1 = rec1.col1

whenever error stop

if sqlca.sqlcode < 0  then
    error "Error ", sqlca.sqlcode, " on select "
    initialize rec1.* to NULL
  end if

return rec1.*

end function
```

In this example, a function is called to retrieve data from the database. The `whenever error continue` statement is placed in the code before the SQL statement is executed. Immediately after the SQL statement, default error checking is restarted using the `whenever error stop` statement. When the SQL statement has been executed, the `sqlca.sqlcode` is examined to determine whether or not the SQL statement succeeded. If it did not succeed, an error message is displayed on the terminal screen using the **error** statement, and the return record is set to NULL to indicate to the calling function that no data was retrieved. The final line of the function returns the record to the calling function.

Error Logging with INFORMIX-4GL

Informix-4GL provides a set of functions to allow error messages to be logged to an ASCII file. This method of error logging has the benefit of storing errors that may occur during the running of a production application. Because end users are notorious for either not noticing or misreading error messages displayed on the terminal screen, error logging enables error messages to be stored for later retrieval and review by technical staff. Error logging also retains a historical list of errors that have occurred, providing a useful debugging tool.

The error log is started using the `startlog` function. Once started, successive errors that occur during the program will produce entries in this file. Entries will contain the date, time, source module name, line number, error number, and error message. Errors are always *appended* to the error log file, making it the programmer's responsibility to occasionally clear this file.

Entries can also be specifically written to the error log file using the **errorlog** function. The following code demonstrates the use of the INFORMIX-4GL error-logging facilities.

```
main

...

call startlog( "prog1.err")

call get_data( key1, key2 )
    returning rec1.*
...

end main

_____

function get_data( key1, key2 )
define rec1 like table1.*

— allow errors to be logged; continue program execution on error
whenever error continue

select col1, col2
into     rec1.*
from    table1
where col1 = key1   and
            col2 = key2

whenever error stop

— write entry to error log indicating function call that failed
— display error message to user just telling user the data  ⇐
        is not there
if sqlca.sqlcode < 0    then
```

```
        errorlog( "The get_data function call failed " )
        error  "Data not available."
                    - display to the terminal screen
        initialize rec1.* to NULL
end if

return rec1.*

end function
```

In this program, the `startlog` function is first called to create the error log in the **current** directory (passing a full path name to the `startlog` function would have created the error log in a specific directory). The function `get_data` is used to retrieve data from the database. When the `get_data` function is called, it first turns off the default error checking and instructs the program to continue when errors are encountered. Because error logging is already turned on at this point, the program will write error information to the error log and continue execution.

In this application, if an error is encountered during the `select` statement, an error will be logged to the error log. After the `select` statement, the `sqlca.sqlcode` is evaluated; if it is less than zero, an error has occurred and additional descriptive information is written to the error log. This will provide additional information to the technical reviewer of the error log.

Trapping Forms and Expression Errors
with whenever any error

Forms errors, which covers both screen form input/output errors and expression errors, are not trapped by the simple form of the `whenever error` statement; the **any** keyword must be used in the `whenever any error` statement. The following code demonstrates the use of this statement:

```
function fix_data( str1, int1, int2 )
define str1 char(10)              - should be a date
define int1, int2 integer         - divide and return the
result
define dte date
define result decimal

whenever any error continue
```

```
— create the date

let dte = date( str1 clipped )
if status < 0 then
    error "Error in date conversion. Date string is ",str1
    let dte = NULL
end if

— perform the division
let result = int1 / int2
if status < 0 then
    error "Error in division. Operands: ",int1, " / ", int2
    let result = NULL
end if

whenever any error stop

return dte, result

end function
```

In this example, the function `fix_data` must convert a string into a date, and divide two integers and return the result. The `whenever any error` trapping provides a convenient method of trapping for errors in expressions. In this case, the `whenever any error` statement uses the `continue` clause to allow program execution to continue on expression errors and let the code after the expression check for errors and respond accordingly.

In the case of the string to date conversion, the expression is evaluated in the form of a function call to the `date` function. After the function call, the `status` variable is checked for a negative value. If the value is negative, a date conversion error is assumed, and an error message is displayed that indicates that an error has occurred in date conversion and displays the offending date string. The `date` variable is then set to NULL.

In the mathematical expression, two integer numbers are divided and the result stored in the result variable. A potential error in this expression is the divide by zero expression error. Expression errors are trapped by examining the status code after the division operation; if it is less than zero, a division error is assumed to have occurred, and an error message is displayed with the offending operands. The **result** variable is then set to NULL.

Note that these examples do not check for specific error codes. It is asserted that if an error occurred, it occurred on the line above where the status code is examined. This is a fairly safe assumption in the previous example, but may not always be the case. Placing the `whenever any error` statement close to where the expression error may occur can decrease the likelihood that an incorrect error could be trapped.

If a specific error number were to be trapped, a `case` statement with several error numbers would have to be placed in the code. In many cases, it may be difficult to tell specifically which error number or numbers to use. Informix documentation does not always specify which error numbers are returned by failed library function calls or expressions. For these reasons, the error-trapping method shown previously is the easiest form to use.

Error Messages

Error messages can be displayed using several methods. The most common of these is the `error` statement. The `error` statement takes a single string argument, rings the terminal bell, and displays the string on the error line (defined in the `options` statement) in reverse video. The current version of the `error` statement does not accept expressions as arguments, only simple data types.

In addition to the `error` statement, there are several functions related to error handling that can be used to display error messages. They are listed in Table 10-1.

Table 10-1 INFORMIX-4GL Error Handling Functions

Function	Purpose
err_print	Prints the error message on the error line in reverse video.
err_get	Takes the error number as an integer argument and returns a character string error message that corresponds to the error number.
err_quit	Takes the error number as an integer argument and prints the error message on the error line and then quits the program.
errorlog	Takes a string as an argument and prints the string in the error log along with the date and time the message was printed. This requires that the startlog function has been called previously.
startlog	Takes a string argument that corresponds to the name and/or full path of the error log file. If a full path is not given, the error log is opened in the current directory. If a full path name is given, the error log is opened in the directory specified in the full path.

Generalized Error-Handling Routines

It is often desirable to have a generalized error-handling routine available for programmers working in a modular application development environment. When necessary, application code can turn off the error handler using the `whenever error continue` statement, and then turn the error handler back on using the `whenever error` statement. The following code demonstrates this method:

```
function err_handler()

whenever error call err_handler
...

function err_handler()

call   errorlog( err_get )
call err_print( sqlca.sqlcode )

end function
```

```
function get_count( key1, key2 )
define key1 like table1.col1
define key2 like table1.col2
define cnt integer

- turn off the default error handler
whenever error continue
select count(*)
into    cnt
from    table1
where   col1 = key1 and
        col2 = key2

if sqlca.sqlcode < 0 then
    let cnt = 0            - rather than null
    call err_handler()    - now call this routine to display  ⇐
        the error message
end if
whenever any error call err_handler

return cnt
```

```
end function
```

In this example, the `whenever error` statement is used to trap all errors with the `err_handler` function. All errors are written to the error log file and then an error message is printed to the terminal screen. This is accomplished using the `errorlog` function, which has as its argument the return value of the `err_get` function. Because the `err_get` function has been called with the error number of the current error, it will return an error message corresponding to the current error; this is the error message that will be written to the error log. The final line of the `err_handler` function calls the `err_print` function with the error number of the current error. This prints the error message for the current error to the terminal screen.

An Error Prompt Function

One minor weakness of the error-handling facilities is that they do not ensure that the user has read them. The message is merely displayed on the screen and/or written to the error log. There is no validation that the user has read the error message.

A dialog box that requires the user to press a key to continue working ensures that the user has at least seen the error message (and, in most cases, has not written the message down). The following code demonstrates the use of a function that opens a window, displays information on the error that has occurred, and then waits for the user to press return before continuing with the program.

```
function err_msg( msg )
define msg      char(80)
define tmpmsg   char(60)
define c1       char(1)

let msg = center( msg, 50 )

open window _ew1 at 10, 5 with 4 rows, 50 columns
          attribute( border, prompt line last )

display msg clipped at 2,2 attribute ( bold )

prompt "Press return to continue " for char c1
```

```
close window _ew1

end function
```

This function accepts a single parameter: the message string. It then opens a window, displays the error message using the bold attribute, and then prompts the user to press return to continue with the program. After the user presses the return key, the window opened is closed and the function returns. The programmer can still choose to end the program at this point, but this function at least requires some interaction from the user, forcing the user to acknowledge the problem.

Help Messages in INFORMIX-4GL

INFORMIX-4GL provides a complete set of help facilities to provide end-user help at runtime. Once a help file has been created using the correct format, it can then be displayed on the screen automatically with certain INFORMIX-4GL statements, or explicitly using the showhelp function. Help messages are created from a delimited text file using a utility called mkmessage. The contents of this text file are entries as follows:

```
.100

This is the error message 100.  When the showhelp function is
called with and integer parameter 100, this message will be
displayed to the screen.

.200

This is the error message 200.  When the showhelp function is
called with and integer parameter 200, this message will be
displayed to the screen.
```

The help file is created using a text editor and should be composed of only simple ASCII characters. It is compiled using the mkmessage utility, which takes arguments as follows:

```
mkmessage input_file output_file
```

This utility does **not** assume or enforce any naming convention for the output file. It takes the input file, processes it, and produces the output file. Beware: if the output file is given the same name as the input file, the output file will be produced from the input file and the output will *overwrite* the original input file quietly, without complaint.

Help messages can be used with certain statements, such as the menu statement or prompt statement. The default key for triggering on-line help with these statements is Control-W, but this can be reassigned using the `options` statement. The following code demonstrates the use of help in INFORMIX-4GL:

```
options help file "menu.hlp"

menu "Input"

        command "Insert"
                help 101

        command "Other"
                call showhelp( 201 )


...
```

In this code fragment, the `menu` statement is used with the `help` clause. Note that the options statement is used to identify the help file. The help file must be identified before being referenced; if not, a runtime error occurs. The `help` clause takes an integer parameter corresponding to the help number for that menu option. When the user presses the help key while the menu is displayed and the cursor rests on that option, the help message corresponding to help key 101 is displayed. This is an example of implicit help.

The `menu` command for the 'Other' menu option has an example of an explicit help message. If this option is chosen, then the function `showhelp` is called to display the help message for the integer help number that has been passed.

This form of explicit help message is frequently used to provide field-level help with the `input` statement. The `input` statement provides for a `help` clause, but it is for the statement in general, not for the specific fields in the `input` statement. In order to provide field-level help, the following strategy is often used:

```
options help file "input.hlp",
            help key  Control-T
...
input rec1.* from scr_rec.*

    on key (Control-W, F1 )
            case
                    when infield( col1 )
                            call showhelp( 101 )
                    when infield( col2 )
                            call showhelp( 102 )
                    when infield( col3 )
                            call showhelp( 103 )
    ....
```

In this example, the options statement is first used to identify the name of the help file and to redefine the standard help key to another key. Next, the input statement is started. When the control key W is pressed, the case statement is executed. Within the case statement, each field is tested using the infield function to determine if that is the current field. Depending on the current field, the showhelp function is then called to display the help message for that field.

The sqlca Record

INFORMIX-4GL tracks errors through the sqlca (SQL communication area) record. This record is used to record both errors and warnings. Errors are generally unexpected events that occur during processing and could adversely affect the application's operation. Warnings are unexpected events that could be considered acceptable during program operation. The distinction between an error and a warning is sometimes nebulous. A programmer must be aware of these distinctions and respond accordingly.

Errors can be returned by the front end or back end. Back-end (or *engine*) errors occur during SQL processing and are returned by the engine at runtime. When an SQL error occurs, the status variable is set to the value of the SQL error code, and the sqlca record is populated with additional information about the error. The elements of the sqlca record are shown in Example 10-1. Table 10-2 lists value ranges of SQL error codes.

Example 10-1 The `sqlca` *Record Structure*

```
define sqlca record
                sqlcode integer,
                sqlerrm char(71),
                sqlerrp char(8),
                sqlerrd array(6) of integer,
                sqlwarn char(8)
end record
```

Table 10-2 SQL Error Code Value Ranges

Error Code	Meaning
1 - 99	Operating system errors..
1- 200	C-ISAM/RSAM errors. These are low-level errors that occur. Usually, `sqlca.sqlerrd[1]` is set for the ISAM error code, if any. This can supply important information about why an operation failed.
0	If SQL operation was successful, this code is set by the engine. All other elements of the record are set dependent on the SQL operation that was being executed.

The `sqlerrd` Array

The `sqlca.sqlerrd` element of the `sqlca` record is an array of six integers that contain information about the last SQL operation executed by the engine. Elements contain information as shown in Table 10-3.

Table 10-3 `sqlerrd` *Array Elements*

`sqlerrd` Element	Purpose
1	Not used at this time..
2	Serial value returned if SQL operation was successful and involved an insert into a table with a serial column. If an SQL error occurred, `sqlca.sqlcode < 0`, this is set to the ISAM error that occurred.
3	The number of rows processed. If an update statement has been executed and the database is not in ANSII mode, this is an indication of whether or not the update succeeded.
4	The estimated CPU cost for the query.
5	The offset of the SQL error into the SQL query statement processed.
6	The `rowid` of the last row selected.

The `sqlwarn` String

The `sqlwarn` element of the `sqlca` record is a character string composed of single characters that indicate the warning generated by the last SQL operation. This string contains useful information on the type of database opened, whether or not logging is being used in the database and whether or not the last SQL statement was an Informix ANSII extension. Elements of this string are set as shown in Table 10-4.

Front-end errors are expression errors that could not be trapped at compile-time, such as division by 0 or numeric overflow. In order for these to be trapped by the application, the `whenever any error` statement must appear in the application before the code that must trap the error.

Table 10-4 `sqlwarn` *Elements*

String Element	Purpose
1	Set to W if one of the other array elements has been set. Interrogating this element effectively provides information on whether or not a warning has occurred.
2	On execution of a database open statement, this is set to W if the database is using transaction logging. If a Select statement has been executed and a character string had to be truncated to fit in an INFORMIX-4GL character variable, this element is set to W. (This does not indicate which variable has been truncated. INFORMIX-4GL currently does not provide a means of doing this.)
3	On execution of a database open statement, this is set to W if the database opened is an ANSI mode database. If a `select` statement has been executed, and an aggregate function within the `select` statement has encountered a NULL, this element is set to W.
4	On execution of a database open statement, this is set to W if the database opened was an Informix-On-line database. If a `select` statement has been executed, this element is set if the number of items in the select list does not match the number of INFORMIX-4GL variables provided to receive the selected data.
5	This element is set to W if float to decimal conversion is used.
6	If the last statement executed as an Informix ANSI extension *and* the DBANSIWARN environment variable is set, this element is set to W.
7	Not used.

Chapter Summary

Using Informix-4GL functions, a programmer can effectively extend the language to perform additional tasks as needed. When used as part of a modular programming effort, a library of functions can be created and then shared by a group of programmers.

When functions are used together to create other functions, programmers effectively reuse code and reduce the number of lines of code required to develop an application. This methodology can shorten the application development process and make maintaining an application easier because program operations are isolated and grouped in an understandable set of modular function libraries.

INFORMIX-4GL provides a useful set of tools for the programmer to make applications respond gracefully to errors. It is up to the programmer to implement these facilities because the INFORMIX-4GL default error checking is probably *not* the preferable method of error checking in a production environment.

Making use of a centralized, generalized error function can make the application more consistent and reduce the amount of coding necessary to develop the application. Such a modular approach will have both short-term and long-term benefits for the application development staff. In the short term, the application will be developed more quickly. In the long term, the application will be easier to modify because nearly all error checking will be maintained in one place.

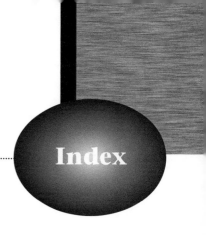

Index

Insert triggers, 310-11
integer, 28, 340-41
Intent locks, 47
Internet development tools, 11
Interprocess communication (IPC), 4
interval data type, 31-33, 344-45
IPX/SPX, 56

Join criteria, 269
Join plan, 201

Language tools, 11
Latch, 44
LBU_PRESERVE parameter, 108
Least recently used (LRU) buffer, 171
    configuration parameters, 175
    decision support system, parameter settings for,
        178
    heavy update load, parameter settings for, 177
    light update load, parameter settings for, 177
    LRU management, 50-52
        tuning, 174-79
    LRU performance, evaluating, 171-74
    LRU tuning, iterative benchmarking for, 178-79
let statement, 300-301
Level 0 archive, 238
Level 1 archive, 238
Level 2 archive, 239
Links, problem with, 120
load statement, 285-86
Local scope, variables, 304
Locking cursor, 376
LOCKS parameter, 94-95
Lock table, 47
Log activity in IDS engine, 167-68
LOGBUFF parameter, 95, 168-69
LOGFILES parameter, 87
Logical disk, 43
    layout, defining, 113-14
Logical log buffers, 48-49
Logical logs, 22, 24-25
    monitoring, 232-34
    status flags, 233
Log performance problems, addressing, 168-69
LOGSIZE parameter, 88, 236
LOGSMAX parameter, 96
Long transaction, 25
Loop join, 201
lpad function, 322
LRU management, 50-52
LRU_MAX_DIRTY parameter, 98, 175-76
LRU_MIN_DIRTY parameter, 98, 175-76

LRU performance, evaluating, 171-79
LRUS parameter, 97-98, 175-76
LTAPEBLK parameter, 90
LTAPEDEV parameter, 90, 234
LTAPESIZE parameter, 91
LTXEHWM parameter, 99
LTXHWM parameter, 98

main program block, table-driven dynamic report,
    440-42
Many-to-many relationship, 247-48
MAXARR integer variable, 354-55
MAX_PDQPRIORITY parameter, 105-6
MAXRECS integer variable, 354-55
Memory leak, 335
Memory problems, addressing, 163-64
Memory-resident tables/indexes, creating, 327-28
Memory usage, monitoring, 161-64
Mirror dbspace, 34, 117-18
Mirroring, 34-35
MIRROROFFSET parameter, 87
MIRROR parameter, 86
MIRRORPATH parameter, 86
mkmessage utility, 476-78
Modified buffers, 45-46
Modified LRU (MLRU) queue, 50
Modular dynamic reports, 423-25
Modularity, 381-82
    in Informix-4GL reports, 428-30
    and screen form interaction, 389-90
Modular programming, with Informix-4GL, 339
money data type, 30, 342-43
Monitoring tools, 10
MSGPATH parameter, 88
MULTIPROCESSOR parameter, 93
Multithreading, 18-20, 54-55, 59
    thread operation, 20-22
    virtual processor (VP), 19-20
Mutex, 21-22, 44

Nested-loop join, 201
NETTYPE parameter, 92
nettype parameter, sqlhosts file, 70
next field statement, 400-401
next size clause, 122
NOAGE parameter, 93-94
Nonprocedural statements, 334
Normalization, 248
NOT IN operator, and SPL conditional expressions,
    290
Null data values, 348-49
NUMAIOVPS parameter, 95
NUMCPUVPS parameter, 93

nvl function, 326

Offline opeating mode, 214
OFF_RECVRY_THREADS parameter, 99-100
onarchive utility, 238, 240
onbar utility, 238, 240
oncheck -pe command, 123
ONCONFIG environment variable, 68, 71, 73
onconfig file:
  changing, 236
  parameters, 81-108
    AFF_NPROC, 94
    ALARMPROGRAM, 89
    BAR_ACT_LOG, 102
    BAR_BSALIB_PATH, 103
    BAR_NB_XPORT_COUNT, 103
    BAR_RETRY, 102-3
    BAR_XFER_BUF_SIZE, 103
    BUFFERS, 95
    CDR_DSLOCKWAIT, 102
    CDR_EVALTHREADS, 101
    CDR_LOGBUFFERS, 101
    CDR_QUEMEM, 102
    CKPTINTVL, 97
    CLEANERS, 96
    CONSOLE, 89
    DATASKIP, 107
    DBSERVERALIASES, 91
    DBSERVERNAME, 91
    DBSPACETEMP, 104
    DEADLOCK_TIMEOUT, 92
    DRAUTO, 100-101
    DRINTERVAL, 101
    DRLOSTANDFOUND, 101
    DS_MAX_QUERIES, 106
    DS_MAX_SCANS, 106
    DS_TOTAL_MEMORY, 106
    DUMPCNT, 105
    DUMPCORE, 104
    DUMPDIR, 104
    DUMPGCORE, 104
    DUMPSHMEM, 104
    FILLFACTOR, 105
    LBU_PRESERVE, 108
    LOCKS, 94-95
    LOGBUFF, 95
    LOGFILES, 87
    LOGSIZE, 88
    LOGSMAX, 96
    LRU_MAX_DIRTY, 98
    LRU_MIN_DIRTY, 98
    LRUS, 97-98
    LTAPEBLK, 90

    LTAPEDEV, 90
    LTAPESIZE, 91
    LTXEHWM, 99
    LTXHWM, 98
    MAX_PDQPRIORITY, 105-6
    MIRROR, 86
    MIRROROFFSET, 87
    MIRRORPATH, 86
    MSGPATH, 88
    MULTIPROCESSOR, 93
    NETTYPE, 92
    NOAGE, 93-94
    NUMAIOVPS, 95
    NUMCPUVPS, 93
    OFF_RECVRY_THREADS, 99-100
    ONDBSPACEDOWN, 107-8
    ON_RECVRY_THREADS, 100
    OPCACHEMAX, 108
    OPTCOMPIND, 107
    PHYSBUFF, 95
    PHYSDBS, 87
    RA_PAGES, 103
    RA_THRESHOLD, 103
    RESIDENT, 93
    ROOTNAME, 82-85
    ROOTOFFSET, 85-86
    ROOTPATH, 85
    ROOTSIZE, 86
    SERVERNUM, 91
    SHMBASE, 96
    SHMVIRTSIZE, 96
    SINGLE_CPU_VP, 93
    STACKSIZE, 99
    STAGEBLOB, 91
    TAPEBLK, 89
    TAPEDEV, 89
    TAPESIZE, 90
    TXTIMEOUT, 99
    USEOSTIME, 105
ONDBSPACEDOWN parameter, 107-8
One-to-many relationship, 247
One-to-one relationship, 247
on every row report block, table-driven
  dynamic report, 446-49
on exception statement, 302-4
oninit command, 213-15
  -i option, 215
  options, 214
Online mode, 214
onmode command, 160-61, 216-26
  -a option, 222-23
  -d option, 224, 226
  -D parameter, 221
  -F option, 223

rpad function, 322-23
rpt_drv function, 432-34, 440-42

sar command, 159-60
Scan threads, 126
Scheduler, Informix IDS/XP, 9
Schema Knowledge tool, 10
Screen fields, 386
Screen form identifiers, 389
Screen forms, 385-407
    current field, highlighting, 402-3
    current window statement, 390-95
    database binding in, 386-87
    display statement, 395-99
        and screen form interaction, 397-99
    formonly screens, 387-88
    input field, moving past, 400-401
    input statement, 399-400
    manipulating in Informix-4GL, 388-89
    modularity and screen form interaction, 389-90
    multiple windows, managing, 390-95
    screen form identifiers, 389
    screen form programming, 386
    screen size, managing, 386
    termcap, 385, 403-5
        adding function keys in termcap file, 404-5
        refining function keys, 403-4
        turning off insert/delete keys, 404
    trapping the interrupt key, 405-6
Scroll cursors, 372-76
    problems with, 374-76
Secondary dbspace, 34
select clause, 268
select permission, 229-30
select statement, 267, 268-81
    display labels, assigning, 270
    from clause, 268-69
    grouping records, 272-73
    maximum number of rows returned, specifying, 271-72
    outer joins, 278
    recursive queries, 276-77
    select clause, 268
    sort order, identifying, 270-71
    table aliasing, 273-74
    union clause, 278-81
Sequential read, index read vs., 198
Serial cursors, 372
Server, 4
Server architecture, 41-56
    components, 41-42
    database memory, 44-54
    disk I/O, 43-44

logical disk, 43
physical disk, 43
SERVERNUM parameter, 91
Session, 180
Session data, 52-53
set debug file statement,306
set explain command, 189-90
set optimization command, 202-3
Shared locks, 46, 47
Shared memory, 69
    buffer pool, 47-48
    buffer table, 45-46
    chunk table, 46
    communications portion of, 44-45, 54
    data replication buffer, 50
    dbspace table, 46
    lock table, 47
    logical log buffers, 48-49
    LRU management, 50-52
    page-cleaner table, 47
    physical log buffers, 49
    resident memory, 44-47
    tblspace table, 47
    transaction table, 47
    user table, 47
    virtual memory, 44-45, 52-54
Shared memory, See also Resident memory; Virtual memory
Shared memory buffer, 18, 22
Shared memory buffer cache, 161
Shared memory communication, 55-56
SHMBASE parameter, 96
SHMVIRTSIZE parameter, 96
SINGLE_CPU_VP parameter, 93
Sleep queue, 21
smallfloat data type, 28, 341
smallint data type, 28, 340
Soft links, using to assign chunks, 119
Sorting pool, 54
Sort-merge—join, 57
Source code modules, 337-38
Special data types, 33-34
sqlca record, 478-79
SQL DDL statements, 248, 250-67
    alter table statement, 249, 260-62
    create database statement, 249, 250-51
    create table statement, 121, 249, 251-53
        column integrity/referential
            constraints, 263-67
        column name, 252
        data types, 252-53
        IDS fragmentation definition, 253-54
        table name, 252
    create view statement, 249, 255-58

Thread data, 53
Threads, 54-55
Trace, 306
trace statement, producing debug output with, 306
Transaction table, 47
trim function, 320
Tuning strategies, for IDS, 149-51
Two-process architecture, 4
TXTIMEOUT parameter, 99, 225

Unbuffered logging, 25, 36
union clause, 278-81
    segmenting values with, 279-81
unload statement, 285-86
Unmodified buffers, 45-46
Update cursors, 376
Update locks, 47
update permission, 229-30
update statement, 25, 282-83
"update statistics" command, 134-35, 206, 254
Update triggers, 313-14
USEOSTIME parameter, 105
User-defined functions, Informix IDS/UD, 9
User roles, 226
    creating/using, 228-29

User session, 67
User table, 47

varchar, 33
Virtual memory, 44-45, 52-54
    big buffers, 52
    dictionary cache, 53
    global pool, 54
    session data, 52-53
    sorting pool, 54
    stored procedure cache, 53
    thread data, 53
Virtual processor (VP), 19-21
vmstat command, 159-60

Wait queue, 21
Warm restores, 238, 241
when clause, using in triggers, 316
whenever any error statement, 471-73
whenever error statement, 467-68
while statement, 294-95, 355
with append clause, set debug file
    statement, 306
with grant option statement, 230-31
wordwrap clause, 412, 420

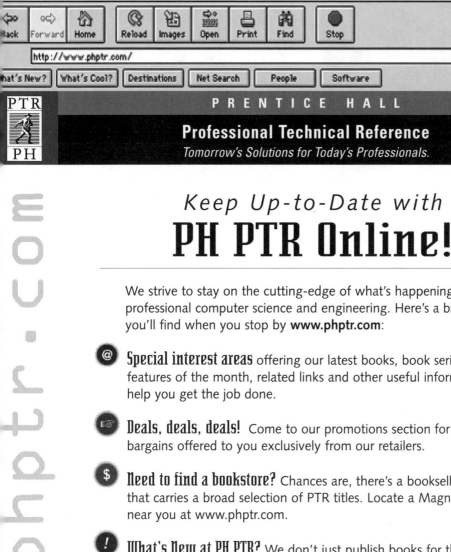

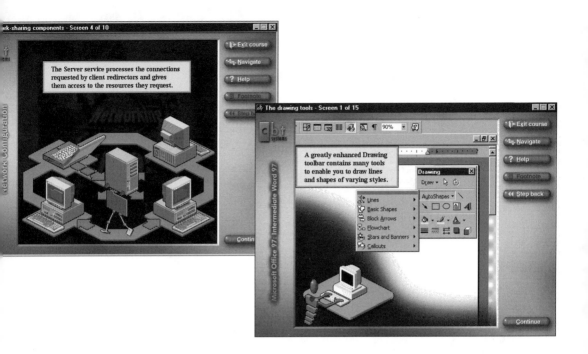

ther curricula available from CBT Systems:

- sco
- formix
- a
- arimba
- icrosoft
- etscape
- ovell

- Oracle
- SAP
- Sybase
- C/C++
- Centura
- Information Technology/
  Core Concepts

- Internet and Intranet
  Skills
- Internetworking
- UNIX

To order additional CBT Systems
courseware today call 800.789.8590 or
visit www.clbooks.com/training/cbt.htm

REAL Books by REAL Authors for REAL Professiona

FROM PRENTICE HALL PTR

NEW!
INFORMIX-OnLine Dynamic Server Handbook
Carlton Doe

Hands-on information that will help INFORMIX-OnLine Dynamic Server administrators get their job done as effectively as possible.This book transforms the dry technical details of Informix documentation into practical, hands-on techniques and ideas for effective administration. It serves the needs of both DBAs and administrators responsible for multiple database environments. This book covers the entire process of starting up and running an INFORMIX-OnLine Dynamic Server database environment, including preparing for initialization; initializing an OnLine Dynamic Server instance; building a database environment; archiving and restoring; monitoring and optimization. It reviews issues related to high availability and distributed transaction environments. There is cogent, careful coverage of how to recover from a crash. The accompanying CD-ROM's extensive library of scripts can save you hundreds of hours by automating many essential administration tasks.

1997, 496pp., paper, 0-13-605296-7

A Book/CD-ROM Package

Informix Performance Tuning, Second Edition
Elizabeth Suto

Maximize the performance of your INFORMIX-OnLine System. This insider's guide to Informix performance has been completely updated to reflect all recent releases of INFORMIX-OnLine, INFORMIX-OnLine Dynamic Server and INFORMIX XMP. No matter which release you're running, this book will walk you through all the performance-related issues you need to understand, including: query optimization, database design, disk layout, memory utilization, and processor usage.

1997, 192 pp., cloth, 0-13-239237-2

NEW!
JDBC Developer's Resource
Art Taylor

JDBC allows developers to create Java applications which fully leverage their existing corporate database resources. This book is the first comprehensive tutorial and reference for learning and using JDBC. The author begins by introducing the JDBC standard and its relationship to ODBC; then shows how JDBC can be used to enable a wide variety of applications. It shows how JDBC provides for enhanced security, through techniques such as trusted applets. There is detailed coverage of Java database access application design, including both two-tiered and three-tiered applications. Techniques for using JDBC are also covered. An extensive tutorial section walks developers through every step of developing three sample applications, demonstrating most of the techniques developers will need, including how to implement multithreading support, register drivers, and execute SQL statements. The book also contains listings of every JDBC class method, with usage examples and tips. All code appears on the accompanying CD-ROM — along with the exciting new Mojo rapid application development environment for Java, and JDBC/ODBC drivers from Visigenic — everything a developer needs to build database-enabled Java applications.

1997, 752pp., paper, 0-13-842352-0

A Book/CD-ROM Package

Informix Stored Procedure Programming
Michael L. Gonzales

Informix stored procedures, which can be used to dramatically improve the performance of SQL code, tighten security, reduce maintenance of permissions, and maximize data integrity, are often difficult to understand. This book offers numerous examples and illustrations that show how stored procedures can be used to optimize code while improving security and data integrity. Also included is a comprehensive SPL syntax reference, as well as more than 20 stored procedures that can be used or adapted as needed.

1996, 200 pp., paper, 0-13-206723-4

CBT SOFTWARE LICENSE AGREEMENT

IF YOU DO NOT AGREE WITH THESE TERMS AND CONDITIONS, DO NOT INSTALL THE SOFTWARE.

This is a legal agreement you and CBT System Ltd. ("Licensor"). The licensor ("Licensor") from whom you have licensed the CBT Group PLC courseware (the "Software"). By installing, copying or otherwise using the Software, you agree to be bound by the terms of this Agreement License Agreement (the "License"). If you do not agree to the terms of this License, the Licensor is unwilling to license the Software to you. In such event, you may not use or copy the Software, and you should promptly contact the Licensor for instructions on the return of the unused Software.

1. Use. Licensor grants to you a non-exclusive, nontransferable license to use Licensor's software product (the "Software") the Software and accompanying documentation in accordance with the terms and conditions of this license agreement ("License") License and as specified in your agreement with Licensor (the "Governing Agreement"). In the event of any conflict between this License and the Governing Agreement, the Governing Agreement shall control.

You may:

a. (if specified as a "personal use" version) install the Software on a single stand-alone computer or a single network node from which node the Software cannot be accessed by another computer, provided that such Software shall be used by only one individual; or

b. (if specified as a "workstation" version) install the Software on a single stand-alone computer or a single network node from which node the Software cannot be accessed by another computer, provided that such Software shall be used by only one individual; or

c. (if specified as a "LAN" version) install the Software on a local area network server that provides access to multiple computers, up to the maximum number of computers or users specified in your Governing Agreement, provided that such Software shall be used only by employees of your organization; or

d. (if specified as an "enterprise" version) install the Software or copies of the Software on multiple local or wide area network servers, intranet servers, stand-alone computers and network nodes (and to make copies of the Software for such purpose) at one or more sites, which servers provide access to a multiple number of users, up to the maximum number of users specified in your Governing Agreement, provided that such Software shall be used only by employees of your organization.

This License is not a sale. Title and copyrights to the Software, accompanying documentation and any copy made by you remain with Licensor or its suppliers or licensors.

2. Intellectual Property. The Software is owned by Licensor or its licensors and is protected by United States and other jurisdictions' copyright laws and international treaty provisions. Therefore, you may not use, copy, or distribute the Software without the express written authorization of CBT Group PLC. This License authorizes you to use the Software for the internal training needs of your employees only, and to make one copy of the Software solely for backup or archival purposes. You may not print copies of any user documentation provided in "online" or electronic form. Licensor retains all rights not expressly granted.

3. Restrictions. You may not transfer, rent, lease, loan or time-share the Software or accompanying documentation. You may not reverse engineer, decompile, or disassemble the Software, except to the extent the foregoing restriction is expressly prohibited by applicable law. You may not modify, or create derivative works based upon the Software in whole or in part.

1. Confidentiality. The Software contains confidential trade secret information belonging to Licensor, and you may use the software only pursuant to the terms of your Governing Agreement, if any, and the license set forth herein. In addition, you may not disclose the Software to any third party.

2. **Limited Liability.** IN NO EVENT WILL THE Licensor's LIABILITY UNDER, ARISING OUT OF OR RELATING TO THIS AGREEMENT EXCEED THE AMOUNT PAID TO LICENSOR FOR THE SOFTWARE. LICENSOR SHALL NOT BE LIABLE FOR ANY SPECIAL, INCIDENTAL, INDIRECT OR CONSEQUENTIAL DAMAGES, HOWEVER CAUSED AND ON ANY THEORY OF LIABILITY., REGARDLESS OR WHETHER LICENSOR HAS BEEN ADVISED OF THE POSSIBILITY OF SUCH DAMAGES. WITHOUT LIMITING THE FOREGOING, LICENSOR WILL NOT BE LIABLE FOR LOST PROFITS, LOSS OF DATA, OR COSTS OF COVER.

3. **Limited Warranty.** LICENSOR WARRANTS THAT SOFTWARE WILL BE FREE FROM DEFECTS IN MATERIALS AND WORKMANSHIP UNDER NORMAL USE FOR A PERIOD OF THIRTY (30) DAYS FROM THE DATE OF RECEIPT. THIS LIMITED WARRANTY IS VOID IF FAILURE OF THE SOFTWARE HAS RESULTED FROM ABUSE OR MISAPPLICATION. ANY REPLACEMENT SOFTWARE WILL BE WARRANTED FOR A PERIOD OF THIRTY (30) DAYS FROM THE DATE OF RECEIPT OF SUCH REPLACEMENT SOFTWARE. THE SOFTWARE AND DOCUMENTATION ARE PROVIDED "AS IS". LICENSOR HEREBY DISCLAIMS ALL OTHER WARRANTIES, EXPRESS, IMPLIED, OR STATUTORY, INCLUDING WITHOUT LIMITATION, THE IMPLIED WARRANTIES OF MERCHANTABILITY AND FITNESS FOR A PARTICULAR PURPOSE.

4. **Exceptions.** SOME STATES DO NOT ALLOW THE LIMITATION OF INCIDENTAL DAMAGES OR LIMITATIONS ON HOW LONG AN IMPLIED WARRANTY LASTS, SO THE ABOVE LIMITATIONS OR EXCLUSIONS MAY NOT APPLY TO YOU. This agreement gives you specific legal rights, and you may also have other rights which vary from state to state.

5. **U.S. Government-Restricted Rights.** The Software and accompanying documentation are deemed to be "commercial computer Software" and "commercial computer Software documentation," respectively, pursuant to FAR Section 227.7202 and FAR Section 12.212, as applicable. Any use, modification, reproduction release, performance, display or disclosure of the Software and accompanying documentation by the U.S. Government shall be governed solely by the terms of this Agreement and shall be prohibited except to the extent expressly permitted by the terms of this Agreement.

6. **Export Restrictions.** You may not download, export, or re-export the Software (a) into, or to a national or resident of, Cuba, Iraq, Libya, Yugoslavia, North Korea, Iran, Syria or any other country to which the United States has embargoed goods, or (b) to anyone on the United States Treasury Department's list of Specially Designated Nations or the U.S. Commerce Department's Table of Deny Orders. By installing or using the Software, you are representing and warranting that you are not located in, under the control of, or a national resident of any such country or on any such list.

7. **General.** This License is governed by the laws of the United States and the State of California, without reference to conflict of laws principles. The parties agree that the United Nations Convention on Contracts for the International Sale of Goods shall not apply to this License. If any provision of this Agreement is held invalid, the remainder of this License shall continue in full force and effect.

8. **More Information.** Should you have any questions concerning this Agreement, or if you desire to contact Licensor for any reason, please contact: CBT Systems USA Ltd., 1005 Hamilton Court, Menlo Park, California 94025, Attn: Chief Legal Officer.

IF YOU DO NOT AGREE WITH THE ABOVE TERMS AND CONDITIONS, SO NOT INSTALL THE SOFTWARE AND RETURN IT TO THE LICENSOR.

LICENSE AGREEMENT AND LIMITED WARRANTY

READ THE FOLLOWING TERMS AND CONDITIONS CAREFULLY BEFORE OPENING THIS DISK PACKAGE. THIS LEGAL DOCUMENT IS AN AGREEMENT BETWEEN YOU AND PRENTICE-HALL, INC. (THE "COMPANY"). BY OPENING THIS SEALED DISK PACKAGE, YOU ARE AGREEING TO BE BOUND BY THESE TERMS AND CONDITIONS. IF YOU DO NOT AGREE WITH THESE TERMS AND CONDITIONS, DO NOT OPEN THE DISK PACKAGE. PROMPTLY RETURN THE UNOPENED DISK PACKAGE AND ALL ACCOMPANYING ITEMS TO THE PLACE YOU OBTAINED THEM FOR A FULL REFUND OF ANY SUMS YOU HAVE PAID.

1. **GRANT OF LICENSE:** In consideration of your payment of the license fee, which is part of the price you paid for this product, and your agreement to abide by the terms and conditions of this Agreement, the Company grants to you a nonexclusive right to use and display the copy of the enclosed software program (hereinafter the "SOFTWARE") on a single computer (i.e., with a single CPU) at a single location so long as you comply with the terms of this Agreement. The Company reserves all rights not expressly granted to you under this Agreement.

2. **OWNERSHIP OF SOFTWARE:** You own only the magnetic or physical media (the enclosed disks) on which the SOFTWARE is recorded or fixed, but the Company retains all the rights, title, and ownership to the SOFTWARE recorded on the original disk copy(ies) and all subsequent copies of the SOFTWARE, regardless of the form or media on which the original or other copies may exist. This license is not a sale of the original SOFTWARE or any copy to you.

3. **COPY RESTRICTIONS:** This SOFTWARE and the accompanying printed materials and user manual (the "Documentation") are the subject of copyright. You may not copy the Documentation or the SOFTWARE, except that you may make a single copy of the SOFTWARE for backup or archival purposes only. You may be held legally responsible for any copying or copyright infringement which is caused or encouraged by your failure to abide by the terms of this restriction.

4. **USE RESTRICTIONS:** You may not network the SOFTWARE or otherwise use it on more than one computer or computer terminal at the same time. You may physically transfer the SOFTWARE from one computer to another provided that the SOFTWARE is used on only one computer at a time. You may not distribute copies of the SOFTWARE or Documentation to others. You may not reverse engineer, disassemble, decompile, modify, adapt, translate, or create derivative works based on the SOFTWARE or the Documentation without the prior written consent of the Company.

5. **TRANSFER RESTRICTIONS:** The enclosed SOFTWARE is licensed only to you and may not be transferred to any one else without the prior written consent of the Company. Any unauthorized transfer of the SOFTWARE shall result in the immediate termination of this Agreement.

6. **TERMINATION:** This license is effective until terminated. This license will terminate automatically without notice from the Company and become null and void if you fail to comply with any provisions or limitations of this license. Upon termination, you shall destroy the Documentation and all copies of the SOFTWARE. All provisions of this Agreement as to warranties, limitation of liability, remedies or damages, and our ownership rights shall survive termination.

7. **MISCELLANEOUS:** This Agreement shall be construed in accordance with the laws of the United States of America and the State of New York and shall benefit the Company, its affiliates, and assignees.

8. **LIMITED WARRANTY AND DISCLAIMER OF WARRANTY:** The Company warrants that the SOFTWARE, when properly used in accordance with the Documentation, will operate

in substantial conformity with the description of the SOFTWARE set forth in the Documentation. The Company does not warrant that the SOFTWARE will meet your requirements or that the operation of the SOFTWARE will be uninterrupted or error-free. The Company warrants that the media on which the SOFTWARE is delivered shall be free from defects in materials and workmanship under normal use for a period of thirty (30) days from the date of your purchase. Your only remedy and the Company's only obligation under these limited warranties is, at the Company's option, return of the warranted item for a refund of any amounts paid by you or replacement of the item. Any replacement of SOFTWARE or media under the warranties shall not extend the original warranty period. The limited warranty set forth above shall not apply to any SOFTWARE which the Company determines in good faith has been subject to misuse, neglect, improper installation, repair, alteration, or damage by you. EXCEPT FOR THE EXPRESSED WARRANTIES SET FORTH ABOVE, THE COMPANY DISCLAIMS ALL WARRANTIES, EXPRESS OR IMPLIED, INCLUDING WITHOUT LIMITATION, THE IMPLIED WARRANTIES OF MERCHANTABILITY AND FITNESS FOR A PARTICULAR PURPOSE. EXCEPT FOR THE EXPRESS WARRANTY SET FORTH ABOVE, THE COMPANY DOES NOT WARRANT, GUARANTEE, OR MAKE ANY REPRESENTATION REGARDING THE USE OR THE RESULTS OF THE USE OF THE SOFTWARE IN TERMS OF ITS CORRECTNESS, ACCURACY, RELIABILITY, CURRENTNESS, OR OTHERWISE.

IN NO EVENT, SHALL THE COMPANY OR ITS EMPLOYEES, AGENTS, SUPPLIERS, OR CONTRACTORS BE LIABLE FOR ANY INCIDENTAL, INDIRECT, SPECIAL, OR CONSEQUENTIAL DAMAGES ARISING OUT OF OR IN CONNECTION WITH THE LICENSE GRANTED UNDER THIS AGREEMENT, OR FOR LOSS OF USE, LOSS OF DATA, LOSS OF INCOME OR PROFIT, OR OTHER LOSSES, SUSTAINED AS A RESULT OF INJURY TO ANY PERSON, OR LOSS OF OR DAMAGE TO PROPERTY, OR CLAIMS OF THIRD PARTIES, EVEN IF THE COMPANY OR AN AUTHORIZED REPRESENTATIVE OF THE COMPANY HAS BEEN ADVISED OF THE POSSIBILITY OF SUCH DAMAGES. IN NO EVENT SHALL LIABILITY OF THE COMPANY FOR DAMAGES WITH RESPECT TO THE SOFTWARE EXCEED THE AMOUNTS ACTUALLY PAID BY YOU, IF ANY, FOR THE SOFTWARE.

SOME JURISDICTIONS DO NOT ALLOW THE LIMITATION OF IMPLIED WARRANTIES OR LIABILITY FOR INCIDENTAL, INDIRECT, SPECIAL, OR CONSEQUENTIAL DAMAGES, SO THE ABOVE LIMITATIONS MAY NOT ALWAYS APPLY. THE WARRANTIES IN THIS AGREEMENT GIVE YOU SPECIFIC LEGAL RIGHTS AND YOU MAY ALSO HAVE OTHER RIGHTS WHICH VARY IN ACCORDANCE WITH LOCAL LAW.

ACKNOWLEDGMENT

YOU ACKNOWLEDGE THAT YOU HAVE READ THIS AGREEMENT, UNDERSTAND IT, AND AGREE TO BE BOUND BY ITS TERMS AND CONDITIONS. YOU ALSO AGREE THAT THIS AGREEMENT IS THE COMPLETE AND EXCLUSIVE STATEMENT OF THE AGREEMENT BETWEEN YOU AND THE COMPANY AND SUPERSEDES ALL PROPOSALS OR PRIOR AGREEMENTS, ORAL, OR WRITTEN, AND ANY OTHER COMMUNICATIONS BETWEEN YOU AND THE COMPANY OR ANY REPRESENTATIVE OF THE COMPANY RELATING TO THE SUBJECT MATTER OF THIS AGREEMENT.

Should you have any questions concerning this Agreement or if you wish to contact the Company for any reason, please contact in writing at the address below.

Robin Short
Prentice Hall PTR
One Lake Street
Upper Saddle River, New Jersey 07458

ABOUT THE CD

The enclosed CD-ROM contains the following computer-based training (CBT) course module from CBT Systems:

INFORMIX OnLine D-S-S Administration: Critical Operations

The CD can be used on Windows 98/95/NT

Technical Support

If you have a problem with the CBT software, please contact CBT Technical Support. In the US call 1 (800) 938-3247. If you are outside the US call 3531-283-0380.

Prentice Hall does not offer technical support for this software. However, if there is a problem with the media, you may obtain a replacement copy by e-mailing us with your problem at: disc_exchange@prenhall.com